John Nichol served in the R... ...On active duty during the first G... ...er was shot down during a missi... ...nd held as a prisoner of war, John ... ...ng worldwide condemnation and leaving one of the most enduring images of the conflict.

John is the bestselling co-author of *Tornado Down* and author of many highly acclaimed Second World War epics including *Spitfire* and *Lancaster*, both of which were *Sunday Times* bestsellers. He has made a number of TV documentaries with Second World War veterans, written for national newspapers and magazines, and is a widely quoted commentator on military affairs.

Praise for *Tornado*

'He has used his extensive knowledge and contacts to create a well-rounded record of the Tornado strike force during the Gulf War. He . . . brings the experience of flying and fighting the aircraft to life in a dramatic but expert fashion . . . Nichol combines a professional eye for the technicalities with the human stories to create a readable and informative work, and a fitting tribute to those who did not come home.' *History of War*

'Nichol superbly interleaves graphic stories of combat with the effects on those left at home. The author describes combat with a superbly written dispassionate voice, relating the technicalities and feelings of modern combat clearly and with a style that takes you seamlessly from the Tornado's cockpit to the fears of those left at home . . . This is a fine book to join his "biographies" of the Spitfire and Lancaster . . . And one of the best pieces of sharp-end military history I have had the privilege and pleasure of reading.' *The Aviation Historian*

TORNADO

In the Eye of the Storm

JOHN NICHOL

SIMON &
SCHUSTER

London · New York · Sydney · Toronto · New Delhi

First published in Great Britain by Simon & Schuster UK Ltd, 2021
This edition published in Great Britain by Simon & Schuster UK Ltd, 2022

1 3 5 7 9 10 8 6 4 2

Simon & Schuster UK Ltd
1st Floor
222 Gray's Inn Road
London WC1X 8HB

www.simonandschuster.co.uk
www.simonandschuster.com.au
www.simonandschuster.co.in

Simon & Schuster Australia, Sydney
Simon & Schuster India, New Delhi

A CIP catalogue record for this book
is available from the British Library

Paperback ISBN: 978-1-4711-8055-2
eBook ISBN: 978-1-4711-8054-5

Typeset in Sabon by M Rules
Printed in the UK by CPI Group (UK) Ltd, Croydon, CR0 4YY

For Sophie

CONTENTS

This book is dedicated to all the courageous, dedicated and skilled men and women involved in the liberation of Kuwait 1990–1991.
Especially those who made the ultimate sacrifice.

Desert Storm Theatre of Operations

Homs

Euphrates

Lake Tharthar

SYRIA

Al Asad

Damascus

Fallujah

Ar Rutbah

H3

Mudaysis

JORDAN

IRAQ

SAUDI ARABIA

Tabuk

RAF Tornado bases

Main Iraqi airbases

Ground invasion major routing

Main roads

Major towns

RED SEA

ACKNOWLEDGEMENTS

Many people willingly offered their valuable time and considerable expertise while I researched and wrote this book. I cannot mention every person individually but I am eternally grateful to you all.

My sincere thanks also go to:

Fellow authors Mike Napier, Ian Black and Charles Allen for their encyclopaedic knowledge of Tornado and Gulf War operations, wonderful collection of photos and access to their vast mine of Tornado-related information and interviews.

Steve Barnes and Steve Barnfield, both former Tornado Qualified Weapons Instructors, for their forensic analysis of early drafts of the book and cover image. Any remaining errors or misinterpretations of tactics or events are mine alone.

Les Hendry, the Dhahran Tornado Detachment Senior Engineering Officer, for access to his incredible database of Gulf War Tornado operations and photos. Dicky James, the IX(B) Squadron Association Historian, for his assistance with locating memoirs, documents and personnel. Matty Mathieson for his help sourcing videos and photographs. And Paul Lenihan for his assistance locating Tornado veterans.

The whole team at my fantastic publisher Simon & Schuster for their encouragement, advice and expertise, and to Thomas Harding for his time and assistance.

I am ever grateful to my friend and agent of thirty years Mark Lucas, who wields his famous red editing pen with laser-guided precision and is always a steadying source of wise counsel.

My wonderful wife Suzannah and daughter Sophie, who are always there with their unstinting love and support.

Finally, I am truly grateful to the countless serving RAF officers and veterans, and their loved ones, who told me their Tornado stories and who appear in this book. It was an incredibly emotional process at times and many tears were shed as long-buried memories were recalled. I was only able to use a fraction of the accounts I heard and it was impossible to detail every mission undertaken. Everyone involved served with courage and dignity, so I hope I have done justice to you all, and to the story of the Tornado at war in 1991.

* * *

I was assisted by many other RAF personnel, researchers, authors and historians, who offered invaluable information and contacts. It is impossible to name them all, but the following provided important leads, accounts, pictures or advice:

Spike Abbott, Colonel Cliff Acree, Colin Adair, Dave Ailano, Brian Armstrong, Vanessa Burgess, Air Commodore Al Byford, Wing Commander Gary Coleman, Gary Eason, Colonel Dave Eberly, Air Vice-Marshal Ian Gale, Paul Giverin, Group Captain Ian Hall, Lyn Hicks, Gillian Howie, Jamie Hunter, Mike Lumb, Rob McCarthy, Lawrie Marshall, Liz Merger, Dave Morris, Stuart Norris, Mark Ranger, Air Commodore Graham Pitchfork, Air Vice-Marshal Pete Rochelle, Tommy Tank, Group Captain Andy Turk, Professor Gordon Turnbull, Berry Vissers, Dame Arabella Warburton, Andy White, Simon Whittaker, Rob Woods.

MAJOR CHARACTERS

Countless Royal Air Force squadrons, units and personnel served in the region from August 1990 to March 1991 and it is impossible to list them all. Almost 200 Tornado aircrew served during the conflict itself;[1] these are just the main characters who feature in the book.

The reader should note that this book's author, John Nichol, appears as a character described in the third person in the same way as the other participants.

MUHARRAQ, BAHRAIN

Nigel Risdale (pilot)
& John Broadbent (navigator, Officer Commanding 15 Squadron[2] and Tornado Detachment Commander)

Nick Heard
& Rob Woods

Rupert Clark
& Steve Hicks

Gordon Buckley
& Paddy Teakle

Pablo Mason
& Gary Stapleton

John Peters (wife, Helen)
& John Nichol

Mark Paisey
& Mike Toft (wife, Sue)

Nigel Elsdon (Officer Commanding 27 Squadron)
& Max Collier

Dave Waddington (mother, Berenice)
& Robbie Stewart (wife, Tange; daughter, Kirsty; son, Scott)

DHAHRAN, SAUDI ARABIA

Cliff Spink, Detachment Commander

Jerry Witts (Officer Commanding 31 Squadron and Tornado
Detachment Commander)
& AJ Smith

Simon (Budgie) Burgess
& Bob Ankerson (wife, Chris; son, Gareth)

Stew Gillies
& Pete Rochelle

Ivor Evans (Officer Commanding 9 Squadron)
& Dicky James

Tabuk, Saudi Arabia

Pete Batson
& Mike Heath (Officer Commanding 20 Squadron)

Trevor Roche
& Dave Bellamy

Mike Warren
& Mal Craghill

Garry Lennox (wife, Anne)
& Kevin Weeks

RAF Marham, Norfolk, UK

Jock Stirrup, Station Commander

Bill Green (Officer Commanding 27 Squadron. Wife, Jenny; son, Jeremy; daughter, Philippa)
& Neil Anderson

GLOSSARY

AAR   Air-to-air refuelling.

ALARM   Air-Launched Anti-Radiation Missile; used to
            attack enemy radar systems.

AWACS   Airborne Warning and Control System; aircraft
            designed to provide over-watch, battlespace manage-
            ment and monitoring across the area of the conflict.

Boz pod   The under-wing pod carried by the Tornado which
            dispensed chaff to confuse radar systems, and
            flares to counter heat-seeking missiles.

Chaff   The strips of metallic fibre ejected from the Boz pod
            which reflected enemy radar signals in an effort to
            avoid detection or break a missile lock. Possibly used
            in conjunction with a missile-break manoeuvre.

CVR   Cockpit Voice Recorder; the so called 'black box'
            which records all intercom and radio conversation
            in the cockpit.

CWP   Central Warning Panel; the in-cockpit system that
                   warns of an aircraft systems failure.

DetCo   Detachment Commander; each major RAF base had
                   a senior officer as the overall DetCo in command
                   of all aspects of operations and support functions.
                   The Tornado unit on each base would have its own
                   DetCo solely in charge of Tornado combat ops.

GLO   Ground Liaison Officer; usually an army officer
                   attached to an RAF squadron to ensure liaison
                   between the services.

HAS   Hardened aircraft shelter; the reinforced bunkers
                   on airfields used to shelter aircraft from attack.

HUD   Head-up Display; a pilot's in-cockpit display which
                   projects crucial information so that it appears in his
                   eyeline as he looks ahead, out of the cockpit.

IFF   Identification, Friend or Foe; an electronic system
                   that is used to tell friendly aircraft from potentially
                   hostile ones.

IP   Initial Point; the point that marks the start of the
                   final run-in towards the target.

LGB   Laser-guided bomb; a munition which has been con-
                   verted to follow laser signals precisely onto a target.

MIA   Missing in action.

Missile break   Aggressive manoeuvres an aircraft makes in an
                   attempt to break a missile lock. Possibly accompa-
                   nied by deploying chaff or flares.

Missile lock	When an enemy SAM system targets a specific aircraft ready to launch and guide a missile in an effort to shoot it down.
MRCA	Multi-Role Combat Aircraft; the initial term by which the Tornado was known before receiving its name.
NBC	Nuclear Biological Chemical.
NVGs	Night-vision goggles.
OLF	Operational low flying; flying down to 100ft above the ground. Only allowed in very specific areas.
Pave Spike	The laser targeting pod used by the Buccaneer aircraft. Daylight only.
PBF	Pilot Briefing Facility; the reinforced building on an airfield aircrews would use to plan and brief missions.
PGM	Precision-Guided Munition; the overall term for any guided weapon.
PLB	Personal Locator Beacon; the emergency radio aircrew carry to use after ejection. When activated, it sends out a signal that can be homed in on.
PTSD	Post-traumatic stress disorder.
QWI	Qualified Weapons Instructor; aircrew who have completed an arduous course to become some of the most highly trained personnel. The role memorably portrayed in the *Top Gun* film.

RHWR   Radar Homing and Warning Receiver; the in-
                cockpit system that warns a crew they are being
                monitored or directly targeted by a potentially
                hostile radar system.

SAM   Surface-to-air missile.

SEAD   Suppression of Enemy Air Defences; this could
                include anti-radar missiles or bombs to attack sites,
                or jamming aircraft to confuse enemy radars.

Sky Shadow   The pod carried by the Tornado under its wing
                which could jam some enemy radar systems.

TFR   Terrain-Following Radar; the forward-looking
                radar system which, when coupled with the
                Tornado's autopilot, allowed the aircraft to 'fly
                itself', with the pilot hands-off the controls, in total
                darkness or bad weather.

TIALD   Thermal Imaging Airborne Laser Designator; the
                improved laser targeting pod rushed into service
                which allowed attacks by both day and night.

TOT   Time on target; the precise time bracket a forma-
                tion was given to get its weapons on the target.

Triple-A   Anti-aircraft artillery, or AAA; intense cannon or
                machine-gun fire from the ground, using 'tracer'
                and explosive rounds which glowed in the dark-
                ness, giving the impression of a sparkling dome of
                light in the desert.

FOREWORD

The RAF Club, Piccadilly, London
20 February 2016

The marbled halls of the Royal Air Force Club in London echoed with excited chatter. Old friends greeted each other with hugs, kisses, and the occasional tear; some had not seen each other since they had fought together many years previously. Amid the grandeur of the Churchill Bar, under the renowned wartime Prime Minister's gaze, drinks were flowing, as were stories of battle, brushes with death, and friends who had made the ultimate sacrifice flying Tornados.

Upstairs, the staff prepared the grand dinner for 110 guests in the huge ballroom, with its mirrored panels and sky-painted ceiling. Polished silverware formed the centrepiece of each long table; legendary RAF aircraft, Spitfire fighters and Lancaster bombers, jostled for space with modern Tornado fast jets. Yellow ribbons, symbolising support of those MIA – missing in action – were tied around the vases. Off to one side, the Salon Orchestra of the Central Band of the RAF was rehearsing the theme tunes from suitably appropriate films – *Those Magnificent Men in Their Flying Machines* and *The Great Escape*.

A security team had already swept the building and armed police bodyguards kept a watchful eye on proceedings, and their two VIPs. The first, the United Kingdom Secretary of State for Defence, was enjoying a pre-dinner glass of champagne with the aircrew and their families. At 7pm, a teenage air cadet sounded her bugle to bring the bar to order and the second VIP, former British Prime Minister, The Right Honourable Sir John Major, stepped forward to speak. He was obviously in some pain, having undergone a hip replacement only a few weeks earlier, and was under doctor's orders to rest. But it was clear to all assembled that he felt it was his duty to attend the event, however briefly, and address those he had sent to war in the Gulf twenty-five years before:

> It is hard to believe that it is twenty-five years since the First Gulf War[1] [which] was, without doubt, a *just* war. Twenty-five years ago we celebrated a victory of freedom over oppression. Tonight's dinner is in honour of the airmen, soldiers and Special Forces who were prisoners during that conflict, which must have been a terrifying experience, especially for those who were, at the time, so young. They must have wondered what the future held, or worse – given whose hands they were in – whether they had any future at all.[2]

Although the dinner was the twenty-fifth annual reunion of the Gulf War prisoners of war, Sir John's words rang true to every single member of the large gathering, especially those who had been at the heart of the 1991 battle to liberate Kuwait from Iraqi occupation.

Some of us had indeed survived being blasted out of hostile skies, been captured, tortured, and endured endless brutality as POWs. But a greater portion of the audience were our friends and colleagues who had shown astonishing bravery and skill, flying countless missions, night after night, under truly deadly fire. They knew what fate awaited them if they too were shot down; they had seen their battered and bruised colleagues paraded as prisoners on Iraqi television. They also knew that a number of their friends had been killed. Carrying on in the face of such adversity had taken a special kind of courage. Collectively, our lives had hung by the narrowest of threads; a situation none of us had ever imagined, or were really prepared for.

* * *

Back in August 1990, when Iraqi forces had invaded neighbouring Kuwait, none of us had any concept of what the future held. Few could have accurately pointed to either country on a map. More importantly, most of us who flew out to the Gulf that year had no real concept of armed conflict. We were Cold War warriors; some at that dinner had joined the military in the 1960s, a few years after the Cuban Missile Crisis had brought the world to the brink of nuclear Armageddon. Our primary concern through the 1970s and 80s was with the threat to Europe and the West from Communism and the Soviet Union. Our training was built around the threat of mass battles, mass casualties and, ultimately, the use of the nuclear weapons. The notion of fighting a focused, regional war in a faraway desert was simply unimaginable. In 1982, as the first Tornados were just entering service, a war had been fought to liberate the Falkland Islands after the Argentinian invasion and many lives had been lost. But at the time it was regarded as perhaps an isolated incident, and, while air power had been crucial, there had not been mass attacks with hundreds of aircraft in the skies at one time.

As a young Tornado navigator in the 1980s I was part of a truly vast, 310,000-strong military machine. The RAF's Tornado force *alone*, which would eventually spearhead the defence of Saudi Arabia and subsequent attacks on Iraq, numbered around 430 bomber and fighter aircraft. The total size of the RAF was astonishing – nearly 94,000 personnel and 1,800 front-line and training aircraft.[3] To give this some context, in 2020 the RAF had around 32,000 personnel and some 570 aircraft.

Regardless of our incredible military might, I had never truly believed the Tornado force would fight any war. We trained endlessly for it, but the reality was far from my mind. Our major focus was on the deployment of nuclear weapons, and, if I had ever taken off on that mission, there would have been little to return to. We were like firefighters who had never fought a blaze, medics who had never attended to an injury.

Then, in August 1990, the brutal Iraqi dictator Saddam Hussein invaded his Gulf neighbour and everything changed. Hussein had thought the world would never intervene. His miscalculation would cost him and his nation dear. And the ramifications of the conflict he ignited still reverberate around the region, and the world, thirty years later. Within weeks of the invasion, United States President George H. W. Bush had built a near-total international coalition intent on evicting Iraq from Kuwait; hundreds of thousands of troops deployed to the region. The American and British military would be in the eye, of what would become, Operation Desert Storm.[4]

* * *

There was another group at the dinner in the RAF Club that night; the friends and relatives of those who had fought. Men and women who had sat at home, waiting for news. In many ways, theirs was the most heart-wrenching and lonely task, watching events unfold on TV, waiting to see if *their* loved one would survive. And a few listening to Sir John had received the dreaded 'knock at the door'; military officers in uniform delivering the worst news possible, as the war drew to its close. The former Prime Minister made it clear he had felt a deep responsibility to those who fought, and those who died:

I have many memories of the conflict. A few days before the war started, I visited Dhahran and when I stood on a lorry to speak to the vast array of troops and airmen gathered around, I saw how truly young so many of *you* were. I knew – though you did not – that the war would begin two or three days later, on January 16.[5] As it happens, that day was my son's sixteenth birthday and, as I looked out at the sea of faces before me, I saw many who were

barely older than him. As I spoke, my own son's face was trans-
posed on each one.

Nothing could have been a more powerful way of demonstrating – *to me* – the momentous task we were asking of *you*.
Older men and women decide on war, but it is younger men and
women who have to fight it, and risk their lives in doing so. And,
sadly, lives were lost. Mercifully few – but even *one* is too many. I
remember staying up night after night to receive reports – and this
was the hardest thing to bear – to learn which, if any, crews had
been lost. Never imagine that ministers do not share the tension
of families sitting at home. We felt every single moment; not least
since *we* were responsible for it.

His recent hip operation meant our principal guest speaker should
only have stayed at the venue for around twenty minutes, but he
spent considerable time chatting to the men and their families. He
was particularly keen to seek out those who had lost a husband,
brother, father or son and talk to them in private.[6] Over an hour
after his arrival, a bodyguard quietly reminded him he was not
meant to be standing at all.

After his departure, the drink flowed and reminiscences
became increasingly noisier. Hands were waved like wings above
the silver aircraft tableware, detailing aerial skirmishes and close
calls with death in the Iraqi skies twenty-five years before. Those
of us who had flown just a couple of missions before being shot
down (in my own case, a single op) were the target of light military ribbing by friends who had flown countless sorties in the
face of deadly fire.

Before things got too riotous, the Secretary of State for Defence,
Michael Fallon, who had come straight from a seventeen-hour flight
from the Falkland Islands, stood up to speak:

Let me start by saying, it's not simply an honour to meet you,
but humbling too. Being Defence Secretary means having to take
hard decisions that can put our people in harm's way. That's never

easy. But it's easier for *me* than it is for *you* – and *your* families. You have to carry out those political choices on the front line. And you have to face the consequences. You had to cope with something entirely new for your generation.

Since the First Gulf War, today's men and women have grown used to the idea of serving in a combat situation. But for you who took part in that seminal conflict things were *very* different. We'd just emerged from the Cold War. You were trained to guard against the hordes who might suddenly emerge from behind the Iron Curtain. You were ever on the alert for nuclear escalation. Tense and terrible though it was, it was predictable. And this shadow boxing had gone on for decades. No one really expected things to change.

And then – seemingly out of nowhere – Saddam Hussein sent 100,000 troops crashing into Kuwait. And you found yourselves part of one of the biggest conflicts of our modern era – well over half a million people assembled in the desert. It was not that you were unprepared. More that it was so unexpected; so unpredictable. That must have come as a huge shock to your system. The sudden knowledge that this wasn't a test. It was happening for real. Yet, despite all that, you remained undaunted. You adjusted. You adapted. You did us proud.

And let me make particular mention of [those] sadly no longer among your number. Their families – some I'm honoured to see here in the room tonight – need to know that we will never forget their sacrifice and service. Their names and their legacies will live on.[7]

A number of dinner guests were in tears as the Defence Secretary made his tribute to the fallen.

* * *

That reunion of colleagues who had fought above the deserts of Iraq was a momentous occasion, not least because it prompted a number of surprising realisations. As individual memories of the war, sometimes painful, often long buried, began to surface, it became obvious to me that, even after all those years, most of us still knew little of our companions' true experiences during the conflict.

Indeed, *I* had never spoken, in any detail, to my fellow prisoners of war, or even my own Tornado Squadron friends, about *their* experiences of captivity or battle; their emotions in the face of fear and possible death. And I had never spoken *at all* to the wives or children who had waited at home, praying for husbands and fathers to safely return.[8] The seeds of this book were sown.

Countless RAF, army and navy units were involved in the liberation of Kuwait and all served with courage and dedication. Nearly 50,000 British personnel deployed to the Gulf region. Of course, I can only tell the stories of a few, but I hope that their interwoven experiences will stand as a tribute to them all.

John Nichol
Hertfordshire
April 2021

PROLOGUE

SEVEN SECONDS

SATURDAY, 19 JANUARY 1991, THE GULF

Robbie Stewart stared into the hotel's polished bathroom mirror at the grey stubble that spread down his cheeks and across his jaw.

He sprayed shaving foam into his hand and saw again the yellow-white explosion of flame with its vicious red heart. Robbie's friend and fellow Tornado navigator Max Collier, and his pilot Nigel Elsdon, the Squadron Boss, had disappeared in an instant. Nigel had only been with them for a few weeks. Both had gone down on the first day of the war to liberate Kuwait from Iraqi occupation, although they were presumed dead there was no official confirmation.

Robbie's own Tornado had been travelling at 600mph, trying to escape the storm of gunfire, when the radio call came to say an aircraft had gone in. At first, he had thought one of their JP233 runway-busting munitions had exploded. Then came the sickening realisation. 'I knew immediately that the huge orange fireball was an aircraft, but there was no time to reflect, we just needed to get out of the target area.'[1] Both men had gone; their Tornado strewn across southern Iraq's desert floor.

Out of immediate danger, reality took hold. 'It was just a hollow feeling that we hadn't all made it, but there was nothing to be done or said.' At first the barrage of deadly triple-A – anti-aircraft artillery, or AAA – streaming skywards had seemed almost like a novelty. Sparkling white and yellow lights cascading over the cockpit like a firework display. Robbie, the Tornado's navigator, had felt strangely cocooned under the thick Perspex canopy. 'You could see all this happening around you, but it's calm and settled inside a Tornado with your helmet on. So quiet you feel isolated from the outside. I didn't feel any fear, I was concentrating on the job. I had one task: to release the weapon at the right point, at the exact time.'

They were now two days into the air campaign that sounded the opening salvo to drive Saddam Hussein's forces out of Kuwait, a sovereign state the Iraqi Republican Guard had invaded six months earlier. They had lost Max and Nigel on their first mission. Days later, they were about to face it all over again, now knowing beyond any doubt that death in war was real. Neither Max nor Nigel would be present at the next briefing. Nor would the grinning faces of other colleagues. The 'Two Johns', Peters and Nichol, had also been shot down earlier that first day, 17 January. All that had been heard of them was Nichol's last cry: 'We're on fire. We might have to get out!'[2] Then silence.

Four aircrew lost in the opening hours of the war.

As Robbie stood in front of the mirror, the intense triple-A barrage, the deadly, never-ending salvoes of exploding shells, the smell of sweat, the grunts, the concentration and exertion from the Tornado's high G-forces all but swamped him. The enemy gunfire had been of unimaginable intensity and volume, and yet somehow they had sailed through it untouched as they attacked the airfield. They had gone to war for the first time *ever*, with an arsenal of *real* weapons under their Tornado, against a *real* enemy who wanted them dead. Robbie's feeling was now very different from the adrenaline charge and apprehension of the first night. 'England and my family seemed a long way away and I was about to enter a hostile country where people would be trying to kill me. Again.'

Until the first jets had been lost, it had seemed they were untouchable. He sighed and slid the razor down his bronzed cheek. *Thank God for Tange*. Talking to his wife – her name was a shortened version of 'Tangerine', her childhood family nickname – the previous evening had released the pressure. The vision of her sitting on their sofa in the snug living room of their Victorian cottage in the quiet Lincolnshire village of Coleby. The bench on the green opposite their front door, the magnificent tower and steeple of All Saints Church. The low hum and familiar smell of the Tempest Arms. 'I'm safe, Tange. I'm okay,' Robbie had told her. He knew that there had been relentless television coverage of the first raids. Tange would have seen reports about Tornados going down, but said nothing. The relief and delight in her voice had made his heart soar.

Robbie had not been able to stop himself from telling her what he had seen and her sympathy was overwhelming. He had felt tears brim. It was time to go. Neither said, but both knew in their hearts that this could be their last conversation. Some of his colleagues had already had *their* final words with loved ones. Her voice had carried in his ears as he had gone back to the bar to drink to Max and Nigel's memory. The beers had the desired effect. He'd slept soundly. Only to wake up a few hours later knowing another mission loomed. Alcohol could not obliterate that. *I can't call her after every raid*. It was too much knowing that every phone call might be their last.

Robbie's young pilot Dave Waddington had also slept well, only to wake up with similar images of that first mission replaying endlessly in his head. Flying in total darkness, before the night had been lit up by the searing flames of the jet hitting the ground. *Max and Nigel gone*. 'I had looked out over my left shoulder to see a huge explosion; a fireball spreading across the desert floor. I knew it was a jet, but I couldn't quite rationalise what I was seeing.'[3] Their Tornado cockpit had been largely silent on the flight out of the combat zone. 'There wasn't much chat, there was little to say. Just a horrible, sinking realisation that we had lost our colleagues and there was nothing we could do about it. The incredible elation of getting out of danger, having done the job for the first time, for real, was quickly consumed by loss. It was really hard to accept, but you knew it had happened because you had seen it with your own eyes.'

Dave listened to the sound of Robbie's ablutions from their hotel bathroom. He was thankful to have such an experienced operator at his back. Their bond had grown over the many months they had flown together. At twenty-four, Dave Waddington was the youngest pilot on the Squadron. His navigator was forty-four, a silver-haired old hand, devoted to his wife and two teenage kids. Robbie's quiet disposition complemented Dave's flying skills, centring his focus on all that mattered – *get in, release the bombs, get out*. 'I was amazed how calm I had been as I gave a running commentary to Robbie in the back seat. All I could see was sparkling lights streaming into the sky towards us. I didn't think about there being three inches of explosive lead bullet behind it all!'

Their return to base presented them with a strange and disconcerting contrast. One moment they had been flying into furious gunfire, the next they were sitting in air-conditioned comfort amid the marbled columns of the Bahrain Sheraton Hotel, their designated quarters for the duration of the deployment in the absence of other military accommodation. They quietly drank cold beers, lancing the pain of their loss. 'When someone is killed in action, there are rituals to be observed by the survivors. It's a Royal Air Force tradition. Either fill up the guy's bar book, or drink whatever he's got in his room. It was very hard. We were drinking their beer and they weren't coming home. We were toasting lost friends, but we all knew that we would soon have to do the same thing again.'

They were in a contest now, that was for sure, where you flew through a wall of bullets and a hail of missiles. Where you either came home or you died. Despite the casualties from the first sorties, Dave pushed away such thoughts. 'I didn't allow myself to acknowledge that I might be killed. I didn't talk about it with my fiancée Claire. I didn't write a last letter. I knew death might happen, but I didn't want to acknowledge it was even a possibility for me.' If his bond with Robbie was tight in the build-up to war, that first night had cast it in steel. 'The reality of what we had been through hit us.

The loss of Max and Nige started to come to the fore in a growing realisation that in the not-too-distant future, together, we would be going again.'

Dave yawned as he dragged himself from the Sheraton's luxury bed. The frenzied conversations with other Tornado aircrew came back to him. Hearing *their* sortie descriptions. What *their* triple-A was like. What *they* had seen. Everyone was thirsting for knowledge, searching for a vital clue on how to survive what was coming next. He sat on the edge of the bed. In just a few hours he would be back up in the air. The memories of the cauldron of triple-A, the tensions and loss, resurfaced. 'A nearby target had been hit by the Americans that turned night into day in a few seconds. I remember thinking, *I can't believe we are going to get through that.* We had lost the Two Johns, Max and Nige, flown through a wall of lead and had a missile shot at us. There was no doubt in my mind the risks were very, very real and it wasn't going to get any easier.'

'Morning.'

Dave looked up as his friend and navigator flicked on the television, already pre-set to CNN 24-hour news. The American channel was the only one with reporters in Baghdad, showing the world the devastating effect of previously unseen precision attacks. It was real-time intelligence for everyone. There was something unreal about watching the reports of raids from the comfort of a hotel bedroom when they would be back over hostile territory in a matter of hours, bombing Iraq themselves.

Clean-shaven, showered and in crisply pressed flying suits, Dave and Robbie took the ten-minute bus ride to work in silence, via the causeway to the island of Muharraq and Bahrain's airfield. Forty-eight hours after the first sortie, it was clear to Robbie that there had already been a tactical rethink. The Tornados were going in for yet another attack on the massive Tallil airbase in southern Iraq. But this time, they would be on their own with just the shroud of darkness for protection; no prior 'softening up' by American bombers. Instead, the thinking went, surprise would catch the Iraqis unprepared. Robbie was unconvinced. 'To gain surprise we were not being supported by the usual myriad American aircraft suppressing surface-to-air missiles – SAMs – and radars. This way, it was hoped, we would avoid the wall-to-wall triple-A which we'd encountered on our first sortie. But I would have preferred the Americans accompanying us; to me, while the triple-A was a horrifying sight, the SAMs were the real threat.'

Instead, the eight-ship would provide their own airfield defence suppression. The first flight of four – call sign 'Belfast formation' – including Robbie and Dave, would go in and drop 20,000lb of high explosive on the gun and missile emplacements, demonstrating the immense skill that RAF crews had developed flying Tornados. A 'loft – or toss – attack' at night from low level was as dangerous as it got. Pulling up steeply from low level while the weapons aiming system calculated the exact point of release, the jet would accurately 'throw' its five 1,000lb bombs forward, towards the target. They were set to detonate over the heads of the Iraqi gunners, blasting shards of shrapnel through weapons and flesh. The hard part was then turning away from the target and manoeuvring the jet back down to low level, in total darkness and under fire.

Dave and Robbie had trained hard for this type of loft attack. *Come in fast and ultra-low, pop up, lob the bombs, get back down to low level and bugger off.* And thoroughly discourage the triple-A gunners from firing at the four-ship coming in behind with the vaunted JP233 weapons system, which would deliver surface crater-ing munitions and scatter anti-personnel mines to shut down Tallil's runways and deter any Iraqi repair teams.

Dave and Robbie listened in the cool of the Operations Room as the briefing moved on to Tallil's air defences. 'We knew there'd be triple-A and we knew there was a Roland missile system on the air-field. We were very apprehensive. Dave and I looked at one another. We didn't need to say much, we just looked.' There was good reason to fear the Roland SAM. Hurtling out at over 1,200mph, its 9kg warhead threw out deadly fragmentation designed to gut aircraft and crew. One of the few foreign-made SAMs purchased by the US,[4] the French-made missiles had taken down numerous Iranian jets during the earlier Iran–Iraq war. The operators in Tallil were old hands. Robbie and the others well understood its significance.

The Tornado at least had the Radar Homing and Warning Receiver. The RHWR was a key defence against any radar-guided missile attack.[5] A small green screen on the right-hand side of both cockpits, it would give an indication, a 'trace', if a radar was looking at them, and from which direction. Cleverer still, it signalled the type of enemy missile system or aircraft. If a radar locked onto the Tornado, the RHWR flashed a line across the screen, a 'strobe', and delivered a high-pitched squawk into the crew's flying helmets to warn of an imminent engagement. An even more urgent siren would sound if a missile was launched, accompanied by 'MG' flashing on the screen, indicating missile guidance. The RHWR was rightly considered a wartime 'no-go' item if it was not functioning correctly.

The intelligence briefing came to an end. Someone asked if there was any update on the Two Johns. There wasn't. Just a reminder to check their own escape and evasion kits. Robbie felt for the tube of gold sovereigns worth around £1,000[6] with which to bribe any locals, and the piece of paper – the so-called 'goolie chit' – which announced in Arabic that the bearer would receive a further £5,000 if a flier was returned to safety in one piece. In previous Middle East wars aircrew had been returned with testicles severed, and there was no indication that times had changed. Especially under the savage rule of Saddam Hussein and, more especially, given the rumours Robbie had heard of torture in Kuwait.

'Our minds were even more focused now because of the losses. I was very aware of checking and rechecking everything – we made sure all the escape kit was correctly positioned to give us the best chance if we ejected into enemy territory. We were not just concentrating on the flying side of ops. We double-checked the search-and-rescue procedures but still wondered if we were ready for the worst.' Some aircrew believed it might be better to perish quickly in the cockpit rather than slowly, at the hands of Saddam's henchmen.

The loss of comrades had really pointed up the dangers for Dave, but he couldn't let it affect him. 'I compartmentalised it, put it out of my mind and kept my focus on our own mission. There was nothing else you could do. You can't just walk away and say, "This is too dangerous." There was also the naivety of youth, probably like our Second World War RAF forebears, you just tell yourself: "It will never happen to me."'

He filed out of the briefing with another crew in their formation whose attack profile took them right over the SAM site. 'There was certainly some anxiety around; we were going very close to a Roland missile site which was a very real threat. I remember that the last thing I said to the other crew before we headed to the aircraft was, "Don't worry about the Roland, it will probably get me before it gets you."'

They all grinned. But then Dave caught Robbie's eye and saw a look of apprehension. They both knew what lay ahead. The odds might improve with the planned element of surprise, but Tallil's air defences were still a very real threat. On the first night the Iraqis seemed to just spray their triple-A randomly into the sky. Intelligence suggested they had now lowered the elevation on their gun barrels to catch the Tornados coming in at their approach height of around 200ft.

* * *

Under a mid-afternoon sun the eight pilots and eight navigators drifted out of the briefing room and headed across the tarmac towards the mess tent for some dinner. On the first night there had been a buzz of anticipation mixed with nervous laughter along the benches and tables. Not any more, reflected Robbie. 'The atmosphere was sombre. We all knew what the reality of this war now meant.'

Fliers and ground crew were all in this together. The Tornados belonged to everyone. The ground crew spent hours on them, carefully attending to every screw, bolt, cable, ramp and nozzle that held the £20 million machine together.[7] To lose an aircraft was to lose a part of themselves. To lose *their* aircrew was unbearable. And it was a very real possibility. Two sets had already been left forlornly gazing into the Arabian dawn, waiting for their jets to return, hearing only the sound of the muezzin's call to prayer. Among the engineers, the fitters, the admin staff and the logistics teams, the atmosphere was muted. Minds were focused.

Dusk was approaching as last-minute adjustments were made. Robbie found himself repeatedly checking every item of kit. The water pouches, the gold, the maps. He pulled out his small Walther PP from the leather shoulder holster and ejected the magazine, checking the eight rounds. He checked everything again then spotted his precious Ray-Bans on a table and, despite the looming darkness, stuffed them into his G-suit pants. The glare of low-level flying over the desert made them a necessity. One last time he went over the search-and-rescue procedures with Dave. Everyone else in the eight-ship was doing the same.

With their pockets bulging, G-suits tightly bound around their legs and thighs, the airmen picked up their helmets and ambled awkwardly to the waiting Tornados.

'Crews walking.' The message was sent out.

They were ready to take over the aircraft from the engineers. Robbie was pleased they were back in 'F for Foxtrot', which had carried them through the first mission unscathed. 'We said farewell to the flying-clothing boys, who wished us well with some concern showing. The jet was just 50 yards from the Operations Room but we walked out like gladiators, our kit clanking and clanging. The five 1,000-pounders already had some graffiti along the side suggesting what Saddam should do with the bombs.'

White chalk messages from the ground crew were often scrawled across the long, dark cylinders: from *One in the eye for you, Sad Man Saddam* to the endearing *Hi Sarah, Love Pete*.[8]

The aircraft loomed menacingly in the shadowed lights of the shelter. The Tornado's black nose contrasted dramatically with the desert pink of its body. Inside the sharply pointed cone was the ground-mapping radar that helped the navigator update the navigation system and identify the targets. Behind it the cockpit swept back over broad, muscular flanks. Intakes on either side of the fuselage fed air back to the powerful engine. The jet-pipes would roar, emitting yellow-blue flame from the reheat. Every fibre of its being yelled power. When the under-wing-points were harnessed with missiles, defensive pods and fuel tanks, and the belly with neatly arrayed bombs, there was no doubt what the Tornado GR1 was about. It exuded menace and meant business. The business of hitting the enemy hard. Fully armed, with its tailfin standing proud, it sent a message of dominance as it shuddered into the air. A war-fighter capable of raining fury upon its enemies, but it was graceful too.

The Tornado was neat and compact, and, for those like Robbie who had seen an aircraft or two in his twenty-five years' service, very, very effective. 'It had everything you could have dreamed of. Great navigation and targeting kit. It could fly at night, in terrible weather, at low level and hands-off. It really was superb, very modern.'

Laden with his helmet, escape equipment and G-suit, Robbie had walked past the sandbagged airfield defences, the tankers and other jets. 'Approaching the dark shape of the Tornado in the gloom, bristling with a full weapons load, ready for war, made you contemplate what you were about to do. There was a palpable sense of apprehension, hoping to God we would survive what was to come but ready for the fight. We knew the drills and were eager to get underway. This was our job, it needed to be done. We pushed all other thoughts aside.'

He mounted the steps, settled into the navigator's rear seat, which sat slightly higher than the pilot's but with instruments in front obscuring some of his forward visibility. He went through the careful ritual of strapping himself into the ejection seat, then checked his watch. Forty minutes to take-off.

Dave completed his final checks on the 30-tonne machine[9] that he was about to launch airborne under the twin thrust of its

Rolls-Royce RB199 engines. He pulled himself up on the jet-pipes to check for any loose articles, then tapped the two under-wing 2,250-litre fuel tanks. He gave the pair of Sidewinder air-to-air missiles a good shake to ensure they were properly locked on. They would be needed if Iraqi fighters showed up. He then made sure that the safety pins had been removed from each of the 1,000lb bombs, knowing his touch would be the last before they became a screaming ball of shrapnel.

Under the shadows cast by the glare of the airfield lighting he reached up to the 'Boz' self-defence pod under the right wing, checking the chaff and flare dispenser.[10]

When activated, 'chaffing' would send thousands of tiny metallic fibres – 60 per cent glass, 40 per cent aluminium, and the thickness of a human hair – into the air. They were designed to reflect and interfere with enemy radar signals, confusing both the systems and their operators. The flares would be pumped out if targeted by heat-seeking missiles; they burned off at an intense temperature, hopefully providing a more attractive target than their jet engines.

Dave examined the Sky Shadow pod on the other wing that was programmed to electronically jam enemy radar systems. They had every possible countermeasure the Tornado was designed to carry. It was reassuring for Dave to feel they were all held firmly in place if he had to throw F for Foxtrot about. 'In reality, the ground crew have already checked all this, then double-checked it, but we all did it again. Everyone had their own idiosyncrasies. I always gave the fuel tanks a tap to ensure they were full. They always were!' Everything was in order outside the aircraft. It was time to board.

Robbie fitted his oxygen pipe, intercom cable and G-suit hose into the personal equipment connector then clipped it onto the side of his seat, plugging himself into the machine's systems. He tightened the straps over his thighs and torso connected to the fastener over his stomach which held him firmly into the Martin Baker ejection seat. His hand brushed against the black and yellow-striped D-shaped ejection handles between his legs as he switched on the inertial navigation system, allowing the gyroscopes and sensors to start up their alignment process. He turned on the main computer and its monitors, and then the radios. Everything was working as advertised and the cockpit came alive with the green and red glow of the equipment. He took out the navigation cassette – the same type used to play music in a Sony Walkman – and loaded it into the main computer. It had been fed with all the information needed to navigate the route to Tallil and back, along with the precise co-ordinates of the target and aiming points.

Dave stepped back from beneath the towering fin that gave the Tornado its nickname, climbed the 9ft steps up to the cockpit and levered himself into the front seat. With his green flying helmet in place, he had the sharp, focused look of a jet pilot. It was the job he had dreamed of since he was seven. The ground crew fussed over him, pulling tight the straps on his harness. 'Give Saddam one from us, sir,' one said before climbing down and removing the steps.

Dave began his well-rehearsed start-up routine. 'There was a comfort in the well-trodden procedures. As I lowered the cockpit canopy, I felt isolated in the Tornado despite the activity outside. We had left plenty of time in case we had any problems. As I went through the checks, my nerves started to dissipate as I became part of the machinery of war. It was exactly like a training sortie, but I knew it was for real.'

Dave found the cockpit spacious compared to other jets and the ejection seat quite comfortable. He used the electric motor to raise his seat an inch, and briefly scanned the ground crew activity. He too attached his oxygen, comms and G-suit into the personal equipment connector and snapped it in place.[11] A glance at his watch told him it was thirty minutes to take-off. Plenty of time to sort out any problems. He rattled through the check list.

His cockpit was dominated by the circular moving map display right in front of him. On his left were the flight instruments, the throttles and lever to move the wings – back for low, fast flight; forward for take-off, medium-altitude flying and landing. His right hand gripped the control column – the 'stick' as it was generally known – between his legs while his left fell naturally on the throttles at mid-thigh level on the console. He paused, breathed in then looked up. The HUD – Head-up Display – dominated the cockpit front and centre. And rightly so. It was his primary flying instrument. When the Tornado was tearing along the desert floor at night, in thick fog or bright sunshine, the HUD projected speed, height, direction, weapon aiming and much more in green symbols on a glass screen.

To the left of the HUD was the Terrain-Following Radar display. TFR was the heart of the Tornado's ability to fly at night and in poor weather at very low level. A radar swept the ground ahead and gave instructions to the TFR computer system which fed the aircraft's autopilot.[12] Once activated, the pilot would remove his hands from the controls and TFR would take over; the Tornado would 'fly itself' at speeds of up to nearly 700mph and just 200ft above the ground. In total darkness or thick cloud. It was an astonishing piece of equipment.

To the right was the RHWR screen, which would warn them of incoming missiles or radar detection. Dave rapidly ran through the checks then muttered a curse. The flashing cockpit 'attention-getters' were mounted left and right of the cockpit coaming, just above the RHWR and TFR screens, and flashed red if there was a problem, attracting the pilot's attention to the Central Warning Panel (CWP) on his right. This, in turn, had more than sixty different captions which illuminated red for primary and amber for secondary-type warnings.[13] A single illuminated word on the CWP indicated the problem, such as 'FUEL', 'TFR' or 'OXY'. It was a bit like the alerts on a car dashboard, bar the fact it contained two captions that read 'L FIRE' and 'R FIRE', informing the crew their left- or right-hand engine had become an inferno. In the event of multiple failures, the CWP might 'light up like a Christmas tree'; a *really* serious problem would trigger an accompanying siren.

They were an important part of the Tornado's safety systems. Unfortunately for Dave and the engineers, F for Foxtrot's attention-getters flashed for no reason, and couldn't be cancelled.

In peacetime, they would simply 'crew out' – leave the aircraft – as it was impractical to fly with red warning lights flashing. But the spare Tornado had already been taken. And leaving F for Foxtrot meant not going on the mission. Dave was caught between a rock and a hard place. 'I knew I should really crew out of the jet; it was the correct thing to do and I certainly wouldn't be facing the dangers ahead. But what would people think of me? Say about me? What was the *right* thing to do? It was a choice, a tension between doing what was acceptable or doing what was *right*. I didn't want to let anyone down.'

The minutes to take-off were counting down. Dave felt his heart start to thud. He looked out at the engineer. 'Any suggestions?' he asked over the external intercom.

'The only thing you can do, sir, is flip up the covers and take out the bulbs.'

A big, ballsy call. Flying fast and low at night into a sky full of gunfire was already risky as hell. To not be alerted to a problem which would normally be signalled by bright lights right in front of his eyes took them a whole lot further along the hazard spectrum. Dave spoke to Robbie over the intercom. 'Shall we take the fault? The engineer said he can take out the bulbs . . .'

Robbie had his own attention-getters in the rear seat so knew they had a safety net.

'Yes,' he said. 'Take it.'

'Okay.'

Dave checked the various modes of the IFF. *Crap!* It wasn't loading up. Now this was critical. It would be suicidal flying without it. IFF – Identification, Friend or Foe – was an electronic system used by the coalition fighters and ground radar to differentiate enemy and friendly aircraft.

The ground crew loaded, re-loaded, and loaded it again. Finally, they got it working. The engineer pocketed the bulbs from the attention-getters, gave the cockpit canopy a quick wipe then closed it once again. With all the technical glitches cleared, or at least overcome, it was time to get airborne.

'Clear for engine start,' Dave said. The engineer gave a thumbs-up and Dave flicked a switch. He listened as a pleasurable low hum became a rumble.[14] The temperature gauges rose steadily from 6°C to 420°C. Even with the canopy shut and his helmet on, he could hear the powering jet engines and feel the shuddering vibration as they built to a roar.

The ground crew removed the chocks, Dave inched the throttles forward, rolled a few yards then tested the brakes by dabbing them and stopping. He taxied to the runway, feeling the heavily laden aircraft bump over the seams in the concrete. Deep blue-yellow flames glared at them from the afterburners of the other jets as they took off ahead. The Rolls-Royce engines generated 30,000lb of thrust, and burned around 600 kilos of fuel a minute at maximum power.[15] Every last ounce of it would be needed to propel the lumbering Tornado off the ground.

Their aircraft shuddered again under the turbulence as jet after jet lifted off Bahrain's friendly tarmac strip into the night sky. Dave lined up and carried out their final checks.

It was time to go.

His left hand eased forward the throttle. There was a surge of power as he pushed the engines into reheat, fully opening the jet-pipe nozzles and pumping fuel at incredible speed onto the engine's hot exhaust gas, where it ignited in a sheet of blue flame, doubling the power and making a sound like thunder.

'Engine's good,' Dave said, glancing at the gauges above his right knee. 'Captions clear.'

There was nothing on the Central Warning Panel to prevent take-off. They both felt the aircraft quiver as the engines went through maximum dry power into reheat.

He released the brakes and the Tornado's acceleration pushed him firmly back into the seat, as if a giant hand was pressing onto his chest.

'Eighty knots, 100 knots,' Dave called as they blasted down the tarmac.

The jet trembled, eager to fly, as the runway lights rushed by.

'One hundred and thirty knots,' Dave breathed. They were pass-ing the last point at which their fully laden Tornado would be able to use its own brakes to bring them safely to a halt.

'Okay.'

The speed in the HUD rapidly increased.

'One hundred and eighty knots [207mph]. Engine's good. Captions clear. Rotating.' With the extra weight he gave himself a bit more speed then eased back the stick.

F for Foxtrot lifted off cleanly.

'Gear up.' He flicked the undercarriage handle to raise the landing gear.

'Two hundred and fifty knots. Out of reheat.'

A moment later, they were climbing through 2,000ft.

The Tornados of Belfast formation sailed through the night sky above the silent waters of the Gulf, turning northwards. Dave focused on the task ahead, a mid-air rendezvous with their tankers at 15,000ft. Air-to-air refuelling at night in total silence and near total darkness was a challenge. Before Saddam invaded Kuwait back in August, barely anyone in the Tornado bomber world had attempted to thread a probe into a swinging drogue basket in a blackout. In the hit parade of piloting skill sets, it was second only to ultra-low flying. The previous night, seven out of eight Italian Air Force Tornados had been forced to turn back from a raid after failing to hook into the tanker drogue. The pilot who had refuelled carried on alone, pelted by the flak surrounding an ammunition dump north of Kuwait City, and dropped his bombs 250ft above the deck. He was hit by triple-A gunfire forty seconds later.[16]

The aircraft had gone down at 4.30am on 18 January and the crew were MIA – missing in action. The third Tornado to be lost in the first twenty-four hours.

Dave's eyes scoured the darkness for the tanker. With a full war load the Tornado sucked up 60kg of fuel a minute in normal condi-tions at low level, ten times that in reheat. They carried enough fuel for perhaps two hours' flying, for a mission that would last twice that. The plan was to refuel just before entering Iraqi air space, then top up again on the way home. After six months of intense training, Dave was ready for the challenge.

'Eight miles. Heading two-seven-zero.' Robbie was the one whose skills were needed at this point. He had identified the tanker aircraft on his radar and talked down the ranges and height on the approach, plotting a course to within a few feet of the hanging basket. It was not until Dave squinted through the darkness that he could finally make out the looming belly of the tanker. They ran through the pre-tanking checks, depressurising the fuel system and extending their refuelling probe.[17]

Dave slipped the Tornado to the right, stabilising a few feet behind their target. The red light under the tanker's wing flicked off and he was cleared to join.

His concentration was all-consuming as he lined up the symbol on the HUD with the pod under the tanker's wings. His grip on the stick tightened and so did his chest with every bump as they edged forward, making tiny corrections to keep aligned. The Tornado's refuelling probe was extended to his right, but he wasn't looking at it; diverting his focus from the looming tanker could be catastrophic. Instead, he was concentrating on flying his aircraft towards a precise point on the tanker itself, knowing that as long as he was accurate the probe – almost unseen on his right – would slip effortlessly into the basket.

Robbie had a far better view of the probe and basket. With the occasional word of guidance from the back seat, Dave's concentration was only broken by the clunk of the probe engaging with the dangling fuel pipe. The feeling of satisfaction as he finally glanced to his right was strong.

But he couldn't relax. Both aircraft were travelling at nearly 350mph, with the nearest Tornado just yards away.

From now on Dave had to fly in precise formation, anticipating any jolts that might rip their connection apart. He edged the nose forward, bending the hose back to trigger the flow of high-octane fuel. The 'traffic light' on the tanker's wing turned green and Dave glanced down at the fuel gauge above his right knee. After a few minutes it showed they were once again ready for combat. He reduced power, backed away from the basket, manoeuvred to the left and joined formation with the other Tornados that had completed their own delicate night-time ballet.

For a brief moment he allowed himself to relax. He flexed his right hand, tingling and numb after gripping the stick so tightly, and fleetingly scanned the dark void below them. *Get down, get it done, go home.*

They slipped away from the tanker well short of the Iraqi border, swept the wings back and accelerated down to low level in radio silence. As they sped through the moonless sky, they completed the checks on their self-defence and attack systems. The Sky Shadow and Boz pods, and RHWR were all active. Dave set his armament safety switches to the 'live' position, ensuring their Sidewinder missiles, the 27mm Mauser cannons and the bombs were all armed and ready for instant use.[18] The fuel tanks under each wing were preselected for jettison just in case an emergency release was needed to evade enemy SAMs or fighters. They checked all external lights were extinguished and did a quick review of the escape and evasion. *Just in case.*

The pilots in the eight Tornados had engaged their TFR systems and removed their hands from the controls. The jets now flew themselves on autopilot through the darkness. They were on parallel track, a strategy developed when flying hands-off on TFR and autopilot in poor weather or at night. The lead Tornado and his wingman followed two separate but parallel flight paths, around 2.5 miles line abreast, as if on rail-tracks, with the second two, also line abreast, around 5 miles behind them, creating a box-shaped formation, all proceeding just 200ft above the desert floor at 7 miles per minute.[19] The crews relied on radar fixes along the route to keep the navigation systems accurate and to ensure the box remained separated.

Robbie had no way of seeing their comrades, but knew they were out there, on the same heading, bonded by the shared objectives, and shared dangers. 'We descended, lights out, into the dark

unknown, heading across the Saudi border. We were totally alone.'
He watched the moving map display tick off the distance, as they
flew in, increasing speed to over 480mph. Then they were 'sausage
side'. They had borrowed the nickname for enemy territory from the
avidly watched BBC classic *Blackadder Goes Forth*. The insanity of
the First World War trenches was beginning to echo uncomfortably
in the current conflict.

The readouts confirmed to Robbie that they were racing along at
just 200ft, the Tornado's TFR automatically adjusting their flight
path to account for every contour and obstacle, but their sensory
isolation seemed to insulate them momentarily from the hostile
world outside the warm glow of the cockpit. 'The night was pitch-
black, so the only indication of our height were the numbers on the
TV monitor. There was still no sign of any Iraqi resistance as we
approached the target. I was relatively calm, bearing in mind what
we were doing. Everything seemed to be going to plan. I had all the
weapons systems checked.'

Up front, Dave had a strong sense of the aircraft powering through
the night. His right hand rested on his lap, away from the control
column, his left hovered near the throttle. Although he was poised to
instantly take control if any problems arose, right now he was simply
monitoring the systems. 'Everyone was in the right place at the right
time. We were moving towards the target and everything was calm.
Our flight time over Iraq was about thirty minutes until we hit the
target. I was relying solely on TFR, the aircraft flying itself. There
were eight aircraft in the formation but it felt like it was just us out
there. Everything was running on rails. No triple-A. All was well.'

Robbie checked their time on target. They were a few seconds
behind schedule. Dave inched the throttles forward to increase the
speed to 630mph to pick up a little time. The HUD now told them
they'd hit Tallil precisely as planned.

In southern Iraq, it was just before 8pm on Saturday, 19
January 1991.

* * *

Back home in England it was 5pm and Robbie's wife Tange Stewart was immersed in the final scenes of the seasonal pantomime, alongside some of the children from the local Sunday school where she taught. This Saturday in mid-January offered them one last, post-Christmas treat. It had become something of a tradition. Fortunately, her teenage daughter Kirsty had been on hand to help shepherd the chirruping youngsters onto the coach for the journey to the theatre in Newark. The dame's buffoonery had the children in stitches, and their enjoyment of his saucy jokes was a welcome distraction from the terrible events unfolding some 3,500 miles to their south-east.

Earlier that day, she had penned another letter to her beloved husband after they had discussed the fateful mission where his Squadron Boss and their friend Max Collier had gone down:

To my dearest darling,[20]

It is the early hours of Saturday morning, sleep seems to elude me yet again. I am afraid last night's news of Max and The Boss was rather a shock. I will buy a card for Max's wife today and drop her a line on our behalf.

It is going to be a sunny day here and Kirsty and I are going to Newark for the pantomime. She is playing in the East of England Netball Tournament next Saturday. Tonight I am going to the Heavers for dinner; I don't know that I'm very good company at present!

Well, darling, all our thoughts and emotions are with you, you are never out of our mind. The kids are coping well but obviously it's difficult for them now. Keep us in your heart but do not worry about us. We have the Stewart grit.

Love you loads.

Tange xxx

Her thoughts drifted away from Iraq and back to the entertainment on stage. Suddenly, Tange stopped laughing. Overwhelmed by a dreadful premonition that Robbie was in terrible danger. She glanced at her watch. Nearly 5pm. She sat back and closed her eyes, trying to let it pass.

'Are you okay?' The woman in the neighbouring seat couldn't keep the anxiety out of her voice.

'Just . . . a little tired,' Tange replied.

The woman smiled and patted her on the arm, doing her best to hide her puzzlement, and failing.

Tange was in turmoil.

When they finally managed to escape the theatre, every traffic light and junction on the winding road home seemed to hold them up. She dialled the Bahrain Sheraton before removing her coat. The receptionist answered politely and put her through to Robbie's room.

No response.

Tange tried again and again, seven or eight times, with the same result.

'I'm sorry, madam,' the receptionist kept repeating. 'There's no answer.'

Tange glanced at her watch. She had a dinner date with friends across the green. On the way out she told her older son Scott to keep trying to call his father. 'Dad would love to hear from you,' were her parting words.

She hid her worries from the children, but could not ignore the dark fear inside. 'My stomach was knotting up. I knew something wasn't right.'

* * *

'Ten miles.'

The jet was still comfortably flying itself as Robbie monitored the distance to the moment when Dave would take their Tornado into the loft attack profile to toss the bombs onto the target. 'I was relatively calm, bearing in mind what we were doing. I had all the weapons systems checked and we started the attack run as planned. Our four-ship formation would complete the night attack from parallel track, lofting the 1,000lb bombs onto the triple-A sites from about 3 miles out. This should discourage the gunners from firing at the aircraft carrying the JP233 airfield denial weapons following behind us.'

In the front seat Dave was concentrating hard, his right hand ready to disengage the autopilot and take control of the jet, his left resting on the throttles, waiting to ram them forward and send the aircraft into a steep climb in order to 'throw' the bombs towards the airfield.

'Five miles,' Robbie called out over the intercom.[21]

'Five hundred and forty knots [621mph].'

They were travelling at 10.35 miles a minute 200 feet above the desert.

Robbie made a rapid calculation. *Just another thirty seconds.* They were on time and on target.

He checked the weapons systems again. No flak ahead, no hint of danger on the warning systems. All quiet. Surprise was on their side.

The Tornados of Belfast formation started their final attack procedures. 'Using the radar, I found and marked the first "offset" which updated the attack system. Suddenly, the RHWR indicated an unknown radar looking at us.'

Dave felt his chest tighten. The RHWR showed a powerful radar system searching from dead ahead, trying to acquire a lock. 'We were just coming to the "pull-up point" and starting our weapons release procedure. Almost immediately we had a missile launch indication and a siren warning screaming in our ears. A missile was in the air.'

The RHWR continued its wail.

Twelve o'clock!

Dave knew it was the worst possible direction that a missile could come from. 'Roland' flashed up on the RHWR. It couldn't be anything else. The best missile the Iraqis had was around 3 miles out, travelling towards them at a third of a mile every second.

They had just seven seconds to save their lives.

Seven seconds.

'Missile launch!' Dave said clearly and calmly. In an instant, he disconnected the autopilot from TFR and took over manual control. The green strobe on the RHWR was still pointing straight at them. Their headsets throbbed with the two-tone scream of the siren, confirming a missile was inbound.

Six seconds.

Now flying manually at over 600mph and just 200ft in total darkness, Dave snapped into a hard-left turn shouting, 'Chaff!' at his navigator. 'All I could see was a flame like a very large firework coming towards me but once I banked the aircraft left, I lost sight of it.'

The Iraqi missile operators had them locked, and the 9kg hollow charge warhead was being guided onto them with pinpoint accuracy.

The warning, like a police siren, continued relentlessly, filling their helmets. Dave's voice still sounded matter-of-fact and calm to Robbie. Their endless training had been there for a reason. It was now his pilot's job to manoeuvre them out of trouble.

Five seconds.

'Chaffing!' Robbie's right hand had moved a split second before he spoke. 'As we turned, I hit the chaff button and the Boz pod blasted out clumps of metallic strands, trying to shroud our presence from the radar-guided missile. There was no time for any fear or panic. Our reactions were hardwired.'

Four seconds.

Dave fought to turn the aircraft, hauling on the control column in the darkness, eyes fixed firmly on the HUD. His only means of knowing what height they were at, what attitude the jet was flying in, if it was climbing or descending towards the ground. 'We had a full weapons load and lots of fuel on board, so the Tornado didn't turn very quickly. It was pitch-black, we were very heavy and I was totally alert to the fact we were very, very close to the desert floor. It was all happening in seconds. It was a trade-off between being hit by a missile and hitting the ground. And the latter was 100 per cent fatal.'

Three seconds.

Dave was making the hardest possible turn, pulling the stick as

tightly as he could into his stomach. The violent manoeuvre, coupled with more chaff, gave them the best chance of breaking the
radar lock, causing the missile to lose guidance and fly blind.

He just needed a bit more time. A second, maybe two.

'Chaff,' Dave said again, as if toasting his companion outside a
country pub.

'Okay ... chaffing ...' There was a hint of urgency in Robbie's
reply as he coaxed the Boz pod to pour more metallic fibres
into the sky.

Two seconds.

'Okay,' Dave responded, still trying to bury the stick in his gut.

Apart from their deep breathing, all was now silent in the cockpit.
The missile was out there somewhere, but the hard turn had left
them blind to its position.

One second.

Time crept by. The turn was nearly complete. Perhaps they had
broken the lock?

Zero ...

Robbie felt an enormous blast rock the Tornado. 'There was a
blinding orange flash as the missile exploded near the front cockpit.'

All Dave saw was searing light. 'The cockpit was consumed by an
enormous flash. Everything happened in just fractions of a second.
I knew I was losing consciousness and I was trying to get my hands
towards the ejection handle, but I just couldn't move them.'

A secondary warning siren now kicked in. This time, a more
urgent tone, like a submarine's crash dive blast, signalling multiple
aircraft systems failures.

Shrapnel shattered the canopy and enveloped the underside of
the Tornado, shredding hydraulic and fuel lines, causing electrical
failure and a massive fireball.

The sirens then ceased as the Tornado started to disintegrate.

Dave felt a hurricane-force wind buffeting his body.

He had one final thought. *It's game over. I'm going to die.*

CHAPTER ONE

THE BIRTH OF 'THE FIN'

1960–1990

Wreckage from Waddington and Stewart's Tornado jutted out of the desert sand. F for Foxtrot's death plunge had created a crater the size of a diving pool. The chaff and flare Boz pod lay at its edge, live flares still clearly visible, chaff dispensing port still open. It had somehow survived the crash intact, but the inferno had stripped away some of the sand-coloured paint, leaving a faint hint of green – its colour a few months earlier when the camouflaged jets had blasted across northern Europe's forests and valleys.

It had now come to rest 200 miles south of Baghdad, and more than 3,000 from its natural habitat.

The Tornado had for almost a decade streaked through dark, wet nights and thick cloud, just a few hundred feet above treetops and valleys. A brainchild of the Cold War, it was able to slip below the radar, avoiding Soviet surface-to-air missiles, then suddenly materialise above an enemy airfield, ready to rain down destruction. But then, in 1989, the Berlin Wall had crumbled, and with it the great Communist alliance. The brilliance of the tactical nuclear bomber was about to be lost. The battle-winner had run out of enemies.

* * *

Robbie Stewart had joined the Royal Air Force in October 1965, six months before the birth of Dave Waddington, the pilot he would go to war with in a Tornado twenty-five years later. All it had taken for the teenage Robbie to decide where his future lay was a couple of flying lessons during the summer holidays. 'I got hooked, and that was it. My career path was set.'[1]

Three years before Robbie joined up, the Cuban Missile Crisis of 1962 had brought the world to the brink of destruction. The US 'Defense Condition' had been raised to its highest ever level: DEFCON 2. Strategic Air Command bombers were readied with nuclear weapons to 'deploy and engage' in less than six hours.[2] Britain had also stood-to its nuclear forces – including the iconic 'Vulcan' bomber that Robbie would soon serve on – at fifteen minutes' readiness. In the midst of the confrontation, an American aircraft, flying over Havana at what intelligence briefs had previously suggested should be above the range of any surface-to-air missile, had been shot down by a Soviet SA2 missile and the pilot killed. The same system had also brought down another American reconnaissance pilot, Gary Powers, two years earlier, under similar circumstances.

Disaster was averted when the Russians backed down and agreed to remove their nuclear missiles from Communist Cuba in return for America's pledge never to attempt an invasion of the island. The Western allies breathed again and lessons were learned. A hotline was established between the White House and the Kremlin for direct communication *in extremis*. And it was now clear that flying incredibly high no longer guaranteed immunity from surface-to-air missile attacks.

To stand a chance of survival, the Vulcan and its V-Force cousins had been developed to fly fast and high in order to deliver their nuclear payload uncontested. The SA2 now clearly undermined that tactic and the Delta-winged bomber was subsequently ordered to fly in beneath the detection capabilities of Soviet radar. It wasn't ideal. The 77-tonne, fully laden Vulcan was challenged by low-level flying; the forces this subjected it to induced metal fatigue, weakening its distinctive wing structure. The RAF decided that something fast, low and capable of operating in northern Europe's grim climatic conditions was required. The search for a new breed of fighter-bomber had begun.

But, in the meantime, the V-Force had to continue its role of policing the Warsaw Pact airspace. The close proximity of atomic Armageddon hadn't really featured in Robbie's youthful fantasies, but that soon changed. 'I had no notion of ever going to war when I joined up, but the reality of the Cold War became clear once I became a navigator on Vulcans. All the exercises we did, preparing for a global nuclear war, you really began to comprehend what it all meant. We all knew that if we ever took off in anger, it would probably be the end of me, my family and the world as we knew it.'

The potentially catastrophic consequences of such a conflict made Robbie and his companions hope and pray that no one would sink to such madness. But hope and prayer are rarely enough to create a place of safety in the international political cauldron. To replace the Vulcans, the RAF needed a fresh, new aircraft. An order for fifty F-111s, the latest low-level American nuclear bomber, was made then axed. Other initiatives came and went. Something custom-built was needed. And it wasn't going to be cheap. Late 1960s Britain was being pummelled by strikes, debt, loss of empire and emasculated productivity. Hobbled by its ageing bomber fleet, the RAF wanted a top-performing, cutting-edge jet that could keep the Soviet threat at bay. If Britain's moribund aircraft industry was to survive, it had to break away from the American monopoly and seek like-minded allies with whom to meet the challenges of the new era. European ones were the obvious – indeed only – option.

In March 1969, Britain entered with gusto into a partnership with Germany and Italy, who also wanted to move away from American dependency and enhance their own industrial base. The concept of the tri-nation 'Multi-Role Combat Aircraft' (MRCA) was born. Britain envisaged a twin-engine, two-man machine that would cost around £1.6 million per airframe.[3] She would build the rear, the Germans the middle and the Italians the wings. The RAF and the Luftwaffe would take 420 each, the Italians 100.

The spirit of optimism surrounding the 1969 'memorandum of understanding', its detractors said, could not possibly last. How could you build three different components in three different countries in which no one spoke the same language, and where one was still using measurements in inches and feet? Then there was the far-fetched idea of assembling all the bits and pieces like a child's Meccano set. How were the Italians going to get their wings to Germany when neutral Austria and Switzerland had barred all overland transportation of military equipment?

Then the Italians insisted on the aircraft being a single-seater. They didn't have any trained backseat navigators in the entire Regia Aeronautica. The Germans were reluctant too, but the argument that two pairs of eyes and hands were better than one, with the solo pilot's workload being partly blamed for the high loss rate of the Luftwaffe's single-seat F-104 Starfighter, won the day. By 1970 all were on board with the idea of two engines and two seats.[4]

A highly complex and innovative design began to take shape. It would have variable-geometry 'swing-wings'. Swept fully forward, the wings were optimised for low-speed flight and manoeuvrability. Swept fully back, the Tornado resembled a dart and was capable of high-speed low-level flight carrying a heavy weapons load.

It would be truly 'fly-by-wire'; the pilot's physical inputs into his controls would actually be sent to a computerised flying system and then digitally on to the aircraft control surfaces. The computer systems ensured that the Tornado's handling characteristics remained almost constant regardless of speed and wing-sweep position. By the standards of the day, it was straightforward to fly and a

smooth, stable weapons platform.[5] In the era before the existence
of composite metals, the MRCA was to be constructed from 71 per
cent light alloy, 18 per cent titanium and 6 per cent steel.[6] The clear
underside could carry a substantial arsenal. Its cockpit was laid out
with plenty of room for the aircrew.

With success vital for all three governments, the pressure was
mounting. The MRCA label also had to be dealt with. No one falls
in love with an acronym. Being fast, low to the ground, nocturnal
and stealth-like, *Panther* seemed a credible choice, but that was also
the name given to the legendary Second World War German panzer,
and a household lavatory cleaner of the time.[7] *Tornado*, on the other
hand, was the same word in all three languages and created the
evocative image of a force of nature that could strike with immense
power and devastation.

It was an era before any form of 'night-vision goggles' (NVGs)
so it would be impossible to fly the aircraft manually – visually –
at low level in darkness. The key to the aircraft's success was the
installation of the highly sophisticated Terrain-Following Radar
system, or TFR, for low-level penetration. Originally developed by
the British company Ferranti in the early 1960s, it swept the flight
path ahead of a fast jet, registering the landscape and even obstacles
like power lines, allowing it to fly at a near-constant altitude above
whatever man or nature could throw its way.[8] The radar returns
were processed to calculate the changes in the terrain, then fed into
its flight computers and harnessed to the autopilot allowing the jet to
fly itself, with almost no input from the crew, and maintain ground
clearance at a constant height of 200ft, soaring over any terrain
at high speed in pitch darkness or thick cloud. Blending into the
landscape or 'terrain hugging' meant the Tornado could hide from
enemy radar, reducing its vulnerability.

But the Tornado would be nothing without the power capable
of complementing these other advances. On the face of it, building
a jet engine was now relatively straightforward. Just get it to suck
in the ambient outside air, squeeze it, heat it with ignited fuel and
chuck it out of the rear pipe a great deal faster than it came in, and

you could achieve remarkable thrust. The Americans were currently dominating the market, but this was a European project. It was time for the boffins at Rolls-Royce to show that Britain could still produce the innovative and the incredible. It was also a moment for the three nations to unite at the frontier of risk.

In 1970 everything depended upon Rolls-Royce's concept for the Tornado's engine. But it only existed, thus far, on paper. Each power plant had to produce 16,000lb of thrust when reheat was engaged for take-off. It had to swallow the huge influx of fuel necessary to produce the energy it took to lift a fully laden bomber. If they failed to conjure up the RB199 from scratch, the whole project would fail.[9]

Smaller than existing engines yet with more strength, it made the complex journey from the drawing board into action in four years and the RB199 demonstrated it possessed the heart of an elephant and the speed of gazelle.

* * *

Tange Webster had been warned to stay away from RAF officers. The older girls at the teacher training college in Lincoln had told her the flyboys might appear a dashing bunch in their smart uniforms and fancy jets, and, yes, they had a bit of spare cash and the whiff of heroism that came with being the vanguard against the Soviet threat, but they rarely hung about. At the student union dance in 1967, however, she actually found trainee officer Robbie Stewart pretty down-to-earth and, in his quiet way, really rather charming.

Four years later, when Tange turned twenty-four, they married and moved into the village of Coleby, with its primary school, two pubs and a church whose foundations went back to Saxon times. Robbie was flying out of RAF Scampton, a half-hour's drive away, with 27 Squadron, the unit with which he would later go to war. As the pleasantly warm summer of 1974 stretched ahead of them, Tange's walks around the village began to shorten with the breathlessness of third trimester pregnancy.

* * *

Seven hundred miles away, it was a humid afternoon on 14 August at Manching military airbase in West Germany, not far from where Messerschmitt 109s had been assembled in their thousands four decades before. Designers, engineers, mechanics and military observers now gathered to witness what they hoped would be a step change in aircraft dynamics.

The massive fin of the Tornado, in its smart red and white livery, immediately caught everyone's eye. Vital to stabilise and steer the bomber through waves of turbulent low-level air, it was as distinctive in its way as the Spitfire's elliptical wings, or the Lancaster's proud nose. For many, it would give the shiny new aircraft its nickname: 'The Fin'.

German, Italian, British and the odd American eye looked on with interest, as did the binoculars and the camera lenses of the Soviet enemy the Tornado was designed to defeat, from somewhere beyond the surrounding pine forests.

The aircraft's components had been concealed beneath tarpaulin and transported 55 miles by road from Munich. Its designers had managed to keep the prototype, P01, hidden from scrutiny, and they were determined to do so until the last moment. Given that its maiden flight was to be here in Germany, it was agreed the pilot would be British. It fell to Paul Millett, formerly of the RAF and the Fleet Air Arm, to take the controls.

After climbing the ladder to P01 and strapping himself in, Millett patiently waited as the two chase jets took off, ready to examine the newcomer at close quarters in case any issues arose mid-flight.

Under clear but muggy skies Millett taxied P01 to the runway. The sound of air molecules being ripped apart filled the deep green forests as he ignited the RB199s. The roar increased to a crescendo as fuel was poured onto the Rolls-Royce engines, throbbing with anticipation at getting airborne for the first time. The livery became a red and white blur as he powered down the runway.

Millett found the aircraft's nose eager to lift at 120 knots. Too eager. He held P01 down, forcing it to gather more speed. The needle passed 160 knots (184mph), he eased back the stick and lifted smoothly into the air. He left the landing gear down as they climbed, in case an emergency landing was called for.[10] But all was well. Then it was time for the Tornado to look like a real combat jet. The undercarriage tucked neatly up into the broad fuselage as it powered effortlessly through the south German skies. Millett levelled off at 10,000ft then settled down to 300 knots (345mph). He was impressed. 'It flew as though this was the environment it had been built for.'[11]

There were gasps and one or two tears as the Tornado, with a chase jet at each wingtip, flew low past the spectators waiting on Manching's airstrip. The wheels liberated themselves once again from the fuselage. The handling on the approach to landing proved to be precisely as the designers had told Millett it would be. This machine flew beautifully at low level.

He took it for a low-altitude pass, then came back round. 'It feels as though it's on rails. You just sit with your hands and feet off and let the aircraft fly itself.' Thirty-three minutes after taking off, its wheels kissed the tarmac once more. 'It really felt like an aircraft that had been flying for many years. For a first flight it was something tremendous. The handling was perfect,' Millett said. 'It cannot be improved upon.'

He might have heard himself echoing the first pilot to fly the Spitfire prototype in 1936, when he said on landing: 'I don't want anything touched . . .'[12]

There was relief all round. The British aerospace and defence industry was rescued, the Germans had set the seal on their engineering prowess, and the Italians had secured a host of proper manufacturing jobs.

* * *

Robbie Stewart, like many others in the RAF, had a vague notion of the Tornado's maiden flight, but he wasn't counting his chickens. Many such projects had got this far before now, and failed. Just days before the Tornado's first flight Robbie was back in his Vulcan, 50,000ft above the North Sea, monitoring Russian maritime activity. The world felt like an unsettled place. Richard Nixon had recently resigned as US President. Willy Brandt, the West German Chancellor, had also quit over the revelation that his personal assistant had been spying for the Stasi, East Germany's intelligence service. Then the Turks invaded northern Cyprus. Spiralling oil prices were crippling the West's economy, and the Soviet Union seemed to be seizing the ascendancy in the competition for global supremacy.

Robbie still got back in time for the birth of his son in late August, and had a few weeks with Scott before he was back on duty with 27 Squadron, flying halfway round the world to Midway Island in the South Pacific, downwind of China, following a recent nuclear test by the People's Republic. The Vulcan also undertook the 'nuclear fallout detection' role – otherwise known as 'sniffing' – collecting air samples for analysis. There were upsides. The return leg home took in a refuelling stop in Hawaii. 'We had a chance to swim at Waikiki Beach; life wasn't all bad.'

His wife Tange understood the realities of service life. Robbie would be there one minute and gone the next. 'I would get the odd phone call in the middle of the night and Robbie would disappear off on exercise for days, sometimes weeks, on end. It was the middle of the Cold War and the world sometimes seemed a dangerous place; but that was all part of our lives.'

Robbie's training roster also seemed to demand an unusual number of cold-weather survival courses. 'I hope you never find yourself in the desert,' she once joked. 'You've not done the course!'

* * *

As the 1970s progressed, the Tornado began to take shape. With all three nations in harmony, the development site outside Munich grew to a workforce of almost 200 people. Three decades on from the Second World War, there had been a few stony silences in the office shared by a veteran German Luftwaffe colonel and a similarly aged RAF squadron leader.[13] Into this somewhat frosty atmosphere was thrown the snippet of information that both had been fighter pilots, one in Messerschmitts, the other Spitfires. Conversation became a touch more animated when it was discovered that each had fought in the same campaign over northern Europe in the latter stages of the conflict. Logbooks were produced, dates aligned and in no time at all the whirling, twisting and twirling hand gestures favoured by fighter pilots revealed that they had indeed shared the same airspace, though fortunately neither had been on the receiving end of the other's bullets. As one onlooker dryly observed, *they were clearly both lousy shots*.

No matter. A lifelong friendship had begun, with the Tornado at its heart. Their business now was to help develop a jet that could fly very low, and very fast. Because it had to. The Soviet defences arrayed against it were numerous and formidable. The most advanced surface-to-air missiles, anti-aircraft guns, radar and fighters. But the Tornado could dip out of sight while travelling at 600mph, 10 miles a minute, armed with the deadliest explosive device mankind had ever invented.

The Tornado project was no longer on the Cold War sidelines. The Russian spymasters in the KGB reportedly viewed it as a very serious threat. One of their top agents in West Germany, Manfred Rotsch, was also head of planning for Messerschmitt-Bölkow-Blohm, the German company building Tornado,[14] and was ordered to pass on everything he could get his hands on. The Soviets pretty much got the lot. And it didn't improve their humour. The West, the KGB discovered, was building a weapon of unsurpassed excellence. The decaying British Empire, the recently defeated Germans and even the haphazardly Communist government of Italy had formed an industrial union. It was all unfathomable to the Soviet mind. But Tornado, the Moscow comrades were told, was a problem. Even the Russian word for it – *Smerch* – suggested something subversive. The bristling defences of Eastern Europe were said to be vulnerable. And this was very serious. They had to know more.

Manfred Rotsch was put on notice. Find out everything you possibly can about *Smerch*.

* * *

In 1975, a year after the Tornado prototype took to the air, Dave Waddington also flew for the first time. His uncle owned a sharp-looking twin-engine Piper Aztec, and Dave was asked if he wanted to fly. 'YES!' was the immediate answer. His excitement grew as he was allowed to sit in the co-pilot's seat. He strapped himself in, trembling with anticipation. The feisty Lycoming piston engines roared as the Aztec sped down the runway. Dave watched the grass rush past as the wheels bounced beneath him, then the vibrations disappeared and they rose into the sky. After they had climbed to a few thousand feet, his uncle asked Dave if he wanted to take over. The 9-year-old's reply was unequivocal. *Yes please!* He reached for the control column, listening intently to the instructions. 'I was smitten. I wanted to fly. That was my dream.'[15] Dave set his heart on becoming a pilot. A fast-jet pilot.

It would be many years before he would get his hands anywhere near the Tornado, which, in the words of British Prime Minister Harold Wilson, was 'one of the wonder birds of aviation'. But his words were barely out of his mouth when the nascent bomber faced the kind of cross-examination that could cast it into the oblivion suffered by many other promising British projects.

It was 1975, and the first solely British Tornado prototype was about to take wing.[16] The gunmetal grey skies of Lancashire had cleared by the time test pilot Paul Millett eased back the control stick and felt P02, the second Tornado to be built, launch itself into the blue with familiar ease. They passed over the green fields and marshland that spread to the sandy banks of the River Ribble below.[17] The picturesque cottages of the nearby village of Fylde shrank as they climbed.

Perfect flying weather.

A blaring alarm interrupted Millett's momentary reverie. Flashing attention-getters and an illuminated caption on the Central

Warning Panel suggested a serious fault. *Low oil pressure. High temperature.* A jet of flame surged out of the right-hand engine.

There was a lengthy silence in the cockpit.

'Okay, Dave, what do you reckon?' Millett's fellow test pilot was in the back seat.

'Can't see anything wrong from here,' came the reply.

Millett waited a few seconds. The temperature continued to build. He throttled the right-hand engine all the way back to idle. The Tornado had more than enough power to fly on one. Easily enough to switch to plan B and ask the tower to check for any visual damage before making a precautionary landing. P02 slowly descended. Then there was another thump, followed by a big bang. Both sets of eyes swivelled left. Flame now blazed out of the remaining engine, which had just ingested a large seagull. More flames danced along the fuselage.

Millett immediately shut down the left engine, and slammed the right from idle straight into reheat to gain maximum power. There was an uncomfortable silence as it failed to respond and the altimeter continued to unwind. The Tornado was sinking fast towards the marshland surrounding Warton. The Ribble was no longer a ribbon. The buildings below them were rapidly increasing in size.

The altimeter passed through 500ft.

The only engine functioning was still refusing to deliver any power.

Millett scanned the gauges. *What could he do?*

Both pilots knew that their options were limited.

Prepare to eject?

And leave the second Tornado ever built, the British Tornado, to bury itself in the Lancastrian marshland?

Three hundred feet.

At least the altimeter was functioning flawlessly.

Fingers brushed the yellow and black ejection handle between their legs.

P02 was doomed.

Time to bail out.

The aircraft rocked and shuddered. Then the right-hand engine burst back into life and Po2 soared skywards.

It had been a *very* close call.

The incident did much to inflame the inevitable detractors around any new aviation project. But Po2, despite a few hair-raising moments which included a partial snapping of the tailfin during spin trials, soon began reaching notable landmarks, including a top speed of 809 knots (930mph).[18]

By July 1979 the first dual-control RAF Tornados rolled out of Warton, ready for instructing new pilots, though the fanfare was muted. During treacherous weather conditions a few weeks earlier, Po8 had plunged into the sea 44 miles off Blackpool during a test flight involving the hazardous 'loft attack' profile. It could be dangerous work at the best of times, and was made worse in this instance by the mist and drizzle over the Irish Sea. There were no survivors.

Despite this fatal accident, the first of many, the Tornado was accepted into service three years later. And while it would certainly suffer a number of ongoing technical issues due to its cutting-edge technology, the aircrew and ground crew worked together to ensure that most tasks were completed as planned. The RAF finally had a fighter-bomber that could hit a target accurately night or day, no matter the weather.

* * *

Robbie Stewart noticed a bit of a difference going from the nuclear-armed Vulcan to the Tornado GR1. 'The Tornado had everything you could have dreamed of for the time. Computerised flying systems, navigation and targeting kit. It could fly at night, in terrible weather, at low level, hands-off. It really was superb.' One of its primary roles was as part of the nation's nuclear deterrent. For Robbie, as a navigator checking his target maps to be used if the Cold War ever turned hot, the idea was deeply unpleasant. 'You checked to see where the target was; what built-up areas it was near. That was quite a curious feeling, knowing if you ever launched, you'd be destroying a huge area. And that the world would be changing beyond recognition.' If the target was more distant, such as in western Poland, the aircraft might carry a single WE177 nuclear bomb under the left shoulder pylon and an extra, third fuel tank on the right.[19] At shorter range, the Tornado could carry two WE177s, bringing the explosive power of many Hiroshimas.

Along with its TFR, only used at night or in bad weather, the GR1's other key attribute was the crew's skill – flying manually and visually, fast and, at 100ft, far below enemy radar or, in a combat situation, even lower. No autopilot had this function so they had to become highly drilled at skimming above rugged terrain trusting their expertise to the maximum.

Fast-jet flying at 100ft and at high speed anywhere near built-up areas was forbidden across most of the UK and all of Germany, so there was no better place to practise this crucial skill than the wilds of Canada, with its deep canyons and jagged peaks. It was a real challenge and the cost in aircraft and aircrew lost bore testimony to the dangers. But those dangers had to be faced and overcome if the pilots were to fly the Tornado through the layers of Soviet air defence, beneath the searching radars, to ensure no missiles or anti-aircraft artillery (triple-A) could be guided onto them. The practice presented a real and deadly challenge, and the crews loved it.

* * *

John Peters had also had a childhood love of flying, and was now a pilot who delighted in nothing more than to be behind the controls of his Tornado. Especially when the RAF was really putting the jet through its paces, practising ultra-low-level flying, or 'operational low flying' (OLF), across the lakes and canyons of Goose Bay in north-east Canada. Usually, the only low-flying aircraft found there were the Beaver seaplanes that took sports anglers for a fortnight's holiday with some outstanding fishing in remote log cabins surrounded by millions of acres of forest, and the occasional bear. With not many souls about, it was also a fine place for some of the most breathtaking and challenging aviation.

Unrestricted by the low-level flying limits of Europe, the Tornados could tear along at ultra-low level and around 700mph in very testing conditions. A key piece of advice was not to go 'too low'. Since a lake's surface mirrored the sky, more than one pilot had become disoriented and dived straight in.[20] For pilots blessed with great vision, Goose Bay provided the clearest atmosphere they'd set eyes on. No pollution or heat haze, just 50 miles of crystalline visibility, unheard of in the Old World.

But for pilots new to Canada like John Peters, when flying over the rock, lichen and smaller and smaller trees of the northern tundra, it could be lethal. 'As the trees begin to imperceptibly decrease in height, there is a real danger of believing that you are flying too high, so you adjust the position of the aircraft lower in the sky to restore that familiar picture. If you are not careful you can find yourself being drawn closer and closer to the ground as the trees, which are normally around 50 feet high, shrink to as little as 10. It is a well-known optical illusion of low flying and everyone is made aware of the potentially fatal dangers.'[21]

The Tornado crews enjoyed some of the most exhilarating flying they ever encountered. John Peters soon discovered that one particular 15-mile-long canyon rapidly narrowed as they sped between the sheer cliff walls. It had been named 'Star Wars Valley' after Luke Skywalker's unforgettable route to the heart of the Death Star. For John, it was the ultimate challenge. 'You have to roll the Tornado onto its side and pull hard, sweeping the wings forward to increase manoeuvrability and squeeze the aircraft around the sheer walls of rock. Finally, you have to say: "No, no further," yank the stick back and pull out. It's sheer seat-of-the-pants flying.'[22]

The concentration needed was so demanding that pilots could barely look anywhere else but straight ahead and the navigator had to do the rest.[23] It took a lot of practice to have the confidence to push the aircraft down to 100ft, the height of two rugby posts. But if it came to war, to survive the Soviets' highly capable air defences in daylight, they were going to have to fly even lower.

It was exciting and exhausting work, which increased in intensity when done on the autopilot coupled to the TFR, which for those in the front seat provided the strange sensation of being on an out-of-control rollercoaster. TFR meant that night-time or low clouds no longer limited RAF attack aircraft. Britain now had the capability to attack at any time of day on any day of the year.[24]

'With the computer autopilot flying the jet, I would sit with my left hand resting on the throttle and my right lying uselessly in my lap, twitching towards the stick every time I saw a rock looming up from the ground below.'

Peters glanced intently at the tiny display screen of the TFR's 'E-scope' which showed an image of the ground in front as the radar in the Tornado's nose swept the terrain of the flight path ahead. 'As the jet soars over a ridge, prompted by the TFR, then plunges down into an unseen valley, our anti-collision lights reflect back from a solid wall of thick, grey cloud. The navigator hunches in the back with only my running commentary to brace himself for the next lurch as the jet twists, soars and swoops, following the terrain as if glued to it.'[25] The jet could continue on TFR for as long as it liked until the pilot moved the paddle bar on the stick that cuts out autopilot to get back onto manual control.

If the Tornado could fly through thick fog, over mountains and at night, it needed to have something special to deliver – other than a nuclear bomb – if it was truly going to make an impact. The new aircraft had been designed to be 'multi-role', from nuclear and conventional bombing to reconnaissance and even, in the guise of the F3 variant, interception.

* * *

In the first few hours of any Cold War conflict, the Tornado's role would be to prevent the enemy from using their airfields, and the unique JP233 'runway denial munition' was specifically designed to meet its profile for fast, below-the-radar attack. Developed during the 1970s, the JP233 was designed to render the Soviet runways built in East Germany or Poland unusable for critical operations with a barrage of cratering weapons and anti-personnel devices.[26]

Each JP233 contained thirty runway-cratering munitions weighing 57lb, designed to penetrate the surface of a runway before then exploding and causing massive 'heave distortion' to the surface area. The blast would force the tarmac upwards in a great spew of broken rubble. To discourage anyone seeking to make repairs, a further 215 anti-personnel bomblets followed on small parachutes, designed to pop up on three legs and arm themselves, detonating if disturbed. A final kicker was that a number of the munitions would continue to detonate randomly for some hours after lying dormant. It was a vicious weapon.

A Tornado could carry two of the 2.5-tonne JP233s, so a single raid by eight jets brought the potent mix of 480 cratering bombs and 3,440 anti-personnel bomblets. It was a brutal and effective method of airfield operating surface denial, with one 'slight' drawback. The scientists who developed it required the Tornado to fly straight and level down the runway, at around 200ft and 520mph, which, the aircrews observed stoically, *greatly* increased the possibility of being shot down.

And the Tornado demonstrated its versatility with other crucial tasks. The GR1A reconnaissance version could sneak behind enemy lines and record images of troop movements, defensive positions or bomb damage. It utilised a revolutionary infra-red video system which allowed image collection by both day and night. It was able to see the heat signature of aircraft on a runway or the heat trace of recently departed jets. This also meant that it was much harder for troops to conceal weapons that required engines, such as giant rocket launchers.[27]

Then there was the adapted Tornado F3, the air defence variant designed to track, intercept and, if necessary, shoot down hostile intruders. If lacking in the manoeuvrability of other, purpose-built fighters, it could still occupy a significant role as an interceptor.

* * *

Dave Waddington's passion had remained undiminished throughout his school years. He joined the RAF straight after his A-levels and by 1988 had fulfilled his dream of flying fast jets. He knew that they were Cold War warriors but felt any major conflict unlikely. 'The idea of global thermo-nuclear war didn't really enter your mind. We were certainly a deterrent, but the feeling was that if the Cold War ever turned hot, it would be so catastrophic as to be unimaginable.' Anyway, there was too much fun to be had flying, alongside a packed social life, to think about Armageddon. 'The Tornado was cutting-edge technology, I was just twenty-two and flying the RAF's most modern, capable fast-jet aircraft. Being on a frontline squadron was simply amazing – the ethos, the camaraderie, the training, the lifestyle was everything I'd hoped it would be. I was living the dream.' Part of that dream was finding himself on the front line, even with only the most distant prospect of conflict.

Nuclear war moved several steps further away one Thursday in November 1989 when the collapse of the Berlin Wall heralded the beginning of the end of the Soviet empire. There was a question mark over whether the RAF would ever be needed for combat now that its chief adversary was gone. What was the point now of the Tornado, primed to break through enemy defences that no longer existed? No one knew what the future held, except the near certainty that the 'peace dividend' would mean the military establishment faced huge cutbacks.

* * *

Seven years earlier, in 1982, Dave Bellamy had joined up after reading about the RAF's new generation of fast jets. At the age of eighteen, he went straight onto the Tornado as a navigator. 'I loved the aircraft and really enjoyed flying it, even if the prospect of any real conflict was remote.'

With the Cold War over, Bellamy could read the tea leaves. A devastating blow to the Tornado force was announced to Parliament just a week before Iraq invaded Kuwait in summer 1990.[28] The RAF was to reduce from 90,000 personnel to 75,000, with the closure of four bases in Germany and the loss of six squadrons. For Dave, 'it was a depressing possibility, so I had decided to leave the RAF early and handed in my notice'. Costs for training a navigator ran into the millions, so his contract meant he would still have to serve another two years. And take a pay cut. That was fine by him. He wanted a new challenge.

Under the government's 'Options for Change' proposals, the British Armed Forces were to be cut by almost a fifth. Gordon Buckley, one of the RAF's top five Tornado pilots in terms of hours flown, was among those who faced an uncertain future. He was based at RAF Laarbruch in northern Germany and his Squadron was in line for the chop. 'When the Iron Curtain slowly crumbled away I really wondered what our role in the RAF might be. I certainly didn't imagine we might soon be fighting a major war.'

Despite the looming cuts to RAF strength, and perhaps because of them, families like Robbie Stewart's felt that by the summer 1990 they deserved a really good holiday. Scott was now sixteen, and their aircraft-mad daughter Kirsty was about to reach her teenage years. The Bavarian foothills of Germany's highest mountain, the Zugspitze, and its forest of conifers offered the adventure-loving Stewarts the ideal location.

The Stewarts packed the car and drove from Lincoln, across Europe then down into southern Germany to camp at Garmisch. The host town of the 1936 Winter Olympics sat in a breathtaking bowl of snow-capped mountains. It was early August, the sky was deep blue and the air fresh. They took the train to the high station. Robbie was in good spirits as they clambered out of their compartment and prepared to embark on the hike to the Zugspitze's 10,000ft peak.

Then something caught his eye at the station gift shop.

In large black letters, an English newspaper headline declared:

'SADDAM INVADES KUWAIT'

CHAPTER TWO

THE GATHERING STORM

AUGUST–NOVEMBER 1990

The former British protectorate of Kuwait was a tiny oil-rich state at the head of the Gulf, sharing just two borders, one with Saudi Arabia to the south and the other with its dominant neighbour Iraq in the north. Shortly after 2am on 2 August 1990, as much of the RAF Tornado force enjoyed their summer holidays, 100,000 of Saddam Hussein's elite troops, the Republican Guard, swept south with 2,000 tanks.[1] Iraqi commandos landed by helicopter and seaborne assault. The 16,000-strong Kuwaiti army and air force put up a stiff resistance. For two days they held firm, until they ran out of ammunition. The bulk of their leadership, including their Emir, fled into the Saudi desert. The last pockets of resistance were overrun, raising their death toll to 420, while their invaders lost 300 men and 39 aircraft.

On 4 August, Kuwait ceased to exist as a state and became, instead, the 19th Governate of Iraq. Events had been set in train which would eventually cost tens of thousands of lives, and reverberate across the region, and the world, for many years to come.

* * *

A decade earlier, Saddam Hussein had made another decision with global consequences when he invaded neighbouring Iran. That war had been about border disputes, religion and Arab–Persian hegemony, and been pursued at great cost. More than half a million soldiers perished in battles frighteningly similar to the trench warfare of the First World War. Iran used human-wave attacks, sending massed infantry against barbed wire and machine-gun nests. Saddam maximised his use of chemical weapons, sending mustard gas clouds that condemned Iranian soldiers hiding in their trenches to an agonising death.

By the end, not a jot of land advantage had been gained by either side, but Iran's Ayatollah Khomeini strengthened his religious revolution and the once-prosperous Iraq was $100 billion in debt.[2] Saddam's financial weakness was compounded in 1990 after a global glut of oil led to prices plummeting. Iraq's main income was under threat because of overproduction and Kuwait was among those overproducing. The dire economic situation was a threat to the Iraqi president and his power base. There had been four assassination attempts in the previous two years. Saddam's reputation – hitherto sustained by a combination of brutality and low cunning – was tumbling as quickly as the price of oil.

Tensions rose when he accused Kuwait of stealing $2 billion by cross-drilling into Iraqi oilfields. Iraqi divisions were ordered to assemble at the border. As last-minute compromise talks were held, Iraq demanded Kuwait pay $10 billion in compensation. The Kuwaitis offered $9 billion but that just insulted Saddam's personal honour. The Kuwaitis would pay in blood and treasure. Saddam invaded and a geopolitical earthquake, with countless aftershocks, was triggered.

Margaret Thatcher was giving her full attention to President George Bush's opening address at a conference at the Aspen Institute in Colorado when news of Saddam's invasion broke. She steadied nerves by ordering the nearest Royal Navy warships to sail to the region. The British Prime Minister showed her experience as a military campaign veteran for whom the lessons of the twentieth century were clear.

The next morning, President Bush asked her: 'Margaret, what do we do?'[3]

Mrs Thatcher, who famously ordered the retaking of the Falkland Islands by military force after the Argentine invasion in 1982, replied: 'Aggression must be stopped. If an aggressor gets away with it, others will want to get away with it too. You cannot gain from your aggression.'

Saddam occupying the country with the sixth largest oil reserves on the planet was already highly troubling, and Mrs Thatcher was in no doubt about what could happen next. 'An immediate question now was whether Saddam Hussein would go over the border and seize Saudi Arabia's oilfields. If [he] were to cross the border into Saudi Arabia he could go right down the Gulf in a matter of days. He would then control 65 per cent of the world's oil reserves and could blackmail us all. Not only did we have to move to stop the aggression, therefore, we had to stop it quickly.'[4]

The prospect of Saddam's battle-hardened Republican Guard rampaging through Saudi Arabia's neatly assembled oil production facilities with its unlimited supply of 'black gold' was deeply unsettling. The land of the holiest Islamic sites of Mecca and Medina had not been invaded for more than twelve centuries. Hysteria grew among the Saudi royal court and their people. King Fahd readily agreed to an audience with senior American officers who came to ask permission to allow their troops into the kingdom for its defence. The Vietnam veteran, General Norman Schwarzkopf, who had a reputation for a short temper and great leadership, was a member of the group. 'Would strictly Islamic Saudi allow Christian soldiers onto their holy soil?' the American asked.[5]

'Yes,' came the immediate response.

Saudi's airbases and ports were immediately opened up to the military might of the world's dominant superpower. There had been little choice. Victorious Iraqi divisions were assembling on the

border. The capital, Riyadh,was six hours' drive away. Saudi lay at
Saddam's mercy.

* * *

Despite the arduous walks that seemed to typify their family
holidays, Robbie Stewart's 12-year-old daughter Kirsty had been
really enjoying the two-week break from school studies. Her dad
was relaxed, there was lots of fun and laughter. There was one
particularly memorable moment with him, lying in the sun by a
stream before building a rock dam. But her idyll had been shattered
when, ready to conquer the Zugspitze, they had seen the newspaper
announcement of Saddam's invasion. Robbie Stewart had stopped,
turned, and reread the first paragraph. His wife Tange glanced
over his shoulder. Then their eyes met. Robbie looked like he'd
been punched in the stomach. 'It hit me like a sledgehammer. I just
knew how it would unfold. And I knew the Tornados I flew would
be involved.'[6]

They had both been aware of the increased tensions in the Gulf
but thought there had been a last-minute compromise. Both immediately understood the implications. The highway from Kuwait led
straight down to Saudi Arabia and its great swathe of oilfields. One
of the world's most ruthless dictators controlling half of the world's
oil was a direct threat to global stability. After decades of atrocities,
gassing Kurds and torturing his own, Saddam had finally crossed a
line that could not be ignored.

'You know what's going to happen, don't you?' Robbie's voice
was tight.

'Yes,' Tange replied quietly.

She had always known war was a *possibility*. 'But this seemed a
world away from everything we knew.'[7]

'I have to call the Squadron,' Robbie said.

They took the train back to the campsite to get a stash of coins
to call RAF Marham from the public phone box. There was relief
on Robbie's face after the call. He'd been told to check in regularly,

but they did not need to rush home early. No immediate plans had been made to deploy Tornados. The Zugspitze still loomed over them but the joy had gone out of their adventure. Every night Robbie tuned in to the news. A confrontation was looming and he was certain Tornados would be in the gathering storm. 'I wasn't really enjoying the holiday as much. Each night I read about rising tensions in the region. Both Tange and I were very aware that I might be heading that way. We had a very real sense that our lives were going to change.'

Tange had the same nagging feeling. 'We continued with our hikes around the mountains during the day, maintaining the air of a normal family holiday, but at night, when the kids had gone to sleep in their own little tent beside ours, Robbie and I would discuss the situation in whispers; the possibility Robbie might be going out there and what that might mean. There was a real sense that war was imminent.' Their quiet chatter did not go unnoticed by Kirsty. 'There were whispered conversations between Mum and Dad, staying up late at night. I had never heard of Saddam Hussein, or even Kuwait, but very soon, those words were part of my regular vocabulary. The holiday suddenly turned serious. It was really odd, because Dad was never like that, he was normally so laid-back.'[8]

Because his service life had begun in the sixties, Robbie and Tange had always known war with the Soviets was a possibility, but this was something entirely different. Fighting, flying and dealing with danger was what RAF fliers were trained to do. It was just that for Robbie the Cold War had ended, yet the prospect of dying in a real war was again staring him in the face. 'I had no doubt in my mind I would deploy and it was certainly worrying. But it was my job, what I had trained to do.'

* * *

A week after the invasion, 130,000 Iraqi troops were massed on the Saudi border itself. To the military analyst's eye, it appeared to be a 'strategic pause', a moment to rest, re-equip and rearm prior to offensive operations. It wasn't just the 1,200 tanks and regiments of heavy artillery that were unnerving the generals. The Iraq Air Force, comprising many veterans of the Iran war, was probing Saudi air space, looking for weaknesses and recording response times.[9] The strongest and quickest response the Americans had was air power. Within days of the invasion, forty-eight heavily armed F-15C Eagle fighters sounded the opening notes of the campaign to protect Saudi Arabia. The F-15s flew straight from the United States, over fourteen hours non-stop, with multiple air-to-air refuelling slots. Each fighter carried eight air-to-air missiles, and were ready to fight their way in if necessary. But the Americans needed more help.

One Tornado Squadron Commander, on leave from Germany, was pruning the roses in his garden when the house phone rang at his cottage in the east of England. 'How long will it take you to get to RAF Cottesmore?' he was asked.[10]

'Half an hour,' he replied.

When the officer pulled up at the airbase, a Tornado from his Squadron was already waiting. He took the backseat spot from the navigator and flew straight back to Germany, then on to Saudi Arabia. Royal Air Force mobilisation was taking place on a scale unparalleled since the summer of 1939.[11]

The RAF's nearest jets were in Cyprus in the eastern Mediterranean – a detachment of Tornado F3s, the interceptor or 'air defence variant' of the GR1 bomber. They were there for the good training weather as well as the odd summer beach barbecue, but were wholly unprepared for war. A few days after the invasion, the aircrew were sipping cold beers in the Mess when an 'Eyes Only' message arrived for the Squadron Boss. The twelve jets that had deployed to the British sovereign base to practise air-to-air combat were now heading to Saudi to stop, or at least slow, the impending Iraqi invasion.

'It felt as though we were going to last two or three days out there and then we'd be overrun,' one pilot said.[12] A fellow navigator described it as a 'nightmare', mainly because the Tornado F3s were only halfway through a major capability enhancement programme.

'We were deploying out to the Gulf with jets that hadn't been modernised for war. We had no chaff, no flares. We didn't have the good missiles on, we didn't have the good radars and a lot of us didn't feel we were going to come back.' Saddam's reputation for murderous chemical warfare meant preparations for Nuclear Biological Chemical (NBC) attack were also taken very seriously. 'The thing that was really worrying us was the NBC because the next time you put your respirator on it could be for nerve gas and that was you gone.'[13]

'Last letters' were written, to be delivered to loved ones if the worst happened, and wills hurriedly filled in. Then it was time to leave, just as visiting military families were arriving at the other end of the Cyprus airfield for their summer holidays on the beach. Only a week after Saddam invaded Kuwait, the twelve Tornado F3s landed at the vast, modern Dhahran airbase, on Saudi's Gulf coast. Within hours they were back in the skies again, flying four-hour combat patrols along the Iraq border, swapping shifts with their US and Saudi counterparts.

RAF Jaguars also arrived, along with shuttle loads of C130 Hercules transporters ferrying in ground crew, support staff and batteries of Rapier surface-to-air missiles. When the Hercules landed in the heat of Dhahran – 30°C at two in the morning – the loadmasters went into overdrive. 'They kicked us out of the back like there was no tomorrow and the Herc was off taxiing before we'd even put our kit down,' recalled one airman. 'At that point I suddenly thought, "My God, this is all getting a little bit tense."'[14] Very quickly the RAF had 1,000 personnel on the ground. But it wasn't enough. They were joined by 4,000 lightly armed American paratroopers rushed in from the 82nd Airborne Division as part of Operation Desert Shield, the rapid deployment of troops to protect Saudi Arabia. In response, more Iraqi divisions poured into Kuwait. At this point the horrific possibility of Saddam grabbing half the world's oil appeared to become a certainty. A few days earlier, an Iraqi officer had defected to Egypt with their invasion plans for Saudi Arabia.

An expression took hold in Saudi that seemed to capture the

allies' precarious predicament. They would be mere 'speed bumps' in an invasion, just a few battalions of lightly armed infantry who would be mercilessly rolled over by the heavy armour of the Republican Guard. The Desert Shield was in place, but reinforcements were rapidly required if it was to hold.

* * *

Feeling the Florida sunshine dry off the last droplets of pool water, Dave Waddington couldn't have been happier. He was twenty-four and a recently qualified pilot on the RAF's most advanced fast jet. The job came with a certain lifestyle that befitted his role on a frontline squadron. Camaraderie, intense training and of course some thoroughly top-notch parties. He shifted on the sunbed and glanced at his partner Claire. After a hectic day in the Florida theme parks where the G-forces were not to be sneered at but some distance from those of a Tornado, they were taking it easy at his sister's West Palm Beach home. It was early August and even after a cooling dip the heat was beginning to become uncomfortable. Somewhere in the distance, beyond the patio doors, he heard the distant ring of a telephone. He closed his eyes, shutting out the world.

'It's for you, David. Someone called Bambi Thwaites.'

He instantly sat up. Thwaites was an executive on 27 Squadron, and not one to call West Palm Beach without good reason. Dave picked up the phone in his sister's dining room and Bambi got straight to the point. He could finish his holiday, but he would be deploying to the Middle East at the end of August in support of Operation Desert Shield. He felt a rush of nervous excitement. 'I was just a Flying Officer, very young, recently qualified, and I had been picked for "the first team". There were older, more experienced hands on the Squadron but they had chosen me.'[15]

The Squadron executives clearly had a lot of faith in Dave Waddington. By 1990 the Tornado force had reached its peak of eleven frontline squadrons, including eight in Germany, and two training units, totalling nearly 230 combat jets. There were scores of other aircrew who would have readily taken his place on operations. Dave knew he was lucky. He tried to contain his exhilaration as he headed back to the pool to tell Claire he was going to war.

* * *

Life in the RAF had treated Tornado navigator Bob Ankerson well. By 1990 he had been promoted to Squadron Leader and, even though he had just turned forty, he was doing something that very few other forty-somethings did. Flying the most amazing and sophisticated aircraft in the RAF. Bob trained for war but never imagined it would happen. Service life was pleasant and he had become happily accustomed to peace. He had joined the RAF almost by accident, in 1973, a year before the Tornado took flight. He had been in Nottingham with his new wife Chris and some friends when they saw an RAF recruiting stand. Bob had recently been working in the aero-engine division of Rolls-Royce but was now between jobs. 'You could always join this lot,' one of his friends joked, pointing at the display stand. Bob had laughed but by the Monday morning had begun seriously considering the idea. Three months later he was in uniform, aged twenty-three, and heading for a career as a navigator. Like Robbie Stewart, he first flew on Vulcans equipped with nuclear weapons that, he hoped, they would never use. 'I didn't really think much about conflict. The RAF was more of a challenging lifestyle, exciting flying, something few people did.'[16]

Bob's life might not have been quite so contented if Chris had listened to her father. The couple were childhood sweethearts. They met when they were sixteen. She was educated at a convent and he at a boys' Catholic school. Chris's dad approved. As an aeronautical engineer, the clean-cut, likeable young man clearly had solid prospects. Then, five months after they were married, he was in the uniform of the RAF. His father-in-law, a Second World War veteran, made it clear to Chris that he did not approve. 'He had seen it all as a teenager and didn't want me married to anyone who might have to go to war.'

'If I had known he was going to join the RAF, he certainly would not have married you!' he admonished. But at least while the Cold War was centre stage, conflict felt unlikely.

Chris found the RAF provided a marvellous life for a young couple. The glamour of fast jets came with a social circuit of house parties and formal functions. 'War was so far from our minds. Even when Bob was on Vulcans, on 24-hour nuclear Quick Reaction Alert duty. I didn't associate any of this with going to war.'[17] And Bob was a calm, easy-going man. Not a gung-ho fighter. 'I always thought of him as a peacekeeper rather than anything else.' In early August 1990 the Ankersons were caravanning in the forests of Eifel in Belgium when they heard about Kuwait. Enjoy your holiday, Bob was told when he called his base to check if he might be needed. There was no chance of the Squadron being called up. And, anyway, 17 Squadron had a key role to play in the Battle of Britain fiftieth anniversary celebrations and flypast later that year. He could relax.

* * *

'This is Northern Fixer on Guard.'

The air traffic controller using the 'Guard' international distress frequency was rare. Gordon Buckley, instantly alert, relaxed his grip on the Tornado's control column, climbed the jet from low level, and instinctively scoured the deep blue of the summer sky above him.

'Repeat, this is Northern Fixer. Leader of Kayak formation, return to base immediately.'

More messages followed.

'Bobcat and Mallet formation, you are to RTB immediately ...' The list of all RAF units flying training sorties over northern Germany went on. Everyone was being recalled. Gordon had a strong idea what the recall was about. It was Wednesday, 8 August. Just four days earlier, Saddam had completed his conquest of Kuwait.

In the modern age, Gordon Buckley would never have been a jet pilot in the RAF. As a teenager, he had made a schoolboy pact with his best friend that as grown-ups they would become airline pilots. But Gordon's grades put paid to that. He left school with just three O-levels, but what he lacked in exam results he made up for in ambition. Aged twenty-two, Gordon was on the road to qualifying as a Post Office engineer, but his desire to fly remained. He followed his instincts and joined the RAF. Those instincts were justified. The RAF identified a naturally skilled pilot and within three years he was flying Jaguars, a fast, single-seat strike-attack aircraft. He didn't want be anywhere else. Until Tornado came along.

The air traffic controller told Gordon to divert to RAF Bruggen, home to four squadrons of Tornados and close to the West German city of Dusseldorf. His instinct about the 'Guard' call was confirmed. It wasn't going to be his last flying for that day.

Air-to-air refuelling (AAR) would be imperative in any attack plan on Iraq. With the East German border just over 200 miles away, the German-based Tornado GR1 bombers could make it to their Warsaw Pact targets and back without having to replenish their tanks. Almost none of the Germany-based crews had ever carried out AAR sorties. But if they were going deep into Iraq, that changed things. They might require at least two air-to-air refuelling slots. The idea of approaching an airborne tanker trailing a long pipe with a small drogue basket at high speed and at night had little appeal. AAR was a chore for the UK-based Tornado squadrons who would have far further to fly if the Cold War had ever turned hot. For that unimaginable conflict, the eight Tornado squadrons spread evenly between the RAF bases of Laarbruch and Bruggen, near the Dutch border, were as combat-ready as they could be. But anyone going out to the Gulf would rapidly require air-refuelling qualification. Planners scoured the records.

Squadron Leader Gordon Buckley, one of the force's most experienced Tornado pilots, was among the tiny handful of RAF aircrew in Germany qualified as an AAR instructor. Hence the call for him on the emergency frequency. 'My jet had barely come to a halt when I was ordered straight onto a Tornado with dual controls and back into the air to train another pilot.'[18] Fortunately, that pilot was a quick learner, mastering the technique that required a slow, careful approach and a dose of confidence. One trip and he was qualified as an instructor. They each then took another pair up, taught them the art of AAR, and by the end of the day RAF Germany had five new instructors.

Gordon Buckley got back to his home at RAF Laarbruch utterly shattered, but also somewhat elated. 'I really wanted to be part of it all; this was what we had trained to do. I didn't want to kill people or to die, but our job on the Tornado was war and I had never thought I might do that job for real. We were not warmongers, but here was the possibility of being ordered to put all that training and all those skills to the test.'

At Laarbruch's War Operations Centre, an urgent briefing had already been given by the Station Commander. 'You need to pack your bags tonight – we're going to war.'[19]

Iraq? Kuwait? The pilots and navigators looked puzzled. Few of the aircrew could easily point to them on a map. Not that they had any maps of the region to examine. The answer was provided by the Tornado squadrons' ground liaison officers, who had photocopied pages out of the *Times World Atlas* then taped together a mosaic of Saudi Arabia, Kuwait and Iraq. It was the only map they had for the entire summer.

What the intelligence officers lacked in cartography, they had made up for in reams of information on Iraqi Air Force capabilities. Saddam had procured a broad range of Soviet jets. He also had complex and integrated surface-to-air missile – SAM – systems, French and Russian, plus 10,000 anti-aircraft artillery guns.

And in a somewhat surreal turnaround of events, some of the RAF aircrews preparing for war already had experience of 'combat' with Iraqi pilots, albeit during practice sorties while training them. When Iraq had been viewed as 'a friend' in the region in the 1970s and 80s, some of its air force pilots had been trained at RAF flying schools,[20] as well as at other prestigious establishments like the British Army's Royal Military Academy Sandhurst.[21]

Those who had worked with the Iraqis in peace knew that, if a conflict ensued, it would not be a walkover.

For Gordon there was also the moral issue of going to war in a far-off country. 'Kuwait had been brutally invaded and we were hearing of some pretty horrific things going on over there. There was a moral question to all this. Surely it was right to help liberate an occupied country?'

* * *

Yet again the Tornado proved itself one of the airshow's top attractions. It was 8 August and the bellow and power of the Rolls-Royce RB199 engines, the muscular airframe, the reheat flames shooting out, thrilled the crowds at RAF St Mawgan in north Cornwall. Hundreds of RAF aircrew stood around their aircraft, chatting to the public, posing for pictures, keeping an eye out for girls to invite to the after-show party in the Officers' Mess.

Navigator John Nichol, a relatively new member of Gordon Buckley's 15 Squadron, had flown in from RAF Laarbruch, one of the perks of the job. 'It was a typical airshow. All your aircrew mates get together the night before, you go to the bar and have a few drinks. The form is fairly easy, all you need is a hard head and a good line in banter.' The banter took a different turn later in the day. 'I was enjoying the sunshine next to my jet, soaking up endless questions, youthful admiration and the Cornish sun when the station Tannoy system barked into life. "*The captain of the Victor tanker is to report to Station Operations immediately.*" Moments later the entire tanker crew were scrambling towards their aircraft. "We're off to the Gulf," they shouted as they passed us. We just stared in disbelief, wondering what was happening.'[22]

Then the call went for another squadron's Tornado crew and thirty minutes later the Tannoy sounded again. '*15 Squadron Tornado crew is to report to Station Operations immediately!*'

After a few minutes, Nichol's pilot came back from the Operations Room.

'We're also on thirty minutes' notice to move,' he gasped. 'To the Gulf!'

'Naah, never. Don't be daft.' Nichol didn't believe a word of it.

'Yes. We've got to get this aircraft ready to go. Now.'

Order followed counter-order as rumours flew around the base. But a few hours later they were all stood down, which, after the initial tensions of the call-out, was taken as a good excuse to have a stiff drink. After a few more of those, Nichol was tearing around the bar with a tea towel on his head pretending to be Lawrence of Arabia. The 'standing down' was going very well and there was much laughter from the assembled aircrew. 'Simon Burgess, a Tornado pilot and mate of mine, called to me across the bar: *"Nichol, you might regret doing that one day!"* When we met again a few months later, in less salubrious circumstances, Simon reminded me of that night.'

* * *

To get on a war footing, Tornado training reached new heights of intensity with the emphasis on low-level flying. It came with great risks.

The weather was fine off Spurn Head on the Yorkshire coast on 14 August. No cloud below 5,000ft and visibility in excess of 6 miles. There was just a hint of summer haze, making it a bit more difficult than usual to see other aircraft in the area. The skies were busy with training sorties. One Tornado had taken off from RAF Honington in Suffolk, and was making a practice bombing run on an east coast weapons' range. Another pair of Tornados, including navigator Gordon Graham, had flown across the North Sea from RAF Laarbruch and were also practising on a nearby weapons range. Not far off Spurn Head, Graham's Tornado had just levelled off at 320ft after detecting a minor systems fault. A few seconds later he spotted a rapidly approaching aircraft dead ahead and shouted 'Break!', the command to instantly turn away. It was too late. Both aircraft were flying at the exact same height in the same place; two seconds later they collided and broke apart. Graham and his pilot ejected into the sea, but the navigator's wounds were fatal. As were the injuries to the crew of the aircraft they collided with. Graham's badly injured pilot was the only one of the four aircrew to survive the collision.[23]

* * *

'Fuck me, Belly, I thought you were dead!' John Nichol declared as he walked into the flat he shared with Dave Bellamy near RAF Laarbruch.

Bellamy looked up from his ironing and registered his fellow Tornado navigator's startled expression. They were barely a week into the intensive war-training. Like Gordon Buckley, Bellamy was one of the few air-to-air refuelling instructors in Germany. 'I had withdrawn my resignation so I could be part of any deployment and was then flying three or four times a day to get the rest of the Squadron AAR qualified. By mid-August, I was absolutely knackered.'[24] That 14 August, Bellamy was meant to be flying the fateful training sortie near Spurn Head, but as two of the four Tornados programmed to fly from Laarbruch had technical problems, Gordon Graham, one of the Squadron's senior officers, told him to go home.

'I was so tired, Gordon said he would lead the sortie with the Boss while I had some downtime. I was really grateful for the rest. I went back to the flat I shared with John Nichol to catch up on some chores.' That afternoon, news of the crash and deaths of three aircrew had reverberated around the Tornado force. 'There had been confusion on some of the other squadrons,' Bellamy remembered. 'The word had gone around that I had been killed in the crash. However, I knew who had been flying in my place and realised it was Gordon who'd died. It was awful.'

'You didn't serve long as fast-jet aircrew before a mate was killed,' Nichol said. 'But this crash really hit home. Gordon Graham had previously served on my Squadron and he was universally regarded as a really decent bloke and a great operator; one of life's good guys. His loss was a massive shock for my Squadron and Dave Bellamy's.'

Across the Tornado force, from RAF Marham to Laarbruch

and Bruggen, people were rushing to prepare for a war no one ever expected. It came at a cost. 'It was a real blow for 20 Squadron,' Bellamy remembered. 'We had lost the Boss, now seriously injured in hospital, and Gordon, one of our Flight Commanders, was dead. We then had Gordon's military funeral to deal with, where a number of our guys acted as pallbearers. It was an awful time.'

The short tribute, later placed in the RAF Laarbruch magazine, said it all:

> As a true Officer and Gentleman, Squadron Leader Gordon Graham will be greatly missed by the members of 20 Squadron, all of whom held a deep respect for him both as a Navigator and Flight Commander. Our sympathies and hopes for the future go to his widow Gael and son Jamie.[25]

The ongoing deaths didn't make Bellamy, twenty-seven, reconsider his decision to withdraw his resignation made in the light of the looming post-Cold War cuts to the RAF. He would not duck the coming combat. Bellamy was also fast becoming the 20 Squadron expert on a brand-new missile that the RAF was rushing into service. The ALARM – Air-Launched Anti-Radiation Missile – was a clever munition. Its primary purpose was to seek out and destroy radar systems. Without them, the enemy could not see incoming jets or guide its surface-to-air missiles onto them. The ALARM was a stand-off, fire-and-forget missile that could be launched from considerable ranges, giving aircrew greater protection from groundfire. Bellamy was more than happy with that. '20 Squadron crews came to realise that they could fire a "smart" missile while avoiding the worst of any hostile defences. ALARM offered the RAF and the Tornado a radical new capability.'

* * *

Bill Green was not going to miss leading his own Squadron to war. As the Boss of 27 Squadron at RAF Marham, he had thoroughly enjoyed his time bringing the fliers and ground crew up to exceptional standards. And he was popular with aircrew and ground crew alike; a frequent visitor to the 'business end' of the Squadron engineering facilities as well as an astute planner in the Operations Room. There was something else that seemed to set him apart from the average officer. He was genuinely in love with flying. 'I would *pay* the Queen to let me fly her aircraft!' he would often quip.

He'd met his wife Jenny when they were both studying at Oxford University. They had married in Christ Church Cathedral soon after finals in 1969. In the following years they had two children and settled into RAF life. Bill and Jenny Green had dealt first hand with death in the fast-jet community on many occasions. Early on in their married life, a close RAF friend was killed in a training aircraft. The previous Sunday, they had christened his 3-month-old son. Jenny was babysitting him at their friends' home when an officer arrived to relay the terrible news. As the deceased pilot's wife was not at home, Jenny later had the crushing duty to inform the young mother that she was now a widow. 'We all understood that the possibility of our husbands dying in a flying accident was always there. You know it can happen, but you never get used to it.'[26]

That aside, RAF routine was fairly predictable. Their children grew into teenagers and squadron life was comfortable. Jenny knew her husband thoroughly enjoyed it. 'Being a Squadron Commander was a wonderful experience for Bill. He was dedicated to his men and especially to the young ground crew who he felt always gave their very best, but were not always properly recognised for their incredible efforts.'

Bill Green was regarded as a thoroughly decent and honourable man. The type whose troops would follow into battle. He also played the piano, church organ, guitar and, if the Squadron band's drummer failed to turn up for rehearsal, percussion too. Many of Bill's contemporaries thought he was destined for high command. He himself realised that the Cold War's conclusion would have significant ramifications. When the Berlin Wall came down in 1989, the countries behind the Iron Curtain experienced the first taste of freedom since Communism had been imposed on them from 1945. Bill understood that great upheaval led to turmoil. 'This is just the beginning, not the end,' he told Jenny. 'The world will now change in a very different way.' Then Saddam decided to invade Kuwait and his Squadron was one of the first to be ordered to the Gulf. Bill was told he was going to be the Detachment Commander for the Tornado bomber force. They would be deploying at the end of August. They had to prepare for war. Fast.

Bill's 17-year-old son Jeremy and 15-year-old daughter Philippa were home from boarding school as preparations ramped up. 'Living on a Tornado base meant that RAF life almost became part of family life,' said Jeremy. 'You were immersed in the day-to-day realities. Dad had known a couple of the guys killed in the crash just a few days before and we had spoken about what it all meant. We then had a conversation about what would happen if he died in any coming war. We had known some of Dad's friends killed in flying accidents over the years, so this was now a greater possibility if he was going to war. I understood those risks; for much of my life I said a nightly prayer, asking God to keep him safe when he was flying.'[27]

Jenny saw Bill take the prospect of action extremely seriously. 'On previous major detachments, there would always be a happy whistling going on as Bill put new strings on his guitar, and checked the piano accordion. None of that happened this time. This one was for real.' And the training had to be very real. As the Boss, Bill was at the forefront of the action, which included continual preparation for night-time, high-speed attack missions. As a pilot he was determined to be at the very top of his game. In the early days of August, while ensuring his Squadron was ready to deploy, he flew hour after hour, honing his flying skills to the highest level. A sortie was set for 16 August as part of the intensive pre-deployment training package. The next day the whole family would head from Norfolk to visit Bill's relatives in Northumberland to say goodbye. 'We were looking forward to spending a few days together as a family and enjoying some long walks on the beach before Bill's departure.'

That morning, Jenny had listened as he played the piano,

accompanying their daughter Philippa on the violin. Jenny had
made lunch and called them to the table. 'I had to chivvy them along
to eat together so we could get away in time to visit my mother over
in Stamford, who was going into hospital for an operation. Bill went
off to work and expected to be back around 11pm.' She spent the
rest of the day with her mother and the children. Returning to their
quarters exhausted, she went to bed, smiling ruefully to herself at
the thought of the long johns Bill would currently be wearing under
his flying suit – they had been dyed pale pink after a red T-shirt had
got mixed up in the wash. At least they would go with the desert
pink colour scheme of the newly painted Tornados they would be
flying in the Gulf.

It was dark when Bill took off with his navigator Neil Anderson
from the long tarmac strip of RAF Marham. After night-time
air-to-air refuelling, they flew over the flat Norfolk landscape for
TFR practice, followed by a bombing run over a range near Hull.
Before returning to base, they headed out to sea, paralleling the
coast. Bill decided to practise the challenging low-level loft – or
toss – bombing manoeuvre that they would inevitably have to use
against Iraqi airfields. They picked up a ship on the radar and chose
it as the target. He flicked the control to take them out of automatic
terrain following and entered a steep climb from 250 feet above the
wave tops, going through a practice bomb release at around 1,200ft
before commencing a recovery back to low level.[28]

* * *

The ringing echoed inside Jenny Green's head. It was far too early
for her alarm. And there it was again. More persistent now. She
opened her eyes. It was still dark. The bedside clock told her it was
1 a.m. 'The doorbell was ringing like mad. My first thought was
that Bill had forgotten his key. I got out of bed and got halfway
downstairs, then wondered if it was actually him, so turned back
to put my dressing gown on.'

Jenny headed back downstairs. 'I got to the bottom step and

paused. If it was Bill, would he not be calling through the door to reassure me?'

Another ring. She could now sense someone standing outside. She flipped open the spyhole cover and caught her breath.

RAF Marham's Station Commander Jock Stirrup was standing outside in full dress uniform. The gold braid of his service cap glinted in the porch light. Jenny took a step back, forcing the bad news that lay on the far side of the door to remain where it was. If she did not answer, everything would still be okay.

'My life changed for ever in a split second. I instantly knew what had happened. I couldn't open the door. I just sat at the bottom of the stairs. Poor Jock had to stand outside while I composed myself.'

It had happened to others and now it had happened to her. No more would the house be filled with Bill's laughter, his music . . . his presence. She heard movement above. The children were at the top of the stairs. She couldn't delay any more. She saw her hand reach for the latch. Group Captain Stirrup spoke gently:

Bill's aircraft is missing . . . over the Wash . . . there's no hope of them being alive . . . I'm so sorry, Jenny . . .

'The rest was a blur, but the next twenty-four hours are still crystal clear, indelibly imprinted on my brain, even though it was over thirty years ago. However much you think you might know what it might be like, because you have seen *others* go through it, it is very different when it happens to you, when it is *your* life.'

Those first moments were also imprinted on Jeremy Green's teenage mind. 'I still remember it all as clear as day,' he said. 'I loved photography and Dad had arranged for me to visit his Squadron *that* night to take some pictures. But because of my grandmother's illness I put it off until another day. There was always going to be another day. If I had been there, waiting on the Squadron, as the news of the crash came in . . . it doesn't bear thinking about. Mum looked broken. We had endless visitors. We drank endless tea. At some point later the TV news showed wreckage of his aircraft being lifted from the sea. Your mind knows the worst, but you don't want to accept it.'

A Military Accident Report[29] subsequently showed that at the peak of his weapons release manoeuvre, Bill Green had rolled the aircraft into a hard bank while entering the challenging recovery phase from the loft attack; aiming to get the Tornado wings level, descending back to low level, and heading away from the target. But something had gone terribly wrong and the Tornado hit the sea at 500 knots (575mph) while still in an 18-degree dive. No attempt had been made to eject and both Bill Green and Neil Anderson were killed instantly. The report concluded that for some reason during the recovery from the loft manoeuvre, the aircraft had entered a steeper than normal dive. The crew might have been somehow distracted. But in many ways it didn't matter, another Tornado was down after just a few weeks of training for a war in the Gulf. And five aircrew were now dead.

Bill Green's body was never recovered from the North Sea and his passing was a bitter blow. He was the type of leader who cared for and loved his men, and that was reciprocated. 27 Squadron was in mourning; it would be difficult to replace 'The Boss'.

* * *

Robbie Stewart's family got back to their home in Lincolnshire on 20 August in reasonable spirits despite the interrupted Bavarian holiday. Robbie phoned his Operations Room to be told he would be deploying with his Squadron. He already knew about the horrific collision off Spurn Head which killed three crewmen on 14 August, but he hadn't heard any names. It was then that he was also given the news about his Boss, Bill Green, and friend Neil Anderson, who had died two days later. 'I just couldn't comprehend what they were saying. Bill was such a wonderful guy. I was totally floored to hear he'd died.'

Tange was in the house when Robbie made the call. As the phone hung limply in his hand, she could see his face crumple. 'Robbie looked at me but couldn't speak. He eventually managed to get out that Bill and Neil had been killed. It was such a terrible shock for all of us.'

Kirsty Stewart saw the hurt on both her parents' faces. She had turned thirteen a few days earlier and her father treated her like a grown-up. 'I still remember both Mum and Dad's reaction and how upset they were, but Dad explained about what it was like to fly at night and how difficult it could be, how you could get disorientated.' The death of close friends brought a grim focus to her father's imminent departure for war. Kirsty was growing up fast. 'There was a creeping realisation that Dad was going away, and it was really serious.'

In between sorties, Robbie had a long list of tasks, from inoculations against Saddam's biological weapons to practising pistol drills. 'We had to start preparing straight away: jabs, medicals, checking our personal weapons. I had a very real sense of what was to come, that we were heading to war. Talking to Tange and the kids was both emotional and hard. Lots of the younger guys were excited but those of us who were older, with families, were a little more realistic about what we faced.'

After long days he would get back late to their four-bedroom cottage in Coleby. Tange managed to sit him down for a few important conversations. 'We tried to sort out what we all wanted if the worst was to happen. We didn't really have much time at all as he was so busy down at Marham and we were up in Coleby. We talked about finances, the children, their education, what Robbie hoped for us all if he didn't come home. But there really wasn't much time to plan anything.'

Despite the intense preparations Robbie's pilot, Dave Waddington, found the time to visit Jenny Green and offer his condolences. 'Bill Green was a great Boss – very experienced, an old-fashioned type of officer and a lovely guy. I said goodbye to Jenny early because we were deploying and I would miss the Boss's funeral. As the youngest guy on the Squadron, there was little I could say to her. It was a very difficult moment.'

Training for war had claimed three Tornados and five lives in just a handful of summer days. The other navigator killed in the Spurn Head collision had been a close friend of Bob Ankerson, as had Neil

Anderson. 'Neil was a good operator, great company and passionate about the RAF.' His passing was a reminder to Bob that war or no war, death was the third passenger every time you flew the Tornado. 'That was the way things happened back then. There was just an acceptance. You got used to deaths in the RAF, but these were the first real friends I had lost to accidents. It highlighted the risks, but you quickly shoved any notion of death into the background, telling yourself, *It'll never happen to me . . .*'[30]

Two weeks after Gordon Graham's death his Squadron celebrated the unit's seventy-fifth anniversary. The guest of honour was 20 Squadron veteran Air Marshal Sir Victor Groom, ninety-two and a First World War ace who had flown the 120mph Bristol F2B fighters in 1918, just fifteen years after the Wright brothers' first ever powered flight. Miraculously, Groom survived the final year of the war while claiming eight 'kills'. David Bellamy was among those watching and he could not help but wonder if his own generation of Tornado aircrew might soon share the same fate as the majority of First World War pilots on the Western Front.

* * *

As the dog days of August 1990 approached, there was a last chance for a bit of family time over the bank holiday weekend. On the Friday before Robbie's departure, Tange Stewart booked a table at the local Beefeater pub in Canwick Hill for a farewell meal. Around them, others enjoyed the summer sunshine. 'It was a lovely family pub and a beautiful sunny day but the four of us were subdued and contemplating the future. I remember just thinking, *These people have no idea what is happening.* The next day my husband and my children's father was heading to war.' As Kirsty watched the other children play, she could not stop feeling uneasy. 'It was a horrible time. There was a sense that my dad was heading off on a very uncertain journey.'

After saying goodbye to them, Robbie left Marham by bus on Sunday, 26 August, heading to one of the RAF's transport bases to begin a series of long flights to the Gulf. 'As we drove off base, lots of the wives and families were standing near the exit, waving. It was sobering to see them, wondering when, or if, we would ever see them again. But there was also a real sense of excitement and anticipation on the bus. This is what we had trained to do. Then I looked out of the window to see the Norfolk countryside flashing by and realised we were heading to a warzone.'

After a two-day journey the aircrew landed at Muharraq airbase on the island of Bahrain, linked to Saudi Arabia by a causeway. In between the build-up for war, Gulf Air passenger jets were still taking off with businessmen and holidaymakers, escaping the intense August heat. Even at 5am it was over 30°C; a dry heat with no hint of any breeze. On the shimmering tarmac, Robbie could see the machinery of war was in full swing. RAF C130 Hercules transporters fought for space with civilian airliners. RAF Regiment Rapier air defence missile batteries bristled along the perimeter as countless transport aircraft flew in endless supplies and RAF tankers took off for vital air-to-air refuelling sorties. Everyone was on their toes, waiting for the enemy attack. 'The build-up at Muharraq as the machinery of war moved in was astonishing. The military had really swung into action.'

Back in Germany, the army was also gearing for war. In September it was announced that the British 7th Armoured Brigade – the Desert Rats – were deploying. The Challenger tanks and Warrior armoured fighting vehicles had turned their turrets away from the Soviet threat in the east, and shipped south to the desert. Reservists were called up. Trombones and flutes of the RAF musicians were exchanged for stretchers and bandages as they adopted their wartime role as medics. In the Gulf, the smell of war-fighting was in the air. The metallic odour of munitions mingled with the stench of aviation fuel as sweating ground crew serviced the aircraft. It was a demanding task, preparing not only for war but for a conflict in which it was clear the Tornado would play a lead role.

It was challenging too. The desert flying, Robbie and Dave agreed, *was exceptional*. No longer did they have to abide by the strict lowest-level limit of 100ft – operational low-level flying, or OLF. They flew as close to the ground as their skills and safety allowed, regularly below 100ft, ultra-low level. Something that was not strictly authorised. Looking on from the rear seat, Robbie found it thrilling. 'The desert flying was fantastic, a chance to hone our skills and practise everything at a really operational level, down at 50 feet and 540 knots [600mph]. You'd be flying across the desert at ultra-low level in gin-clear skies then suddenly a herd of camels would loom up in front of you. It was the most advanced flying we had ever done.' Very soon they were carrying full war loads, testing the Tornado to its maximum, practising air-to-air refuelling and low-level attacks. But for Robbie the excitement could not hide what they were there for. 'There was an inevitability about it all. The sense of a relentless march to war.'

Enhancements were rapidly being made to the Tornados to bring them fully onto a war footing. Radar absorbent paint was applied to try to hide them from Iraqi air defence systems.[31] HaveQuick radios, resistant to electronic jamming, were fitted, along with secure IFF systems that would easily distinguish between friendly and potentially hostile aircraft across any future battle space. Given the long combat sorties from the Gulf into Iraq, it was decided that, for many missions, the two 1,500-litre drop tanks under the wings should be replaced by the larger 2,250-litre tanks, increasing fuel load and range. The additional kit created different aerodynamics with extra drag on the aircraft, especially when carrying a full war load.

The American build-up was relentless too, and accompanied by the most sophisticated aerial weapons systems in history.[32] Western allies and Arabs were also joining the growing force. French troops and aircraft arrived, along with eight Italian Tornados, plus Egyptians, Pakistanis and Moroccans. There was even a contingent of 500 Niger soldiers to protect the holy sites of Mecca and Medina.

The build-up was a success and the immediate threat of an Iraqi invasion of Saudi Arabia subsided. The US influx had been truly astonishing. Within six weeks they had brought in the 24th Marine Expeditionary Force and the 101st Airborne Division, along with scores of Apache attack helicopters and the A-10 'tank-buster' air-craft. The Desert Shield was firmly in place. The Iraqis knew it too. Satellite photographs had shown that rather than being poised on the border, they were now digging in and waiting.

In November 1990, after three months of non-stop preparation, 27 Squadron was ordered home. It was time for others to come in and share the load. Waiting to take the flight out, Dave Waddington did not particularly mind the prospect of missing any future war. Yes, it would have been exciting, but he had been selected for the choice posting of the 'Qualified Weapons Instructor' course and the honour to become a 'Top Gun' pilot. If he passed, he was going to be the youngest Tornado QWI pilot. A big professional fillip and a career marker for greater things to come.

After the emotion of their rapid departure, Robbie Stewart was also only too happy to be home for Christmas. He was not one of the young guns, eager to be part of any upcoming war. He would do it if necessary, but Coleby, Lincolnshire, with Tange and his children, was the place he loved.

CHAPTER THREE

'EVERYTHING'S CHANGED!'

NOVEMBER 1990–15 JANUARY 1991

The intensity of training for war had drawn the individual Tornado squadrons closer together. Comprising around 130 engineers and support personnel, with some twelve jets and eighteen crews,[1] each squadron was tight-knit, with its own traditions and proud past. As they practised for war, the bonds grew deeper with the prospect that they too might make their own bit of history. The likelihood of battle was becoming an unnerving reality. They had trained hard since early August, they had taken casualties, but they were ready to face whatever lay ahead.

At RAF Laarbruch in Germany, after four months of relentless training, a good party was in order. Usually it would be the annual 'Lunch of the Year' around Christmas time, but because of the urgent deployments, this had to be brought forward. It fell to 15 Squadron's more junior crew, pilot John Peters, twenty-nine, and navigator John Nichol, twenty-seven, to organise what would be their final social event before heading to the Gulf. The 'Two Johns' had a few experienced hands to fall back on for advice. Among them was navigator Mike Toft who, with a wife and young family, was feeling the tension grow as the days to deployment counted down. The in-depth briefing on the Iraqi air defences, similar to the Soviet ones they knew only too well, had taken on a grave tone. 'We had really feared going up against them in the Cold War. The prospect now was formidable. And worrying.'[2]

That worry turned to anger in a pub one night back in England, when a couple of bikers sat down at the next table. Mike could not help but overhear the loud complaints about how tensions in the Gulf had dramatically increased petrol prices. He could barely control his anger. 'I thought, "You *bastards*! Are *you* putting *your* balls on the line to bring the prices down?" It was almost surreal. We were heading to war and those outside our bubble had not a jot of understanding about what we were going to do.'

There was at least comfort in flying the Tornado. Mike had originally been a navigator on the Canberra, the RAF's first jet bomber. It was a step change crossing over to the Tornado with its new technology and capability. 'The radar was bloody awesome at low level – really easy to use and fantastic for identifying everything from large radio masts right down to turns in fence lines. And while there were occasional issues with bits of kit not working as advertised, we all completely trusted the jet.' If Mike was going to go to war, then Tornado was the best option. After months of hard work, he was ready for a good party.

There was another wise old hand that the Two Johns could turn to for advice, and not just on hosting parties. Since joining the RAF a decade earlier, Nige Risdale had absorbed all he could about the RAF's brand-new Tornado 'electric jet' while going through training and his heart had been set on flying the aircraft. With scores of Tornados coming into service, he had been rewarded with a 'boy in a sweetshop moment' after landing at RAF Marham in late 1982, aged twenty-three. 'We were shown into one of the giant hangars and it was chock-full of brand-new, shiny Tornados. They looked amazing; a complete flying machine which really looked as though it meant business.'[3]

Nige was hooked and did not want to fly anything else. He was not one of the hotshot pilots who favoured the single-seat Harriers and Jaguars. He preferred the comfort of another set of hands and eyes in the back seat, especially the 'older' experienced navigators who could offer advice and airmanship. It was a mature quality in a young flier, and one that over the years marked Nige Risdale out to be one of the most trusted pilots on the Squadron. After completing the tough QWI 'Top Gun' course, he also had real experience and knowledge. Quiet and reserved, Risdale was a hugely talented officer, particularly respected by the younger aircrew. It was why, at just thirty-one years old, he was the designated pilot for the Squadron Boss, John Broadbent. Together, they would lead the Squadron's initial combat missions. It was a job that needed a clear head and exceptional flying ability.

The Squadron's more experienced officers were an important source of knowledge, social and professional, to newcomers like John Nichol. He had joined the RAF aged seventeen in 1981 as a communications technician, and after four years had worked his way up to the rank of Corporal.[4] An ambition took hold that perhaps he could advance further up the RAF's command ladder, so he applied for a commission as an officer, then trained as a Tornado navigator. The organisational skills he had learned in the ranks were now put to good use.

The 15 Squadron 'Lunch of the Year' 1990 felt more than usually significant. 'Even then, with war mentioned daily in the headlines, I was still convinced it was not going to involve me,' Nichol recalled. 'I just couldn't comprehend how it would all end in battle. Surely Saddam would see the madness of trying to take on the world's most modern armies and air forces? And I certainly wasn't one of those hungry for combat.' All the same, the TV reports were full of images of the build-up in the Gulf. 'We were heading in that direction, so John Peters and I decided to lay on a daytime version of the "Last Supper".' They decked out the crew room in black sheets, played mournful church recordings, had Bible readings, then got everyone to dress in their flying suits with sandals instead of boots. Each officer entered the crew room solemnly carrying a lit candle and walked to chairs at the end of the room where the Boss, John Broadbent, and Flight Commander Gordon Buckley ritually scrubbed their feet in a bowl of soapy water with the biggest, filthiest brushes the Two Johns could find.

There was a fair bit of drink taken and much laughter. Mike Toft demonstrated his legendary talents as a Cossack dancer. The occasional bread roll was launched, like a surface-to-air missile, across the crew room. The senior aircrew, like Nige Risdale and Gordon Buckley, looked on as though indulging recalcitrant children. It was a moment to forget both what lay ahead and those they were leaving behind. For Nichol, in among the fun was a more sobering thought that there was a chance, no matter how remote, that some of them might not be present at next year's lunch. 'People were letting off steam and most of us got a little the worse for wear. But there was a breath of something in the air, of people coming to terms with events. It was as if the religious ritual provided some sort of answer to a question we had not yet even asked ourselves.'[5]

Across the airfield, final gatherings were also taking place for Laarbruch's other squadrons selected to deploy. Nichol's flatmate and fellow Tornado navigator Dave Bellamy had finally cancelled the five-week Chilean travel adventure he had booked with his girlfriend. Instead of trekking the Atacama he would be flying over another desert. Before deploying to the Gulf, Bellamy made one last trip home. His mother's parting words were that she had been praying hard, and 'God has promised you will be safe'.

Bellamy told his pilot Trevor Roche that this divine intervention would happily extend to him, as they were in the same aircraft. Then the rest of the formation heard about 'Dave's heavenly safety'. Superstitions grew. Perhaps if they flew close to Dave and Trevor's aircraft, they too would fall under the Good Lord's umbrella? Word spread and other members of 20 Squadron asked if they could join the formation that was clearly going to be 'watched over'. While it became a bit of a standing joke, there was just a hint of seriousness behind the smiles. How *would* they survive what was coming?

It was now late November, and 20 Squadron was deploying two weeks earlier than Nichol's 15 Squadron. Bellamy was chuffed they had 'beaten' them to the punch but there was a downside: last-minute packing. He had put on a clothes wash, and with no time to dry his long johns and T-shirts, he reached for Nichol's prized microwave, trusted purveyor of so many gourmet baked bean dinners. He placed his flying long johns and T-shirts reverently inside and turned up the dial. A few minutes later there was a satisfying ping. But his delight was short-lived. 'Unfortunately, my plan hadn't worked so I stuffed the laundry, warm but still wet, in a plastic bag. The funny thing was that the process sterilised my clothes so two weeks later when my kit arrived, I had fresh but damp clothes and no mildew. John, on the other hand, had baked beans tasting of Persil Automatic.' As Bellamy threw his clothes into his kitbag he spotted handwritten notes among the unwashed crockery on the kitchen table. His flatmates had decided to write a couple of encouraging goodbye messages.

'*Bydsee bye Dave,*' Nichol had scrawled on the back of an envelope. '*Look after ya'self and check six. See ya when we collect our medals! I'll drop ya a line. All the best, John.*'

Their fellow flat-sharing navigator, who would also soon deploy to the warzone, cheerfully wrote: '*Dave, I love you dearly. Please don't leave me! Take care you twat. Luv, Glyn.*'

When Bellamy rose before dawn he tucked the notes into his trousers then proceeded to pick up his pilot from the married quarters. As Trevor Roche got into the car, his wife Katie rushed out to say a final goodbye. 'Belly, promise me you will look after him, promise me you will bring him back to me?'

'I promise,' Bellamy replied with no idea if he could honour the pledge, merely hoping against hope that his mum's conversation with God really was going to come up trumps.

* * *

Arriving at Tabuk in Saudi Arabia, Bellamy found there were washing lines for his damp kit, but little else by way of comfort, especially not microwaves. In the far north-west of the country, they were closer to the splendid reefs of the Red Sea than the arid deserts of Iraq. The enemy border lay 300 miles to the east and Baghdad another 200 miles beyond.

Tabuk was a military airbase; functional and spartan, it had a sense of purpose. There was no swimming pool or bar – nothing to distract them from the job in hand. There was little to choose from in the way of accommodation, although, as usual, the officers seemed to fare better than the airmen. It was something that was – generally – taken with good grace by the RAF rankers. The officers, after all, were the ones who went into battle. But the aircrew also understood that without the ground crew, there would be no flying; they kept the jets airworthy. Their shared mission was a mutual bond. The officers took over the little wooden villas belonging to British Aerospace (the major defence contractor – BAe) with six to a room, whereas the airmen's quarters were more basic, and twice as crowded. Dave Bellamy's formation was even luckier. There were no villas left when they arrived so they were given rooms in a single-men's block still used by BAe personnel. There was a feeling that the Saudis on the base, while generally friendly, were not overly enamoured with having a bunch of foreigners on their land. Initial co-operation had been 'difficult' at best.

The Tabuk detachment was substantial, with aircrew from a number of the RAF's UK and Germany Tornado squadrons. The base was surrounded by hundreds of miles of desert, which for the aircrew was perfect. 'The flying out there was absolutely fantastic, the best I've ever done in the air force. Most of the Saudi desert is absolutely flat but here there were fantastic valleys, mountains, volcanoes and standing stones ... and we were told we could fly as low and as fast as we needed to go.'[6] They shared the base with the resident members of the Royal Saudi and US Air Forces, which allowed the Tornados to fly mock combat sorties against the highly capable Saudi F-15s, whose pilots proved to be 'very, very good'.

Which prompted a mildly disturbing thought: *Maybe the Iraqis are just as good.*[7]

That worry was compounded by the Iraqis having the sixth largest air force in the world, with 900 jet aircraft. They would present a formidable foe.

* * *

While the earlier 'Last Supper' party had parked his troubles for one afternoon, navigator Mike Toft, still waiting at RAF Laarbruch to deploy, could not shake off the concern of leaving behind his toddler daughter and a wife who was six months pregnant. Mike was returning from his sorties to a worried partner and playful 2-year-old. *How the hell are we going to get through this?* he thought. While many of the young, single aircrew brimmed with excitement, married men like Mike were more introspective. 'It was a sense of duty that carried me through. I did not particularly *want* to go, but that's what I'd signed up to do. Was I excited? I don't think so. Was I worried? Hell yes, especially for Sue and our 1.6 kids. Leaving them behind for the unknown was damned hard.'

Mike Toft and the other 50,000 British soldiers, sailors and airmen sent to the region were under military orders. Even if it meant leaving a young family behind. The crosses being marked on the family calendar leading up to 2 December 1990 seemed to speed up as his departure date drew closer. The last forty-eight hours were the worst. 'We both knew what was going to happen and just wanted to get it over with.' To pass the time they took their daughter to a local petting zoo. It didn't help. 'It was really striking; the normality of wandering around this little park, feeding the goats and the sheep, a seemingly happy family. But amid the crowds, only Sue and I knew that I'd soon be putting my life on the line 3,000 miles away.'

Toft was flying out to replace the likes of Robbie Stewart and Dave Waddington, hurriedly spirited to the Gulf in August. He would be joining Gordon Buckley on 15 Squadron. While the prospect of war was daunting, some weight was taken off their minds when they were told their destination was Bahrain – and that they would be billeted in the five-star Sheraton in the middle of town. It had excellent rooms, air conditioning, swimming pools and, unlike Saudi Arabia, alcohol. The aircrews were told to pack their dinner jackets. When they arrived at the hotel, each pilot and navigator pair was given a room to share for the duration.

The genial expat community were eager to befriend the glamorous new arrivals and proved themselves generous hosts. During the day there was rigorous planning and preparation for war but then along came the party invitations. Gordon Buckley found it curiously unsettling. 'There was a lot of socialising with the locals joining us in the hotel bar for a drink and inviting us to their homes. It was really strange to be living the life of a businessman in a five-star hotel while preparing for war.' And he was not alone in still questioning whether there would actually be open hostilities, especially now the coalition force had grown to 800,000. 'I presumed we would threaten, have a bit of sabre-rattling and then Saddam would back down.'[8]

With the distractions of a full social life, including horse riding and windsurfing in the Gulf, interspersed with flying demanding training sorties, their surreal existence continued. Sometimes it was only the dawn chant of the muezzin calling the faithful to prayer that reminded them where they were. And why.

* * *

Nige Risdale definitely wanted to ensure that the Tornado's leading role would achieve maximum impact with the minimum risk. Only he and 15 Squadron's Boss, Wing Commander John Broadbent, who would be leading any initial attack, were given access to the US-controlled, top-secret planning. 'The missions for the first seventy-two hours of offensive operations were all to be pre-planned. The Americans controlled the show and decided that in order to keep the security lid tight, access to the raids would be limited to one crew per detachment.' Leaving behind clear-headed veterans like Gordon Buckley and Mike Toft, Nige found planning for missions that presented grave dangers a taxing and lonely affair. The Tornado was clearly among the best qualified coalition bombers to do the low-level missions and the attack plan was to use the unique runway-busting JP233 to knock the Iraqi airbases out of action – and that came with considerable risk. In any all-out war of national survival against the Soviets, high casualties had been expected and accepted. But this was a relatively parochial battle for someone else's country. Did they have to put so many lives on the line?

As one of the most qualified pilots, Nige Risdale knew better than most about the Tornado's potential. He had previously served on 20 Squadron, which had trained in dropping laser-guided bombs – LGBs – onto their targets via the Pave Spike designating pod on another very capable aircraft, the Buccaneer. Using these assets, Nige had initially thought, the Tornados could drop their 1,000lb bombs with clinical accuracy. 'I thought, *We should be using LGBs*. I'd dropped many live LGBs so I knew exactly what they were capable of. I thought we should get the Buccaneers out so we'd have precision weapons to attack the airfields.' The response to Risdale's suggestion was unambiguous. 'I was told that this was not going to happen. The sense I had got in the initial stages of deployment was that the RAF's Tornado had been "*sold*" to the Americans by "high command" as an airfield-busting force using JP233s to put airfields out of action. Which of course, was exactly the role we had trained for, so it made sense.'

In fact, while it was undoubtedly true that the RAF had been earmarked for its airfield attack capability, the idea of bringing in Buccaneers to provide precision targeting was also being discussed. And dismissed. As Air Vice-Marshal Bill Wratten, the British Air Commander, later recalled. 'Most airfields were very overcrowded, with some, such as Bahrain, particularly so. But we wanted to introduce the Buccaneer into theatre to provide ourselves with a laser target-marking capability. This led to a spirited debate in which Horner [General Chuck Horner; the overall Air Commander] made his position quite clear – the Brits simply did not need to import any more aeroplanes because the USAF could provide all the designation that might be needed.'[9]

It was decided; the JP233 would be the RAF's main contribution. It had been developed specifically for Tornados to sneak through Soviet defences then deliver their devastating ordnance via a high-speed, low-level overflight.[10] The Iraqi Air Force was able to operate from a number of very large and well-prepared bases, and the USAF lacked dedicated airfield-denial munitions, so the Americans warmly embraced the British offer of employing Tornado GR1s to complete the job.

But Nige knew that the JP233 was going to present a challenge, particularly to get enough aircraft over the target to achieve the requisite damage. The weapon had been designed to decimate Warsaw Pact runways. Punching through their thick layers built on dense northern European clay subsoil, the cratering munitions would bury themselves then explode, 'heaving' the runway surface upwards and causing massive damage. 'The tactics we had always used dictated that knocking out an 8,000ft Soviet runway on "Day One" of the Cold War going hot would require one Tornado eight-ship formation, each carrying two JP233s, attacking that single airfield. Those of us who survived that initial assault would return to base, reload, refuel and then repeat the attack about four hours later with another eight aircraft loaded with JP233s. We would have deployed thirty-two JP233s: nearly 1,000 cratering munitions and 7,000 anti-personnel bomblets. For *one single* 8,000ft runway.'

Nige was told their first target in Iraq would be the giant military airbase of Tallil, near Nasiriyah, about 150 miles north-west of Iraq's second city, Basra. It was a tough proposition. 'Tallil had *two* parallel 12,000ft runways – about the same length as Heathrow airport's – and *two* taxiways which could also be used for take-off and landing if required. Tallil effectively had *four 12,000ft* runways! There were also HAS [hardened aircraft shelter] sites in each corner of the airfield with individual access direct to the runways. During all those Cold War exercises, we never imagined we would truly have to do it for real, so the "numbers game" hadn't really mattered. That had all now changed. It was going to be a big ask.'

The old, Cold War missions had also been planned over familiar and accurately mapped terrain. Iraq was an entirely different proposition. Unlike Europe, the vast deserts were bereft of landmarks for the navigation system which fed the Tornado's main computer. The Tornado was not equipped with a 'global positioning system' – similar to a car's 'sat nav'.[11] It used an 'inertial navigation' device which was programmed with an exact 'start point' when on the ground. It then used a complex system of sensors to continuously monitor the speed, height, orientation and direction of movement of the aircraft to keep its position updated and fed into the main computer.

But inertial systems lose accuracy over time so the navigator needed to regularly update the main computer with a precise location. For the most part, they would use the ground-mapping radar to identify a prominent feature such as a radio mast, bridge or coastal outline whose exact co-ordinates had been previously fed into the system. With the point carefully identified by radar, the navigator would 'mark' its location relative to the aircraft by clicking his hand controller. In simple terms, the Tornado main computer knew exactly where the known feature was, so could precisely calculate its own position in relation to it, and the main computer would be updated with incredible accuracy.

Now, with few reliable fixing points in the Iraqi desert, and before any 'night vision' devices were widely available or in operational use on the Tornado,[12] Nige Risdale was struggling to find a way of getting the aircraft safely and accurately on target in total darkness. He sought permission to bring 15 Squadron's most experienced navigator, and his fellow Qualified Weapons Instructor, into the confidential process.

In Paddy Teakle, 15 Squadron had a highly talented and accomplished mission planner. A big, universally respected character, he had flown Victor tankers on the famous Black Buck bombing raids during the Falklands War eight years earlier. While Paddy was not easily fazed, he quickly recognised the complexity of Nige's challenges, and their need to change their Iron Curtain-centric thinking.

'The task of planning every sortie for my own Squadron would have been enough, but to plan for all of the other Muharraq-based Tornado units as well was a different challenge altogether. What exactly was our credibility with the other units? Would they understand our thought processes and the tactics we would employ? Had they undertaken the same extensive work-up training? What were their strengths and weaknesses? Unfortunately, due to the highly confidential nature of our work, these were questions that remained largely unanswered, yet they niggled away at me constantly. I tried to make the plans as simple as possible. Minimise the threat, maintain accuracy and provide an element of surprise.'[13]

Together, they began to work on how they were going to take out Tallil. In theory, they might need *hundreds* of JP233 attacks to put this single airfield out of action. 'Iraq then had countless more of these massive airbases,' said Risdale. 'We were also really concerned about our ability to produce the accuracy that we would need for these missions to be anything close to successful.'[14]

They re-examined the best maps they had of southern Iraq and saw an oil pipeline that ran along Saudi's northern border, along with a series of telecommunication masts. That was enough to give the attackers an accurate navigational fix as they crossed into enemy territory. But once inside Iraq the systems would need further radar-identifiable landmarks to feed the computer. Going back to the maps under the strip lights of the planning room at Muharraq airbase – while the rest of the squadron enjoyed nights out – Nige and Paddy saw that the Iraqis surrounded their bases with a massive metal fence whose corners provided a really useful aiming feature, easily identifiable on radar. It was a great find. But only if the 20-year-old maps were still accurate, and the Iraqis had not moved any fences.

* * *

The JP233 was not only unproven in battle; there was barely a Tornado pilot who had flown with one. A live drop had been undertaken during its early testing, and in 1988 two crews had flown with a fully armed and JP233-loaded aircraft to test the handling capabilities at the aircraft's maximum permissible weight,[15] but this very expensive and highly secret weapon was not authorised to be deployed for normal peacetime training. The restrictions were quickly lifted. Nige flew his first ever sortie with two live JP233s on 17 December to check how the war-laden Tornado coped with the weapons – a total of almost 5 tonnes – under its belly, at low level, before people began shooting at them for real. 'In some ways, the Tornado was a fish out of water in the desert. It had been designed for the European theatre of operations to fly at low level and in a cool climate. Now we were flying it in incredible heat, which meant the engines were less efficient.'

But the Tornado still performed well, even if it was thirsty work for its engines. As Nige and Paddy prepared the first missions of any imminent engagement, the rest of the Muharraq detachment, excluded from the secret planning, continued its training – and socialising – oblivious to what their colleagues were doing. 'I had absolutely no idea whatsoever that planning was at such an advanced stage,' remembered John Nichol. 'It was never mentioned or discussed. We simply carried on training for an event I personally thought would never take place. And, in our downtime, we continued to enjoy the nightlife of Bahrain!'

* * *

In the lead-up to war a curious cultural contrast became apparent between the British and their closest ally. American audiences exceeding 14 million, including President George Bush and the overall Allied Military Commander General Norman Schwarzkopf, had been gripped by *The Civil War,* a documentary series that captured the nation's imagination with brutal imagery of that elemental 1860s conflict. The film-makers had employed the novel technique of using the camera to slowly pan over graphic contemporary photos. Accompanied by the mournful tune of the 'Ashokan Farewell', and with a voiceover by Morgan Freeman and others, it was an instant hit when first shown on the Public Broadcasting Service that

September. A Vietnam veteran, Schwarzkopf ensured his officers watched it to better understand the nature of war. But the show was also having a negative effect on morale back home. With the prospect of mass casualties, public support for an invasion began to diminish. 'The Civil War series on TV has had a sobering effect on many,' Schwarzkopf noted.[16]

Gordon Buckley and the rest of 15 Squadron were among those from the British military who were engrossed in something entirely different. The videos of the iconic series Blackadder Goes Forth had just been released. The Two Johns, Mike Toft and, on the occasional night off from planning, Nige Risdale and Buckley's veteran navigator Paddy Teakle, gathered in a room at the Sheraton for some light relief. Laughter echoed down the corridor during the moments of blackest humour when the insanity and carnage of First World War trench warfare contrasted with trenchant comedy. But the show also had poignancy and resonance for those about to go into action. Particularly the last instalment, when Captain Blackadder, played by Rowan Atkinson, was ordered to lead his men 'over the top' – or 'sausage side' – in a doomed assault. Captain Blackadder knows 'Operation Certain Death' can only end one way. He attempts to feign madness, placing a pair of underpants on his head and pencils up his nose, telling his sidekick Baldrick to ask him questions. 'Wibble,' responds Blackadder to each in turn. The ruse doesn't work and in the final moments before leaving the trench he reflects on the insanity of war: 'Who would have noticed another madman around here?'

The whistles sound, the men go over the top, the outcome is inevitable. The final scene, shot in slow motion, is as stark and sobering as they come as the main characters are mown down by machine-gun fire.

It had a profound effect on Buckley and the watching aircrew. 'The room just fell silent at the end. It was really quite moving. It became an unwritten rule that this last episode should not be played again. The rest of them, however, were played relentlessly and most of us could recite the lines by heart. "Wibble" and "sausage side" became well-worn phrases heard while we were flying. It seemed to reflect the reality of our own approaching war.'

* * *

Not long after Gordon and his flight had arrived in the Gulf, a seismic event occurred back home that shook both the British military and their allies. During more than a decade in power Mrs Thatcher had made many enemies, not least within her own Conservative Party. Her fading political instincts failed to detect the knives now being unsheathed by her own tribe, determined to oust her at any cost. On 22 November she resigned and was replaced by John Major. The establishment was rocked and Saddam delighted. George Bush was not. The US President was handed a note during a visit to a warship in the Gulf. General Schwarzkopf noticed an instant change. 'He was stunned. Thatcher was his closest friend and staunchest ally, and had helped him the most in the early days of the Gulf crisis.'[17]

Back in Britain things weren't pretty for John Major either. Loyal to the end, he had seen his mentor brutally dispatched. But that was politics, a brutal business. The reality for Major was a tricky inheritance. Inflation was in double figures, interest rates at 14 per cent, unemployment rising by 50,000 a month and house prices falling.[18] Recession loomed as he now led Britain towards its most formidable military operation since the Second World War.

While war, diplomacy and high politics had people glued to their televisions and newspapers, at home at RAF Bruggen that November navigator Bob Ankerson got on with day-to-day tasks as a Flight Commander on 17 Squadron. Soft-spoken and avuncular, Bob was a well-liked and trusted navigator with three decades of service. So he had felt a touch put out that after so long on the Cold War front line, he was going to miss out on the real thing. He had been selected to remain on base and look after affairs while the majority of the Squadron deployed. If battle casualties started to occur as expected, a steady hand would be needed to steer the Squadron through trying times.

His wife Chris could sense his disappointment. 'He had trained all his career for this moment and didn't want to be left behind. I thought it would be tough for him, but I also felt a sense of guilt that all my friends' husbands were deploying and mine would be safe at home.' At least they could spend more time with their 12-year-old son Gareth who would soon be back from boarding school in England. In early December, Bob was back on a training course at RAF Cranwell in Lincolnshire. He was passing the delightful neo-classical main building on his way from a good lunch in the Officers' Mess when he was called to the telephone. There was little small talk. His Squadron Boss, Wing Commander Dusty Miller, got straight to the point. Another navigator had been pulled from the deployment. Family circumstances. 'You've had your last beer for a while, Bob; you're booked on a flight back to Germany first thing tomorrow. You're going out to the Gulf at the end of the month.'

'Okay, Boss.' Bob Ankerson put down the phone, told his instructors he was leaving the course immediately, went back to his room and packed his bags for war.

In their married quarters, Chris was contemplating their Christmas plans when she got the call.

'Everything's changed,' Bob told her. 'I'm deploying to the war-zone with the rest of the Squadron in a few weeks.'

For a moment she found it difficult to speak. Everything really had changed. 'But your mum and dad are coming over in a few weeks for New Year,' she said, knowing full well that family plans made no difference to war orders. Bob arrived back in Germany the next day. With so much to do, there was no time to discuss what it all meant and the implications for their future. They managed a few snatched conversations about life insurance and bank accounts, but Bob's view was everything was in order, *you'll be fine*. Chris understood. 'He was on a war footing, preparing to fly out to the Gulf. My naive thought was, *The worst won't happen to Robert; things like that don't happen to us. He'll be quite safe, do his bit, come home and we'll carry on as normal.*'

Bob's new pilot was the young but extremely likeable Simon

Burgess. In between vaccination jabs, small arms training and gath-ering personal kit, they managed a few sorties together. Bob quickly understood why Simon was popular. His charm on the ground was matched by smoothness in the air. Whereas most of the Squadron had had a good few months to prepare, Bob and Simon had just a few days to build their partnership. Flying low, fast, at night into enemy fire required extraordinary co-operation between pilot and navigator. Any of the usual aircrew jibes of 'talking ballast' and 'stick monkey' – navigator and pilot – were quickly parked. The pressure of flying, navigating and getting bombs on target was immense. Co-operation was everything, monitoring actions and correcting each other's mistakes. Anticipate. Communicate. They learned to work the Tornado together. 'We were flying intensively, building trust, preparing for war together; the personal relationship was going to be crucial. Although I was a Flight Commander and senior officer, once in the air, all of that was forgotten. We became a finely honed team. Developing that relationship was crucial, so that when the chips were down, we each had total trust in the other's decisions.'

* * *

Bob and Simon were training for the war while Nige Risdale and Paddy Teakle were in the midst of planning it 3,000 miles away. Standing in the Operations Room at Muharraq, arms folded, they looked over their mission planning notes, the Top Secret US Air Tasking Order, and countless charts spread across the table before them. On the area map it looked easy. Head roughly north-west and their first target, Tallil airbase, was around 500 miles from Bahrain. Perhaps sixty minutes' flight time. But you'd arrive with little fuel left in the tanks. There was no way the Tornados were going to fly from Bahrain or Dhahran directly into Iraq, or over Kuwait and its complex SAM defences. They traced a more westerly route over Saudi Arabia, along what would become known as the 'tanker trail' paralleling the border. Here, scores of jets would meet up to refuel before heading into Iraqi airspace. To attack Tallil, Nige decided on a route that began with them heading 500 miles west. 'We would have around an hour's transit from Bahrain, paralleling the Saudi border, taking on fuel, until we dropped to low level to penetrate Iraq where it was least defended. We then might have around an hour at low level to and from the target. So we also needed to refuel on the way home.' With 700 combat aircraft assembling to go into Iraq on 'Night One', at intervals timed to the nearest five seconds, the tanker rendezvous timings had to be precise.

It was all very different from what now seemed like the fairly straightforward Soviet strategy. Even the jets had changed colour from the shiny new green, grey and black Nige had seen at RAF Marham eight years earlier, to their current desert-sand. The new kit inside the Tornado, the massive new fuel tanks, the live JP233s; it had all happened very quickly. He sighed. It seemed that changes were happening so fast there was no time to absorb the impact or implications. 'Paddy and I realised we just had to ditch our Cold War mentality and re-evaluate all the tactics and procedures we had ever used in Germany. We had never really trained or prepared for the coming scenario and I had a sense of somewhat hoping for the best. We had major fuel considerations and the real possibility of less-than-accurate navigation and weapons aiming systems.'

The best they could do, Nige and Paddy concluded, was to employ the JP233 to 'harass' the Iraqi airbase's operations. 'We came up with a plan to use the JP233 to cut across the runways, access points and taxiways. Hopefully the anti-personnel mines would then hamper any repairs.' These bomblets were both vicious and cunningly designed. They would shred anyone who disturbed them. And if a bulldozer attempted their clearance, they would tip over and fire a shaped-charge slug of metal through the blade and into the driver's cab. Eight aircraft each carrying two of the 2.5-tonne devices would bring a deadly mix of cratering munitions and anti-personnel bomblets to Tallil.

Knowing that American bombers were also going to 'bomb the crap out of the airfield before we arrived', Paddy agreed that it wasn't going to be necessary to cover the entire area with JP233 munitions. 'We chose points where we could have maximum impact – taxiway and runway intersections. Break up the runway there, and you could theoretically stop aircraft entering the runway and taking off.'[19] After several submissions the plan was given the go-ahead.

While the pair spent long nights planning in secrecy, the younger officers were also hard at work ensuring the Squadron's social reputation remained intact. Indeed, on his second night in Bahrain, with senior officers missing at a meeting, John Nichol and others were ordered to take up their formal invitations to a cocktail party at the British Club. 'The club was packed out with expats eager to greet us and thank the RAF for what they were doing. From that moment on our social engagements blossomed.'

For Paddy and Nige the long nights in front of maps meant they often missed out. 'We did lots of the planning in the evenings when most of our formations were relaxing at our favourite restaurants – Señor Paco's Mexican or the Up A Tree Cup A Tea Thai. I knew Buckers was confused that I wasn't around in the evenings to socialise.' The level of secrecy imposed by the Americans had meant that even Gordon Buckley, who would actually lead a formation of Tornados with Paddy, could not be told what his navigator was doing. 'I knew Paddy was up to something, but he never told me what. He would just get up out of his bed in the morning on a day off, and say he was going to work.'

The parties and socialising were a diversion from the realities that lay ahead. If it was war then young aircrew like Peters and Nichol wanted to sharpen their skills to have a chance of surviving. That meant some of the best and most challenging training of their lives. Peters' mentor was a squadron leader who had been in the Gulf for some months. 'He briefed us on the hazards of desert flying. He made sure we took on board the ways in which the sun can deceive and disorientate, and gave us tips on how to fly low, safely, in a flat and featureless environment. It was really tricky gauging height under certain combinations of terrain and light. So we kept it careful to begin with, nothing too gung-ho. But as the days went past, and we got used to the conditions, we began winding the aircraft gradually downwards towards the deck, foot by foot, inch by inch, until we were all hammering along just above the sand, right down at 40 feet.'

On a visit to Tabuk airbase in the west of Saudi Arabia, Nichol experienced something not unlike Peters had during his *Star Wars* moments in Canada. 'We went through narrow gorges, so narrow that it seemed John Peters was continually having to roll the Tornado onto its side to squeeze through the sheer sandstone cliffs soaring high above us. We flew through the most fantastic rock formations, sculpted by sandstorms. To look at it, it was stunning. To fly through, a joy.'[20]

And flying low over Saudi Arabia, John Peters got a true sense of the scale of the assembling invasion force. 'Below us in the desert were scores of allied tanks parked in the sand along with huge piles of equipment, ammunition dumps, supply dumps and fuel bowers. On the road there was convoy after convoy of armour and supply trucks, the traffic almost continuous with vehicles chucking up huge dust plumes.'

The build-up was continuing apace.

* * *

War was far from Tange Stewart's mind. She could not hide her joy at the promise of a family festive season with her Tornado navigator husband Robbie now back home. The long, painful days and clammy August nights listening to the BBC World Service reports on the panicked reaction to Kuwait's invasion had become a memory. She was pleased, *really* pleased that Robbie had returned home after three months in the Gulf. He had been away many times before on exercises around the world but this time it had been different. Now he was back for good. Robbie was also delighted to fit back into family life with the prospect of battle banished. 'I wasn't one of those desperate to go to war. I was ready to do it if necessary, but was not hugely disappointed if not. I quickly went back to normality, enjoying family life with no thoughts of war.' In mid-December, Robbie even had time to visit Tange's village primary school to chat about the Gulf region. Dressed in his flying suit, he had chatted to the wide-eyed children about the desert geography and rock formations, although it was his videos of ultra-low flying that attracted the most attention.

Delighted with the children's reaction, he arrived back home in Coleby in good spirits. He gave his teenage daughter Kirsty a kiss and was about to get changed when the phone rang. Standing beside him as he picked up the receiver, Kirsty couldn't really hear what was said. But she didn't need to. Lowering the phone, her beloved father simply said, 'I'm going back out to the Gulf.'

'Dad's face was ashen. We knew that our lives had changed at that moment. I could see him trying to hold back tears. Not wanting to show too much emotion.'[21] It was horrible. Her dad was her idol. A constant figure of love and support. Now Kirsty only saw worry and fear. Instinctively she knew the bedrock foundation of him always being there was gone.

Tange had barely got through the front door when Kirsty and her older brother Scott fell on her. 'Dad's going back out to the Gulf . . .' The looks on their young faces confirmed her fears. 'It felt like a fist to my stomach,' Tange remembered. 'I know it was his job and his duty, but it was a real shock that after just coming home from the warzone for Christmas, he was going to have to return. As an RAF wife, I knew that in reality if anyone should be going back out, it should be him. But as a civilian wife and mother it was hard. I had to hand over my husband to the RAF again and it felt as though things were getting very, very serious.'[22] She paced the house as Robbie talked through the implications. 'I was really upset discussing it with Tange. We both had no doubt that war was just weeks away, and I was going to be part of it. It was a huge thing for the family to come to terms with. The kids were upset because they could see we were upset.' The whole family knew the reality. The Tornados would be at the forefront of the action. A small number of men would be taking immeasurable risks going into battle against a foe who would do everything they could to kill them.

The children were old enough to be told the harsh realities. Kirsty appreciated their honesty. 'It was horrible to see my parents affected like this. The people you look up to for stability, who you trust to be there for you. I could see Dad was truly concerned. There were tough conversations about what we would do if Dad was killed – how we should stay at our schools, how Mum would ensure everything would continue as normal.' Her father also explained the exact nature of a Tornado strike mission and when the war might start, that 16 January was a new moon and total darkness would cloak any potential attack. He spoke of the danger but also of the Tornado's brute strength and resilience. He explained why the RAF's job was so important. To protect as far as possible the lives of the young soldiers fighting on the ground. Robbie also arranged to meet his insurance broker friend to discuss changes to his life insurance policy. Just in case. The seeds of danger and reality which had been sown back in August were now fully grown. But 13-year-old Kirsty was grateful for being treated as an adult. 'I'm pleased we discussed it all. We could see it happening on the news and it was important we knew the reality. There was a sense we were all in this together and I would probably need to grow up a bit.'

For the Stewart family, Christmas 1990 would not be the joyous occasion they had hoped for.

* * *

David Bellamy wanted to do his best to conjure the warm feeling of Christmas back home in the flat, featureless terrain surrounding Tabuk airbase in Saudi Arabia; of lights, decorated trees and cosy carol services in village churches. The base lay 900 miles due west of Bahrain and was a similar distance in terms of comfort.[23] It had become the RAF's biggest Tornado deployment with nineteen jets and personnel from a number of squadrons. Bellamy and some of his colleagues sought solace and a moment of serenity amid the austerity. On Christmas Eve a small room converted into a chapel filled with those keen for a reminder of home and oneness with God.

To the accompaniment of a piano, they sang 'Once in Royal David's City' and a sense of Christmas enveloped the small community. The emotion of 'Silent Night', with its link to the trenches of the First World War, was followed by the uplifting 'Hark! The Herald Angels Sing', with pertinent references to 'death', 'salvation' and 'resurrection'. 'O Little Town of Bethlehem' brought the service to a close and those with families could not help thinking about children opening presents with fathers absent. Warm handshakes were exchanged as the service sheets were handed back in. Most obeying the instruction typed in bold at the top and bottom of the paper: 'NOT TO BE TAKEN AWAY'. Holding a non-Islamic religious service in Saudi Arabia was against the law.

It was now after midnight, so with formalities out of the way, the pilots and navigators retired to Bellamy's room and settled down to an alcohol-free beer. After a show of hands, it was agreed to open one of the ten-riyal (£4) presents they had bought one another from the local market. It was a curious collection. A toy Uzi machine gun, a non-leather wallet and a bottle of 'Sexy Musk Oil'. Bellamy's gift at least provided some practical use – a tape of Saudi music.

Despite its austerity, Tabuk had its own oasis. British Aerospace had built accommodation around a quadrangle with a lawn that the previous occupants had kept in good order. When the boom of Rolls-Royce Tornado engines was silent, it became a small corner of calm and relaxation. You could tread on soft, green grass, listen to the fountain and contemplate fish in the pond. A serene spot for the fliers to open their family presents on Christmas morning before heading off to the compound to serve the airmen Christmas dinner.

An old hand at the tradition of officers serving the junior ranks, Bellamy wore an unwashed flying suit for the inevitable food fight that broke out deploying Brussels sprout missiles tipped with deadly brandy sauce. After watching a football match between the RAF and a Saudi XI, the officers assembled at 7pm for their own dinner. It was a smart affair; most had packed their cummerbunds and black bow ties. The menu showed they were also in for a treat. The starter was a shrimp cocktail or French onion soup, followed by roast turkey or beef Wellington, served with the usual trimmings of baked, roasted or croquette potatoes, broccoli and, of course, Brussels sprouts.

For the fliers there was an extra treat. The BAe contractors had produced some 'altered' grape juice – homemade wine – which disappeared at an alarming rate as soon as the 'Amen' had followed the Padre's grace. The room filled with banter and goodwill, a near equal to the merriest of Christmas tables. After dessert of cake and ice-cream, and with the memories of the carol service still fresh, Bellamy felt the vocal cords stir, recording in his diary, 'I had a need to sing. Quite soon it is a riotous and joyful 20 Squadron yelling at our rivals from RAF Laarbruch, 16 Squadron. Everyone felt quite merry so we headed off to the BAe "Lightning Club" to make a night of it. Several jugs of home-brew later, our voices had turned hoarse from singing Christmas pop songs.' It was like a scene from another war, when the drink flowed and officers gathered around the Mess piano as a fire blazed during a bleak winter's day on the Western Front.

Dave Bellamy got away from the party in good order at 11pm, only to be woken up hours later by his pilot Trevor Roche crashing into their room, a good few sheets to the wind. 'This will be a short night and I bet I will be crabby tomorrow,' Bellamy noted in his diary.

* * *

For Norman Schwarzkopf, the man in charge of the effort to eject Saddam Hussein's Iraqi invaders from Kuwait, Christmas 1990 was a solitary time, contemplating the possibility that for perhaps many hundreds of young men under his command, it could be their last. The latest intelligence showed the Iraqis had built up a defensive force of 545,000 troops in and around Kuwait. In response, the coalition of the Arab world and the West had grown to 800,000 troops, one of the most powerful ground forces in history, with the very latest tanks, armoured vehicles and artillery designed to defeat the once-mighty Soviet Union.[24] General Schwarzkopf also had 2,000 combat aircraft at his disposal which would be the tip of his spear when the fighting began.

As the lights on his plastic Christmas tree twinkled and carols played from his tape machine, he drifted off to sleep. Suddenly the red telephone next to his bed gave a shrill ring. The warm voice was instantly recognisable. 'I couldn't let this day go by without calling to wish you and all the men and women under your command a Merry Christmas,' President Bush said. 'I know that you are far away from your loved ones, but I want you to know that our thoughts and prayers are with you. You now know the course we are on. Our prayers will stay with you during the coming days.'

Schwarzkopf now knew that war, and all that came with it, was imminent.

The next day he sat alone opening presents from his wife and three children. His 20-year-old daughter Cindy had written him a poem titled 'You Are My Hero'. It brought home his loneliness. 'It was the most desolate hour I had spent in Saudi Arabia. At other times I'd felt harassed, exhausted, browbeaten, burdened, now I simply missed my family.'[25]

John Major, who had only been Prime Minister for five weeks, spent the weekend before Christmas with President Bush and his wife Barbara at Camp David, discussing options for the coming battle. The President disclosed his preferred start date – the moonless night of 16 January. 'He did not glory in war or in the military might of the United States. He was a reluctant but convinced warrior.'[26] Camp David, deep in the wooded hills of Maryland, was a long way from the deserts of Iraq, and for a moment Major managed to escape his troubling thoughts. 'Work over, George and Barbara Bush gave us a delightful weekend, full of log fires, good food, Christmas songs from a small male-voice army choir and the occasional film.'

* * *

After receiving the unwelcome news of Robbie Stewart's deployment, his wife Tange had tried to keep everything as normal as possible over Christmas, visiting friends and family and outwardly maintaining the British stoicism and reserve that 'everything would be fine'. But not so far beneath the surface she was worried. 'Rob was leaving us again and that sense of the unknown hung over us all.' Only once did Robbie's mask of calm slip. Just after Christmas, the *Sunday Times* ran a huge feature on the Tornado's capabilities, weapons and potential targets the aircrews would be attacking. It included a map with all the bases in the Gulf and the type of aircraft and tactics used. He was livid. 'This is just the bloody sort of information an enemy interrogator will use against a captured airman.'

There was anger too, at the petty military officialdom facing those about to go into combat. With a wife, who was seven months pregnant, and toddler back home, Mike Toft couldn't help dwelling on the 'what ifs'.[27] Before leaving home, he'd had *the conversation* with Sue. The conversation that had happened over the centuries, when a husband going to war made provision for failing to return, usually caveated with 'should the worst happen . . .' There was one small hitch that Mike wanted to resolve before it was too late. As he was an officer on a 'Short Service Commission' contract, Sue would only be entitled to a widow's pension and a lump sum payment of around twice his salary if he was killed. But, Mike discovered, if he was on a '*Permanent* Commission' when killed, she would receive nearly *four* times his salary. It was money for nothing; Mike had always intended to stay in the RAF for life anyway, but had not yet got around to changing his short-term commission status. He quickly filled out the necessary paperwork but heard nothing in the weeks leading up to Christmas out in the Gulf. Now the deadline for war was just weeks away and still the paperwork had not been processed.

Between the ultra-low-level training sorties over the pancake-flat deserts of Saudi, Mike used his spare time to chase up the clerks. Their answer was always the same: 'It's being processed, sir.' His concern grew and he decided extreme measures were required. The issue *had to be* resolved before he went to war. Mike stormed into the admin Portakabin, and with the merest hint of a smile, carefully removed his pistol from its shoulder holster and placed it on the clerk's desk. 'Is the paperwork for my Permanent Commission sorted out yet?'

The clerk glanced from pistol to officer.

'But sir—'

'No more BUTs!' Mike firmly interjected. 'I need this to be sorted. Now!'

'But, sir, it's Boxing Day in the UK. No one is working . . .'

For a moment there was silence, then they both laughed. Mike holstered his pistol, his concerns somewhat dissipated. A week later the clerk called with news. 'Congratulations, sir, you now have a Permanent Commission!' It was just two weeks to Saddam's deadline to withdraw. Should the worst happen, Sue Toft would now receive some reasonable compensation.

Mike Toft was not the only one considering the looming realities of war. His pilot Mark Paisey had already taken into account what 'the worst happening' to him would mean and taken action. Paisey was a late addition to the deployment from another squadron but he and Mike had bonded well. 'I think it was probably much more difficult for the married guys with kids. I was quite relaxed about deploying to the Gulf. I'd had a bit of a rough time in the previous months with the end of a relationship so this new phase, while it might present dangers, was something I was quite calm about. I had no real concerns. I had ensured all my affairs were in order and had written a "last letter" to my mum and dad to be delivered if I was killed, setting out my final thoughts and feelings so that they had something from me. I sealed it in an envelope and propped it on the desk in my room back at Laarbruch.'[28]

Knowing everything was as settled as possible, Mike and Mark slept a little easier as the Christmas memories, good or ill, were already fading and 1991 began.

* * *

As the fireworks detonated over the married quarters at RAF Bruggen that New Year's Eve, Chris Ankerson stared up at the bursting stars. 'I was standing outside the front door watching the fireworks, thinking, *I wonder what 1991 is going to hold in store for us all?* Another wife and I exchanged a look. We didn't say anything, but we each understood.'[29] Her neighbour's husband had already deployed. Her own husband, Bob, would soon follow. Events were now beyond their control; they had entrusted their husbands to the RAF.

Bob's parents had flown to Germany to celebrate New Year but were not told about his impending deployment. Throughout the holiday period Bob and Chris could barely conceal the strain while pretending everything was normal. Just before they left for the airport, Bob informed his parents that he was going to war. His father's eyes welled up. He too had served in combat during the Second World War and knew that the difference between death and life was measured by a hair's breadth. Bob had rarely seen his father cry. As they stood amid the civilians heading to less challenging destinations at Dusseldorf airport, tears slipped down his father's cheeks. 'Please be careful, son,' he whispered.

A few hours later, at 2am on 2 January 1991, there was another emotional farewell. This time Bob Ankerson was on the doorstep of his home, hugging and kissing Chris and his young son one last time before bidding them farewell. Her arms wrapped around his chest, the grip made awkward by the pistol carried in her husband's shoulder holster, an intrusion on the life they had built together, where war was something that had previously existed in another world.

* * *

In early January Robbie Stewart and Dave Waddington trickled back to Bahrain with other new arrivals to bolster the Tornado force, pinching themselves again at the sight of the Sheraton's marble floors, crystal chandeliers and polite receptionists. The warm welcome from both locals and expats was complemented by the temperate climate of the Gulf. Blue skies and low humidity, ideal for shorts, sandals and the pool, the equivalent of a perfect English summer's day. Even when they left the hotel's comforts, the facilities at Muharraq airbase were, in military terms, five-star. The crew room was a fully air-conditioned Portakabin with armchairs and a fridge crammed with cold drinks and chocolate.

Across the causeway in Saudi Arabia, the hum of aircraft engines, the assembly of military vehicles and shouted commands to new-comers fresh into 'theatre' told Bob Ankerson and his pilot Simon Burgess that they were very much in a new world. It was last light on 4 January when they stepped onto the tarmac of Dhahran air-base and the RAF personnel had never seen anything quite like it. 'It was well ahead of anything we had in Europe. Seven runways, the most modern hardened shelters, underground bunkers, all mod cons, a very impressive set-up,' an engineer recalled.[30] Others were also stunned by what they were witnessing. 'The first day we saw 550 helicopters all lined up. All the US Marines, the Army, the 82nd Airborne, were coming through.' Norman Schwarzkopf's mighty army was poised to implement the United Nations resolution to use 'all necessary means' to restore Kuwait's sovereignty. The task would require brute force and Saddam's invasion had been mistimed on several counts. In the last half of the 1980s, American aerial bombing technology had achieved astonishing advances. The US had the most sophisticated aerial arsenal in history.[31]

At the forefront were the F-117 Nighthawk stealth fighters accom-panied by B-52 bombers carrying air-launched cruise missiles, along with advanced F-15 and F-16 fighters. Beyond the glamour of the jet fighters the Americans had key assets such as the Airborne Warning and Control System (AWACS), whose radars could see every air-craft flying for hundreds of miles. They also supplied countless air tankers, critical to allowing deep strikes into Iraqi territory, and an armada of helicopters. As the 'ally of choice', British officers in Saudi, like Nige Risdale over in Bahrain, had already been allowed into a highly secretive group, based at the coalition headquarters in Riyadh, that was preparing the Master Air Attack Plan. Rigorous and detailed organisation was required to send wave after wave of aircraft into enemy airspace. The Tornados and their ultra-low-level tactics were put at the forefront of Operation Desert Storm, the plan to remove Saddam from Kuwait. Even the American fast-talking, high-fiving fighter jocks felt admiration for the Brits when it dawned on them what they *really* did. Very fast, very low at night and right over the enemy's heads. *That took balls.*

For Wing Commander John Broadbent, the Tornado Detachment Commander at Muharraq, there was no doubt about their tactics. 'I had twenty years' experience on the RAF's front line and, as far as I was concerned, nobody was seriously considering going to war in a Tornado at medium level until we had established air superiority.' If established, that dominance of the skies would negate the much-feared threat from the Iraqis' own fighters. 'Until that condition had been fulfilled, it would have been wrong, even foolhardy, to contemplate such an option. We were up against the Iraqi Air Force, powerful and battle-hardened by several years of war with Iran. We fully expected them to be ready and willing to fight and we had to judge them on their *capability*, not guess at their *intentions*.'[32]

And the Americans were not the only ones to pass comment on the dangers. Before leaving home, Gordon Buckley's wife Dawn had laid down the law. 'Whatever you do, *do not* take any risks when you are out there!' she ordered. Gordon had to take note. Dawn had previously stopped him from applying to the Red Arrows aerobatic display team because she didn't want him to take 'more risks' than he already needed to flying fast jets. But Gordon also knew the time was approaching when he would have to defy Dawn's instructions.

* * *

In those early days of January 1991, Bob Ankerson and Simon Burgess soon got down to work, trying to catch up with those who had been training for months. Nerves were certainly required. And, sometimes, it was best not to draw too heavily on one's well of courage by seeing how much was really needed. During one night sortie, flying over the Saudi desert on autopilot at a steady 200ft in complete darkness, Bob and Simon decided to pop one of their high-heat anti-missile flares. 'The area around us lit up so brightly and we could see the ground rushing past at indecently close range. We decided not to repeat the exercise but to continue along in darkness and blissful ignorance!' Not that they had much chance for practice. As the 15 January deadline approached for Iraqi forces to leave Kuwait, they managed to squeeze in only five training sorties. 'The brief was that we were cleared to 100ft but to remember that we could be going to war any day and so to make the most of the opportunity. We flew over the desert at 40ft, almost level with the top of the palm trees, flashing over herds of camels out in the bleakness. It was a truly memorable experience.'

They practised more anti-missile drills, using chaff and flares, then spent hours on the ground reading the intelligence reports on Iraqi SAM systems. It was a bonding experience for Simon and Bob, thrown together just days before deploying. 'We were flying together, working together, building up that level of trust and relationship. We both needed to know that we could rely on each other regardless of what was thrown at us. It didn't matter what flying we were doing, practice bombing, intense low-level TFR at night, tanking; the important thing was that we were flying *together*. Getting to know each other, how we worked, finding out how the other person "thought". Building confidence before we headed into the unknown beyond Saudi's border.'

On 8 January, exactly a week before the deadline expired, they were told the British Prime Minister John Major would be visiting Dhahran airbase to meet the troops. The question many asked was: would the PM go to the effort of visiting if they weren't going to war? Bob Ankerson and Simon Burgess could ask him personally. They were his designated hosts on the Tornado. It was late afternoon as the pair took him through the aircraft's functions. Major asked a few questions about the Tornado's capabilities then climbed down from the cockpit and stood on a box as the troops gathered round him in a large horseshoe. John Major was not a military man and was troubled by war. 'As a non-soldier I was uneasy at sending others to war even though I had no doubt it was right to do so.'[33] His own son James was just about to turn sixteen. Many of the men before him were only a year or two older. Major knew that he would be sending some of them into a battle from which they would not return. War was all but inevitable, and he did his best to steel the soldiers and airmen. They were going to be at 'the sharp end of whatever may happen in due course'.

One senior officer present had an inkling of what was afoot. 'Something in the way he said it made me think he knew something I didn't.'[34] There were some in the crowd, and many families back home, who hoped a last-ditch meeting between US Secretary of State James Baker and Iraqi Foreign Minister Tariq Aziz might head off the possibility of conflict. That meeting, Major told them, was not about negotiation or compromise. It was to make it 'absolutely certain, beyond a shadow of a doubt, that the Iraqis understand that the allied forces are serious; that, if they do not withdraw from Kuwait and go back to Iraq, at some stage we will use the force'. That evening, Bob featured prominently on the television news and his wife Chris was overjoyed. 'I actually saw Bob on TV as he and Simon showed the Prime Minister around a Tornado. It was lovely to see him and to have that small glimpse of my husband, a tiny connection, however distant.'

As John Major left the troops he was about to send to war he was reminded again of their age. 'There is nothing impersonal about war. It is about sending young people out to fight and perhaps to die, for a cause older men decide is worthwhile.'

The odds were clearly shortening. There was quiet chatter among the troops as the gathering broke up. Beyond a miracle, fighting was now close to certain.

* * *

On 9 January 1991 the world's attention focused on Geneva's Intercontinental Hotel.

President Bush had insisted on 'going the extra mile for peace', offering the chance for Saddam to leave Kuwait without a fight. America was also facing its biggest military challenge since the humiliation and soul-searching of the Vietnam War. The US President wanted to demonstrate he was doing his best to avoid war and to reassure the public, especially those watching the graphic and bloody deaths depicted in *The Civil War* TV series.

The talks failed and at 8.55pm Tariq Aziz, Iraq's smooth-talking Foreign Minister, took to the podium to address the world's media. He spoke for thirty minutes, conveying Saddam's final threat: if America and its allies attacked, Iraq would retaliate by attacking Israel. Clearly, the dictator had not lost the cunning that had allowed him to dominate Iraq since 1968. Drawing the Jewish state into the conflict would make America's Arab coalition allies extremely uncomfortable. Aziz's final warning shot that Iraq was 'preparing for war' left little doubt about what was coming next.

The RAF aircrews in Bahrain had decided to turn in early rather than stay up till past midnight to hear news. Shortly after dawn the next day, Gordon Buckley woke up to the sound of the local newspaper being shoved under the door of his hotel room. The glum faces of Aziz and US Secretary of State James Baker staring from the front page told their own story. No compromise. No peace. 'I think we are going in, Paddy ...' he said, dropping the paper onto his navigator Paddy Teakle's bed.

The atmosphere across the region was nervously expectant. Military hardware was everywhere. A constant reminder of Saddam's unpredictable nature were the respirators, or 'gas masks', carried by every serviceman and their proximity to their NBC – Nuclear Biological Chemical – suits. The NBC kit was there to protect against any deadly chemical or biological agents Saddam might deploy via one of his Scud missiles or air force bombers. In 1988, he had dropped a lethal cocktail of mustard gas, VX and sarin onto Iraqi Kurdistan. More than 5,000 Kurds died from a ghastly cyanide-type poisoning. Saddam had stockpiled up to 4,000 tonnes of deadly chemicals and intelligence spoke of 800 Scud B missiles with a range of 500 miles able to deliver them.[35] The press reported that chemical warfare was not only likely; it was inevitable.

John Broadbent was in no doubt about what might happen. 'We were charged with planning an air campaign to ensure that, as far as possible, Iraq's air power could not be brought to bear either on the thousands of friendly troops massing in the desert or on packed Saudi airfields and infrastructure. There was a real fear that Iraqi aircraft carrying chemical or biological weapons would attack our airfields or vulnerable ground forces.'

In fact, Saddam had been warned in private that any use of chemicals on either civilians or military would be met with the most robust response.[36] During his long meeting with Aziz, James Baker had told him: 'If conflict ensues and you use chemical or biological weapons against US forces, the American people will demand vengeance. And we have the means to exact it . . . This is not a threat, it is a promise.'[37]

It was widely known that the armouries of US aircraft carriers in the region held nuclear weapons.

* * *

The preparations intensified in the remaining days before the deadline. On 13 January, a last training sortie of three Tornados flew out of Dhahran military airbase for a simulated low-level attack. There they were to test their flares against heat-seeking missiles while flying at ultra-low level, followed by one last exhilarating run through the valleys in northern Oman.[38] Soon after the flares were deployed, a radio call went out for the number four aircraft, flown by pilot Kieran Duffy and navigator Norman Dent, to check in. There was no response. Again, the call went out. Fliers began frantically scanning the skies around them. 'After several attempts with no reply and still with no sign of No 4, we spotted a large plume of black smoke several miles behind us,' the formation leader recalled. 'We immediately turned around and headed for the smoke. To our horror we found a very obvious scrape across the desert floor several kilometres long, the smoke rapidly dispersing and numerous unrecognisable items of debris scattered along the line.'[39]

There had been no Mayday call, no parachutes, no distress beacons activated and no word on the emergency frequency. Even without enemy fire, ultra-low-level – well below 100ft – flying came with extreme danger. Exactly two months earlier, Jaguar pilot Keith Collister, twenty-six, had been killed when his aircraft hit the crest of a sand dune in Saudi Arabia.[40]

The later investigation showed that during a hard left-hand turn at ultra-low level, travelling at almost 600mph, the wingtip of Kieran and Norman's Tornado brushed the sand and the air-craft cartwheeled into the desert. Pilot and navigator were killed instantly. Their Squadron Commander was deeply saddened by the loss. 'It was such a waste. That was what gave me more personal grief than anything else. They were two young lads with lots of spirit but they were gentlemen, great friends of everyone, the leading lights in the Squadron "junta"; the young men who are the Squadron personalities.'[41]

The crash was a devastating blow to morale in Dhahran, par-ticularly for close friends of the pair. 'It really knocked people who were just about to go to war themselves. Particularly the ground crew, who'll never forget that they started the aircraft up and waved goodbye as it went off.' The news of Dent and Duffy's passing had been broken to the rest of the Dhahran contingent by the Tornado Detachment Commander, Jerry Witts: 'We have sadly lost two colleagues and two friends. But we have to concentrate on the job in hand as the war may well be starting very soon. We will mourn their passing later.'[42] There was little more to be said.

Dave Waddington heard the terrible news after his own last train-ing sortie with Robbie Stewart in Bahrain. 'If you lose a friend or colleague in training like Kieran Duffy and Norman Dent, you just have to put it out of your mind. There is nothing you can do about it. There is a sorrow that someone has died, but you have to go on. You get into a Tornado full of excitement, you never think, *Crikey, I might die on this sortie*. Of course, the possibility is always there, but if you thought that way you would never go flying. Logic tells you there is a risk, but emotionally you put that aside.'[43]

News of yet another fatal training accident arrived back at the crew's home base of RAF Bruggen, where four Tornado squadrons were located. Chris Ankerson saw how the deaths affected the whole station, but she also felt something else, something possibly every other wife experienced. 'There was a terrible sense of loss and sadness, especially as they were so young, but other than expressing sympathy, there was little you could say to their friends. There was also a quite selfish notion at the back of your mind – *thank God it's not my husband*. You feel terrible about that. But it's the way things were if your husband flew fast jets.'

The two deaths brought the total in the Tornado force since August to seven, they were unlikely to be the last. No one doubted the extraordinary demands about to be asked of them.

* * *

The deaths so close to the 15 January deadline made the prospect of war and its consequences a sobering reality for the young military men. Tensions rose too. Now six weeks into the shared hotel room with John Peters, John Nichol found himself angry at his pilot's constant interruptions while he was trying to listen to the recording of messages from home his young nieces had sent along with his Christmas presents. 'I just snapped, then threw on my shorts and went for a long run along the seafront. I sat alone on a rock for an hour or so staring out to sea. It had suddenly dawned on me, in its full and horrible reality, that I was going to war. There was no turning back. It had not really hit me before then, but the message from my nieces back home had pulled the emotional trigger. After my sojourn on the rock I felt better about it, I had come to terms with it.' Peters had gone for a long run too. They had lunch together and no mention was made of the flare-up. Each understood. The time was approaching when they would be among the few in the heart of enemy territory.

The same day Duffy and Dent were killed, Mark Paisey, who
would be flying alongside Peters and Nichol, sat in the Muharraq
Operations Room penning his regular letter to his mother back in
the UK. The light-hearted details of his formation's social life were
no longer relevant. He had already told her where his 'last letter' –
only to be opened if he was killed – was located and he now turned
to the stark analysis of what might soon happen:

Dear Mum,

*The time is 0430 and I find myself drinking black coffee
and contemplating the days ahead. All of the peace initiatives
have failed and by the time you read this I expect we will be
at war. It seems almost incomprehensible that, in 1991, such
an undertaking is necessary. Everyone held out the hope that
the fighting would never really happen. Many seem surprised
it now will, and no one is prepared for the sacrifices which
lie ahead.*

*We are now on a shift system and I work from 0100 to 1300.
Today it has rained since midnight and everywhere is flooding
which seems really strange. With all the sandbags and puddles,
I am reminded of the [First World War] trenches.*

*Despite the immediate prospects, morale is high. Much
emphasis has been placed on our training and equipment but
that is all an echo of times past. Undoubtedly we are prepared,
but even the best-laid plans have the habit of running amok.
Let's hope the war is decisive and short, though I can't see
it myself.*

*Since this is probably my last letter until war breaks out, I
just want to tell you that the last couple of weeks have been
very happy for me. I will write whenever I can but circumstances might overtake me. Be brave yourself, I love you very
much and am proud to be your son.*

*Hopefully nothing will happen to me – or I will be
very angry!*[44]

As aircrew across the region assembled for the final briefings, they were given an overview of what General Schwarzkopf wanted to achieve. The air attack plan had originally been given four phases. A doubling of aircraft strength from November meant the massive air armada could now achieve all four at once.[45]

The main objectives were to gain air superiority, destroy Saddam's Scud missile sites and chemical warfare locations and disrupt command and control. At the same time, and this was where Tornado came in, they were to suppress the Iraqi Air Force's capability which meant smashing their airfields. Everyone would then focus on going after the tanks and troops dug in around Kuwait, paving the way for the ground invasion.

In Bahrain, the Tornado crews were given an eve-of-battle pep talk by a senior officer who had flown in specially for the task. It proved less than inspiring. 15 Squadron Flight Commander Gordon Buckley, seated at the front of the briefing room, remembered that, 'the gist of it went along the lines of "how lucky you all are to be going to fight the Iraqis and how I wish I could be coming with you". But the VIP spoke so quietly that most of the audience couldn't hear him!' None of those present thought of themselves as 'lucky'. Not when going up against the world's sixth largest air force and defences bristling with multiple SAM systems. It was, thought Buckley, 'a massive prospect and I certainly did not *feel lucky* at all!' The officer, who had kept his service cap on throughout the briefing, promptly left. Few at the back of the room had actually been able to hear the not-so-rousing motivational speech.

'Why was he talking so quietly?' one asked.

'Because what he was saying was secret!' came the tart reply.

Buckley left the meeting convinced that never had a 'call-to-arms' speech done more to discourage people to fight.

As the hours ticked past, Gordon and the rest of the aircrew were now left to contemplate their immediate future. 'I began to think, *What the hell are we going up against here?*'

CHAPTER FOUR

THE WOLFPACK

16–17 JANUARY 1991

The senior officer arrived at Tabuk airbase direct from Air Headquarters in Riyadh, carrying a briefcase handcuffed to his wrist. He was waved through security and moments later entered the briefing room with the 16 and 20 Squadron formation leaders. Senior navigator Dave Bellamy watched him remove, with a flourish, a folder marked 'Top Secret' from his briefcase. 'He somewhat bigged himself up as he briefed us on the plan for the first twenty-four hours of the war. But there was no real detail on our targets or what the hell we would actually be doing.'[1] Retaining his solemn demeanour, the officer placed the secret papers back in the case, handcuffed himself to it and left.

'Dave, it's best you reserve some planning space for your formation,' one of the Flight Commanders quietly told him afterwards.

'Aha. Roger that,' Bellamy replied.

It was the morning of 16 January, the day after the UN deadline for Saddam to leave Kuwait had expired. Something was definitely on the cards for Bellamy's Squadron equipped with the ALARM anti-radar missile. The message of peace and goodwill from the Christmas service he had organised a few weeks previously was a distant memory. After breakfast the aircrew assembled in the Operations Room where maps of Iraq and Saudi lined the wall. Bellamy sensed growing excitement as the rumours of imminent operations took hold. 'Everyone was chit-chatting and laughing like little schoolboys. Some were smiling excitedly, treating it as a school outing, while still trying to acknowledge the seriousness of their situation. The Detachment Commander walked in and set it all out in simple words. Training was over, the jets were being loaded for war. It was happening.'

As lead planner for 20 Squadron, it was Bellamy's job to organise the details for the ALARM attack against their target, a major Iraqi airbase. 16 Squadron would follow in their wake with the JP233 runway-busting weapons. Al Asad lay 100 miles west of Baghdad, and a few miles from the meandering waters of the Euphrates. It was built on top of an oasis known locally as 'Abraham's Well', which was now covered with tonnes of asphalt forming two 13,000ft runways. It was a key installation housing the Iraqi Air Force fighters that protected Baghdad from a Western attack. It was strongly defended. Batteries of SA-6 SAMs, which had proven their worth against both modern Israeli jets and US fighters in Vietnam, defended the area. Each unit consisted of three missiles mounted on a tracked vehicle making it mobile as well as deadly. The SA-6 missile had a range of 15 miles, could reach 46,000ft and travel at more than 2,000mph.[2] The half-dozen launchers per battery were controlled by a single radar vehicle that could track aircraft almost 50 miles away.

The system's strength was also its weakness. To track aircraft, the radar vehicle had to emit a strong radiation signal. British defence scientists had recognised the guided SAM threat and invented something clever to counter it. The ALARM – Air-Launched Anti-Radiation Missile – could detect an enemy radar system from a range of more than 50 miles and home in on the signal. Just before impact a laser fuse would set off the high explosive warhead to demolish the equipment, and any exposed personnel.[3] While enemy SAM operators could theoretically turn off their radar to break the lock[4] of other incoming anti-radiation missiles such as the American HARM, ALARM had a clever ploy to counter the tactic. If the targeting information was lost, it would use a rocket to zoom-climb to over 50,000ft and deploy a parachute, taking up to ten minutes to descend as it waited for the ground radar site to switch on again.[5] Immediately it did so, the ALARM would update its target's position, jettison the parachute and dive down onto the target.

ALARM had been rushed into the Gulf and few had witnessed its effectiveness. Dave Bellamy knew more than most, as he had trained everyone on the system since October. 'As a stand-off, fire-and-forget missile, ALARM offered the Tornado a radical new capability. It could be launched at considerable ranges and hit any of a number of radars.' Two Tornados, each carrying three ALARMs, were to fly the 500 miles from Tabuk to Al Asad and take out the SA-6 radars guarding the airbase. If they failed, then the four Tornados from 16 Squadron following a few miles behind were going to have a rough ride delivering their JP233s onto its long runways.

Navigator Mal Craghill, twenty-two, would be one of those bombers following Bellamy's formation and hoping it had severely degraded Al Asad's defences. One of the youngest aircrew in theatre, Craghill 'had presumed Saddam would not be so stupid as to risk any sort of confrontation with the incredible forces ranged against him across the region. I thought he would back down at the last minute and we would not be required. I now knew I had been wrong.'[6] But he was now ready for the fight. 'I don't remember any real nerves at all. We were well trained and had prepared as much as possible. There was certainly a sense of trepidation; but it was more about how I might perform; not wanting to let anyone down.'

Craghill and all of the Tabuk crews were about to discover just how prepared they actually were.

* * *

Some 900 miles to the west of Tabuk, sixteen aircrew from the lead formations of 15 Squadron in Bahrain were gathering in the War

Operations Room for a similar briefing. The previous day Nige Risdale's detailed attack plan had been presented, so the crews were familiar with the task ahead. But a tight lid was kept on the precise date and timing of the attack. Early that 16 January, Gordon Buckley, leading the second half of the formation of the initial eight-ship, had detected that Wing Commander John Broadbent, the Tornado Detachment Commander and Risdale's navigator, was 'acting a bit twitchy'. Gordon was direct. 'Are we going in tonight, Boss?'[7]

Broadbent's reply was less so. 'I've heard nothing to say we aren't . . .'[8]

Risdale was only partway through his update when the Boss was called out of the room. A 'Top Secret' communication had just been received:

---

16 Jan 1991
From:
HQ British Forces Middle East

TO:
RAF Detachment Tabuk
RAF Detachment Dhahran
RAF Detachment Muharraq

TOP SECRET EXCLUSIVE

For Detachment Commander from Air Commander

SUBJECT: WOLFPACK EXECUTE ORDER

THIS IS THE EXECUTE ORDER

H HOUR IS DECLARED AS 0000Z 17 Jan 91

Acknowledge by FLASH Signal to Air Commander and personally by Secure Speech[9]

War was authorised and the attack start time, 'H-Hour', was set for midnight ('Zulu' or Greenwich Mean Time) that evening, 0300 local time in Baghdad. For Buckley and his companions, the impact was electric. 'It was an incredible feeling, just to look around the room and see the guys' eyes really widen. We were actually going to do it.'

Eight Tornados would be going into Tallil, each carrying two JP233s to rain down a fearsome load of runway-cratering munitions and anti-personnel mines. John Broadbent, too, was struck by the enormity of the journey they were all about to embark on: 'As I gave the brief that first night, the thing that worried me most was how I would react under fire. How would any of us feel when we saw the flak for the first time and realised that someone was actually trying to kill us? Would the training kick in and allow us to just shrug it off as of little consequence? Or would our guts turn to liquid and the urge to turn and run be irresistible? Would the fact that this was far from being the war that we'd all signed up for – to defend the "White Cliffs of Dover" – make a difference to our resolve and preparedness to make the ultimate sacrifice? I for one couldn't be sure of the answer, but we were all going to find out soon enough.'

Later, the Ground Liaison Officer (GLO), an army major, gave the final intelligence brief. This particularly popular GLO had invented a 15 Squadron tradition during Cold War exercises in Germany, in which comic lyrics he had written to the tune of 'It's a Long Way to Tipperary' were sung as any *practice* war entered its final, catastrophic nuclear phase. As their first ever *real* war mission briefing drew to a close, the GLO turned to Broadbent with a slight raising of his eyebrows: 'Squadron song, Boss?'

There was a moment's silence. Given the circumstances, it appeared an audacious question.

'Why not?' Broadbent replied.

The raucous singing was heard by navigator John Nichol as he approached the Intelligence Room for the regular evening update. He had spent the day lounging around the Sheraton's pool and marbled foyer waiting to hear news of any attack before driving to Muharraq in the late afternoon with the rest of his formation. He instantly understood what it meant. 'A tight feeling of apprehension grabbed me; I felt almost sick with anticipation. The first attack wave had their mission! I presumed we, on the second wave, would soon follow. It was a truly momentous realisation.'[10]

Unable to restrain his curiosity, Nichol knocked on the door and entered. 'I saw all my mates, in full war kit, trying very hard to deafen one another with the infamous Squadron war song. As the singing stopped, the GLO said, 'Give us twenty minutes, John, we're still briefing.' I knew then for sure, from the tone of his voice, that I had just been looking at the aircrew on the first RAF attack wave of the Gulf War.' Nichol closed the door as his pilot John Peters appeared in the corridor. 'Shit, we're really going to do this,' he said. 'It's really happening. We're going in.'

Inside the room Buckley had noticed one of the female Intelligence Officers wipe tears from her eye as the song came to an end. 'It was a strange sensation, standing there singing a ridiculous song as we were about to embark on the type of mission we had flown end-lessly on Cold War exercises, but were now doing for real. Were we all going to get back okay? Was I going to be able to carry out the attack successfully?'

Buckley, and the rest of the Tornado force, would soon find out.

* * *

Similar scenes were playing out across the RAF's Gulf bases. At Dhahran, with its recent influx of GR1A recce jets, now the largest force in the region, Wing Commander Jerry Witts, the Tornado Detachment Commander, was off duty in the house he shared with other senior officers. 'We were watching CNN and chatting. I thought that now Saddam had faced-off past the deadline, he'd start to pull out. Then my phone rang.'

It was his Operations Officer. 'Can you come into work, Boss? Straight away!'

'I just grabbed my kit and drove in. I was absolutely terrified. I remember my knees were trembling, my foot was shaking on the

accelerator. I was thinking, "I can't believe this! I can't believe this!"
I was looking at other motorists and thinking, "I wonder if they
know where I'm going?"'[11]

One of the Victor tanker pilots who would shepherd the
Tornados into battle also received a phone call. 'We had particular
coded messages – if the caller said, "The mail is *out*", it meant you
were not needed. If the caller said, "The mail is *in*", it meant you
needed to bring your crew in.' The tanker Captain's coded message
was abundantly clear. 'We all came in and it suddenly dawned on
everyone that we were about to do something unstoppable.'[12]

Over at Tabuk, Dave Bellamy and his pilot Trevor Roche had
completed the planning for their first war mission, so returned to
their room to try to relax while awaiting the phone call that would
send them airborne. 'We discussed what to do if we were shot down,
how we would try to get together, where we were going to keep our
guns. And the circumstances where we might use them. We cut off
our identity badges from our flying suits as a final act before going
to war. I pondered whether to write to my girlfriend Anna, but
decided not. We were both apprehensive but not scared enough to
be gibbering wrecks.'

Trevor suggested they listen to some music. They put on Dire
Straits' *Brothers in Arms* and for a moment were transported by
the title song, written about the 1982 Falklands War, describing a
soldier's need for solidarity in battle. With combat now imminent,
its resonance was stark. From the haunting guitar opening to its
'fields of destruction and baptism of fire' lyrics, to the sad soldier's
adieu 'let me bid you farewell', it took on a very vivid poignancy.
Both men were quiet as they contemplated what lay ahead. They
turned on the BBC World Service and heard Douglas Hurd, the
British Foreign Secretary, suggest that there was still a chance of
peace, which produced a chuckle.

Trevor shook his head. 'If there's a positive chance for peace, my
cock's a kipper.'

A moment later their Squadron Boss entered the room. 'It's game
on. You guys will lead the first attack. Tonight. Get some rest.'

A fully armed Tornado from RAF Marham during a test flight in 1988. The large JP233 runway denial weapons are clearly visible on the underside.

Looking down into the cockpit of a Tornado at low level. In the front, the pilot can be seen with his right hand on the control column and his left on the throttles. In the rear seat, the navigator has a map in his left hand and more mission notes on his knee and to his right.

Bob, Gareth and Chris Ankerson celebrate Christmas at RAF Bruggen in Germany in 1990. Tornado navigator Bob would deploy to the Gulf a few days later, it would be many months before his family saw him again.

Mike Toft and Mark Paisey swap seats in their Tornado. Navigator Toft sits in the front seat whilst his pilot takes the navigator's position.

The Tornado's twin Rolls Royce engines producing maximum power with afterburners, or reheat, engaged ready for take-off.

Navigator Dave Bellamy (left) and his pilot Trevor Roche, prepare for a mission by their Tornado armed with laser-guided bombs. Both are wearing their G-suits, and the blue leg-restraints which hold their legs against the ejection seats can also be seen. The iconic artwork began to be added to the aircraft after the first missions.

Prime Minister John Major addresses personnel at the Dhahran detachment a few days before the conflict began. The Detachment Commander, Cliff Spink, is on the left wearing his cap.

Dave Waddington, right, and Robbie Stewart, smiling, pictured in the Operations Room before their first mission on 17 January 1991. Nigel Elsdon and Max Collier would not return from this sortie.

A formation from the Muharraq detachment in Bahrain after landing from a night training sortie. All those pictured would see action just a few days later, not all survived the conflict. Left to right: Rob Woods, Nick Heard, Ricci Cobelli, 'Tommy' Tank, John Broadbent (The 'Boss'), Nige Risdale, Steve Hicks, Rupert Clark.

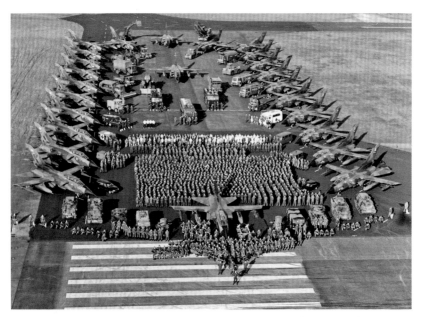

Just a fraction of RAF Laarbruch assembles at the end of the runway for a group photograph in 1989. Around half the base's Tornados are present, and perhaps a quarter of station personnel.

A pair of Tornados take on fuel from a Victor tanker during a training sortie before the commencement of hostilities.

Engineers from the 'bomb dump' at Dhahran make adjustments to live 1000lb bombs as they convert them into laser-guided bombs ready for use during the conflict.

Tornado pilot and Officer Commanding 27 Squadron Bill Green, with his wife Jenny, at the RAF Marham Officers' Mess Summer Ball in July 1990. Bill would be killed in a flying accident just a few weeks later.

Paddy Teakle, left, with his pilot Gordon Buckley prepare for a mission over Iraq. Their 'Personal Equipment Connectors', or PECs, can be seen hanging in front of them. The metal unit has connections for their G-suits, oxygen supply and communications, and clips directly onto their ejection seats.

A fully armed Tornado at the Muharraq detachment. The Boz chaff & flare pod can be seen under the wing on the far left, then an external fuel tank with a Sidewinder missile mounted above. The air-to-air refuelling probe is extended next to the open cockpit canopy. Two JP233 runway denial munitions are mounted under the fuselage. On the far right, the Sky Shadow electronic countermeasures pod, covered by a tarpaulin, is next to another under-wing fuel tank and Sidewinder.

The Navigator's cockpit of a Tornado GR1

1 Altimeter
2 Air Speed Indicator
3 Moving map and ground mapping radar display
4 TV Tabs which show navigation and target information
5 Cockpit 'attention-getters', which flash red to indicate a systems problem
6 Stores jettison selection panel
7 Undercarriage position indicator
8 Weapon selection panel
9 Radar control panel
10 Navigation mode selection panel
11 Radar Homing and Warning Receiver
12 Weapon and attack mode selection panel
13 Navigator's hand controller used for

updating navigation systems and during target attacks
14 Navigator's ejection seat
15 Ejection seat harness lap straps
16 Sky Shadow electronic countermeasures pod controls
17 Boz pod chaff and flare controls
18 Central Warning Panel which gives precise details of systems failures
19 Cassette system for navigation and target data entry
20 Main computer control panel
21 Radio and intercom controls
22 Inertial navigation system
23 Radio boxes
24 Cockpit lighting controls

The Pilot's cockpit of a Tornado GR4

1 Head Up Display
2 Autopilot selection panel
3 Cockpit 'attention-getters'
4 Late Arm switch
5 Head Up Display controls
6 Master Armament Safety Switch
7 Terrain Following Radar screen
8 Radar Homing and Warning Receiver
  screen
9 Flight instruments
10 Multi-Function Display
11 Engine gauges
12 Fuel gauges
13 Undercarriage lever

14 Pilot's control column
15 Central Warning Panel
16 Throttles
17 Wing sweep lever
18 Pilot weapon aiming controller
19 TFR settings control panel
20 Computerised flight systems controls
21 Radio and intercom controls
22 Mounting position for pilot's ejection seat
23 TFR system panel
24 Engine & generator control panel
25 RHWR controls
26 Cockpit lighting controls
27 Fuel temperature gauges

The waiting was over.

'The show is finally on the road,' Bellamy wrote in his diary. 'Godspeed.'

* * *

Waiting was all that American General Norman Schwarzkopf, in overall command of all troops in the region, could now do. Every part of the giant military 'chessboard' he had constructed was in place, the various pieces waiting to be moved. In a few hours he was about to launch the biggest air attack ever attempted. He was ordering men into battle. He knew only too well what that meant, and nothing he could do now would change the outcome. He went to his office in the headquarters bunker in Riyadh. 'I sat down and did what soldiers going to war do. I wrote to my family, saying how much I loved them.'

> *My dearest Wife and Children,*
> *The war clouds have gathered on the horizon and I have*
> *already issued the terrible orders that will let the monster*
> *loose ... we will soon be at war.*[13]

After the final verse of 15 Squadron's rousing song had been belted out, the briefing room momentarily fell silent. A few glances were shared between men preparing themselves for combat. They opened the door to see the faces of the eight aircrew readying themselves for the next mission, among them the Two Johns, navigator Mike Toft and their moustachioed leader, Pablo Mason. 'Good luck!' was the chorus as they all shook hands. 'Give it to them!' Buckley led his formation into the clothing section where the safety equipment specialists kept their flying kit in pristine order. He had already taken off his wedding ring and put it in a plastic bag, remembering his wife Dawn's request for him not to take risks. He then removed all other personal effects that might compromise him if taken prisoner. It was all part of the 'sanitising' process. All the pilots and navigators now carried for personal identity was a card with their name, rank and service number, and their indestructible 'dog tags' with basic information to identify their bodies.

On the way out to the aircraft, one of the airmen took Buckley aside and passed him a hip flask. 'Here you are, sir, one for the road.'

'Thanks,' Buckley smiled. 'But I'd better not.'

Gordon checked his Walther PP in its leather shoulder holster, then the £1,000 in gold sovereigns to negotiate safe passage with local tribes if they were shot down inside Iraq. He had the 'goolie chit', appropriately enough, in his pocket.

As they left, the message 'Crews walking!' went out.

Just before 0100 on 17 January 1991, kitted up in G-suits, helmets in hand, the fliers walked purposefully to the eight waiting Tornados.

This was it – they were going to war.

Nick Heard, 15 Squadron's Qualified Flying Instructor, was in the lead four-ship of the formation, with Risdale and Broadbent. Calm, likeable and an experienced and trusted flier, the 31-year-old was a well-respected figure on the Squadron. He had sat quietly during the briefings, keeping his thoughts of the approaching danger to himself.

The intelligence had been stark. Iraq had amassed an astonishing defence network. The country was defended by 154 SAM sites and 16,000 missiles, alongside almost 10,000 anti-aircraft guns.[14] 'My stomach dropped at what we were about to do. I thought, *Bloody hell!*' Outwardly, Nick had maintained a brave face. 'But inside, I had a fatalistic view; there was a very real chance I would not come back. I never mentioned it to anyone, it just sat at the back of my mind. Regardless of how good the Tornado was, the Iraqi air defence system was also very good and we would be very vulnerable.'[15]

Now he was in the cockpit of an overladen bomber, looking across to Risdale's Tornado that was about to lead them off to war. Finally, in total radio silence, they taxied out, ready for take-off at 0200. 'I watched Nige's reheat ignite and he rolled down the runway.

Ten seconds later we followed. The Tornado was heavy with eight tonnes of fuel but we got airborne safely and I started easing in on the leader's navigation lights to take up my position on his wing. Night-time close formation had become yet another newly acquired skill in the previous few months.'

Gordon Buckley and his navigator Paddy Teakle had completed their own pre-flight checks and also started up without a hitch. As leader of the second half of the formation, they would attack Tallil one minute after Nige Risdale's assault. Gordon watched the first four Tornados roll forward in full reheat then power up into the darkness over the Arabian Gulf.[16] Buckley rumbled down to the now vacant take-off point. To his right, under the airfield lights, he saw an unforgettable tableau. 'There were people everywhere, waving, standing on the walls, on cars, anything they could climb on to see us off. It was incredibly uplifting, seeing all the troops wishing us well, in the same way the ground crews had done back in the Second World War as the bombers set off on a mission. The sense of pride was immense.' He was fully focused on getting his heavy aircraft into the air. It began to shudder and shake as he increased the power. 'It really felt as though we were doing the right thing. We were about to take off in one of the most sophisticated jets in the world to help liberate an occupied country. This is what my career in the RAF had been about. It had all led to this point.'

He waited for his number two pilot to give him the thumbs-up signalling that the rest of the formation was lined up. The digit emerged and Gordon immediately pushed the throttles through the gate into minimum reheat, all the while holding the aircraft stationary. 'When I was happy, I released the brakes and rammed the throttles open to full reheat. The aircraft roared down the runway, quickly reaching the speed that would let it take to the sky.' Just as Nige Risdale had planned, the eight-ship formed up ready to refuel before heading into Iraq via the 'back door' out to the west, and entering the fray. The thunder of aircraft taking off into the night echoed across every coalition airbase.

In the giant field hospital in Bahrain, the British medics readied themselves for the inevitable casualties. 'We were sitting outside and the noise was spectacular,' one recalled. 'I went away from everybody else and just sat and listened. It was a horrible feeling, really eerie. We all knew then that something was going to happen. Some people had a few tears.'[17] The hospital commander had equally ominous thoughts. 'Everyone was apprehensive and you could feel it. Later, there was a briefing with the Detachment Commander who said, "In five minutes' time the first aircraft will hit Baghdad. You can tell your troops." The biggest fear was, would we be able to do the job if a lot of horrible casualties came in?' All those not involved in getting jets airborne got into their NBC suits in expectation of a retaliatory Iraqi Scud attack, potentially with deadly chemicals. Some of the nurses asked the Padre to say a prayer with them. As he did so, many were in tears.[18]

Elsewhere, thousands of other fliers were readying themselves for combat. Giant B-52 bombers had already taken off from the USA on a 35-hour round trip; the longest bombing raid in history. F-18 Hornets and A-6 Intruders launched from aircraft carriers in the Gulf and Red Sea, F-117 Stealth fighters were inbound to Baghdad on a 1,000-mile flight from their southern Saudi base. It would be the first real test of their famed 'radar invisibility'. From bases all over Saudi Arabia, Oman and Bahrain, aircraft from tankers to fighters and bombers were powering into the night sky, joining a 2,000-strong armada that would descend on Iraq that first day.

Part of that armada was the Tornado force that had been given the most dangerous job: hitting Iraqi airfields from low level. As well as the squadrons from Muharraq and Tabuk, more Tornados from Dhahran were flying fast towards Mudaysis, 150 miles south-west of Baghdad. They were led into combat for the first time by their universally popular Tornado Detachment Commander, 41-year-old Wing Commander Jerry Witts. 'We were apprehensive, but there was no time to brood about it, no time to worry. We just got on with the job. I began to get quite excited; I thought it was fantastic. There were hundreds and hundreds of planes up there. We were going to stuff this bloke and he deserved it.'[19]

The Wolfpack had been unleashed.

Back in London, British Prime Minister John Major had gone to bed with mixed emotions. He knew that all the options had narrowed to this single course of action, but he was still anxious about sending young men to war. 'I wondered what would be in the minds of the young aircraft crews as, for the first time, they launched themselves into action. I found it hard to imagine, but my visit to them had convinced me that they were ready for the fight and would do their duty with distinction.'[20]

* * *

Mind firmly fixed on what lay ahead, Nick Heard climbed to 12,000ft for the first refuelling rendezvous. The fully loaded aircraft was being tested to the full, but Nick found it responding with good grace as he moved towards the right-hand hose of the VC10 tanker, unseen in the darkness ahead. 'I stabilised around 10 feet behind the basket. With a bit of power I moved in and plugged in first time; a satisfying result. Fuel flowed and we were quickly full, so we unplugged and moved to the left wing to watch the other Tornados take theirs.' As they proceeded up the 'tanker trail' paralleling the border with Iraq they were able to relax a little. Nick's navigator Rob Woods tuned one of the aircraft's radios in to the BBC World Service. The BBC was just hours away from clearing its service to become a rolling news and comment channel during the war. But for the moment, no one, bar those in the air, was aware that war was minutes away.

'It was totally surreal. We were listening to something totally innocuous like *Gardeners' Question Time*, waiting for the final moment when we would head over the border and start a war. At least we still had the element of surprise. Then the broadcast was interrupted to announce that there were explosions in Baghdad. We turned the radio off.' Nick then monitored all the other aircraft checking in with AWACS, the great eyes and ears in the sky. 'I knew there was a huge armada of aircraft gathering; part of the massive initial attack and it was incredible to be part of it.'

The converted Boeing 707 Airborne Warning and Control System, topped by its distinctive saucer-like radar dome, gave the coalition forces hundreds of miles of sight over the aerial battlefield. The massive fleet now approaching Iraq required four AWACS constantly in the air, spotting both enemy and friendly aircraft many miles away. If an Iraqi jet homed in on a coalition aircraft, it was up to AWACS to warn the fliers and provide them with protection.[21] If the AWACS controller broadcast the message 'picture clear', it meant there were no immediate threats at hand. It was a phrase that Tornado crews, particularly vulnerable at low level in the flat desert, were always pleased to hear.

The opening shots of the war were to be fired by Apache attack helicopters hovering over the southern Iraq desert.[22] Their task was to destroy two early-warning radars, creating a corridor down which the hundreds of aircraft could travel en route to strike airbases, power plants, communication centres and Baghdad itself. The attack was timed for 0240 local.[23] At 0239.30, the US Army pilots waited, stationary in the hover, peering into the darkness. There was no movement.

Ten seconds to go.

There was a sudden flurry of heat signatures as Iraqi personnel scurried around the buildings. The clock ticked down to 0240. The crosshairs of Apache weapons systems settled on their targets and a volley of Hellfire missiles speared away. The attack helicopters edged closer, loosing off rockets, then moved in closer still, engaging anything still standing with their 30mm cannon. Fire rose from buildings, trucks burst into flames with bodies slumped around them. During four minutes of unfettered destruction, the Apaches unleashed 27 Hellfires, 100 rockets and 4,000 cannon rounds. The Iraqi radars – and many of the personnel – were obliterated. The 'back door' had been kicked open.

A few hundred miles from Baghdad, thirty-five cruise missiles had been launched from the squadron of B-52 bombers that had flown from their base in Louisiana. Scores more cruise missiles, launched from warships in the Gulf and Red Sea, were zeroing in on the Iraqi capital. They were the opening notes in a symphony of destruction that was about to thunder through Saddam Hussein's night.[24]

The Tornados topped up with a final load of fuel before casting off and descending into enemy territory. Nick Heard was at the front of the formation. 'I felt confident as we prepared for combat. I set the weapon armament switches to live, arming the two 27mm Mauser cannon and the two AIM9L air-to-air missiles, then turned off the external lights. Rob Woods, my navigator, set up the Radar Homing and Warning Receiver, Sky Shadow electronic jamming and Boz chaff and flare dispenser pods and checked that the JP233s were correctly set up.' As they descended to 1,500ft Nick turned the TFR onto autopilot to check the system was working then reset the minimum height in stages all the way down to 200ft. 'The Tornado settled beautifully at 420 knots [480mph] over the invisible Saudi desert. On my moving map display in the cockpit, I noticed the border approaching. On one side it said "SAUDI ARABIA" and on the other "IRAQ". This was for real. I was just about to enter the airspace of a hostile, foreign country at high speed, low level and fully armed. I was about to start a war. At any point the Iraqis were now entitled to defend themselves by shooting us down. I was suddenly struck by the enormity of it all.'

A few seconds later they crossed the Iraq border. All was quiet in the desert below. They were on track and at the right speed to be over Tallil within the strict 'time-on-target' arrival of plus or minus five seconds. Despite being on autopilot, Nick concentrated hard on what lay ahead. 'I had my hands off the controls as the Tornado flew itself at around 500mph towards the target. The jet was solid as a rock. I suddenly thought, *This is amazing*, the Tornado was taking Rob and me into the heart of the Iraqi defences in total darkness and I wasn't even flying it!' Nick listened intently to the AWACS frequency and the reassuring calls of 'picture clear' from the American air controller. With ten minutes to go there were no Iraqi fighters incoming.

* * *

Far out to the west, the Tabuk formations, including Dave Bellamy and Mal Craghill, were also in the air. But problems had already started to surface. In their JP233-armed Tornado, Craghill and his 25-year-old friend and pilot Mike Warren were struggling. 'Back on the ground we'd had a failure in the weapons system which meant we shouldn't have taken off. But we decided to launch anyway; these things did happen but often cleared up once airborne. More importantly, we didn't want to be seen to be chickening out on the first ever mission. And we had no idea how quickly Saddam Hussein might capitulate – this could be our only chance to fly a war sortie!' Desperately trying to reset the system, they continued towards the border. But things got worse. 'The radar then packed up so we now had two major faults making us a liability to the other formation members. We were useless; there was no way we could continue so we left the formation and reduced weight before returning to Tabuk. I was devastated.'

David Bellamy was leading his formation of two Tornados, each carrying three ALARM anti-radar missiles to protect the three remaining bombers. After air-to-air tanking they plunged down from 10,000ft to 200ft and crossed into Iraq. Unfortunately, there was no 'picture clear' in their skies; the Iraqi Air Force had come out to defend their homeland. An AWACS air controller urgently vectored F-15s onto an Iraqi Mirage that was among the 120 enemy fighters launched to counter the initial allied attack. Within a few minutes, Dave saw what seemed like a very bright flare slowly descending from the darkness above him, which turned out to be an Iraqi fighter shot down at 30,000ft by a Sparrow air-to-air missile fired from an American F-15.

Battle had been joined.

Bellamy's formation powered through the night, allowing the TFR to do the work as they hurtled towards Al Asad. With no night-vision equipment to show the way, the only relief from the cloak of darkness they enjoyed was illuminated ground features. 'Once we were over Iraq it was all so unreal. It was mostly pitch-black but if lights were on, you could make out streets and petrol stations.'

Passing close to a brightly lit military airfield halfway to Al Asad, the crews could see Iraqi Mirage jets being hurriedly towed into hardened shelters. Sensing a potential opportunity, his pilot Trevor Roche asked, 'Shall we strafe them?'

'Nah, it's probably someone else's target,' Bellamy quickly replied. But he couldn't quite believe that the enemy appeared totally unaware that the war had started. As they dashed past the base, he knew that would soon change. Leaving the bright lights behind them, Bellamy calculated that they would be firing live weapons onto the enemy in just ten minutes. As they got closer, the sky to their right lit up as huge shock waves expanded outwards. The F-117 Stealth fighters were going to town over Baghdad, unseen by the sixty SAM sites and 3,000 triple-A cannons protecting the capital.[25] The stealth technology had worked. The Iraqis had no clue what had hit them as 2,000lb Paveway bombs, precisely guided by the F-117's infra-red and laser targeting system, plummeted from the night sky. The key objective of the first night's attack on Baghdad was to knock out the Iraqi air defence and military command and control systems so that their response to the aerial assault would be – hopefully – significantly less successful. But for Norman Schwarzkopf and his staff back at the headquarters in Riyadh, there was no way of knowing if the Stealth attacks had worked because strict radio silence had to be observed. There was, however, another way of finding out. The main target was Baghdad's International Communications Centre, which accounted for half the airwave traffic out of the capital. It was also the key transmission point for CNN's live TV stream. Soon after 0300 the CNN pictures from Baghdad went off air.[26] The BBC World Service managed some on-the-spot reports of 'flak over Baghdad' and 'bombs falling from nowhere' before their lines also went dead. Within ten minutes, all TV and radio broadcasts had ceased. There was cheering in Riyadh; the Stealth had worked, as had the countless Tomahawk cruise missiles detonating across the city. By 0400 Baghdad was plunged into near-darkness after its main power plants were struck.

Dave Bellamy's attention was drawn away from the inferno

around Baghdad as they closed on their target. He could feel the sweat run through his cropped hair, down onto his nose and cheeks. Briefly wiping it away with a gloved hand, they made their final checks. 'TFR out!' Trevor called on the final approach, switching from terrain-following mode and taking manual control in readiness for missile launch. Bellamy completed the attack routine ready for the first ever combat firing of the British-made anti-radiation missiles, their targets the SA-6 radars defending Al Asad. His formation was in exactly the right place to ensure the coverage and protection for the three Tornado bombers armed with JP233 following close behind.

'All switches confirmed live.' The missiles were ready to go.

'Stand by.'

There was one last warning Bellamy had to give before launching: 'Don't look at the flash!'

The seconds ticked down to the precise moment for launch.

'Five, four, three, two, one. Commit!'

The three missiles blasted off the Tornado's belly. A triple whoosh was followed by a huge blaze. Bellamy neglected to turn away. 'I was momentarily blinded by the rocket motors igniting.' When his vision cleared, he realised the attack had gone horribly wrong. 'I looked down to see two ALARM missiles flying out in front of the aircraft. They started to accelerate away but then immediately flew nose down and hit the desert in a flash of sparks. To say it was disappointing would be an understatement. Two failures on the first ever mission!' The third missile took off into the night, heading towards its target. But the failures raised questions which would undoubtedly need investigating.

* * *

The Tornados in Nick Heard's formation again heard the comforting AWACS 'picture clear'. In their part of Iraq there were no fighters airborne and ready to fire air-to-air missiles their overburdened aircraft would struggle to evade. In the darkness to his left, flying unseen in parallel track 4 miles away, was Nige Risdale and his navigator, John Broadbent, 'the Boss'. A few miles behind them, as if on tramlines, also unseen, were the two other Tornados. Then a minute behind them, were Gordon Buckley and Paddy Teakle, leading their four-ship in a similar box formation. Without night-vision goggles to check any positioning by sight, each crew simply presumed and trusted that the seven others were in the right place, at the right time, and at the right speed. As the eight aircraft flew themselves automatically on TFR, Buckley's thoughts were filled with the looming reality. 'None of us felt comfortable due to the war environment we were going into. But I didn't have any fear or nerves, we just didn't know what to expect. No one had ever done this before! We were the first crews ever to fly the Tornado in anger. Low-level, TFR and night-war ops. It was incredible.'

'Let me know when we're *sausage side*,' he said to Paddy Teakle, repeating the well-worn *Blackadder* phrase which would become the norm. Like Nick Heard a few miles in front, the HUD told Gordon that he was flying at 500mph, around 200ft above the vast Iraqi desert, black as velvet. There was no sight of the ground. It was like driving on a busy motorway in thick fog, at a fraction over seven times the speed limit, trusting your car's computer systems to safely navigate any obstacles ahead. At the very front of the formation, Nige Risdale peered into the impenetrable blackness, content that his plans had finally evolved into a real attack. 'I looked around, occasionally glancing in to check the cockpit indications that everything was running smoothly. The aircraft was flying itself, we were on track, on time; everything was going as planned. I wasn't nervous by that point, there was so much to be done. As the lead aircraft of eight Tornados, we were checking timings, positioning, defensive aids, speed, height and weapons selection.' [27] He also had to ensure the aircraft was serviceable, checking the fuel gauges and engine indications. Then, he noticed some bright lights on the horizon up ahead, framed against the dark. 'Someone's getting plastered in our 10 o'clock. Very impressive triple-A barrage,' he told John Broadbent in the rear seat.

'Yes, mate,' the Squadron Boss dryly replied. 'That's where we're going!'

A second later the jet turned itself left onto the final attack track, its nose pointing directly at Tallil airfield and the triple-A barrage, now in full flow.

The Tornados' 'time on target' bracket started at 0408,[28] following on from an attack by an American package of A-6 Intruders and F-18 Hornet strike aircraft. Paddy Teakle's instinct during the planning with Nige Risdale weeks earlier that the Americans would 'bomb the crap out of the airfield before we arrived' had proven correct. The US crews were targeting the Scud missile storage facilities and did not hold back.[29] The problem, Nige quickly realised, was that their attacks had 'stirred up a furious response', with the anti-aircraft cannons firing wildly into the sky. Small dots and dashes going up in spirals from small arms fire were followed by the larger and deadlier lines of triple-A explosive shells from multi-barrelled cannons.

The Tornados were 30 miles out, and in a few minutes they would hit the sphere of triple-A glowering over Tallil. 'It was obvious that it wasn't actually *aimed* at us,' John Broadbent remembered. 'Tallil's defences were not even aware of our presence yet. The guns were all firing at the Americans, thousands of feet above us. But you try telling your sphincter that! At least I was able to focus on the attack systems, so could legitimately keep my eyes in the cockpit as the white balls of fire rose up!'

Nick Heard allowed himself a brief smile. The Tornado really was superb. Here they were, directly over enemy territory, eating up a mile every seven seconds and just a few hundred feet above the ground. Then his brow furrowed briefly as he too caught sight of the staggering amount of triple-A going in his '10.30' position, just out to his left. *Glad we're not going there.* The thought had barely formed when the aircraft, still on autopilot, turned left on its next pre-programmed track. Suddenly they were heading directly towards the yellow 'inverted funnel' of fire hovering over the desert. 'It was then that the horrible truth dawned on me – that cauldron of fire *was* Tallil! I stared at the interlocking mesh of triple-A and my mouth went completely dry. A stab of fear hit me.' Nick wondered if it might be his last few minutes of flying. And living. 'There appeared no way through that gunfire, the barrage was incredible and any hit from those shells would blow us to bits. It sprayed upwards in snaking lines, a ferocious mix of coloured fire. I could see no way of getting through it unscathed. We were quite invisible in the darkness but I could not see how they could miss us with that intense barrage.'

His navigator Rob Woods was not seeing quite as much of the danger ahead as he concentrated on the attack run-in. He found and marked the target's pre-planned 'offset' positions on his ground-mapping radar, which updated the weapon-aiming computer with the exact range and bearing onto the target.[30] Racing towards the airfield Nick found himself suddenly enveloped by the gunfire. 'I was astounded to see that we were still over a minute away from weapons release. It was going to be a long minute.'

Somewhere to their left, flying just a few miles apart, Nige Risdale was similarly preoccupied. 'I thought the barrage would diminish as time went on but it just stayed the same, an intense firework display of white and red interweaving lines forming an impenetrable wall. It seemed like a solid mass.' In the rear seat, John Broadbent glanced up from his radar display. 'It was like driving through snow flurries in your car. The flakes come rushing towards you and, if you focus on one, at the last second it sweeps past the windscreen. But these exploding balls of bright light were not snowflakes!'

Gordon Buckley, one of the most experienced pilots in the entire Tornado force, felt a creeping realisation that extreme danger lay ahead. 'A truly unbelievable eruption of green and red lit up the night sky, a huge barrage.' His reactions were swift. *We're not going through that lot.* He flicked off the autopilot to try to fly around it. 'No matter where I steered the aircraft, the target pointer simply stayed on the barrage. The triple-A *was* our target! *Oh shit! We're going to have to go straight through it!*' Resigning himself to fate, he went back to autopilot. 'We were in a bloody great steam train of jets that wasn't stopping or turning around. We were going to fly into the heart of that barrage and complete the mission. No other thought entered my head.'

What had started as a small dome of light in the distance loomed ominously ahead as Nige Risdale closed on the target, ready to drop the first ever Tornado munitions in combat. For six weeks he had planned this attack, visualising what it would be like skimming over Tallil, but he had never imagined it would be like this. At 3 miles out, Nige increased engine power, throttling up to around 600mph. But he had to keep the aircraft at 'maximum dry' power, giving the fastest speed possible without engaging reheat and its long, tell-tale tongue of flame that really would draw groundfire.

'Eighteen seconds,' Broadbent called.

Nick Heard's intense concentration was momentarily broken by cannon fire blasting just past the cockpit from below and to their right, no further than 100 yards away. 'The gunfire went blindly straight up. In daylight I would have looked into the gunner's eyes, he was that close. It was an astonishing sensation. We were still a few miles from the target and the triple-A was right underneath us. But there was nothing to be done, we had to fly through the middle of it. Nothing was said in the cockpit; there wasn't the slightest thought in our minds of breaking off the attack.' Despite the intensity of the barrage, they could hear no external noise of gunfire. 'I was in a warm, quiet Tornado cockpit, yet we were surrounded by bullets. The noise around the airfield must have been astonishing but it was all quiet in our jet.'

'Ten seconds to release.' *This is it.* Nige Risdale flicked off the TFR autopilot and took manual control of the Tornado. The TFR could, if it detected an obstruction ahead such as an airfield's metal boundary fence, force the jet into a sudden pull-up, not something to be desired while dropping weapons over the target in the midst of heavy triple-A.[31] Checking his 'radalt' – radar altimeter – readings, Nige carefully nosed the Tornado down to 180ft to deliver the JP233. Gunfire was flicking past the cockpit. But he barely noticed it as they closed in on the runways.

Five seconds.

'Committing!' pilot and navigator said together, both pressing the weapons release button to give the computerised aiming system the authority to launch the munitions at the precise moment.

Four, three, two, one . . .

The two JP233s started spraying the airfield below. For five seconds Nige listened as the weapon rumbled while sixty runway-cratering munitions and 430 anti-personnel bomblets fell away. 'It was like driving over endless speed bumps; I could feel the whole thing rattle off right under my backside.' He was not prepared for what came next as the two huge, now empty canisters, automatically fell away. 'The jet ballooned upwards. Carrying the canisters was like flying with two huge wardrobes under the jet and the change in flying characteristics when they jettisoned was significant! I had to push quite hard to prevent ballooning too much and get back down to low level.' Nige recovered the aircraft then quickly re-engaged the TFR to allow the jet to fly itself as they streaked away from the furnace of Tallil.

Nick Heard had been coming in alongside, just out to his right. 'I noticed their JP233 munitions detonating exactly on time, slightly ahead and to our left. It was the first indication that he was there at all.' Their own Tornado flew across the runway almost parallel with Risdale's, scattering destruction onto every surface and exposed personnel before also leaping forward as the giant canisters jettisoned. 'I quickly re-engaged autopilot so I would not inadvertently fly into the ground in the excitement. I trusted the Tornado autopilot more than myself at that moment.' Seconds later they emerged from the cauldron of groundfire to the north of Tallil.

Paddy Teakle was one of the few aircrew who had previously experienced the pressure of a wartime sortie. Eight years earlier he had been a navigator on the Victor tankers that flew far over the South Atlantic, refuelling the Vulcan bombers deployed to strike the Falkland Islands' main airstrip at Port Stanley. But this was very different. People were now shooting at him, wanting him dead. As they ran towards Tallil, he calmly identified the offset marks on the radar and updated the weapons system in the main computer. They were on time and on target.

In the front seat, Gordon Buckley tripped out the TFR in case it reacted to any structure over the airbase and took manual control. It was time to go ultra-low. 'We were flying right into a huge barrage of triple-A with blue and red lines tearing past the cockpit. I had been taught right from the start of my frontline career on the Jaguar that if you encounter triple-A, go as low and as fast as you can.' Buckley did just that, descending the aircraft in darkness until the 'radalt' stopped reading out his height. He knew that it would trip off at 100ft, so he was now confident he was flying the Tornado himself in total darkness around 100ft above the ground. 'It was a very dangerous thing to do, but I had confidence in the aircraft, and our approach to the target was flat. Even at that great weight the Tornado was rock-solid because this was what it was designed to do.'

He glanced at the time to target on the HUD. They were seconds away. He climbed back up to 200ft. Right over the runway they released the JP233 which deployed with the sound of a machine gun firing. Then, like Heard and Risdale, he felt the jet shoot forward as the giant canisters fell away. Gordon did not want to hang about and poured on the power, going to maximum speed and banking hard to the right to get back down to ultra-low level and away from danger. 'The noise and response of the aircraft to the sudden release of the 5-tonne weapon load was completely unexpected. Coupled with my desire to return to ultra-low level, it felt like we were going over the edge of a large rollercoaster ride. The jet leapt forward and it really shocked me. I had to really push to get it back down to 100ft and stay at low level. It was an amazing sensation but, on reflection, manually flying back down to 100ft in darkness after an attack was not the most sensible thing to do. I didn't do it again.'

Nick Heard took a moment to look back at Tallil to see how the other crews were doing in a sky filled with gunfire and explosions. Tallil was erupting under the multiple blasts of JP233 strikes from eight Tornados in a scene of chaos, confusion and high-tech destruction. Their 480 57lb SG-357 runway-cratering devices had floated down on large parachutes. Each detonated just above the ground, firing a shaped charge that went through the tarmac, buried itself then exploded, heaving the concrete upwards and forming a large crater. On smaller parachutes the formation's 3,440 small anti-personnel mines landed without exploding, instead deploying tiny metal legs to set themselves upright, forming a giant minefield, ready to detonate and dissuade anyone from trying to repair the craters.[32]

'It had been as scary as hell,' remembered John Broadbent. 'Getting through the flak felt like trying to run through a shower without getting wet. Those few seconds it took to overfly the target were the longest of my life.' Taking a deep breath, he called for a radio check on the entire formation. '*Two*,' Nick Heard instantly responded, listening anxiously to hear if others would follow.

'*Three . . .*'

'*Four . . .*'

'*Five . . .*'

'*Six . . .*'

'*Seven . . .*'

'*And eight*,' the final aircraft acknowledged.

All the Tornados made it through in one piece. Nick was delighted if not incredulous. 'The relief, not just for our own success and safety but for that of colleagues, was massive. It was incredible that we had all got through it unscathed.' Danger still lurked from above and below as they dashed across enemy terrain to the safety of Saudi Arabia. Eventually Nick's tight grip on the stick relaxed at the 'beautiful sight' of the VC10 refuelling tanker on the other side of the border 'faithfully waiting for us for a short top-up for the trip back to Bahrain'. A huge grin spread across his face as the sun came up over the Gulf. It had been a remarkable night. 'I was now a *combat* pilot! I'd done something very few pilots serving in the RAF at that time had ever done.'

Nick Heard and the other Tornado crews were among the 2,775 coalition sorties flown against Iraqi targets in the first twenty-four hours of the war. Nineteen coalition aircraft were damaged or lost. The Iraqi Air Force flew just 120 sorties and lost eight of its aircraft. Countless more were destroyed in the plethora of bombing raids.[33]

The Wolfpack had been successful.

* * *

As the Tornado bombers from Jerry Witts' Dhahran formation flew back to the safety of the border from their attack south-west of Baghdad, it seemed like an age before the brown line marking the international border on their moving map display approached. 'I suppressed the irrational desire to laugh as the aircraft symbol tracked over the printed notice on the map:

WARNING:
FLIGHT IN IRAQ OUTSIDE
CONTROLLED AIRSPACE
IS STRICTLY PROHIBITED

'Just as suddenly, we were over the line. We're alive! We're safe! My God, we've done it!' Witts performed a few 'celebratory barrel rolls' and began dreaming of the perfect English breakfast. 'I had never felt so high in my life.'[34]

Not everyone was feeling so joyful. Mal Craghill and his pilot Mike Warren had had to return to Tabuk with their weapons unused after suffering multiple technical failures. Like most complex fast jets tested to the limit on a daily basis, the Tornado did suffer from equipment and aircraft failures. It was frustrating for both the aircrews who had to deal with them, and the engineers who had to fix them. But this was no comfort to Mal and Mike; they were both devastated at not being part of that historic first raid. 'It was definitely the biggest feeling of disappointment I have ever had,' Warren later recalled. 'Once you are there, there's nothing worse than coming back and saying, "Yes, I was on the first night but had to turn back because of problems."[35] His young navigator Mal Craghill was unequivocal. 'I really felt a sense of letting my mates down. It had been our big chance to show what we could do and, because of equipment failure, we'd been unsuccessful. At the back of my mind, I also wondered if people might think I'd perhaps used the technical issues to avoid the challenge we faced. I was one of the most junior guys out there; what would people say about my actions? How would they judge me? Would anyone think I had bottled out?'

Like Jerry Witts, Gordon Buckley was also 'absolutely buzzing' as he headed homewards. 'If I had been taken out of the cockpit there and then and strapped to a heart monitor, the results would have been extraordinary.' As the miles grew between his Tornado and the devastation they had left behind, he turned his armament switches to the 'safe' position and began to reflect on what had happened. 'We had done an incredible job as part of the RAF's first war sorties since the Falklands War. Everything had run on rails. I thought, *Yeah, we can really do this!*' Landing back at Muharraq, Buckley and Paddy Teakle headed to the debriefing room, experiencing a massive wave of relief and satisfaction. 'We were exhilarated and our ground crews were ecstatic too,' Teakle said. 'The engineers' shifts had changed but our team refused to go home until they counted all eight of *their* jets back in. There was hugging and handshakes all round; a tremendous welcome!'[36]

Later that morning, the elated crews headed back to the hotel through the largely empty streets of Bahrain. The adrenaline surge from intense combat showed no sign of abating. Everything had changed from the world they had known twenty-four hours earlier, and no one was ready for bed. Gordon and Paddy invited everyone back to their room for breakfast drinks. The cold beers slipped down their throats with ease as they fed off each other's high-octane experiences. 'The banter was gushing – we were all on a high,' Gordon recalled. For Nick Heard, the reason was obvious. 'We had just taken part in the largest air operation for decades and become combat-proven crews. The change in attitude and confidence was clear.' They also knew that the Iraqi Air Force had taken a real pounding and Nick wondered if it could sustain that level of punishment for long. All three Tornado missions on the first night, from Muharraq, Dhahran and Tabuk, had succeeded without any losses.

Nige Risdale was simply content that his and Paddy's long nights of planning had come to successful fruition. But he knew, too, that alongside their hard-earned skills, a bucketful of luck had been involved.

* * *

Waiting for his friends to return to Tabuk, Mal Craghill was still worrying about his own unsuccessful sortie. 'We felt deflated, and despite there being no other decision we could have taken, Mike and I felt like we had abandoned the rest of our formation. We sat quietly in the Operations Room, waiting, talking very little, reading the technical manuals to see if there was anything we could have done differently (there wasn't), playing chess to occupy the time and wondering how our formation mates were getting on. Eventually the radio burst into life and familiar voices checked in to report a successful mission and notify the ground crew that they would be back on the ground in fifteen minutes. A feeling of enormous relief washed over us both. They had all survived. Our next thought was more selfish: when would *we* get a chance to prove ourselves in battle?'

David Bellamy landed back at Tabuk airbase after three hours and fifteen minutes of intense and gruelling excitement. 'It was a combination of high-velocity adrenaline and nerves but we survived.' The excitement finally caught up with him as they opened the cockpit canopy to the dawn sky stretching into the desert around Tabuk. Climbing down the steps he stumbled, his legs weak from the adrenaline overload. One of the ground crew helped him up, then gave him a 'glorious-tasting carton of pineapple juice'. Inside their quarters the excitement among the aircrew overflowed. 'We were chirping away like little birds. It was a joyous melee of excited schoolkids telling three different versions of that same night.' Bellamy also noticed something else from those untested aircrew who had not flown on the first missions. 'The other guys wanted to get stuck in, to get that first sortie under their belt, to prove they could do it too.'

John Nichol and John Peters, heading out to their Tornado for *their* first sortie on the second wave of attacks, had seen that same confidence of success shining in Gordon Buckley as he had walked back into the Operations Room after his first combat mission that dawn morning. 'He was showing a curious combination of excitement and slight shock. He was hyped-up from the mission, but at the same time he had seen something that had really affected him,' Peters remembered. Seeing the Two Johns staring at him, Buckley at first tried to pass it off with a quip. 'I am stirred, but not shaken,' he said dryly.[37] His navigator Paddy Teakle then loomed behind him. 'You should have seen the fucking airfield.' A cigarette shook slightly in his hands as he spoke. 'Lit up like a bloody Christmas tree. Flak everywhere. Tubes of bloody molten metal.' Paddy suddenly realised that Peters and Nichol were about to face the same thing themselves. 'Oh, but don't worry. You'll be okay.'

Buckley caught Nichol's eye. 'You'll be fine . . .' He hesitated. 'It's a piece of cake.'

'Yeah . . . thanks, sir.' John Nichol had a feeling his Flight Commander was probably not telling the whole truth.

CHAPTER FIVE

GIN-CLEAR SKIES

17 JANUARY, MORNING

As Paddy Teakle's formation had headed back to the Sheraton Hotel
and some post-mission beers at dawn, his wife Sonia and most of the
15 Squadron spouses were glued to the television news back at their
RAF Laarbruch base in Germany. Sonia had been woken at 1.40am
by an uncle calling breathlessly from Wales. 'Do you know the war
has broken out?'[1] She immediately phoned a number of the other
wives at Laarbruch, including Helen Peters, whose Tornado pilot
husband John was preparing for his first mission. They gathered in
Sonia and Paddy's married quarters for the first of endless mugs of tea
and watched the hostilities unfolding on TV. Film of triple-A arcing
over Baghdad abruptly switched to footage of Tornados returning
to 15 Squadron's Muharraq base. The wives leaned in closer to the
screen as each jet landed. The camera zoomed in as the crews clambered out of their cockpits and down onto the tarmac. Off came their
helmets to reveal the sweat-plastered faces of her husband's formation. But Paddy and his pilot Gordon Buckley were missing.

Sonia's hand went to her mouth. The others looked at her with growing trepidation. Then the phone rang. Sonia snatched the receiver from its cradle. *Thank God. It's Paddy!* He'd arrived earlier than the rest of the crews and avoided the press. 'I was very relieved and said I hoped he would show his face on camera next time!'

* * *

Readying himself for his first war mission later that night, Dave Waddington, one of the youngest pilots in the region, sought out a friend from 15 Squadron, now tucking into breakfast in the Sheraton's five-star restaurant after returning from the attack on Tallil. *What had it been like?* The navigator, normally laid-back to the point of supine, was excitable. 'As he described the immense wall of triple-A they had faced, I could see it had been a hell of an experience for them, and realised that I too would soon be flying into a similar barrage.'[2]

They were joined by Dave's crewmate, Robbie Stewart, who had spent most of the previous evening writing 'last letters'. It hadn't been easy. 'How do you distil into a few paragraphs how you feel about your children and your wife? I had said our memories and love would always last, but it was really emotional to put those words on paper – even the thought that they might be opened. There was a sense of everything closing in on us.'[3] After sealing the envelopes, Robbie had asked fellow navigator Max Collier to join them for a drink, but he hadn't been in the mood. Before going to sleep, Robbie had sipped a glass of Southern Comfort and looked at pictures of Tange, Kirsty and Scott, doing his best to dismiss thoughts of what the following day might bring. Now he was finding it awkward sitting at breakfast with men who had just been in combat. He had switched on CNN first thing that morning to see the breathless reports set against the backdrop of explosions over Baghdad. 'I didn't particularly want to go to war, but it was my job; I was an RAF Officer, a professional; it was my duty and what was required of me.'

He decided to go back to his room and write another letter to his wife – one she could read immediately.

Thurs 17 Jan

 My Dearest Darling,[4]

 Well, it has all started as you know. I heard the Tornados go out this morning and was greatly relieved to hear that they all got back safely. I spoke to some of them this morning and they said it was like a firework display – a lot of Flak over the target but it was not directed. The TV is currently showing the results and they seem very impressive. We are waiting to go in shortly and complete our mission. I hope things will go as well for us as they have for the others. I am not sure when you will get this; not too long I hope. Look after yourself darling, I need and love you very much.

 All my love,

 Rob

He signed off the letter with ten kisses.

Nick Heard was also tucking into a Full English downstairs after a quick shower and change into 'civvies'. His sights were firmly fixed on the temazepam sleeping tablet he would soon take to help push away the memories of a night sky torn apart by triple-A. 'It was a surreal moment. Just a few hours earlier, my life had been on the line. Now I was enjoying bacon and eggs in the Sheraton.'[5] He really wanted to call his wife Jane, to connect with someone outside the military bubble. But she was skiing with friends in the French Alps, a long way from a phone. He smiled ruefully then swallowed the pill and headed for bed. The powerful medication had been issued by the Squadron doctor to allow aircrew to sleep soundly during the day in preparation for overnight sorties. They worked their magic in a matter of moments, so it took Nick some time to register the shrill, unrelenting ring at his bedside. With aching muscles, dry mouth and groggy head he reached for the receiver.

Jane had been in the queue for the first ski lift of the day, determined to make the most of the virgin snow, when she heard people around her talking excitedly about '*la guerre*'. She had rushed to the nearest call box and, with trembling fingers, pumped a fistful of francs into the slot. She was clearly overjoyed to hear his voice, and as Nick cleared his head, they discussed what he had done in the first few hours of the war. 'Then we chatted about how the snow was on the ski slopes and what they were all doing out in France. But the phone started bleeping and the line went dead – her money had run out!' For a moment he had been spirited away from the desert battlefield and onto the freshly pisted slopes of Val d'Isère. He blotted out the memory of the burning cone of deadly anti-aircraft fire above Tallil and slumped back into an uninterrupted sleep.

Gordon Buckley also wanted to hear his wife's voice. 'I was desperate to talk to Dawn, to let her know that all was okay. I went into our bathroom where there was a telephone and rang her in Germany, even though it was very early morning her time.'[6]

'What's the matter?' Dawn asked sleepily. Not everyone had been glued to their TV sets in the early hours. A world away from the Gulf, life was going on as normal.

'"We went in last night," I told her. We had just faced the real possibility of death, and almost certainly caused death, but no one knew what we had been doing. I began to realise the enormity of it all. Prior to that, it was all military guys doing the job we had trained to do; now I had made the person I loved most come into the picture.' He put down the handset and went back into the room he shared with Paddy, glad of its anonymity. 'I didn't want any pictures to remind me of home and normality. I just wouldn't have been able to handle the incredible contrast between what we were doing, war and death, then seeing pictures of my family smiling back home.'

He also began to understand that it was going to be 'a hellish time for the wives'. Unlike those fighting, they had little information about what was going on, except via highly colourful television accounts. He was too hyped to sleep. Even though their Squadron Boss, John Broadbent, had told them to stay in the hotel, Gordon had to get out. 'I was about to explode every time I thought of what I had done the night before.' He walked to a souk near the hotel, seeking some kind of normality, but the usual hustle and bustle was gone. He asked a shopkeeper leaning against a wall why it was so quiet. 'They went in last night to bomb Iraq,' he said. 'Didn't you know?'

* * *

Back in the Operations Room at Muharraq, navigators Mike Toft and John Nichol were finalising the plans for their own attack. It was still dark, but the 0730 take-off time was approaching. Their target was Ar Rumaylah airfield in the middle of the desert, about 50 miles west of Basra. As a Dispersed Operating Base a fraction north of the Kuwait border, its main function was to provide close air support to troops on the ground. Taking it out would mean the Iraqi Air Force had one less base from which to launch attacks against tanks and infantry when the coalition eventually invaded Kuwait. Mike Toft shared a look with his pilot Mark Paisey. *This is it; we're going to war.*[7] The pair had got to know each other well since another member of the Squadron was withdrawn from the deployment in November and Mark had stepped in as a late replacement.

Those moments before take-off are still imprinted on Paisey's mind. 'As we began the brief for the mission, the Group Captain walked in to see us. To this day, I can still hear the noise the metal legs of those orange plastic chairs made as they scraped along the floor when we all stood up. He talked to us about what was to come and ended by saying, "Extraordinary times require extraordinary men. You are all *in* the Royal Air Force, and today you *are* the Royal Air Force." His words really struck home.'[8] Mike Toft was also moved. 'Our time had come. The banter had ceased. My thoughts were with my eight-months pregnant wife and 2-year-old daughter back home. She would soon discover that war had broken out and her worrying would intensify.' He could not help wondering if he'd ever see his unborn child.

As a single man, John Nichol did not have to worry about dependants, but he was still more than a mite concerned. 'We were going on a low-level daylight raid. The first ever by a Tornado.' The bomber had been designed primarily to fly in darkness, through heavy cloud and through valleys and hills. Not in bright sunshine across a desert as flat as a billiard table. The earlier vision of hard-ened characters like Gordon Buckley and Paddy Teakle rocked by their experience was alarmingly fresh in his mind. Nichol could not shake off the gut-wrenching feeling that something momentous was about to happen.

That feeling showed no sign of abating as the intelligence briefer detailed the defences they would face in a few hours. He did not hold back. SA-3 and SA-6 missile sites covered Ar Rumaylah air-base, interspersed with numerous triple-A defences, including Iraqi troops armed with the latest Soviet-made handheld surface-to-air, heat-seeking missiles. In daylight, these would pose a serious threat, so it had been decided that flying straight over the runway for five long seconds dispensing the JP233 at 180ft was far too dangerous. Instead, each Tornado in the four-ship formation would use eight 1,000lb bombs to be 'thrown' in the loft manoeuvre from the safer distance of 3 miles out. The 32,000lb of explosives were to be aimed at two sets of Iraqi hardened aircraft shelters (HASs) at each end of the mile-and-a-half runway. The four aircraft would attack in a box-shaped formation, with the lead pair flying around a mile lat-erally apart and the next some fifteen seconds behind. They would be flying manually and visually for the entire sortie, testing their low-flying skills to the limit.

Like the mission that had just finished, the four-ship would head westwards from Muharraq, with a refuelling rendezvous in Saudi, then drop to low level before entering Iraq. Once sausage side, the route zigzagged across the desert in order to keep the enemy guess-ing as to their target. The small Tornado force would attack each HAS site shortly after 9.30am, a few minutes after twenty-four US Marine Corps F-18 Hornets had pummelled the SA-6 missile sites to the east of Ar Rumaylah.[9] Hopefully, this would take the edge off coming in from a flat desert framed against blue skies. And doing the loft manoeuvre in daylight did at least mean you could see your proximity to the ground more clearly in the recovery phase.

Their army Ground Liaison Officer (GLO) issued the mission

briefing, emphasising the emerging triple-A threat, then, with the same lyric sheet used ten hours earlier, they launched into the Squadron song to the tune of 'It's a Long Way to Tipperary'. John Nichol suddenly clammed up with emotion. 'There was a huge lump in my throat. Singing on exercise had been one thing, but now on the point of flying into heavily defended enemy territory, with the very real prospect of not coming back, it was entirely different. I might never see some of the men singing in that room again. Ever.'[10]

The waves of emotion surfaced for his pilot John Peters when he began 'sanitising' – removing all personal items that might give the enemy useful details of their families or personal lives if they were captured. Everything was taken from the aircrew, from lucky charms to photographs and credit cards. Removing the signet ring he'd received from his parents on his eighteenth birthday and then his wedding ring proved hardest of all. 'Thinking of Helen and the kids made me pause for a moment. Here was my life going into this little plastic bag, to be kept in case I was shot down. This was no longer make-believe; this was beginning to feel really serious.'

But it was the moment Nichol had been training for ever since he joined the RAF. 'I wanted to prove that I could do it. It was the most important day of my life. At the same time, I was only human, and the challenges seemed immense, almost insurmountable.' The need to succeed was heightened by the knowledge that people around the world were watching events unfold, scrutinising their every action. 'The expectations were massive, but the dominant pressure is the one you put on yourself. *I will not screw up. I will not let anyone down. I will be a success.*'

'Crew walking!' The announcement the ground crews had been waiting for.

Dawn was fast approaching as the eight airmen crossed the tarmac to their Tornados and carried out their final safety checks. As Mike Toft boarded to set up the navigation systems, Mark Paisey went through his fastidious scrutiny of the aircraft. Checking all around the airframe for anything out of the ordinary, levering the flaps and slats on the wings, then inspecting each 1,000lb bomb under the Tornado's belly, ensuring that all safety pins had been removed. He counted the red-flagged pins – double-checking – with the ground crew. Everything was in order, and Paisey climbed into the cockpit. The airfield was a hive of activity as the desert-pink Tornados were prepared for action. Formation leader Pablo Mason chatted with his ground crew as they made their own final checks. They were the backbone of every squadron and they cared for their aircraft like personal family heirlooms. Without the skill and dedication of the engineers, nothing would fly. 'Our ground crews were clearly nervous as we walked out to them in the half-light. Everything seemed tuned to perfection. I had walked around my aircraft and trusted her, and the men who took such loving care of her.'[11]

Beyond them, the slightly scorched jets that had just returned from war were already being prepared for Dave Waddington and Robbie Stewart's upcoming night-time operation.

* * *

First light over Baghdad revealed the consequences of Saddam Hussein's actions to the Iraqi population. Hundreds of dogs howling at the moonless sky had been the earliest hint of the potent force heading towards them; their ears pricking up at the high-pitched shriek that presaged falling bombs. Moments later the air-raid sirens had sent thousands scurrying to the shelters as the relentless barrage rained down on the capital. Emerging at dawn, the Iraqis had seen plumes of smoke by the dozen across the centre of Baghdad. The stench of burned buildings, electrical and oil fires hung in the air. The civilians crept back into their homes, fear and uncertainty fuelled by the knowledge that they were at war with the greatest military power ever known. And this was just the start. The bombing would go on until the question of Kuwait had been settled. But they kept any doubts to themselves, such was the pernicious nature of Saddam's regime and his secret police, the Mukhabarat. Few had the courage to argue against their leader's strident words. 'The great duel, the mother of all battles has begun,' Saddam declared on the early-morning broadcasts. 'The dawn of victory nears as this great showdown begins.'[12]

But dawn did not bring respite from the night-time rage. Formations of American, French and Saudi aircraft better suited to daytime fighting had been refuelling, ready to streak into Iraq at sunrise. Alongside RAF Jaguars and Tornados, the second wave was about to strike.

* * *

Amid light scattered cloud, the three Tornados of the Two Johns' formation joined up with the two Victor tankers which would shepherd them towards the Iraqi border. One Tornado had been left behind on the ground when its Sky Shadow electronic countermeasures pod malfunctioned, its crew bereft at missing their first op. The jets dropped from the tankers down into gin-clear skies and tore towards the Iraq border at around 100ft. Setting their armament switches to 'live', they streaked through the radar gap created by the Apache gunships that morning, turned east and, picking up speeds of 550mph, headed towards Ar Rumaylah.

Pablo now led the three-ship in a rough 'arrowhead formation'. Nichol and Peters followed, flying around a mile apart from Mike Toft and his pilot Mark Paisey. There was no use of autopilot or TFR; the pilots employed their ultra-low-level flying skills, tracking visually just above the desert, all in sight of each other. 'That's it then, no turning back now,' Nichol said from the back seat. 'After all the preparations and planning we were left to our own devices. From now on, the Iraqis would do everything they could to stop us. I did not really consider them the "enemy". I knew they were normal people with normal lives, with wives, children, lovers and friends. We were attacking their land and they were defending it.' In the broad expanse of the Western Desert, the three pilots instinctively took their aircraft down from 100ft to 50ft, even 30ft at times, speeding across the landscape at 9 miles a minute.

Mark Paisey, his right hand making the most minuscule of inputs on the control column, concentrated solely on the sand flashing past. Mike Toft could occasionally make out Pablo's jet tearing ahead and, looking left, Nichol and Peters roughly parallel with them. He couldn't help thinking how vulnerable they all were, canopies glinting and wings flashing in the bright sunshine. Their Tornado began bouncing hard as it was hit by the low-altitude turbulence caused by the sun beating down on the hardened desert floor. The formations of F-15 fighters, unseen high above them, provided some reassurance, ready as they were to be guided by the all-seeing eye of the AWACS onto any Iraqi aircraft attempting to repel the invaders. But still the crew could not help feeling exposed, with every Iraqi eye reporting their approach. Toft contemplated with some unease what might lie ahead. 'Heartbeats became closer together, the adrenaline pumped, and the fear of the unknown was soon to become the fear of the known. We felt exposed and very vulnerable, even at 50 feet. But we simply pressed on.'

'What the hell is that on the nose, Tofty?' Paisey asked abruptly.

Toft squinted into the haze. A large black patch that looked like an oil slick lay dead ahead. 'No idea – but it's not military.'

It mattered not; they were travelling so fast they were virtually on top of it. The 'slick' revealed itself to be a huge herd of goats shepherded by Bedouin tribesmen. As the jets tore along a few feet above their heads, the startled beasts stampeded in every direction.

Pablo Mason was relishing the rush of ultra-low-level flying, pushing the jet to 600mph around 30ft above the desert. 'I had never flown that low in my whole life. There was not much between the bottom of my jet and the ground. I could feel the rush of air through the space in between.'[13] Nichol and Peters could almost reach out and touch the faces of the Bedouin as the Tornados roared over their tented communities. It was a strange moment for Peters. 'Here we were, going to bomb the shit out of their country, and these people were looking up at us, close enough to spit.' A few minutes later, less friendly faces glared up at the three bomb-laden jets as they crossed the major north–south highway from Baghdad, only feet above a vast military convoy trundling southwards to take up defensive positions. Seeing the enemy so close suddenly made it all seem very real. The men below were there to kill them. And the reverse was also true.

'Okay. Quiet, boys,' Pablo said over the secure radio. 'Let's get to work.'

Adrenaline coursed through the airmen as the Tornados sped towards Ar Rumaylah airfield. The continued 'picture clear' calls from the American AWACS encouraged them to prepare for the daylight loft manoeuvre which would catapult their jets out of the relative safety of low level. Even though it was from 3 miles out, they would still be within range of SAMs and triple-A around the perimeter. Hopefully, the Americans were taking care of the SA-6 threat with the two dozen F-18 Hornets pummelling them hard. Hopefully.

Nichol and Peters' Tornado reached the 'Initial Point', or 'IP', a pre-selected ground feature marking the start of the target run. Peters knew that at 600mph they were just under a minute from the pull-up point, where the attack system would direct him into a steep climb. The main computer constantly fed his HUD with the aircraft's speed, height and time to the target. 'We were now flat out, at fifty feet, the desert looking close enough to touch, fizzing past like a speeded-up film.'[14] He increased speed, manoeuvring the jet further left and widening the space between them and Pablo Mason, still slightly forward and now a couple of miles away to their right, with Paisey and Toft close behind him. They would now be attacking within a matter of seconds of each other.[15]

Nichol checked the switches, preparing the aircraft for the moment the computer would direct the pull-up and calculate the exact release point to launch the bombs on their brief flight to the target. Peters made his stick-top 'live', exposing the weapon 'commit' button, and rechecked the arming and safety systems were all correctly set. Looking through the HUD, he could see all the information he required projected on the glass screen 'floating' in front of him. Their position and time on target were all good. The green, hair-thin vertical bomb-fall line and target bars showed precisely where their explosives would strike. The 'time to pull' clock was unwinding anti-clockwise. They were 8 miles out and forty-eight seconds to pull-up. Everything was in order.

Nichol was wrapped in his own routine, setting the computer into the attack profile, then head in the radar looking for the first 'offset', the topographical feature that updated the computer's navigation and aiming calculations. The three offsets were key to fixing the target exactly in space and time, relative to the aircraft, eliminating any navigational errors.[16] Once each was successfully marked it would mean the lofted bombs should land within a few metres of the target. Nichol easily found the first offset, a large metal radio mast, on the radar and marked it, clicking his hand controller to update the systems.

'Looking at offset two,' Nichol called, fixing a building halfway down the target run. 'Cancel your offset.'

'My offset is cancelled,' Peters calmly replied, thumbing the button. They had 5 miles to the pull-up point. Another thirty seconds.

The third offset was a corner of the huge metal fence the Iraqis had helpfully built around the airfield. The hard edge shone out from the radar display. Nichol marked it, giving the computer a final, precise update. It was now accurate to within a matter of feet. Peters' HUD display jumped slightly, bringing the target bars left to sit directly on where the HASs and taxiways lay unseen in the distance. He nudged the aircraft gently a few metres left to correct their track onto the updated position.

They were on time and on target.

Nichol could now see the objective clearly on radar and placed his marker in the centre of the taxiways. He then double-checked the settings for the eight 1,000lb bombs to be spread over the area in a devastating concussion of explosive power. There were no threats showing on the RHWR, and the Sky Shadow was functioning. A brief search of the burning blue skies outside the cockpit showed no enemy fighters ready to pounce.

All was set.

They were perfectly aligned for the final pull-up prior to bomb release.

Ten seconds to go.

* * *

Flying about 2 miles abeam and a few seconds ahead, Pablo began his loft manoeuvre against the hardened air shelters at the southern end of the runway. 'We were bang on target as I pressed the weapons release button, letting go of 8,000lbs of bombs. Dropping them had meant leaving the sanctuary of ultra-low level and now life started to get very interesting indeed.'[17] The Iraqi triple-A was onto them. It was daylight and the bombers presented ample targets. All hell broke loose. 'The sky suddenly changed as though someone was pulling a dark curtain across my eyes.' All around them the sky filled with exploding triple-A shells as Pablo threw the gunners off their aim by banking the Tornado hard to the right and south, and continuing the high-G turn until they were heading west, directly away from the target and back in the direction from which they had approached.

The blue horizon ahead of Peters and Nichol was abruptly torn by streaks of gunfire blazing upwards. Shells exploded around the cockpit in bursts of black and white smoke, sending shards of shrapnel spearing through the sky. Despite the maelstrom around them there was no noise inside the cockpit. John Peters had an unenviable grandstand view of the incoming threats. 'The buggers were shooting at us! Explosions were peppering up in continuous streams, right across the span of sky over the target. For every glowing tracer ball I could see, there were nine accompanying live gobbets of explosive-tipped lead that I couldn't. They looked terminally close. It was the first time we had been under fire and it was horrifying.' In the back seat, Nichol focused on the screens, the defensive aids and the switches he needed to press prior to attack, constantly firing out the metallic chaff fibres in case an enemy radar tried to lock onto them. He briefly glanced out the cockpit and spotted decoy flares spewing off Pablo's aircraft as their jet recovered from the attack. 'Happy with the target,' Nichol said, his voice calm. 'You're clear to commit.'

'Stick-top live,' Peters responded. 'Three, two, one. Pull!'

He hauled the control column into his stomach.

* * *

Flying a few seconds behind Pablo Mason, Mike Toft knew they needed to increase speed to power upwards while lugging 4 tonnes of bombs. 'We would need to use reheat which was a worry as it would provide an ideal target for any infra-red missiles out there. We made a wild guess when it would be most appropriate, the reheat kicked in and we were soon up around 630mph, ready for the pull-up. I took a quick squint at the radar and identified the aiming point.'

They were seconds away.

As they went through all the arming and firing sequences, Mike made sure all the switches were double- and triple-checked on the approach. 'This was definitely not the time to screw up as we exposed ourselves to the airfield defences.' Mark Paisey sent their Tornado soaring from 30ft into the storm. 'Out to my left I could see the decoy flares pumping out of John Nichol's jet then black puffs of smoke appeared in my peripheral vision as I concentrated on the instruments in front of me. Perhaps it was best to pretend to be in the simulator!'

Climbing through 1,300ft, the cigar-shaped green bombs were released, catapulting forwards by the jet's sharp upward trajectory. The 1,000-pounders reached the top of their gentle ballistic arc then fell to earth with increasing kinetic energy, quickly gathering speed to reach a terminal velocity that allowed them to drill several feet through concrete and tarmac. A split second later they detonated, sending an explosive ripple upwards that buckled tarmac and crippled concrete.[18]

Peters had also pulled the stick back and the Tornado's nose tipped towards the heavens. He jammed his thumb hard on the red weapons switch, and kept holding it down to launch the bombs onto the northern end of the airfield. Nichol had already begun to fire out decoy flares to confuse any incoming heat-seeking missiles.

'Committed!'

There was a pause.

Then another.

'Shit, shit, shit.'

Nothing was happening. The bombs were still glued to the Tornado's belly.

'I haven't got a package,' Peters yelled. 'I haven't got a package!'

His pilot's rising anxiety was impossible for Nichol to ignore. *But why the hell is he talking about a package?* The 'package' was the way the 1,000-pounders had been selected on the weapons system. He checked the panel indications, wondering what the hell was going on. *'Eight 1,000lb bombs at 80 metres' spacing ...'*

Peters realised the mistake he'd made in the turmoil of combat. 'I haven't got a *pull-up!*'

The words came out strangled, and Nichol well understood why. This was horrendous. The bombs weren't coming off. They had messed up. Horribly. 'A number of weapon selection switches set up the attack sequence, and you're meant to make a final selection on the system just before you enter the loft manoeuvre. I probably hadn't hit the final button, so the computer hadn't gone into full attack mode. It was stuck in approach – not final weapons release – profile. *One small button which I'd failed to press!* Perhaps something else had gone wrong? But despite years of intense training, I knew in my heart that I'd made a straightforward, terrible mistake.'

The cockpit was filled with cursing and swearing. Although only a couple of seconds had actually passed since the pull-up point, chaos was taking hold. As Peters had waited for the bombs to come off, the Tornado soared above 1,500ft, then higher. They were now perilously exposed. Peters banked hard to the left, almost inverting them in his attempt to get back to low level. He prayed the sudden drop in height would make them harder to hit. Burdened with nearly

4 tonnes of bombs on its belly, the Tornado made heavy weather of levelling out, and was heading fast towards the desert floor.

'Recover, recover! Recover!' Nichol yelled from the back seat.

'I'm trying to!' Peters shouted, now heading away from the target. Dismay, failure and fear were taking root inside the cockpit. 'Fucking hell! What a cock-up!'

'We can't fail. Let's re-attack!' Nichol was desperate not to fail on their first ever operation. Too desperate. 'I was compounding my initial error with another. You never, ever go around for a second attack. It's a cardinal rule. Every gunslinger on the ground would be ready for us, fingers on triggers, hammering the sky. But this was the worst feeling in our lives. We were going to be the only Tornado crew who had failed! Everyone in the eight-ship on Tallil had been successful. Everyone on our formation had released. Except us. It was a major, major issue. But I also knew it would be madness to re-attack. We were in a very unhealthy situation and it was descending into chaos, confusion and panic.'

'Bugger it!' Nichol said. 'We've got to dump the bombs.' It had just gone 9.30 on the first morning of the war. There would be other opportunities. He hit the bomb jettison button and the Tornado, instantly freed of its dead weight, lurched forwards and upwards while morale plummeted in the cockpit. 'Our efforts had failure written all over them. We were already beating ourselves up hard over what other people would say. Our greatest concern was not for our lives but for our reputations.'

* * *

'Check in! Check in!' Pablo's voice broke through to the fretting aircrew. After so much time over the airfield, they were now lagging far behind their formation leader and Toft and Paisey.

'We've had a problem . . .' Nichol tried to hide the disappointment in his voice.

'Don't worry about it. Just get home.'

Mike Toft detected the sweat and fear in Nichol's response

as Paisey pushed their now substantially lighter aircraft to maximum power.

Peters also poured on more power to get away, descending again to 30ft as the smoke from their colleagues' 16,000lb payload rose over Ar Rumaylah. A scan around the cockpit instruments indicated everything was in order as they made good their egress from the target area. A few miles on, he spotted a group of Iraqi soldiers next to what looked like a communication site. He banked hard, pulling the jet in a tight 4G turn, standing it on one wing to fly wide of the threat.

'Suddenly there was an almighty *whump!* and my teeth rattled. The Tornado jumped across the sky like a scalded cat.'

The stick went dead; warning sirens blared in their ears.

They'd been hit.

The right engine was on fire.

Nichol felt their jet being shoved violently sideways, like a car shunted by an express train at a level crossing. 'It almost flipped us over. One moment I was looking up at blue sky then, *bang,* the aircraft was tumbling like a sycamore leaf and I was looking *up* at brown sand. I was in a state-of-the-art £20 million jet, and a guy on the ground with a glorified pea-shooter had just nailed us.'

The huge, juddering force of the blast knocked the wind out of Peters. Gasping for air and hanging off the seat straps, he yelled: 'What the hell was that?'

They'd been struck by a handheld, heat-seeking missile which had homed in on their fuel-burning engines. There had been no warning on the RHWR. The missile, travelling at nearly twice the speed of the Tornado, had detonated inside the RB199, blasting shrapnel in every direction. But this supreme example of Rolls-Royce engineering was encased inside a titanium shell which, despite the 1.15kg of high-explosive that had torn it apart, might still contain the blaze until it could be extinguished. And they had another fully functioning engine. On full thrust, it was easily enough power to keep them flying safely.

But their aircraft was severely wounded. With the computerised fly-by-wire system destroyed, Peters was essentially left with his control column connected to the tailplanes by metal rods, little different from those used to pilot a Second World War Lancaster bomber. 'The fly-by-wire loss sent us tumbling, the stick falling dead in my hands, a terrifying feeling for a pilot. I was pushing the controls frantically, the Tornado falling out of the sky, the ground ballooning up sickeningly in my windshield.' Nichol looked on helplessly as they wobbled towards the deck, thankful for Peters' superlative flying skills. 'We nearly hit the ground and would have been killed instantly, but John managed to recover the aircraft and get hold of it, even though it was flying like a metal bedframe.'

Peters was struggling to keep them in controlled flight. The stick was giving him nothing. 'Prepare to eject! Prepare to eject!' he shouted. 'I can't hold it.'

'Don't you bloody well eject!' Nichol rasped. 'Just get hold of it!'

He wasn't ready to give up. The Saudi border was less than 100 miles away. Every metre they made south was another metre closer to the US Special Forces Search and Rescue teams in their Black Hawk helicopters. If they could make it to a reserve airfield just over the Saudi border, or at least eject over friendly territory, they still might get home.

The Tornado staggered drunkenly, then slowly steadied. Peters nursed the stick to gain some precious altitude. If he could get a grip of the stricken jet, they might be able to limp over the border, then back to the Sheraton, some cold beers and stories that would need little embellishment. His attention was abruptly diverted to the bank of red lights glowing brightly on the Central Warning Panel at his right knee. Their Tornado was telling them something was very badly wrong. Triple-A fire hammered up towards them and struck the right-hand Sidewinder air-to-air missile, igniting its propellant as it sat on its launcher beneath the wing. Nichol watched a ray of intense flame cutting up through the metal with the intensity of a welding torch. 'Our computer-controlled environment started falling apart. We were on fire. The fly-by-wire technology was down. The live ammunition we were carrying was in danger of igniting.

The Iraqis were laying into us with a vengeance and the Sidewinder was hard at work severing the wing. An item truly crucial for flight.'

He then looked behind the cockpit and uttered a garbled expletive. 'The back of the aircraft was ablaze and the tailfin had almost disappeared. The flames were about 3 feet away and marching steadily towards where I was sitting. The engine was still burning, we had catastrophic airframe failure and we were sitting in an aircraft full of fuel and ammunition. The Tornado was nanoseconds away from blowing itself and us to smithereens. This was it. We had to get out. I shouted "We're on fire!" to JP in the front seat.'

'I know we're on fire!' Peters said, still focused on keeping the jet airborne. He hadn't had time to turn his head.

'No!' Nichol yelled. 'We've got to get out of here. Look outside!'

Now Peters could see the giant orange fireball that was rampaging down the aircraft's spine towards them. Nichol made one last call to his formation. 'We're on fire. We have to get out!' He then selected the emergency frequency monitored by all aircraft and broadcast their call sign and position. Peters pulled back on the stick to climb the jet and give them the best chance of a safe ejection. As the inferno engulfed the wing and fuselage, he shouted, 'Prepare to eject, prepare to eject ... Three, two, one ... Eject! Eject!'

They pulled the ejection-seat handles between their legs simultaneously.

There was a faint mechanical click, but nothing seemed to happen.

Then, just one hundredth of a second later, everything moved very quickly indeed. The straps and harness tightened around Nichol's torso and limbs, pulling him firmly against the seat. Rockets fired, the Perspex cockpit canopy above their heads was jettisoned and a giant hand seemed to reach down and yank him out of the cockpit at thirty times the force of gravity, accelerating him upwards from 0 to around 200mph in a second. The cacophony of blasting rockets was drowned by the slipstream thudding into him at 400mph and ripping through his flying suit. He tumbled, over and over, before the seat initiated the launch of a small stabilising parachute, which stopped the spinning. There was a loud crack as the main parachute then deployed leaving Nichol suspended beneath its large and comforting canopy.

The whole process, from pulling the handle, had taken a second and a half.

'I'd been catapulted from an air-conditioned, computer-controlled environment, through flames and explosions, fear and confusion. A whiplash as the parachute opens, then silence, and I was floating down.'

As he hung onto his harness straps, Nichol scanned the vast expanse of enemy desert he was descending towards. In the distance, the billowing fireball of their Tornado plunged into the desert floor, throwing up a ball of flame, followed by a column of smoke which reached for the sky. 'I knew there was something I should remember about landing. I tried to collect my thoughts, still reeling from the intensity of the attack, being hit, the fire and bailing out. I had to be quick; the ground was fast approaching.' He unlatched the 20lb survival pack attached to his harness to give him a lighter landing and just had time to bring his feet and knees together before hitting the ground. 'I landed with a bang on my backside, and the impact drove the air from my diaphragm.' The column of smoke marking the Tornado's position seemed perilously close. Nichol stood and surveyed the featureless brown terrain. 'If ejecting makes you feel out of control, it's a picnic compared to the feeling of being behind the lines, deep in enemy territory.'

* * *

'Check in!' Pablo repeated the call. He hadn't heard Nichol's final transmission. 'Check in number two.'

No reply, just the white hiss of a silent radio.

Mike Toft listened in as their formation leader then reported the loss to the AWACS crew overhead. If they had ejected and AWACS picked up their position, there was a chance they could be picked up. 'But we all knew this was unlikely. It was early morning, daylight, and, like us, the combat search-and-rescue boys also preferred to operate in the relative safety of darkness.' Every minute took them another 10 miles away from their friends, and increased their sense of devastation as the two surviving Tornados flew back to the safety of the tankers waiting across the border. Reluctantly returning his armament switches to the 'safe' setting, the thought of abandoning his men in enemy territory was unbearable for Pablo Mason. 'We wanted to turn back to help, to do whatever we could to get our two boys home, but it was hopeless. There was nothing we could do to save them.'[19] After refuelling, they sadly set course for home.

'Apart from the routine system checks, Mark and I hardly spoke,' Mike Toft remembered. 'Our thoughts were with the buddies that we had left behind in Iraq. Had they managed to eject or had they gone down with the aircraft? There was no way of knowing.' After a four-hour mission, they landed at Muharraq, relieved to make it back alive. News of Nichol and Peters' failure to return had already reached the ground crew. 'They were really distraught and were clearly asking themselves the question, *Was it something to do with us?* We could only tell them it wouldn't have been a problem with the Tornado.' Mark Paisey, too, felt their devastation. 'The overriding image I still have is the ground crew simply staring at an empty parking spot where the Two Johns' Tornado should be, refusing to leave, hoping they might eventually limp home. Our ground crew were an integral part of the overall operation; we were a family and they took the loss personally.'

The aircrew walked slowly back to the hut to sign the jets in. The Squadron Warrant Officer recognised their dejection. 'Corporal,' he called to one of his engineers, 'chairs and tea for the officers.' The war had struck the Squadron to the core. The first RAF combat losses of the war and they were two of their own; a number of men were in tears. 'We were in pieces,' remembered Mike Toft. 'They were both colourful characters and at the heart of Squadron life. It was only bloody "Day One" and we'd already lost friends. Were they dead? How the hell was this all going to pan out?'

* * *

Back in London, the Prime Minister had already received the news of the night's events and the morning loss of a Tornado. He sat at his desk in Number Ten Downing Street and wrote a parliamentary address. A few hours later, he stood up before a packed House of Commons and was granted the Speaker's permission to make a statement.

'In the small hours of this morning, aircraft of the multinational force began attacks on military targets in Iraq . . . the action is continuing. Attacks have been directed at Iraq's military capability, in particular airfields, aircraft, missile sites, nuclear and chemical facilities.' The attacks had been successful and allied losses low. He paused. 'I regret to inform the House that one RAF Tornado from later raids is reported missing . . .'

For those with husbands, fathers and sons flying Tornados into battle, the final part of John Major's speech was lost in a fog of fear and worry. The rest of the nation heard him say that Britain had only gone to war after 'all peaceful means had failed', and in response to Saddam's intransigence. 'We have no quarrel with the people of Iraq,' the Prime Minister continued. 'We hope very much for a speedy end to hostilities.' His final words resonated with those viewers and listeners who had a serious stake in events. 'Most of all, our thoughts go to the men and women of our forces and their families who wait anxiously at home. They have our wholehearted support and our prayers for a safe return home.'[20]

Tange Stewart was one of those waiting anxiously at home as her navigator husband Robbie was preparing for his first mission. She was on her own at the family cottage in Lincolnshire as their children Kirsty and Scott were at boarding school. She had woken to the news that hostilities had begun and knew that the Tornados, and her husband, would be at the forefront of the action. Now she felt the first tremors of anxiety. Then came the Prime Minister's announcement. 'Suddenly it was all horrifyingly real – an RAF crew was missing. We had all discussed what might happen, but here was the reality writ large and it was horrendous. RAF Tornados were going down in action.' Television commentators had suggested that the aircrew might have ejected, and had gone on to discuss the possibility of them becoming prisoners of war. That scared Tange. 'We'd heard terms like that from the previous wartime generation, but it wasn't something any of us had given any real thought to. It was a terrifying prospect.'[21]

Kirsty Stewart had been woken at seven that morning in her dormitory at Stamford High School in Lincolnshire. Everyone had been hugely sympathetic to her since the beginning of the term; there were a lot of military children there, and they all knew her father was going to be close to the action. There were lots of questions about how she was feeling. 'It was a weird experience, which only served to increase my sense of apprehension. Up to then it had been a family experience, but now everyone knew what we might be facing.'[22] Shortly after the wake-up bell, the matron came in, as usual, to turn on the lights. Then she walked directly over to Kirsty's bunk bed, bent down and whispered into her ear: 'Kirsty, the war started last night.'

'It was all very surreal. I just went into classes as normal – chemistry, maths and English.' Later that day she heard about the missing Tornado. 'I knew then that things might get bad. The worst had happened. We had lost a Tornado. It was real, we were losing people, and it looked as though things were going to be as awful as we thought.'

As his daughter did her best to focus on her maths lesson, Robbie Stewart and his pilot Dave Waddington were hard at work in the Muharraq Operations Room, going over their own final calculations for their first attack. The 27 Squadron crews had arrived late morning and worked hard on the details for the raid later that night. Shaibah was an airfield south-west of Basra. It needed to be knocked out. A minute before they planned to do so, an American package of F-18 Hornets and other jets would take out an oil refinery about 4 miles away, creating enough confusion, it was hoped, for the four Tornados to unleash their JP233s undisturbed. As they pored over the maps, news came in that a Tornado had gone in with the loss of Peters and Nichol. Robbie was shocked. 'Perhaps I was naive, but I really thought that the Tornado at low level, especially TFR at night, was a pretty fabulous piece of kit. Those first ops were so well supported by defence-suppression aircraft attacking missile and radar sites, I thought we might be relatively safe. It appeared my confidence might have been misplaced.'

Dave Waddington felt his heartbeat quicken at the loss. 'Nichol and Peters had not made it home, so now we understood the nature of the task; there was a realistic threat that we might not come back.'

He took a moment, then continued preparing for his first combat sortie.

* * *

The last of the 15 Squadron wives had left Sonia Teakle's married quarters in RAF Laarbruch at 11am, after their ten-hour TV news-watching marathon. Still elated after Paddy telling her that he'd got through his first combat sortie unscathed, she went to bed, hoping to catch an hour's rest. But sleep eluded her, so she turned on the TV only to be confronted by the news that a Tornado had gone missing. Her heart began thumping as she got up and pulled the curtains aside. She saw the Station Commander's car pulling up outside Helen Peters' house across the road. 'That could only mean one thing. The Station Commander calls in full uniform for one reason only. I knew then who was missing.'[23]

The Station Commander was accompanied by the 15 Squadron Boss's wife, Maggie Broadbent. They knocked at Helen Peters' door. She knew what was coming: 'It was very bad news. Seeing them there, I immediately thought the boys were dead because that was what the arrival of the Station Commander usually meant.'[24] Helen froze as she was told that her husband was missing in action. Seeing her shock, Maggie Broadbent placed a hand on her shoulder. 'John's aircraft has failed to return. That's all we know, Helen.'

Sonia Teakle left it a few moments before crossing the street to comfort her friend. They were all fighting this war together. The television and kettle went back on. More cups of tea were called for. She also knew it would only be a matter of time before her and Paddy's young daughter Kimberly heard the news. She sat her down and delivered it herself. 'You know Mr Peters and John Nichol?' The little girl nodded. The Two Johns were at the heart of the Squadron's social activities.

'Their Tornado has crashed.'

'Are they dead?' Kimberly asked.

'I don't know. They probably managed to get out. We just have to wait and see.'

'But what about my daddy? Could something like that happen to him?'

'Of course it could,' Sonia replied. 'But we must hope it won't.'

CHAPTER SIX

'MY GOD, WE'VE LOST ANOTHER ONE'

17 JANUARY, AFTERNOON–18 JANUARY, MORNING

The only landmarks in the empty desert were the black smoke rising from the downed Tornado a mile away, and the billowing white and orange parachutes. John Nichol took off his helmet, rubbed his eyes and got to his feet, grateful that, bar a stiff back and throbbing knee, he'd suffered minimal injuries after being rocketed out of a fighter-bomber travelling at 400mph a few hundred feet above the ground. He walked towards his friend John Peters, sprawled 100 yards away.

'You look bloody messy,' he said helpfully. His pilot's film star looks had taken a beating. Blood poured from a cut above his left eye.

'What are we going to do now?' Peters replied groggily.

'I don't want to worry you,' Nichol said. 'But we're in Iraq! Can you believe it?'[1]

For a moment Peters just looked at him, absorbing the curious nature of their situation. A few hours earlier, they had been among friends in the bustle of Muharraq airbase. Just a few minutes ago they had been in a multimillion-pound Tornado, ready to tick off their first combat mission. The idea of parachuting into enemy territory that morning had been a remote one. Now they were right in the middle of it, in daylight, many miles from friendly lines, each armed solely with a small pistol and eighteen rounds of ammunition. Nichol chuckled, then they both started laughing hysterically. 'Suddenly it all seemed desperately funny. We were struck by the absurdity of it all and once we had started laughing, it was difficult to stop.'

'Let's get out of here,' Nichol suggested as the feeling of merriment subsided. Their downed-aircrew combat survival drills kicked in. Nichol made a brief transmission on his Personal Locator Beacon to say they were both down but alive, and to give their bearing and distance from a pre-briefed 'search-and-rescue point'. If rescue teams were in the area, there was the faintest chance they might come running. They needed key items from the bright yellow fibreglass survival box attached to their life jackets. But getting to their water, food and extra clothing was far from straightforward. 'The way everything was packed meant we had to inflate the dinghies to get the haversacks out. We watched helplessly as the bright orange inflatables careered out of the packs. We could hardly have been more conspicuous if we'd had a Royal Marine band playing!'

After stabbing the emergency dinghies with Peters' Swiss Army penknife, they set off south, leaving behind the glaring evidence of their arrival scattered across the sand. There was nowhere to conceal them and no time to bury the equipment. They needed to run, to get away from the immediate area; any onlooker would already have seen the jet go in. The good news was Peters' status as a regular half-marathon runner; the bad was that he had torn his knee ligaments on ejection and was hobbling painfully. With haversacks on their backs and Walther pistols loaded with nine-round clips, the two hurried away from the landing site as quickly as they could. Even tramping through hot, treacle-like sand didn't completely drain Nichol of hope. 'Perhaps if we moved fast enough away from the billowing pyre, we might get lucky. It was worth a try; we certainly couldn't simply give in and wait for circumstances to overtake us!'

After a few steps, he stopped. Although they had both been 'sanitised' for sensitive and personal items before take-off, it dawned on him to double-check. He still had his route map in a pocket with the combat search-and-rescue reference points clearly marked. If the enemy found those, it could put any rescue teams in real danger. Nichol tore up the map and, as downed airmen had done in many preceding wars, stuffed it into his mouth and began chewing. The sight of his navigator eating a map was clearly a source of amusement for Peters who snorted with laughter again. They set off once more across the barren landscape.

It was approaching midday and they had been walking for more than an hour when Nichol abruptly halted again. 'I suddenly got a bad feeling. We both had this sensation down the backs of our necks that we were being watched. I could feel my scalp prickling.' Instinctively they crouched as they walked, quickening their pace. A few minutes later, the unmistakable sound of an engine cut through the desert silence. They dropped to their bellies, leopard-crawling to a dip in the sand. Peeking through a parched bush, Nichol saw movement. 'It was definitely people coming our way. We took out our pistols. I checked that we both had a round up the spout. A vehicle moved closer; clanking through the desert. Then the real horror, a group of figures shimmered on the horizon, advancing towards us.'

A red pickup truck drove past them, less than half a mile away. Then a volley of shots rang out. *What are they shooting at? Us?* Rounds zipped overhead. It was as if the searchers were trying to flush them out like game birds. Nichol's heart rate quickened. 'I remained perfectly still, my chest hammering, praying the line would turn and move away. Then there was a loud yell. We'd been spotted.'

It was the first time Nichol and Peters had experienced hostile fire outside the cockpit. The Tornado was sealed off from the outside world; even in the heaviest of triple-A, only their eyes registered the threat. It was very different on the ground. 'I'd never been shot at like this; it was very personal and there is nothing more frightening. My guts were churning. They had automatic rifles, AK-47s, the guerrilla's friend. Being torn open by one of those was not the way I wanted to go. The noise was unbelievable, endless whip cracks, a deafening *crack! crack! crack!* The clump of twigs we were lying behind was 18 inches high, but bullets were buzzing through it, swarming angrily over our heads, kicking up jets of sand around our position.' Then AK-47 rounds began puckering the ground close to Nichol's head. 'In my fear I began digging a shallow grave with my elbows, knees and face, driving my whole body down into the sand, the grains in my mouth and nose. Anything, anything to get down below the bullets, to avoid that final, shattering impact.'

A few weeks before deploying, relaxing over a beer at John and Helen Peters' comfortable home at RAF Laarbruch, the two friends had discussed – more seriously than they were prepared to admit – committing suicide rather than being captured and tortured to death. 'It all came flashing back to me,' Nichol said. 'We had joked about capture, about suicide. Saddam had promised to tear any downed aircrew "limb from limb" and we all knew the brutal way they had treated their own people. But did we really want to kill ourselves? Wouldn't that, too, amount to failure, albeit of a rather different kind? I looked at John. Now it came right down to it, could I shoot him before shooting myself? I didn't much fancy killing him. It seemed absurd; we had known each other for a long time. The moment was here – could I do it?'

Nichol turned to Peters. 'Look,' he said. 'They are going to come and get us anyway, shall we go out with a bang?

'I was suggesting we charge towards them, try to take a few of them with us before being killed ourselves; making a fight of it. Why not? It looked certain we were about to be killed anyway.'

Still dazed, Peters looked at the pistol Nichol waved towards the enemy. 'No,' he said, with surprising warmth in his voice. 'There's always hope.'

Nichol knew he was right. 'The odds were way too heavily

stacked against us. There were at least twelve of them and they had automatic rifles. There were two of us with popguns, one injured. All we could have done was stand up and loose off a couple of rounds. In return they would have split our bellies open with their AKs.' They both stood, arms raised, then immediately dropped to their bellies as gunfire erupted around them again. 'They were charging towards us, screaming, shooting wildly less than a hundred yards away. Hearts thumping, ears pounding, we tensed ourselves for the kill. This was it.'

Then the firing stopped.

Very slowly, the airmen hauled themselves upright once more, hands in the air. Another fusillade tore up the desert floor around their feet. 'They had let loose again! It was stupid, but made me realise they were as scared of us as we were of them.' Everything went quiet, apart from an Iraqi officer firing his pistol into the air. He shouted repeatedly in English, 'No, no, no, stop, give yourself up! It's okay . . . up, up, up!'

Alongside him were three Bedouin trackers, including a boy aged about twelve, and a section of Iraqi Air Force personnel. 'As they got to us we expected the worst. I was rock-taut, waiting for another hail of bullets. We were both trembling.' The older, bearded Bedouin shouted dementedly at Nichol, punching him in the face. The Iraqi officer intervened again. 'We were very lucky he was there. Without him it was clear as day they would have killed us on the spot. He was shouting at them continuously in Arabic, at the top of his voice, still very worried they might kill us.'

The fliers were stripped of all their possessions, including, to the Bedouin's delight, the £1,000 tubes of gold sovereigns. The two prisoners then had their hands tied behind their backs and were prodded at gunpoint into the rear of the pickup truck. As they drove off, the young Bedouin boy brandished one of their aircrew pistols, grinned gleefully at Nichol, and drew his finger across his throat.

* * *

In the safety of his Saudi airbase, John Nichol's flatmate and fellow Tornado navigator Dave Bellamy rolled out of bed, trying to shake off the haze of nearly five hours of temazepam-induced sleep. It was approaching lunchtime at Tabuk. He had not long returned from his own first combat sortie, and his emotions were about to be challenged again.

The Detachment Commander called the aircrew into a meeting and announced that a Tornado had gone down, with the crew missing in action. He solemnly read out the names: 'John Peters and John Nichol.'[2] There was no news about whether they had ejected or been killed but everyone thought the worst. Bellamy was devastated. 'I said nothing and left the room to help plan another mission.' One of his formation, knowing Nichol was a good friend of Bellamy, came to offer his sympathies. 'I told him, as a favour, not to mention John Nichol's apparent death in my presence. I didn't want to have to deal with the extra emotion while we were already in the midst of a maelstrom. But I – unlike some of the others – would not give up hope that John had got out of his Tornado alive.'[3]

Although Bellamy was not required that night, many of his friends would be. His colleagues Squadron Leader Pete Batson and their cheerful Squadron Boss, Wing Commander Mike Heath, were preparing for their first outing. Dusk was approaching when Batson and Heath gathered the crews of their eight-ship for the briefing. The RAF was going in to strike Al Asad airbase again, following the same route as Dave Bellamy's formation a few hours earlier, targeting the home of dozens of Iraqi aircraft, including the French-made Mirage fighters. They already knew from Bellamy and the others about the heavy groundfire. The intelligence update only emphasised the growing and unexpected triple-A threat, particularly to those flying low level.

Batson had been a frontline pilot flying Vulcan nuclear bombers and Tornados since 1978, and although this was his first combat mission, he wasn't experiencing any nerves. 'I was going to do something that I had always trained for. Although it was to be in Iraq and not Eastern Europe, the only real difference between this flight and the thousands of training sorties I'd completed was that this time someone would be shooting back with heavy triple-A.[4]

Batson and his colleagues would be part of the ongoing and relentless pummelling of Iraqi forces before the land invasion required to liberate occupied Kuwait. The air campaign was not yet twenty-four hours old, yet raids had been continuous since the first airstrikes at 2am – part of General Norman Schwarzkopf's air plan to knock out the Iraqi Air Force so there would be no threat to his fliers and ground troops from above. As part of the unremitting second wave of attacks, hundreds of aircraft were flying from dawn to dusk, and beyond. They were conducting a similar campaign to that of the Germans in 1940 – knocking out radar and communication sites while battering the air defences, airfields and air force itself into total submission. During the Battle of Britain, the Luftwaffe had failed in its mission to dominate the skies. Fifty years later, Norman Schwarzkopf was determined his air forces would prevail. And he was not holding back. Since dawn that 17 January, his F-14 Tomcats equipped with TARPS – Tactical Air Reconnaissance Pod System – had been surveying the targets hit during the night.[5] They came back with hundreds of pictures of the extensive damage caused during the first wave. But it was just the opening phase of Schwarzkopf's plan.

Batson and Heath at Tabuk in Saudi Arabia, and Robbie Stewart and his pilot David Waddington at Muharraq in Bahrain were part of that ongoing wave of destruction. Readying themselves for their first mission, Robbie and Dave went over the defensive measures they could use against groundfire threats. They had dozens of flares they could deploy as decoys for heat-seeking missiles, bundles of chaff to confuse radar guidance, plus the Sky Shadow radar-jamming system and the heavy punch of the US jets going in before them. Dave had previously been convinced the American-provided SEAD – Suppression of Enemy Air Defences – was sufficient, but now he had his doubts.

'It quickly became clear that we were in a very real fight. Before, I was not really concerned about our own attrition, but the loss of a Tornado really brought home the dangers we faced. Personally, I compartmentalised it; put it out of my mind and kept my focus on our own mission. There was nothing else to be done. You can't just walk away and say, "This is too dangerous; I'm not doing it any more." There was also a naivety of youth. You feel invincible, and, like our Second World War RAF forebears who flew the wartime bombers, you just think, *It will never happen to me.*'

Robbie had previously hoped that the Tornado force might survive the war unscathed. But that had changed within a matter of hours. 'It was a real wake-up call to hear a Tornado had gone down. It focused our minds on the reality as we prepared for our turn to continue the attack.' He collected the navigation tapes with the routing and target information recorded for the Tornado's computer, and headed off to the dining room. Dusk was settling over Bahrain as he walked alongside Wing Commander Nigel Elsdon, who had taken over 27 Squadron after Bill Green's death in August during a practice night-time loft manoeuvre.

Elsdon had less Tornado experience, but shared his predecessor's talent for calm leadership, as his immense RAF pedigree had promised. His grandfather had flown in the First World War and his father had become a Spitfire ace at the height of the Battle of Britain. 'I bet you didn't expect this a few months ago?'[6] Robbie mused as they walked into the dining tent. Elsdon smiled in acknowledgement as his avuncular, 42-year-old navigator joined them. Max Collier had smiling eyes, a fine quiff of dark hair, and two decades of flying experience. A degree of disquiet blunted Robbie's appetite, so he quickly finished his supper and left Nigel and Max talking quietly. Darkness had fallen as he and Waddington strode out to F for Foxtrot. They both felt a mixture of emotions. 'Walking out to the aircraft for that first sortie was incredible,' Waddington recalled. 'No one wants to visit death and destruction on anyone, but this was what we had always trained for, and it was going to be my ultimate professional test as a Tornado pilot.'[7]

Robbie was ready too. 'As I strapped in, ready to go, all apprehensions were forced out of my mind – we were going to work as normal. You became part of the aircraft, part of the machinery of war. You turn off any fears and worries.'

* * *

As Waddington and Stewart readied their Tornado for battle, John Nichol and John Peters' war in the air was already over. They were bundled into captivity at gunpoint, preparing for a test of their own inner strength and resolve. *These people are not going to be happy to see us*, Nichol knew. 'How would *our* ground crew treat an *Iraqi* pilot who had just dropped an awful lot of high explosive on them and killed their mates?'

The impressive array of Iraqi anti-aircraft equipment became even more hideously apparent as they were driven to a nearby airfield. 'There was triple-A everywhere. Quite literally hundreds of gun emplacements. It was staggering. There was a French-made Roland radar-guided SAM system, gun-pits with quadruple-barrelled cannons and tanks with anti-aircraft guns mounted on their turrets, alongside infantry armed with handheld missiles. Nobody on the intelligence side had foreseen this amount of triple-A, or any Roland missiles! Or if they had, we had certainly not been briefed about it. Its sheer weight of numbers meant that somebody was always going to get lucky at our expense.'[8]

The prisoners were driven around the base to great fanfare. 'Our captors paraded us, tooting and waving as if we were some sort of travelling sideshow. As they dragged us out of the vehicle we saw a huge crowd standing around waiting for us. There was loathing in their eyes, a burning intense glare of pure hatred.' Nichol remembered stories of captured aircrew in Vietnam being tortured to death and of RAF men bailing out over Germany being bludgeoned with spades. It was only when they were handed over to the officers in charge that things began to calm down. Many Iraqis had trained in Britain and spoke good English, and, with traditional Arab courtesy, they treated the pair as if they were visiting fellow fliers. They were shocked at the injury to Peters' eye. 'Who hurt you? Who hit you?' one pilot asked, assuming he had been beaten up.

Maintaining their interrogation procedures, the Two Johns did not respond. When the air-raid sirens sounded, the officers hurried them down to an underground bunker where they were introduced to the Base Commander, who proudly sported the ubiquitous Saddam moustache. 'How are they treating you? Do you want anything? Coffee?'

Again, the pair did not respond.

'Don't worry. You are safe now. Would you like some water?'

It was mid-afternoon. They had been shot down at 9.32am and were parched. Both nodded. The Iraqis brought in plates of dates, cake and oranges along with the water. Despite their hunger, Nichol and Peters refused any food, fearing it might be drugged. Moments later they heard bombs exploding in the distance. As soon as the raid ended, they were jostled into another vehicle which headed along a highway signposted to Baghdad. An hour later, they pulled into a site with a giant image of Saddam Hussein at its entrance. *This is where the fun starts*, Nichol thought as their captors became more aggressive. 'They kept banging our heads with rifles to keep them down, presumably so that we wouldn't see any aircraft or the layout of the base.' They were led down into another bunker and blindfolded. 'The atmosphere had suddenly become a lot less friendly. They kept poking us with the guns.' The questioning was more menacing, even though the interrogators were still Iraqi Air Force. 'What did you fly? Where are you from? Which base?'

The prisoners simply responded with their name, rank and number.

'You must answer our questions now or we will have to send you to the nasty people!'

Both of them knew they were referring to Saddam's Mukhabarat security service thugs. The prospect was not a pleasant one, and the outcome certain.

'We are all pilots together,' the Iraqi airmen persisted. 'Although we are at war, we have the same job to do. Talk to us, it will be better for you.'

Still they remained silent.

'If you do not tell us we will send you to Baghdad. They will hit you in Baghdad, they will put you on television, you will not like it.' That immediately struck an uncomfortable note for Nichol. 'Did that mean we were going to be paraded for propaganda purposes? Or would we be held as "human shield" hostages at a high-value target and displayed to reduce the probability of an air raid?' Saddam had no boundaries when it came to human rights. Still they remained silent. Now blindfolded and handcuffed, the pair were bundled into a station wagon and driven north for many hours, finally arriving in Baghdad.

'As the main gate of a third airfield swam up out of the inky desert blackness, there was a sudden flash of light, brilliant even through the crepe blindfold, followed by a tremendous explosion that shook the car,' Nichol recalled. 'The earth erupted around our ears, debris spattering down on the roof.' They were experiencing first hand Schwarzkopf's plan to totally destroy Iraqi military capability. Nichol could make out images in the gap under his blindfold, and in a break between bombs the station wagon sped through the gates and parked next to a concrete blast wall.

He could already hear the next wave of aircraft coming in. 'The bombs rippled across the ground, creeping towards us, crump after terrifying crump.' They were momentarily grateful to be hustled into a bunker. But seconds later, 'The noise curved across space to meet us, winding up to a furious high-pitched whistle, louder and louder as it scythed in. Everybody in the room could tell it was going to be a direct hit. Everything went deathly quiet. Then the bomb hit with a shattering roar.'

Peters and Nichol dived to the floor as the roof fell in and furniture went flying amid great clouds of dust. They could both feel the atmosphere of hostility and aggression grow. The Iraqis had in their midst two of the very enemy who were currently bringing death and destruction to their land and people. They were hauled to their feet. The barked words, the shoving; the abrupt orders increased. Nichol heard Peters being dragged out and he was alone with the guards. The room grew silent. No questions were asked. 'There was a horrible presence in the room, an aura of hatred. I could smell the sharp body odour of the surrounding guards and I could feel their enmity. I sensed a gauntlet of hostility – silent, brooding, expectant savouring of my helplessness. It was time. There was a sudden rush and they fell on me.'

* * *

If the two RAF prisoners were taking a pummelling in Baghdad, it was nothing compared to the hammering that was about to descend across Iraq for a second night. Nichol and Peters had experienced just one bombardment of the hundreds that were going in, with sorties eventually ramping up from 2,000 to 3,000 a day; a bombing raid every few minutes.[9] 'The vast majority of us thought nothing would ever equal the air power of day one,' one RAF navigator said. 'Well, it did – from day two through to day 40! If anything, it got more and more. You couldn't fly for 20 seconds without seeing at least another dozen airplanes flying past you.'[10] Some had hoped that the massive first day of airstrikes would make Saddam Hussein realise he had no hope of winning, and back down with some honour, and his military infrastructure intact. 'I thought we'd all go in on the first night, hit him for six, and he'd realise he'd bitten off more than he could chew and stop the war,' recalled Wing Commander Jerry Witts, the Tornado Commander at Dhahran airbase.

The losses were already stacking up for Saddam on the first day, with eight Iraqi fighters downed in air-to-air combat, mostly with the USAF's powerful F-15 Eagles.[11] But Saddam remained defiant, which meant Dave Waddington and Robbie Stewart's attack on Shaibah airbase would go ahead as planned. 'Time on target' was early evening, 7.30pm local time. The formation would strike after a brisk sixty-minute run, heading north from Bahrain, up through the Gulf. Shaibah was south-west of Basra and a few hundred miles south of where Nichol and Peters were being held. After taking off, all four Tornados rendezvoused with the tanker, then slipped down to low level above the warm, shallow waters of the Gulf. They headed up between the shores of Kuwait and Iran, the shortest way from Bahrain into Iraq. Moments later, the smooth ride through the darkness on TFR and autopilot was interrupted by a stream of light puncturing the sky ahead. 'Got some triple-A going out to the right,' Waddington called to Stewart in the back seat. 'I was amazed at how calm I was, as I'd never seen anything like it! It was incredible, there was so much that I was picking a route through, slaloming the aircraft at 200ft between the streaks of gunfire using the heading control dial on the autopilot. A bit like a video game.'[12]

'Speed's good at four-seven-zero. Height good, 200. Fuel fine,' Robbie said from the back seat. Few words were wasted; unlike some other crews, they kept any cockpit chat to the bare minimum. Robbie looked up from his instruments. 'The triple-A was snaking skywards, trying to hit the F-18s and A-6s which were wreaking havoc on the missile sites. You could see the odd surface-to-air missile taking off in the distance and arcing into the sky. I glanced to the port side as we swept smoothly past a triple-A site 50 yards away and could make out a moving car with its headlights on.'

Dave continued to manoeuvre the aircraft around the massed triple-A which almost had a celebratory quality, sparkling like a firework display, but one which they both knew, given Nichol and Peters' presumed capture, could have a deadly outcome. 'Left three-two-zero,' Robbie called. Dave turned the aircraft slightly to port, registering their speed at 535mph. The silence in the cockpit was punctuated by the gentle background whine of electronics and the odd 'bip-bip' made by the new HaveQuick secure radios. As they crossed from Kuwait into Iraq, Robbie could see that 200 feet below, life seemed to be going on as normal. 'It was truly surreal; we were at war and I was looking down at people on the ground as we flashed by. I actually saw one guy standing half out of his car, resting on the open door looking up at the noise of the aircraft above.'

They began the attack run, one minute out. Right on cue the

night sky to their right erupted in bright orange flames, lighting up the moonless sky. The Americans had struck home on the oil refinery in devastating fashion. 'Triple-A off to the right, just coming left now,' Dave said. The Tornado had turned onto its final approach and on a direct bearing towards the rising groundfire. 'Height good. All switches confirmed live. Three seconds from committing.'

* * *

As the Muharraq Tornados began their attack on Shaibah, Peter Batson made small talk with his Boss Mike Heath before take-off from Tabuk. 'It felt like one of our training sorties rather than the start of a war mission.'

The eight Tornados, four from 20 Squadron and four from 16 Squadron, flew to the tanker rendezvous just inside the border, then descended to low level, narrowly avoiding a flight of helicopters, fortunately a little lower and with their lights still on, heading towards Iraq on their own mission. As they crossed 'sausage side', Batson saw what he presumed was a flaming aircraft wreckage with Special Forces helicopters circling above it, firing at targets on the ground. *Perhaps a dramatic search-and-rescue mission for downed aircrew?*

As they headed west towards Al Asad airfield, something odd began to happen every time the formation crossed a highway. 'A spotlight positioned on the road would spark up. Not at us, but straight into the sky. We just couldn't understand why these searchlights were pointing upwards in the middle of the desert as we flew over.' In fact, the Iraqis had developed a simple but effective early-warning system that did not rely on the radars or electronics which were attracting hostile fire. Soldiers had been stationed at regular points across the network of desert roads, and ordered to switch on the lights whenever an aircraft passed low overhead. It had an unnerving effect on those going into battle. 'They were well spaced, giving a beam to our left and right, forming a surreal corridor; columns of light marking our progress into Iraq. It was a very basic, but very effective alert for the Iraqi gunners awaiting us!'

* * *

Dave and Robbie's Tornado heading to Shaibah was treated to a different welcome. Streams of yellow and white tracer from multiple gun systems around the airfield shot up to greet them as their formation closed on the target. Waddington took the aircraft from TFR autopilot into manual control. 'The triple-A formed a bright dome of fire; we were heading straight towards this incredible curtain of exploding lead bracketed with darkness on either side. Rationally we wanted to turn away from it, but the job was to deliver the weapons on target. I didn't say anything to Robbie, but I certainly thought, *How the hell will we get through this?*' Robbie heard the JP233 spew out its deadly contents as they crossed the runway. 'It fired like a Mauser cannon with a rapid staccato. You could hear the 57lb cratering munitions eject from the canisters then all the anti-personnel bomblets exploding out.'

'The JP233 sounded like a machine gun going off under my backside,' Dave said, 'like driving at great speed over a cobbled road.' With the weapons gone they made a hard turn 90 degrees north out of the target area. Some of the intense pressure fell away. 'I said to Robbie, "Did you see that!" It was an amazing experience. We weren't scared because we were too busy but I thought, *My God, have we just done that?*'

All four Tornados made it through the maelstrom and began their race home.

Moments later, out to Dave's left, a huge fireball erupted and spread across the desert, like a detonating bomb.

A shout came over the radio, 'Aircraft down!'

Before Dave could properly react, the tell-tale white streak of a missile leapt up towards them. 'SAM!' he yelled, immediately throttling back while simultaneously pulling a hard left turn to break any missile lock.[13] 'We were flying at just 200 feet, in total darkness, no NVGs – it was an incredibly dangerous manoeuvre.'

It was about to get a lot more dangerous. Up ahead, the formation leader also spotted another missile hunting his own jet. He broke hard right. Both Tornados were now curving in towards each other, just a few hundred feet above ground, travelling at a combined speed of almost 1,200mph in the void. Dave's aircraft suddenly bumped and bounced in heavy turbulence. It was the formation leader's Tornado hurtling unseen over their cockpit. 'We just crossed in the dark, totally blind, and had no idea how close we came to collision. It was quite disconcerting.'

As they headed to safety the formation leader called on the radio to the number three aircraft, call sign 'Charlie', crewed by the new Squadron Boss Nigel Elsdon and his navigator Max Collier:

'Charlie, are you with us?'

Silence.

'Charlie are you with us . . .?'

The calls went unanswered.

As they crossed the border and climbed towards the waiting tankers, Robbie radioed the AWACS operator for clarification. 'Can you see three or four aircraft?'

After a brief pause to check his screens, the American answered. 'There are only three.'

'The awful truth began to sink in. *My God, we've just lost another one.*'

* * *

Another Tornado had gone down, but the raids pressed on. Four hundred miles to the north-west of where Elsdon and Collier had crashed, the eight aircraft led by Pete Batson and Mike Heath were undertaking their own low-level night-time attack at Al Asad airbase. Batson lined up for the bombing run. He was the first in the stream, hoping that they might be able to get in and out before the Iraqis knew they were there. Speed was of the essence. 'The closer we got to the target the faster we went, progressing up to about 500 knots [575mph] and needing small bursts of reheat to overcome the drag effect of the JP233.' They were about 8 miles out when his attention was drawn to an astonishing sight on the horizon.

He squinted to double-check what was coming out of the darkness ahead. And no, his mind wasn't playing tricks. 'Every single airfield light was on. It was like being back home at RAF Laarbruch on a busy night of flying training. The runway lights, airfield approach lights, taxiway lights, everything, the whole place was lit up.'

'We can't be going there . . .' Mike Heath said from the back seat.

But they were.

Batson did another double-take. An aircraft was flying around the airbase at about 1,000ft doing practice approaches in what appeared to be night-time training. 'It was something we had all done many times before, just not in the middle of a war. The aircraft had its red anti-collision lights flashing and, because we were so low, we were looking up at it. I really couldn't believe what I was seeing.' They were one minute away from the target. 'Mike and I rapidly discussed the threat it could be to the rest of our formation. We didn't know what it was, as we couldn't identify the type, but it could pose a very real threat if armed with missiles – so I attempted to lock my own air-to-air missile onto it, but no reassuring growl came back.' For some reason his missiles had failed to lock on. But by selecting the air-to-air combat option when they were in ground-attack mode, Batson had now cancelled the carefully crafted attack profile. 'That was a bit of a shocker. We were now about thirty seconds out with no weapon steering in the HUD.'

The Iraqis' searchlight warning system must have worked. The Tornado glittered in the bright white light of the enemy shells erupting around them. Red and orange darts speared upwards, seeking its soft belly. But the cockpit remained strangely remote from the incoming threat for these newcomers to war. 'It was totally surreal to see all the exploding, flashing light around us, but all in relative silence.' Batson now had no choice but to carry out the attack run himself, by hitting the pilot weapon aiming 'Target of Opportunity' switch. 'I now had complete control of the weapons system. Aiming wasn't going to be a problem as, with the airfield lights still on, I could see the runway quite clearly. I manually manoeuvred the aircraft to ensure the JP233 munitions would spread over it.'

Then another challenge presented itself.

'Out of the corner of my eye I spotted the aircraft that had been in the circuit, rolling down to land on the runway we were targeting.' Batson quickly brought it within the target markers in his HUD, and seconds later the JP233 delivered its cocktail of anti-personnel mines and cratering devices which detonated across both the runway and the Iraqi jet. 'Many years later, I would think back to my actions that night, but in that moment all I was thinking was that it was an enemy aircraft and at any point, now or in the future, it could pose a threat to my own forces.'[14] In the centre of the airfield the triple-A abruptly stopped. 'That moment of calm in the midst of the inferno is seared in my mind. But we still had to get out the other side and two seconds later we were back in the middle of it all!'

A missile launched dead ahead of them. With very little room for error so low to the ground, Batson hauled the Tornado into a violent turn. 'At this point, I was flying manually at about 150ft in a hard manoeuvre to the left. The missile disappeared so I returned to track and we exited the target area at high speed and raced for the border.' It had been a chaotic few minutes for a first wartime operation. 'I plugged the TFR back in and let it take control for a moment as we headed to safety. At last, I could draw a breath. Our gaggle set track to leave Iraqi airspace. Crossing the border I set the armament switches to safe and our quietly ecstatic formation climbed to medium level. I checked them in on the radio.'

All aircraft responded.

* * *

It was a very different atmosphere in Dave Waddington and Robbie Stewart's jet as their three surviving aircraft landed back at Muharraq. Those waiting watched for the second time in nine hours as another Tornado failed to return from a mission.

Dave taxied in, shut down the engines, opened the canopy and felt the warm air from the Gulf wash over him. Robbie slowly made his way down the steps where he was met by their ground crew. After handshakes and some chatter, he made his way over to the shelter where Elsdon and Collier's ground crew were waiting, their pale faces and white eyes amplified under the harsh lights. Robbie brought them into a huddle. 'We lost the Boss and Max,' he told them. 'I'm sorry.' The young engineers looked on mutely, unable to believe that they had lost another jet and its crew. Their jet. Their crew. 'The loss hit them hard and they didn't want to leave the airfield, hoping against hope we were wrong.' Robbie joined the survivors in the debriefing room inside the Operations Room. They glanced at each other, barely registering their surroundings, trying to understand what had just happened and grappling with the complex challenges of loss and survival. Some were in tears. 'It was our first bombing mission and we'd seen a crash and friends killed right in front of us. It was a very severe baptism of war.'

As news of the second loss spread, the shock waves were felt throughout the Tornado force across the three Gulf airbases, especially for those who would continue the fight. 'If you go to war, people are going to be killed,' said one navigator. 'It's one of those facts that you have to accept. So I had to get on with the job and try not to let it affect me.'[15] It was easier said than done and everyone was quiet on the bus back to the Sheraton. Then they gathered in the cellar bar to drink to the memory of the fallen. Dave Waddington felt the alcohol release the tension and pain of loss. 'It was then that the reality of what we had been through and the growing realisation of Max and Nigel's loss came to the fore. And the utter certainty that in the not-too-distant future, we would have to do it all again.'

'I had known Max for a long time,' Robbie reflected. 'He was quiet, sincere, a good operator; a really nice bloke.' He finished his beer and went to call his wife. 'Obviously, I couldn't mention anything about Max and the Boss as their next of kin may not yet have been informed. But I really needed to talk.'

* * *

Back home in Lincolnshire, Tange replaced the phone on its cradle and took a deep breath. After listening to Robbie's first experiences of war, she took out her pen.

> *Thursday 17th January*
>
> > *To my very dearest darling,*[16]
>
> > *Well, the waiting is over and that is a relief, but a new sort of terror drains us all. It is 11.30pm and, for the first time, the telephone has stopped ringing and I am on my own in the peace and quiet to be with you. It was lovely to hear your voice; things must be indescribable for you all out there and you are in everyone's thoughts and prayers. I spoke to the children's school boarding houses this morning and they had both been told of the outbreak of hostilities. I will collect them tomorrow as planned. Scott is having a friend over for the day on Saturday, Kirsty and I are going to the pantomime – aren't we lucky! But then I'm lucky in so many ways – I've got two lovely kids and I've got you, darling.*
>
> > *Please come back to us safely. We will send photographs this weekend and a flight magazine will be posted with this letter.*
>
> > *Please don't worry about us, we are coping. I just couldn't cope with losing you. Our prayers are with you.*
>
> > *All my love,*
> > *Tange xxxxxx*

Onlookers across the world were now glued to their television sets, astonished at the level of firepower being deployed over Iraq. But back at his home in Bolton, Dave Waddington's mother Berenice had decided to turn off the TV for good, to avoid hearing any more about the Tornado lost on the first morning of war. The endless reports that Peters and Nichol had gone missing were too much to bear. An interview with a retired admiral had finally made her reach for the off switch. He had shared his thoughts on how Saddam could counter the Tornado raids. 'I couldn't believe my ears! During the Second World War we had all the posters about "careless talk costs lives", yet here was this man now telling the Iraqis how best to attack our own boys!'[17] Berenice hated the thought of her son in danger. The grinning 9-year-old who had vowed to become a pilot. She gazed at his framed photograph, taken after King Hussein of Jordan had taken the salute at his graduation parade. 'We were so proud; he'd achieved so much, our little boy presented with his pilot wings – especially a lad from Bolton. When he started flying Tornados, my husband Jack and I never thought he might go to war. We were children of the Second World War and the thought of a war in the 1990s never entered our heads.

'We spent a lot of time praying David would come home safely, as I imagined lots of mothers and fathers were doing. We didn't know what the future might hold, but we knew that our sons were in grave danger after the first Tornado was lost.'

Helen Peters had already been told that her husband and his navigator John Nichol were missing in action. The following day, 18 January, the Station Commander arrived back at her front door, again in full uniform. She was enjoying more tea with a group of the other wives. 'They all looked at me in horror as he drew me gently into the kitchen. Gravely he told me the boys had probably been captured. He said intelligence sources from inside Iraq, which he was unable to discuss, had reported sighting two captured British airmen. At that point, John and John were the only two airmen missing. So it had to be them.

'At first, this seemed like the worst thing that could have happened. I knew deep down that they were both more afraid of capture than of dying. I could understand that. They were prepared for death, for the quick death; when the missile hits and the world goes white, then black. We were all as prepared for that to happen as anyone could be. They were paid to take that risk. But capture was different. We all expected the Iraqis to use their prisoners horribly. In one way, though, I was relieved. At least they hadn't carried out that mad, half-formed suicide pact. It was probably just as well, as John was never much good at DIY!

'This was the only time I cried. At least when somebody you

love dies, you know what has happened to them. You can mourn them. Now, I was facing the prospect of not knowing what had happened to John for weeks, months, perhaps for years. Perhaps never knowing ...'[18]

CHAPTER SEVEN

'THE BAD STUFF'

18–19 JANUARY

Helen Peters remains grateful that she didn't really know what had been happening to her husband in those early hours.

Now a prisoner in Baghdad, John Peters had been isolated from his navigator John Nichol and was being led from the bunker shattered by the coalition attack a short while earlier. His next stop would be the place the friendly Iraqi Air Force officers who first questioned them had warned was where '*the bad stuff*' happened. The air was cool but he was sweating as he was shepherded into yet another concrete chamber. He barely had time to draw breath before the violence began. 'They jumped at me, initially using just boots. They laughed and joked about it, among themselves. The helplessness was a big part of it, humiliating, sordid and degrading.'

Peters steeled himself mentally. *I'm not the one degraded here.* But it was hard, especially when a boot smashed into his knee ligaments, injured while ejecting. 'I had to depend on my integrity, believe in my own worth. What were my worst fears? Suppose they

gang-raped me? Under the circumstances, it seemed only too likely.'
Through the pain he made one promise to himself: 'I'm not going
to let the bastards change me. If I come through this I'm going to
go home to Helen and my son Guy and daughter Toni. I am going
to pick up my ordinary, happy life.'[1]

The questions, and violence, continued.

As Peters suffered, so did the Iraqi people. The aerial bombardment raged on. The doubling of coalition air strength since
November allowed General Norman Schwarzkopf to pursue a
broader range of targets. By the second day he ordered the bombing of the Iraqi army on the ground, and further sites in Baghdad
itself. B-52s and A-10 tank-busters struck again and again at enemy
troops and armour in the desert.[2] Iraqi airbases like the one in which
Nichol and Peters were being held prisoner became the focus for
raids of increasing intensity. A significant number of Iraqi bombers
were destroyed on the ground, and American fighters blasted two
more of their jets out of the sky. F-111s opened a second line of
attack from Turkey, and another 200 Tomahawk cruise missiles
were launched from warships in the Gulf region. Perhaps inevitably,
the stream of US successes did not come without cost. Only two of
the six aircrew manning the three American jets downed on the
second day survived – and would now face the gruelling challenges
which currently confronted Peters and Nichol: whether to break
under interrogation and tell all they knew, or to hold their tongue
in the face of relentless torture.

While John Peters had been dragged from the crumbling bunker,
John Nichol had been left surrounded by guards. Their hostility
was as acrid as their body odour, and it quickly turned physical.
A bunched fist landed on his jaw, and was rapidly followed by
repeated kicks and punches from every quarter. 'I was trying to
hold my head down to protect my face, and my legs together to
protect my balls. They crowded around me, kicking and punching,
their blows driving in from all angles. Blood spurted from my nose,
thick and grimy on my tongue and teeth. I couldn't protect myself,
hard as I tried. They had total control. They could do anything

they damn well liked to me, and they could take as long as they liked doing it.[3]

'Only hours ago, I'd been a significant part of the biggest high-tech military offensive in history; now I was just a speck of dirt in a Third World desert, trampled underfoot, surrounded by an implacable enemy.'

Almost unbearable loneliness combined with immense pain as the savagery continued, until Nichol's aggressors finally tired and left him curled up in a corner. 'There was no sense of time. I was in an endless pitch-black vacuum.' He was not alone for long. Nichol soon found himself back alongside Peters. His blindfold was removed and he was shocked by what he saw. 'JP looked wrecked. He did not seem aware of his surroundings or appear to be taking much in, as though he had had a very thorough going-over, worse than my own.' Both were behind a long table, under bright lights, and confronted by a new Iraqi interrogator. The man was flanked by two obese thugs, 'stock villains straight out of central casting', complete with greasy hair, brown plastic shoes and, more curiously, squeezed into RAF flying suits. The interrogator waited in silence for a minute, then a tirade of questions began. What was their mission? What did they know of other missions? What aircraft were they flying?

Sticking to the standard formula, the aviators replied with name, rank and service number, and the only other approved phrase: 'I cannot answer that question.'

The questions stopped. An order was given in Arabic. One of the thugs pulled Nichol to his feet and hustled him out of the room. 'I had a horrible feeling in the pit of my stomach, that it was about to intensify. As I was dragged away I glanced back at JP, my chum of the last four years. Surrounded by the sadistic bastards, he was being re-blindfolded. I could tell they were getting ready to start on him in earnest yet again. What would they do next? Were they going to do it to me when they'd finished with him? Would I be able to hear him scream? How much could or would he take? How much could I?'

The two friends were now entering the classic routine: beating followed by questioning, followed by more beating. It would go on through the night and into the next day. Countless hours which would only stop when severe injury, death or co-operation was achieved.

Hands still cuffed behind his back, Peters was about to learn how relentless and uncompromising his captors could be. 'They grabbed me by the hair and threw my head against the wall for a few minutes. It felt terribly flat and cold, my features tried to mould themselves to whatever surface they encountered. All the time I was thinking how to protect myself, how not to give in, doubling over, twisting away from the direction of the blows.' But his captors, with many years of experience, were experts at their trade.

As the hours passed, and tiring of the exertion required, they graduated from fists and boots to sticks and lengths of hard plastic hosepipe. Violence followed by questions. Peters' eye, gashed during the ejection, became one of their favourite targets. 'It was extremely squelchy, like a wet sponge, where the face was expanding out. The more it swelled, the more they concentrated on hitting it, smashing down with some sort of pole or cane onto my eyes.' Peters hoped the swelling might at least protect his vision. But his biggest fear was letting down his service, his comrades, his friends and family, and losing his honour and integrity.

The process stretched on, the conclusion inevitable. In the short breaks between sessions, he discovered that the key was to grunt as the blows landed but never to scream. 'Once you have cried out they've got you.'

But the interrogators hadn't taken long to recognise that his badly damaged knee was his point of greatest vulnerability. They went to work on it with karate chops, heel stamps and toecaps. 'A massive arc of pain surged up through me in waves, stabbing into my armpit, jabbing up into my head, welling up through the whole side of my body.'

Then he did yelp.

'I don't know how long it went on but the kicks became more

frenzied, hammering down relentlessly onto my knee. Every time my leg gave way they wrenched me back up onto it, forcing my body weight over it, ready for the next boot heel to come smashing down onto the same spot. Over time, a question penetrated the mist. The same one I had refused to answer for the past eternity.'

'Are you a pilot or navigator?'

'Pilot . . .' Peters finally gasped.

They dropped him to the floor.

'I had broken.'

He had given in, and the effect was devastating. 'A sense of utter failure took hold of me. An overwhelming sense of shame that I had failed.'

The questions came thick and fast, now, as the interrogators pressed home their advantage. But, astonishingly, they were encyclo-paedic rather than considered. They wanted to know how the Tornado operated, its bombload and their target. Nothing of major strategic significance, nothing that had not already been reported in the newspapers. Peters realised they didn't seem to understand the value of the information he could reveal. 'I knew the sequence of signals that would call in a search-and-rescue mission. These codes were good for a week. If the Iraqis had found them out, they could have invented a "rescue mission", with a good English speaker pretending to be a pilot, and simply ambushed it, shot it to pieces.'

Their failure, however, hardly consoled him. 'What mattered was having broken at all – it seemed too soon. When I was left on my own again after answering the questions the most unbearable feeling of desperation and self-loathing swept through me.'

* * *

As Peters and Nichol underwent further rounds of interrogation in Baghdad, Saddam Hussein ordered a salvo of Scuds into the night sky. The Iraqi version of the Soviet missile had been adapted to travel 375 miles carrying 330lb of explosive, which, when used against Tehran in the 1980s, had caused a level of terror that was disproportionate to its size. Most worryingly for the coalition, some variants of the weapon had been adapted to carry chemical warheads. Saddam had always promised the 'mother of all battles', as well as to 'burn half of Israel', and the threat of nerve agents was ever present.

At 3am on 18 January, surveillance systems had detected seven surface-to-surface missiles heading for Tel Aviv. It was 9pm in Washington, and primetime television was being set alight by correspondents in gas masks reporting Scud strikes in the target city. There was a collective intake of breath. Squadrons of Israeli jets prepared to take to the air for a massive strike on Iraq. It was a nightmare scenario. If the Jewish state joined the conflict, the Arab anti-Saddam coalition would quickly disintegrate.

But the Israelis were not interested in coalition sensibilities, and planned their own counterstrike. The plan would involve Israeli aircraft encroaching into Saudi airspace. General Schwarzkopf was horrified by the prospect and immediately called General Colin Powell, the Chairman of the Joint Chiefs of Staff. 'The Saudis will never buy this and you can't sneak it by them. They have people up in our AWACS and they're gonna know.'[4]

An hour later another Scud was fired from the western Iraqi desert, and hurtled towards Dhahran in eastern Saudi, another major hub for the Tornado force. Eighteen of the F3 fighter variant operated from the base's seven runways, alongside six GR1A reconnaissance Tornados and the squadron of GR1 bombers. Countless other RAF aircraft, from Hercules transporters to Chinook helicopters, and 800 RAF personnel were also deployed at the base. The troops had trained exhaustively for the much-feared possibility of a warhead packed with chemicals landing in their midst.

A Victor tanker pilot heading into Dhahran saw a massive flash on the ground below him. 'A few seconds later this yellow flare was coming up skywards and getting stronger. I said, quite loudly, that it looked like a missile and veered the plane away very, very quickly, though I'm not sure it would have done any good. It went right in front of us, rose to about 8,000ft then started to dip down. There was this massive ball of flame as it exploded.'[5] The fast-travelling flare was in fact a Patriot air defence missile, never before tested in battle. The interceptor had blasted into life and powered up to 3,000mph to meet the incoming Scud.

A Tornado F3 navigator who had just returned from a six-hour patrol stumbled from his aircraft as the ground shuddered from the outgoing blast. 'I was looking up at my pilot when there was this bang and – *whoosh* – the sudden realisation that a Patriot had been fired. It zoomed through the clouds and there was a huge flash of lightning as it hit the Scud right over our heads.' The pilot was so shocked by the explosion that he let go of the steps and tumbled down onto his navigator. And both suddenly realised the threat of fallout from the Scud's chemical warhead – if it had one. 'We were rolling round on the floor desperately trying to get our respirators on. Then we ran like hell to this pickup vehicle which had rushed to us, then over to the air-raid shelters, where we dived in absolutely scared out of our heads.'

The Al-Hussein Scud might have had an explosive only a third of the size of a Tornado's 1,000-pounder, but it carried the threat of an even more horrendous death.[6] Below the missile's ballistic arc, all service personnel were struggling into their full NBC – Nuclear Biological Chemical – kit, complete with gas masks, gloves and protective suits.

Three years earlier, Iraqi jets had saturated the Kurdish town of Halabja with mustard gas and nerve agents, massacring 5,000 adults and children. Stark images of the dead lying in the streets were flashed around the world and came to symbolise Saddam's brutality. Those who survived would never forget his latest attempt at genocide. 'I saw people lying on the ground, vomiting a green-coloured liquid, while others became hysterical, falling motionless onto the ground. Later, I smelled an aroma that reminded me of apples and I lost consciousness. When I awoke, there were hundreds of bodies scattered around me. Your loved ones, your friends; you see them walking and then falling like leaves to the ground. It is a situation that cannot be described.'[7]

The deployment of nerve agents, even anthrax and plague, had been taken very seriously by the allies. Hundreds of thousands of troops had been given vaccinations against a range of biological weapons. During the months of NBC drills, they had plenty of opportunity to dwell on the horrific possibilities of an attack. 'It may sound stupid, but I decided that if I got a whiff of it, I was going to shoot myself with the weapon I had,' one serviceman said. 'There was no way I was going to flip about on the floor like a kipper for 40 minutes.'[8] The fear was contagious. A corporal sharing a room with five other medics had woken to the scream of the air-raid sirens. 'We felt the fear and horror that war was upon us. That was the time I was thankful we'd done our ground defence training. However, what with the confusion of six bodies all jumping out of bed at once in their boxer shorts and scrabbling around, it must have taken me about 30 seconds to get my respirator and another five minutes to get my NBC suit on.'[9] With no shelter in which to take refuge, the medics put their mattresses against the window in the vain hope it might partially seal them off from the deadly fumes. They then sat around telling jokes and hoping for the best.

'NBC Black!' would be the Tannoy's coded warning for the detection of chemical agents in any warhead. The loudspeakers remained silent in Dhahran. In Tel Aviv, initial reports that the missiles had chemical warheads were quickly discredited. Following the private warning he had been given before war broke out, Saddam had grasped the fact that the Americans were not bluffing about nuclear retaliation. But the Scuds pushed the Israelis to the point where their jets were in the air, poised to attack. 'Israel has the strongest military forces of any Middle Eastern country, and has said that any attack by Iraq would bring "massive punishment",' the BBC reported. Their jets were only cajoled back down by the private pleas of General Colin Powell and a public appeal from President Bush. The Israelis remained bent on retribution; the Scud threat would have to be contained.[10]

General Schwarzkopf now came under pressure from Washington to allow Israeli officers into his Saudi headquarters to identify the best targets. His response was blunt. 'How can anybody think the Israelis have better target information than our Air Force? We've been studying that part of Iraq with the most sophisticated intelligence gathering technology ever invented.'[11] And inviting Israelis into the home of Islam was 'a dumb idea'.

But the fear of chemical attack was striking terror into both civilian and military hearts, and Schwarzkopf was under direct orders to do something about it.

* * *

Iraq's 'H3' airbase lay a few miles east of Jordan and 60 miles north of the Saudi border. US Intelligence had discovered that Saddam's chemical weapons were stored in a bunker on the old RAF airfield, ready for immediate deployment.[12] It was a priority target for the coalition, and boasted sophisticated defensive systems. F-117 Stealth fighters had attacked it in the opening hours of war and, at 11pm on 17 January, a squadron of American A-6 Intruders also launched a bombing raid on the base from a carrier in the Red Sea. As they came in, low and fast, a volley of Roland missiles rose to meet them. One struck home, forcing the pilot and weapons systems officer (the US equivalent of the navigator) to eject seconds before their jet blew apart. They would soon join Peters and Nichol under interrogation in Baghdad.

Less than twenty-four hours later, the Tornados from nearby Tabuk were tasked with shutting down its runway with JP233s. Having been forced to turn back on the first night of the war with technical failures, 22-year-old navigator Mal Craghill remained determined to notch up a combat mission, but his initial excitement was now being tempered by a more profound understanding of the consequences.

On the morning of the 18th, he had been relaxing in their shared accommodation at Tabuk with fellow aircrew, unwinding after the initial sorties, when one of their number collapsed. As Craghill rose to help him, the airman began to have a fit. 'He suddenly went stiff as a board and started having convulsions. His feet shot out, taking the leg off the coffee table. Then he went absolutely pale and lay there. I thought he was dead. My concern was that he'd swallowed his tongue. I tried to open his mouth, at which point he started lashing out at us.'[13] The medics arrived within minutes, as he was in the process of coming round. He had no recollection whatsoever of what had just happened. 'They thought it might be due to lack of food and sleep – and the stress of exposure to enemy fire'.[14] Without a clearer diagnosis, he would not be able to fly on operations again. It was a disturbing insight into the mental strains they were all experiencing. It would not be the last incident of this kind.

Craghill helped clear up the shattered coffee table then sat back down on the sofa to contemplate the mission which lay ahead that night. Try as hard as he might, he couldn't help wondering what his friend had seen that sent him over the edge. He and his pilot Mike Warren knew that H3 had rapidly garnered a tough reputation, 'heavily defended by an aggressive mixture of surface-to-air missiles and anti-aircraft artillery', and he had to fight to dismiss the image of his fellow flier convulsing on the floor. The words of the Squadron Boss before war broke out still rang in his head. 'His personal opinion was that it wouldn't be difficult convincing guys to go on the first night. It would be the second trip and thereafter that would be difficult, because then we'd all know what it was like to be fired at.'

Craghill's Boss's pre-war assessment of the effects of combat were already showing. Dean Wood was a young engineer based at Tabuk and part of his role was as the 'see-off' crew for the Tornados; helping the aircrew ready their aircraft for battle. After the first few missions, he began to notice a change in their demeanour. 'My crew were very quiet; the pilot stayed on his own while the navigator came for a smoke and a chat with us. He talked about how they'd been lucky to get back from the previous trip, how the triple-A looked like a firework display where you knew that each sparkle might kill you. It's hard to explain the feeling you get when you're talking to someone, knowing you may be one of the last to see them alive.

'What really sticks in my memory was the amount of time they now took getting into the aircraft. Previously, crews had just jumped in and were away. Now they checked everything, stood on their seats, looked around, stretching, delaying the moment that they had to go. I had never seen aircrew do this kind of thing before. It was as if they knew it might be the last time they had the chance to take in their surroundings. You don't say anything, but I was simply thinking, *God, I hope they make it back. I hope their luck stays with them.* When all the aircraft eventually taxied, everyone just stood in silence and watched them all take off, nobody said a word.'[15]

Craghill's four-ship took off into the night without incident, but one Tornado was forced to return to base almost immediately with a technical fault. The rest of his formation joined the precisely choreographed refuelling operation. 'We could see dozens of aircraft, tanking with their lights on to minimise the risk of mid-air collisions. We felt like we were part of a much bigger operation.' One by one the lights flicked out as the jets dropped down towards the border. 'Where once we had seen many, we now saw none. It felt lonely, but we knew we were far from alone and we streaked over the border at 200 feet.' H3 was only a fifteen-minute dash away, and for navigator and pilot it wasn't hard to find. 'Already we could see sporadic bursts of tracer fire. There was very little chat in the cockpit but we weren't particularly nervous. We were in a familiar environment and had trained hard for what was coming up.'

Despite the threat of anti-radiation missiles, the operators at H3 did not hesitate to employ their radars in the search for targets. The airfield defences went active. 'SAM warnings began to show on our RHWR as short "spikes" pointing in the direction of the signal's origin. Then the triple-A became more intense, forming an odd-looking light show as tracer rounds arced into the air from numerous different sites. A dome of triple-A formed over the area of H3, leaving us in no doubt where our target lay.'

Mike and Mal went through the pre-attack checks, readying the JP233s, then turned east, using the Baghdad to Jordan highway to orientate them. 'H3 was now alight with dense tracer fire up to 4,000 feet. SAM radars were searching us out.' Their RHWR was giving them warnings of the Roland, and other SAMs. Mal began dispensing chaff from the Boz pod to confuse the enemy systems. They were now heading to a target with SAM radars already tracking them, and the sky above it reverberating with gunfire. It was becoming an increasingly daunting prospect.

Eight miles ahead of them, Craghill's Tornado Squadron Boss was seconds away from his final run into H3. The defensive barrage protecting the base – a dense cloud of missile, cannon and machine-gun fire – was now truly formidable. Even at a distance, the triple-A looked impenetrable.

'Abort attack!' the formation leader ordered. 'We won't make it through that. Find a dump target.'[16]

Despite his relative youth, Craghill was well aware of the significance of what he was hearing. 'The Boss could see no way of prosecuting a successful attack due to the incredible concentration of triple-A. He clearly thought we would all be shot down. He'd seen it the night before and was able, with that very limited experience, to say that it was now very much worse. It was the best decision he could have made and took incredible courage.'

Their Boss was risking his own reputation by turning his formation away to ensure his men would live to fight another day. But he wasn't waving a magic wand. No plan had been put in place for abandoning the target run in total darkness. 'You were always expected to make it to the target, and no "abort" route was ever considered. So the "big sky" theory now came into effect! An assumption that with just three aircraft scattering at low level, we were, hopefully, unlikely to hit each other . . .'

As they turned away in the inky blackness, only fractionally above the desert floor, Craghill's radar warning alarm sounded again. 'SA-8 target tracker' was emblazoned on his screen. Another siren screeched. He ensured the Sky Shadow pod was jamming, dispensed chaff and called for Mike to roll out, heading north. Almost immediately they were 'spiked' again by the SA-8 radar. His pilot rapidly tightened the turn through another 90 degrees. 'In a sharp turn like this the radar altimeter can't be relied on, so Mike climbed slightly to ensure separation from the desert floor a few hundred feet below while I used the radar to confirm the path ahead of us was clear.' With the warning sirens and radar clear, they turned south and descended once again to 200ft. They now had no idea of the location of the other two Tornados. One of H3's secondary airstrips was now 10 miles on their nose and offered Mal and Mike an opportunity to make their first operational attack. 'We made a snap decision between us and I quickly found it on the radar, Mike lined us up, and we prepared for weapons release using a "Target of Opportunity" profile. It was certainly something we had not briefed, especially with a weapon like JP233.'

Undaunted, they scattered their munitions over the sole runway. Carrying the JP233s back to Saudi would create a real problem with fuel consumption. Mal could see lights sparkling to his right as another set of JP233s was released on an unsuspecting target.

Back at base, Craghill entered the Tabuk debrief room to hear their commander's summation. 'He was in no doubt that we would not have made it safely across the target. For a Squadron Boss to have terminated an attack sent a powerful message to all of our crews that the war was likely to be protracted and we could only fight it if we didn't unnecessarily risk our aircraft and people. In many ways, the Boss's decision was one of the best pieces of leadership I have ever seen.' The crews who had been on the very first raids were in agreement – the groundfire over H3 was 'catastrophically worse'. A frank discussion followed about their level of personal risk. 'We were all in no doubt that we would be called upon to face intense danger. Possibly to make the ultimate sacrifice, depending on the circumstances. But the war looked set to be one of attrition and there was no point in losing a lot of jets in the first few nights.'

Their Squadron Commander was right to be concerned about losses. The war was barely two days old and three Tornados, including an Italian version, had already gone down. They accounted for a third of the coalition combat aircraft losses, which included some of the very latest and most sophisticated multi-role types: the F-15E Strike Eagle and F/A-18 Hornet. Although it was yet to be officially confirmed, seven aircrew had already been killed and nine taken prisoner.

Jerry Witts, the wise Tornado Commander at Dhahran, endorsed the increasingly widely held view that the 'White Cliffs of Dover' syndrome – fliers committed to defend the gateway to their home-land with their lives – simply did not apply. 'The brief that I had been given was that we were to use our assets as efficiently as possible without losing aircraft or lives. I think our outlook was slightly different to how it would have been had we been defending British territory. We were there to do a job of work, and we were quite happy to do it. But none of us intended to die in the process.'[17]

The perils for the Tornado force were beginning to build. Several thousand sorties had already been flown by the coalition, and the RAF's GR1 – small formations flying close to the ground into devastating gunfire – was suffering the worst attrition rate. Those without a combat sortie were still eager to test their mettle, but others, like Witts, were beginning to realise that the losses they were taking during low-level attacks were unsustainable. 'We were cer-tainly suffering a bit in the Tornado world. We'd lost three planes, which, in percentage terms, did not look very good.'

* * *

Sitting in Baghdad, and already out of that aerial fight, John Nichol was in no doubt that several of the men nearby were eager to hurt him yet again. He braced himself on a steel and vinyl chair for the next beating.

'It's okay, we don't want to know any information. Don't worry.' The voice was warm, almost gentle. The Iraqis had sent in 'Mister Nice' to extract information without the brutality enjoyed by 'Mister Nasty'. Now it was time for the wheedling appeals to logic and reason, more subtle and undermining. Nichol was offered food and drink. He declined. The questions began; simple ones about what aircraft he flew, where he came from. It was a more professional approach and every question was answered with the same stock phrase, 'I cannot answer that question.' The interrogator changed tack.

'You are dropping chemical weapons onto my country, aren't you?'

Nichol was startled by the accusation, but blocked him again with the standard, 'I cannot answer that question.'

'Okay. I know you cannot answer these questions, but you know that you will answer them . . . eventually . . . I know you will talk to me, you know, you will talk to me.'

Nichol could not disagree; it was just a question of how much longer he could hold out. *At some point I'm going to tell him what he wants*. The man now twisted the psychological knife. He did not need to ask the questions because he already knew the answers.

'I can tell you that you are a navigator.'

Shit, how does he know that? Nichol thought. It could have been a guess.

'I can tell you that you are from 15 Squadron.'

Nichol was now worried. 'He knew things about me. Where had he got them from? I had a feeling that he'd got them from John. What had they done to him to get the info? The same or worse? Worse, surely. When will I get it? What would it be like? What did they do?'

'I know you are from Bahrain.'

He could still be guessing, or have read it in the British press; his Squadron had featured heavily in pre-war coverage.

'I know that your attack did not work. I know you did not get the bombs off and that you ditched your bombs in my desert.'

Oh fuck! A cold feeling ran through Nichol; there was only one person this information could have come from. *John . . . What the hell had happened to him? Where is he, how is he?* 'I was worried about him, but even more worried about myself. Deep down I was glad that whatever had led him to talk had not yet happened to me.'

The questioning progressed, zigzagging between the cajolery of

Mr Nice and the belligerence of Mr Nasty. He was re-blindfolded and dragged off to another room. 'I knew something very unpleasant was going to happen.' But it wasn't what he expected. Instead of a straightforward beating he was left to contemplate the mental and physical pain of a stress position. 'My forehead was flat against the wall, my feet about 20 inches away from it. I was stretched right up onto my toes. Arms handcuffed behind my back. My forehead was supporting my entire body weight, against the cold surface.' Every time he tried to shift position a fist slammed into him. 'I tried to move my head. Somebody smacked it hard against the wall, a staggering blow. I tried to move my arms, manacled behind my back. The handcuffs were of the ratchet type and, because of the beatings, were racked up tight to the last notch, biting into my wrists, a cold insistent metallic cutting agony.'

Every muscle in his body now screamed with the impossible effort of maintaining the posture. It seemed to go on for hours. He could have been struck thirty times or a thousand. Disorientated and in torment, Nichol lost count. 'Nobody asked me anything after this. Nothing at all. Now dazed, and stunned like a chicken before its throat is cut, I was worried. I had lost track of how they were going to interrogate me. This was not going by the book any more.'

A few minutes later a guard transferred Nichol to a room where he was blindfolded and handcuffed to an iron bedstead. He could hear other coalition prisoners being interrogated and realised more coalition jets must have been shot down. Air raids raged overhead. The triple-A on the roof hammered away. Bombs crumped and rattled nearby.

The day stretched on as further interrogators loomed over him; a kick to the ribs to get his full attention.

'Where did you come from?'

'I cannot answer that question.'

'You *will* be sorry, you know that, don't you, Nichol?'

'I cannot answer that question.'

'We will come back for you soon. You will be sorry!'

I know I'm going to be sorry! I'm already bloody sorry!

It didn't take long. As night drew in again, they came for him. He was blindfolded once more, handcuffed and taken outside, dragged around to disorientate him, then brought back into a room and pushed into the hard chair. One guard held his right arm, another gripped his left. Nichol's chest pounded. 'I knew in my heart of hearts that this was the time; it was going to get really tough now.'

'What squadron are you from?'

'I cannot answer that . . .'

A fist thudded into his face. Blood poured onto his lap, warm against his thighs. He could feel the drips through his flying suit, chemical suit and long johns. The punches went into his head, over and over. Then another question.

'I cannot . . .'

'My head rang to the blows like some kind of bell. There were brilliant lights flashing behind the blindfold. I really did see stars. I was in the middle of the Milky Way.'

Another demand, met by Nichol's stubborn response.

Somebody wrenched off his boots.

What on earth are they going to do to me now?

The interrogators then pulled out what he would learn was a favoured device. A hard plastic pipe was whacked viciously across his shins.

Again, the interrogator spoke. Again, he got the same reply.

'I cannot answer that question.'

Someone grabbed the nape of his neck and stuffed tissue paper down the back of his T-shirt. A multitude of panic-stricken questions raced through his mind. 'This was terrifying now. I'm in a darkened room in the middle of enemy territory, and somebody had just stuffed tissue paper down the back of my neck. What the hell for?'

Shit, they are going to set me on fire!

'Now I really want him to ask me another question. I want to say something. I want to tell him something, anything. But he didn't ask me a question. He just set fire to the paper.'

Nichol threw his head violently from side to side, desperate to escape the burning, to shake the tissue paper clear of his head. His aggressors continued to hammer his shins with the rubber hose as the paper burned. Mercifully, someone finally slapped out the flames.

'What squadron are you from?'

'Fifteen.'

Nichol had broken.

Like Peters, he found the simplicity of the questions curious. These were trained interrogators who could have extracted a ream of useful information, but instead the demands were simplistic. What weapons did the Tornado carry? What was the main weapon used against runways? How did they drop bombs?

'What is the countermeasures pod called?'

'Sky Shadow.'

The name seemed enough. The interrogator failed to ask what electronic countermeasures it contained, or which radars its complex electronics could defeat. After all the skill and enthusiasm they had demonstrated in the process of causing pain, it was bizarre that they were so hapless at asking questions that might yield real intelligence. They didn't know what they wanted to know. The captured aircrew were at their mercy, yet insipid queries were the best they could come up with.

'Why have you come to our country?'

'Err . . . Because we were ordered to?'

The answer, however true, provoked rage and another flurry of punches.

* * *

It was just two days into the war, but Iraq, reported *The Guardian* newspaper in London, had already 'suffered the most sustained and devastating aerial and missile bombardment in history'. It added that the White House 'insisted there would be no pause for diplomacy and the pounding would go on until Saddam Hussein left Kuwait'. The BBC reported that President Bush had told Congressional leaders at the White House: 'No one should assume the conflict will be short or easy.' The front page of the *Daily Express* screamed: 'Iraq Blitz on Israel'.

Its back pages were filled with Tottenham Hotspur's footballing woes and unsubstantiated rumours of a sale of their star midfielder, Paul Gascoigne, to an Italian club. '£8m for Gazza', the headline said, and 'Napoli bid as Spurs' chief tackles debt'. The gossip came to nothing and, away from the ferocity of battle and interrogation, life continued as normal.

Those about to undertake the continuing Tornado low-level missions would have probably welcomed the distraction of 'real world' news as they contemplated flying into the intense hail of triple-A and missiles, knowing the odds against them surviving were shortening with each raid. No one could survive that scale of fire for ever.

It was late on 18 January when Robbie Stewart managed to call his wife. Tange had had a fretful day at the school where she taught as news of the losses filtered through. 'All I could imagine was an RAF officer arriving in uniform to tell me Robbie was missing ... or worse.' The joy of speaking to her husband diminished as he recounted their first night's attack, during which Nigel Elsdon and Max Collier had been killed. 'It was such a great shock to hear about Nigel and Max. We knew Max and his wife well and I had spent some time chatting to him before the deployment. It was all so desperately sad.'

Robbie knew the pitfalls of telephone calls home. 'I wanted to say that I was safe even though I realised the dangers of calling after each raid. I knew a call *after* a raid was also a call *before* the next one. A raid from which I might not return.'

But Tange understood. She was now painfully aware of the very real dangers Robbie confronted, had seen the increasing losses announced in the media. But she was still delighted to hear from him. 'I think we were avoiding talking about the reality of what we all faced. The kids would write him letters telling him normal things about school and I wrote every day about what was going on in the village, the weather, our plans for the future. We were trying to convince each other everything would be fine.'

Robbie found the last moments of their phone call difficult. 'We didn't say it, but we both knew in our hearts it could be our last ever conversation.'

The next day, he and his pilot Dave Waddington would embark on what would become their final mission.

CHAPTER EIGHT

'PLEASE LET HIM BE DEAD'

19 JANUARY, EVENING–20 JANUARY

A few hours before taking off on the attack that would see him blasted from Iraq's night skies, Robbie Stewart had spent a quiet moment penning another letter to his wife and children.[1]

It began, '*My Dearest Darlings, I thought I would drop you a line, though I do not know when you will get this. The initial euphoria of day one has been replaced by a more cautious mood.*'

As he had during the previous night's call home, he went on to describe the crash that had claimed the lives of Nigel Elsdon and Max Collier, then finished:

> *We were soon clear and we both breathed easier but our thoughts were with the Boss and Max. My thoughts now are with you and the kids, darling. The nightmare continues and I just look forward to seeing you all again. I know you are brave and I am so lucky having someone with such great strength. I have told you about that sortie as I thought you would prefer [to know].*

I love you and will do always,
Rob

He signed off with the usual ten kisses, little knowing what fate had in store for him, and his family.

* * *

'CHAFFING ...!'

Robbie sprayed the sky with the metallic strands, determined to shake off the radar-guided Roland missile spearing towards them.

The fifth major wave of RAF Tornado attacks saw him and Dave Waddington targeting southern Iraq's massive Tallil airbase. Each member of their four-ship carried five 1,000lb bombs to pound its defences and pave the way for the runway-busting JP233s. This time, the Tornados were on their own, gambling that the lack of American suppressive support would not alert the Iraqi gunners, giving them the benefit of surprise. It hadn't. With F for Foxtrot only seconds from the target, running through the darkness at high speed and 200 feet, a Roland surface-to-air missile had been launched from dead ahead. Now they were banking hard, G-suits tightening, as Dave tried to break the missile lock. More chaff burst out of the Tornado's Boz pod into the night sky. A cloud of metallic confusion, striving to give the incoming weapon's radar guidance system a juicier target than the speeding Tornado. Dave was pulling the stick hard into his stomach, doing everything possible to persuade the overladen jet to turn. It wasn't enough.

Robbie watched the blinding orange flash envelop the cockpit. The exploding warhead shredded the jet and the warble of the threat warning changed instantly to the shriek of the multiple system failures siren. 'There was no time to think, only to react. I pulled the ejection handle and felt a huge detonation and a whoosh as the seat's rockets fired under my backside. That was the last thing I remember.'[2]

* * *

Am I dead?

Dave Waddington lay on a hard surface surrounded by blackness and silence. A breath of air glided across his cheek. The searing flash, the screaming sirens, the flashing warning lights, the crush of G-force were gone.

Is this what death feels like?

He tried to move his right arm, but felt a sharp jab of pain in his shoulder. He tried the same with his left. Another stab of agony shot from his elbow. 'I was concussed and completely confused. I had been in the Tornado with an absolute certainty I was going to die.'[3] He blinked, his dark brown eyes catching a star overhead and a distant memory of the missile strike. 'Everything had happened in a fraction of a second. I was losing consciousness ... I had tried to get my hands towards the ejection handle ... they wouldn't move ... then an enormous wind and my last thought of, *Game over, I'm going to die*. It now appeared I hadn't!' Dave twisted painfully and glimpsed the white and orange parachute on the sand behind him. The breeze brushing his face then began to fill the canopy.

Oh God, Robbie must have ejected us!

His navigator's lightning reactions had saved their lives as the Tornado disintegrated. He turned his head to see where his friend was. There was no sign except some nearby footprints in the sand. 'I just presumed Robbie was in far better shape than me and had already started his escape and evasion while I was unconscious on the ground.' Dave tried to withdraw his Personal Locator Beacon (PLB) from its pouch in his life jacket but couldn't move his right arm. The shoulder had dislocated. Again, he tried to move his left. Pain speared up his arm. The elbow joint was sticking out at a distorted angle. The pair had ejected at around 600mph, blasted out of the cockpit to be hit by a force four times greater than the most destructive hurricane. They were lucky to be alive. Waddington rolled onto his right shoulder and it popped partially back into place. Enough to let him get up. 'I had a sense of being totally alone, wondering where Robbie was then realising that, despite my injuries, I needed to get going. Once on my feet,

I didn't feel much pain as long as I didn't move my arms; I was in total shock.'

He touched his cheeks, swollen and wet with blood. 'Although I didn't know it at the time, I had tiny bits of Roland missile warhead splattered in my face, along with pieces of my helmet's Perspex visor and other debris from the jet.' The parachute now ballooned behind him, a trembling day-glo signal in the surrounding darkness. Painfully, Dave released the harness. 'My arms were so weak I couldn't overcome the force of the canopy being inflated so just had to let it blow away across the desert. More importantly, my injuries also meant I couldn't get to my pistol or use the PLB properly either. I was in serious trouble.'

With just a small amount of water, near-useless arms, and still dazed from the missile explosion and high-speed ejection, Dave Waddington set off into the night. A few miles to the east he watched the tracer still arcing into the sky over Tallil.

* * *

Back in Lincolnshire, the bullets had just stopped flying in *Stakeout*, the Richard Dreyfuss cop comedy, when Robbie's teenage children, Kirsty and Scott, heard whistling, and a familiar sound on the front path. It was 11pm. Their mother was out with some neighbours. They were alone at their Coleby home with two friends. Kirsty recognised the sound outside all too well. It was the metallic *click, click, click* of steel-tipped shoes. Her heart sank. Military shoes. Her father had often worn them on the parade ground.

There was a knock at the door. A Wing Commander in full dress uniform. 'We looked up at him; he looked at us. I think we were all somewhat shocked. He clearly wasn't expecting to be faced with four teenagers!'

The RAF officer recovered first. 'Could you tell me where Mrs Stewart is?'

'She's having dinner with friends,' Kirsty replied, giving him directions to the house along the village lane. 'We really felt it was important he got to Mum quickly, although we had no real idea why.' The officer clicked his way back down the path, leaving young Kirsty to close the door. Wide-eyed, she leaned against the kitchen counter. 'It was surreal. We didn't really say anything, but Scott and I knew something must have happened. We just didn't want to put the words out there for fear of making them come true.'[4]

Earlier that afternoon, Tange Stewart had been overwhelmed by the sense that her beloved husband Robbie was in terrible danger. Now at dinner with her neighbours, she still couldn't shake off that feeling of dread. She did her best to hold a normal conversation with the two other couples around the table. The kids were at home, less than 150 yards away. She tried not to keep glancing out of the window. 'My stomach was really knotting up. I just knew something wasn't right.' As the main course was cleared away, the doorbell rang. Her host left the table to answer it. A moment later she returned, and leaned down to whisper in her ear. 'There's an RAF officer in the lounge, Tange.' She paused. 'He needs to speak to you.'

You couldn't be the wife of a fast-jet aviator without knowing exactly what this meant. 'Every military spouse would. There was apprehension and dread. My earlier premonitions were coming true. I had been in turmoil since the afternoon panto in Newark, so in a strange way it was a relief to have an answer. No matter how bad it was.'[5] She made her way to where a man in RAF 'blues' stood waiting. The rings on his sleeve showed his rank. Forgetting her manners, Tange didn't give him the chance to speak first. 'Tell me he's not dead,' she demanded. The Wing Commander looked her straight in the eye. 'Mrs Stewart, I'm sorry to tell you that your husband hasn't returned from his mission over Iraq tonight. There's nothing else that we know at the moment.'

Tange paced around the room, as she had done when Robbie had told her a month ago that he was going back to the warzone. Pacing was her default setting for stress and fear. The officer stood there awkwardly, unsure what to say next. 'It was all such a shock but I had the tiniest glimmer of hope, he hadn't *actually* been able to say they were dead. I held onto that. If no one could confirm Robbie was dead, surely there had to be some hope?' Suddenly, she recalled Robbie's conversation with the children just before he deployed after Christmas. *If anything happens to me, someone in full uniform will arrive at the house with the news ...*

'I have to get home and tell Kirsty and Scott!' She barely had time to register her friends' shock and concern as she ran to the door. 'Sorry for missing dessert and ruining the evening!' As she walked down the lane under the dim light of its single lamp, the crescent moon stopped her in her tracks. *Wherever you are, Robbie, my love, we are all under the same moon together.* 'I didn't know it then, but that thought would repeat itself many, many times over the coming weeks.'

There was no easy way to tell her children. 'Dad's missing . . . He didn't come back from his mission.'

Kirsty struggled to take in what was being said. 'I really can't remember much about it all. It was almost like a dream, as though it was happening to someone else and I was watching it unfold.'

People started arriving at the house as the news spread. Tange's dinner-party friends came over, along with the vicar and the officer who had given her the news. They crowded into the living room, where a brass etching of an RAF Vulcan hung on the wood-panelled wall near the stone fireplace. On went the kettle, and endless pots of tea were produced from the kitchen. Tange's mothering instincts now took over. She had to protect the children. But they knew so little about what had happened to Robbie. 'I was in uncharted waters with no idea about what to do or how to react. How long would it go on for? How was I meant to cope? I quickly realised that in reality, and despite the turmoil, I would just have to.'

Kirsty's young mind was already racing. 'I loved reading Second World War and Cold War novels. I was fascinated by spy stories and people working behind enemy lines but I'd also read a lot of interrogation and torture scenes. My brain started heading down a million roads.' As other people in the living room discussed whether he was on the run or had been captured, all Kirsty could think about was her father stranded in enemy territory. She couldn't help herself, and her thoughts turned dark.

Please let him be dead ...

'It seems terrible to think back on it now, but I wanted him to be dead. I was desperately worried and just couldn't bear the thought of him being tortured and interrogated.'

Even amid her darkest fears, 13-year-old Kirsty could have had no concept of the horrors unfolding for her father and his pilot in Iraq.

* * *

The man who had shared a Tornado cockpit with Kirsty's father looked up at the night sky. He picked a star to guide his escape route and headed south towards the Iraq–Saudi border, 140 miles in the distance. Attempting another radio call, he lost his positioning so chose a new star, but a wire fence now blocked his way. With both arms dislocated, there was no way to climb over. Dazed, staggering and weakened, he followed the fence to a busy road. 'I was simply trying to put distance between me and the crash site. After four or five hours, I saw some triple-A coming from an airfield in front of me and thought, *Ah, there must be another airfield around here.*' Exhausted and in pain, he sat and took a swig from a packet of water retrieved from the only leg pocket of his G-suit that had survived the violent ejection. Dawn was approaching. *I have to get out of sight before first light.* He tried to dig a hole but his arms were useless. A sliver of sunshine appeared on the horizon. He had to find somewhere to hide. He remembered the four key words from their downed-aircrew survival course: *Protection. Location. Water. Food.*

He spotted twin 4ft-high oil pipelines nearby and crawled under them. Using his boot heels, he scraped a shallow trench, lay down and activated the emergency locator beacon, 'hoping that any guys flying overhead would hear it'. He attempted another distress call on the radio, fighting the frustration when his ineffectual hands found themselves unable to attach the aerial. Hope of rescue was diminishing. 'I had previously believed that there was the possibility of a mission being launched, helicopters coming in to get me, but when none of my calls were answered, that belief started to fade. I hadn't yet rationalised a long-term plan, only to evade capture for as long as possible.'

It was now around nine hours since they had been blasted out of the sky. Soon his family and fiancée he had recently proposed to would know they had not come back from the mission. 'The thought of my mum and Claire being told was absolutely horrendous; very, very hard for me mentally. I was alive, but they wouldn't know that. Back in England, calls would soon be being made and doors knocked on.'

After despairing at the TV coverage of the war, Dave's mother Berenice Waddington had taken to listening to the radio news at their terraced home in Bolton, a few miles north of Manchester. Late that night of 19 January, the BBC had reported that yet another Tornado had been lost. She took little notice and went to bed; it couldn't possibly be her son. A few hours later she awoke from a fitful sleep. Someone was knocking on the front door.

'Who's that?' Berenice asked her husband, Jack. Their clock told her it was 1.30am. Jack got out of bed, shrugged on his dressing gown and headed down the hall as she sat at the top of the stairs, fearful of what was about to unfold. He opened the door and she could see two RAF officers in smart light-blue uniforms.

'Are you the parents of Flight Lieutenant David Waddington?' one asked.

'Yes,' Jack responded.

'Can we come in?'

Reluctant to move, Berenice watched from her vantage point as they stepped inside. 'I just thought, *Oh no, this is bad . . .*' Then she took another sharp breath. 'They had brought our parish priest! I now knew it was *very* bad news.'[6]

They all sat down in the living room. One of the officers said David was missing in action after a mission over Iraq. There was no other information, no indication if he was alive or dead. Sitting

A Tornado practises the 'loft – or toss – attack' at a coastal weapons' range. With the target accurately identified by the navigator, the system releases the bombs as the aircraft climbs steeply from low-level so that they are 'thrown' forward, arcing towards the target.

Mike Toft's formation sitting on a Tornado armed with laser-guided bombs. The bomb symbols on the nose denote the tally of missions the aircraft has flown.
From left: Chris Lunt, Pablo Mason (standing), Colin Ayton, Gary Stapleton, Bob Brownlow & Jack Calder (the crew who replaced John Peters and John Nichol after they were shot down), Mike Toft, Mark Paisey.

A test drop of the JP233 runway denial weapon in 1983. The cratering munitions can be seen deploying from the large rear pod then descending by parachute. The anti-personnel mines can be seen spraying from the front pod.

RAF groundcrew training in full Nuclear Biological Chemical protective equipment in the run up to the war.

Kev Weeks, left, and his pilot Garry Lennox, centre, planning a mission at the Tabuk detachment in the run up to the conflict. They are both carrying pistols in shoulder holsters. Sadly, both would be killed during the war.

Mal Craghill, left, and his pilot Mike Warren about to head out on another mission. Mal is wearing a life jacket which contains much of his survival equipment, including his Personal Locator Beacon. Mal and Mike would eventually drop the RAF's last bombs of the war.

Anti-Aircraft fire lights up the sky over Baghdad on 17 January 1991. The triple-A over the Iraqi airfields the Tornados initially attacked was considerably more intense than this.

Mike Heath, OC 20 Squadron, at Tabuk.

Pete Batson, Mike Heath's pilot, preparing for a flight in late 1990. They would both have to eject from their Tornado in the early days of the war after a technical failure.

A smiling Steve Hicks in his navigator's seat in the Tornado he shared with Rupert Clark. Sadly, Steve would be killed during the war.

Kirsty, Tange and Scott Stewart meet Her Majesty the Queen in the Officers' Mess bar at RAF Marham in February 1991. At this point, they did not know if Robbie was alive or dead.

Chris Ankerson meets Diana, Princess of Wales, at RAF Bruggen. It was the morning after she had tearfully asked her friend, 'am I a wife or a widow?' It would be many weeks before she would know the answer.

Some of the delighted RAF POWs descend from the Red Cross aircraft on landing at Riyadh airbase in Saudi Arabia after being released from captivity. From top, John Nichol, Rupert Clark, Dave Waddington, Robbie Stewart.

John Nichol re-visits one of the cells where he was held in Baghdad during a visit in 2000 to make a TV documentary. The writing from countless previous prisoners is clearly visible on the pockmarked walls.

The site near Tallil airbase in Iraq where Dave Waddington and Robbie Stewart's Tornado hit the ground at high speed. Wreckage can be seen scattered around the crater and the Boz chaff and flare pod is clearly visible on the left edge, with live flares still primed ready for use.

John Nichol, right, next to Rupert Clark on the VC10 transport aircraft which took the newly liberated prisoners to the medical facilities in Cyprus. Bruises from the attack by guards at Abu Ghraib prison are still visible on his face. Sitting opposite from left are Gordon Buckley, Chris Lunt and Nick Heard, who were part of the team which volunteered to escort the POWs to safety.

A single Tornado races across the desert at high speed and at ultra low-level, probably below fifty feet, during a training sortie before the war.

in her young son's childhood home, surrounded by pictures of Dave in his RAF uniform, Berenice found the news impossible to take in. 'I was just rocking back and forwards as if in a trance.' Someone rang their son John, a fireman on duty a few miles away, and he rushed back home. Then it dawned on them that no one had told Dave's fiancée, Claire. As they were not married, his parents were his legal 'next of kin'; the only people who could be officially informed. It had gone 2am when Dave's other brother Gerard set off for Claire's home in Cambridgeshire. In the event, a friend from Dave's Squadron at RAF Marham had also been dispatched to deliver the bad news to her.

Berenice and Jack sat staring at the photo of their son. 'There was little we could do as a family. It was like being in a dream, totally unreal. But it was all so very, very real.'

The childhood and military pictures at John Nichol's family home outside Newcastle also gazed down on parents trying to come to terms with the thought that they might never see their son again. The RAF navigator's mother and father had struggled for two days with the unreal news of having their boy 'missing in action'. They were at the centre of a media storm as speculation and comment, much of it ill-informed, raged around them. There were moments of hope. One newspaper reported that the airmen were alive behind enemy lines after a satellite had supposedly picked up their Personal Locator Beacons. It was totally untrue.

There were also moments of utter despair. In one radio broadcast, the Armed Forces Minister Archie Hamilton had all but declared their son dead. 'On the whole it is bad news if we have *not* heard anything about them, and the presumption has to be that they are *not alive*,' the politician told BBC Radio 4.[7] His crisply delivered words were met with disbelief in the Nichol council house in North Shields. John's father had kept his dignity, telling the media camped outside that all they knew was that his son was missing and 'we are keeping as calm as possible'. The headline of their local newspaper, meanwhile, proclaimed: 'NORTH AIRMAN PRESUMED DEAD'.[8]

* * *

Robbie Stewart felt the sun warm his face as it rose over the sand-coloured horizon. He had been unconscious for many hours. He blinked in the light, trying to recall the events of the previous night; the explosion, the ejection. His parachute ruffled in the wind nearby. He breathed in the fresh, early-morning air. *Thank God, I'm alive!* Then the scale of his predicament dawned on him. *Poor Tange and the kids! They've got no idea what's happened to me!* Lying spread-eagled on the desert floor, far from home, Robbie began to cry. 'I had just escaped death by the skin of my teeth and only I knew of my living state. Tears flooded down my face.'

He knew he had to move. Although his back ached badly, it was the lack of movement in his right leg that caused him most concern. He looked down. Blood was seeping through his flying suit. It didn't look good. 'The leg was numb, snapped and sticking out at right angles to my body. I couldn't feel any pain at that point, but the blood clearly indicated that the broken bone had penetrated the skin. It was a very serious problem.' He needed help. His left hand was clutching the PLB, his right the mini flares, and a packet of water was on his chest. Robbie wrongly assumed that his pilot had seen him unconscious and helped out as best he could. *Good old Dave, great lad. He's seen me lying here, put this kit out for me and then made his own escape.*

Robbie turned his head. Fifty yards away, cars and trucks carrying people to work along a busy road. The sudden movement now sent pain searing through his body and he lost consciousness again. 'I kept passing out as intense, almost unimaginable pain pulsed through me. I would later discover that I had a broken shoulder, crushed vertebrae and a leg broken in three places.'

Coming around again, he began to wonder if anyone had actually helped him, or if he had got the kit out himself, despite his appalling injuries. In reality, he had clearly done everything himself at some point during the night, including, incredibly, removing the tight-fitting G-suit. Not an easy operation at the best of times, even without a shattered leg. 'I really felt like there had been someone sitting on my shoulder helping me with the water, radio, flares and the complex task of attaching the PLB battery and aerial, all at night. I knew I couldn't escape, but it was as though God had said, "Robbie, you're going to need these." Especially as, by now, I was in no doubt that if I didn't get help I would die where I lay.'

He started transmitting on the radio but there was no reply on the distress frequencies. Blood continued to flow from his punctured leg and Robbie knew that any medical help would have to come from the very people he had been trying to kill only a few hours earlier. 'Of course, we had heard things on the news before the war about how Saddam was telling people to tear us limb from limb, but I just didn't believe it. I have an innate faith in the decency of people.'

Robbie now put that faith to the test. As a lorry approached he rapidly fired two mini flares into the air. The vehicle stopped and two Iraqi civilians got out. They indicated that the airman should raise his hands in surrender, but Robbie could barely move. The pair approached cautiously, chatting in Arabic. It appeared they were looking for weapons. Robbie painfully pointed to the Walther in its shoulder holster. One man carefully removed the pistol and threw it aside. Then both tried to lift him onto his feet. Robbie screamed in agony. 'The pain from my right leg flopping around stabbed through my body. They put me back on the ground and one guy disappeared while the other took off his head-dress and tied my legs together. Every movement now sparked unbearable bolts of pain.' The first man reappeared with a large tarpaulin and together they gently carried him to what turned out to be a cattle truck with a tailgate and wooden slatted sides. The two men lifted him carefully into the back. One took off his own jacket and eased it under Robbie's head.

The road was relatively smooth and the journey to the nearest military barracks lasted less than an hour. The tailgate dropped and Robbie was lifted down by several young conscripts clad in green uniforms, all sporting imitations of Saddam Hussein's distinctive moustache. 'They were looking on with curiosity at this British flier who was now their prisoner.' The soldiers forced him onto the back seat of a station wagon. A smirking conscript abruptly opened the door and prodded his broken leg. Robbie grimaced, fighting back a scream. 'It was a strange pain, not sharp, just constant and deep-seated. My real fear was that I was now face to face with the people we had been bombing relentlessly. All I could hope was that they wouldn't kill me. Still, there was nothing I could do about it. I certainly couldn't run away!' The conscript jabbed at his leg again. The shattered bones grated against each other. 'To his delight, I now screamed out in agony and started to vomit because of the pain.'

Grinning, the Iraqi closed the door, satisfied at his success.

They drove through the town along potholed roads. Robbie vomited again as his leg flopped and the broken bones scraped beneath the skin. An hour later, they arrived at a bunker with camouflage netting over the entrance. The Iraqis pulled him out of the car by his shoulders, allowing his shattered leg to bounce across the tarmac then kerb. He screamed again.

Robbie was blindfolded and taken to a room where another prisoner was being brutally interrogated. 'In many ways, this was worse than if it was happening to me, because your mind plays tricks. It sounded like he was being beaten half to death. It was terrible. He was saying, "Oh don't, DON'T! Stop!" It was awful to endure and my imagination ran wild. *That's going to be me next. Can I take it?*' The man was eventually removed and Robbie knew it was his turn. He was placed on a table with his feet towards the interrogator, who he could now see through the gap in his blindfold. 'He had a really thin face and, unusually, no moustache. He started asking me questions, but quickly became frustrated with me refusing to answer. So he began prodding at my broken leg, moving it around, telling me he could easily break the other leg. I was screaming in pain every time he jabbed me, desperate not to answer his questions. I knew it was going to get worse but luckily the pain became too much and I simply passed out.'

* * *

As Robbie suffered what he knew was going to be his severest test, the comrades he had left back in Bahrain underwent intense scrutiny from the press. As more Tornados were lost, the media interest had rapidly grown. With a number of bombers already confirmed missing from Muharraq, the journalists were eager to get the crews' reactions. An RAF press officer ushered a handful of reporters onto the airbase and lined up some of the airmen who had been at the forefront of the action. Without any media training, the fliers, standing in front of their Tornados, spoke freely.[9]

Pablo Mason had led the first daylight formation which attacked Ar Rumaylah airbase on the first day, when John Nichol and John Peters had been shot down. Dressed in his sand-coloured flying suit and green rollneck jumper, and sporting a tremendous 'Biggles-like' handlebar moustache, Pablo provided them with some highly charged commentary. 'There is a constant awareness that in a few seconds' time you might not exist.' Already visibly fighting to retain his composure, he went on: 'You train to control your emotions when it really matters ...' He had finally broken down in tears. 'I'm responsible for my whole crew. You feel guilty that you have survived and they haven't. We work together, play together and live together. Hopefully, we won't die together.'

Perhaps aware that emotions needed to be tempered, Nigel Risdale, the pilot who had helped plan the first missions, tried to put the aircrews' risk into perspective. 'It's equally hazardous driving around the M25 motorway every day,' he suggested. 'Thousands are killed on Britain's roads each year, but when one aircraft is lost it is news.' Risdale was one of the Squadron's most highly respected fliers, and renowned for his coolness under stress. Speaking with a sand-coloured Tornado fin visible behind him, he added: 'You've survived one sortie, but you know that calming yourself down is important so you can get to sleep, knowing that you've got another task to do in ten hours' time.'

Other aviators had also quickly parked their distress at the losses and wanted to even the score. 'Some on the Squadron were extremely angry,' recalled navigator Paddy Teakle. 'The losses motivated them. They wanted to take the fight to Saddam. This was real and they wanted payback for comrades being shot down.'[10] Mark Paisey, the pilot who had flown alongside Peters and Nichol on their mission, was also candid with his feelings after the Tornado's first ever, and never to be repeated, low-level daylight attack. 'I was in tears when I got back – we had lost our wingman and friends,' he told the journalists. 'At the moment, I'm going through the full range of emotions, from elation right down to dread and fear of dying.'

Paisey also articulated what was going through the minds of most airmen who faced a return to the battlefield. 'Next time, it's going to be harder, because you're aware it could be you . . .'

* * *

For Dave Waddington, the words 'it could be you' had become an uncomfortable reality. Badly injured and on the run in southern Iraq, he knew his chances of escape were diminishing. After scraping out a thin trench around dawn, he had managed to lie down and sleep despite the pain from his dislocated shoulder and elbow. The screech of large birds feeding from stagnant water nearby penetrated his slumber. The sound of gunfire then shook him fully awake. Bullets started pinging into the muddy sand just a few yards from where he lay. 'It was totally unreal, not something I had ever expected to encounter. It was at this point I began to realise I could very easily die.' He glanced up from his meagre cover. Two men in green military trousers and civilian coats, one young, one old, loosed off more rounds as they advanced towards him. 'As they got to within about 30 yards of my position, I really wondered if they were going to kill me.'

The Iraqis kept their distance, gesturing for him to raise his hands. With both arms dislocated it was impossible, so instead he started shouting, '*Salaam alaikum*' – 'peace be upon you'. 'It seemed odd given that I'd just been bombing their country, but it was all the Arabic I knew.'

The older Iraqi tried to soothe the younger as he yelled aggressively at the enemy invader. They gestured again for Dave to put his hands up. 'I thought, this was going to be such a stupid way to die! Just because I couldn't get my arms in the air. It was all getting very, very tense.' They eventually stopped firing and moved closer. Dave pointed to the Walther pistol in its shoulder holster which he had still been unable to reach. The younger man then began manhandling him, using the rifle butt to push him around. Again, he was calmed by the older Iraqi. Dave wondered what his fate might be. 'What was I going to go through before it ended? Being alive was a bit of a bonus as only a few hours earlier I had thought I had died. So there was still hope. At the back of the mind, however, there was also the thought that in the not-too-distant future, perhaps I might wish I really was dead.'

The pair marched Dave off at gunpoint. Astonishingly, he was soon back on the outskirts of Tallil. He now realised that during his night evasion, because of his concussion he had completed a long U-turn and ended up on the other side of the airbase. He was taken to some low buildings close to the runway he had so recently been attacking and dragged down into a pit. 'It was 7ft deep, with sides that sloped in. There were a dozen Iraqis all with rifles staring down at me. It was all very menacing. I thought, *God, what's going to happen here?*' The soldiers stepped down and searched him. 'They pretty much stripped me of everything of value and just left me with my flying suit and boots.' He was left with an older man with no teeth and a wrinkled, sunburned face who took his time searching, eventually finding the gold sovereigns the others had missed. 'His face lit up, looking like he'd won the lottery!'

As Dave was driven from the base he spotted what looked like a baked-bean can on three legs by the side of the road. It was one of the JP233 anti-personnel mines dropped by a Tornado and designed to explode if disturbed by any repair crews. *Shit! If that goes off we'll all be killed!* He pushed himself back into the seat between the two guards 'so their bodies might protect me from the blast and shrapnel if it detonated'. They pulled up at a military camp in the nearby town of Nasiriyah where a huge group of soldiers wearing red berets gathered around the vehicle. 'I was absolutely terrified. If I was going to be lynched, it was going to happen now. It felt like I was a serial killer being taken into court while an angry mob waited outside. There was a lot of noise, jostling and shouted commands. Then I was shoved back in the car and driven to a nearby medical facility.'

Dave was placed on a treatment table where a medic began digging bits of shrapnel out of his face. 'At one stage they were going to give me an anaesthetic, because my face was in absolute agony, but my military guard stopped them. I began to wonder why they might need to avoid giving me pain-suppressing drugs . . .' A medic grabbed his dislocated left arm, put his knee where the elbow was dislocated and levered it back into position. 'It was incredibly painful and I groaned loudly, but he just looked down at me and hissed, "Be a man!" It was all deeply unpleasant.'

'They cleaned up my face and plastered up my dislocated elbow. I was beginning to get really worried. I had no doubt I'd be tortured; there was an inevitability about it. The easy thing would have been to tell them what they wanted to know straight away. But doing the "right thing" was important to me. Even though I knew what that meant in reality.' As they drove towards Baghdad, Dave's arm became excruciatingly painful. The plaster cast that the Iraqi medics had put around his left elbow was so tight that it had restricted the blood flow. They stopped at another medical centre where a female doctor cut off part of the cast. Just before leaving, she edged closer to him so the guards couldn't see her, then, slipping something in his pocket, whispered quietly in his ear: 'For when you need them, Mr David.' 'I later found out it was a strip of fifteen painkillers. It was a remarkable act of kindness and really incredible bravery. She was risking her own safety to help me; I was truly indebted to her.'

* * *

The pain Robbie Stewart was enduring under interrogation had already caused him to pass out a number of times. Returning to consciousness, he squinted under his blindfold as the Iraqi interrogator began prodding his fractured leg again. Despite the intense pain, he still refused to respond.

'Mr Stewart! You're not answering our questions.' His tormentor's tone changed. 'If you continue, somebody else will come!'

The man left the room. When he returned, he spoke in a deeper voice, pretending to be a different, more threatening interrogator. But Robbie could see it was the same person through the gap in his blindfold. 'It was quite funny really; a ludicrous situation! But, unfortunately, he had also brought in his mate carrying a large pole with a ball attached.

'Now I was really scared. There was a lot of fear; a sense of anticipation about what was to come. I knew things were going to get worse, but there was nothing I could do about it. I was just waiting for it to happen. He started laying about me with this pole, repeatedly beating me across my body and legs.' As the blows rained down, Robbie fell in and out of consciousness once more. 'I was in such incredible pain from my leg I doubled up and vomited again into my hanky while trying to keep it off my uniform. Ridiculously, I was still trying to keep clean in this appalling situation! The pain was strange. It came on so quickly and was so powerful, that I simply passed out. Then when I came round they started again. I passed out so many times, it was a way of escaping.'

Despite the ordeal, in his mind Robbie continued the fight. 'I have no idea how many hours it went on for but I was still going through my options, trying to resist. I was determined to try to hold out as long as possible and not give anything away that could harm others. Of course, every time I passed out they had to stop and wait for me to come round before they could start again, which also helped prolong my resistance.

'At some point they told me with great glee that they had captured Dave. I was so relieved. Obviously, I hoped he had escaped, but hearing he was at least confirmed alive was a great boost to morale, better than any painkilling tablet they could have given me.'

The Iraqis knew Robbie had a great vulnerability and didn't waste their time. The interrogator finally wrapped his hands around the airman's shattered leg and began twisting it, grating the broken bones together. 'The pain was agonising and I began to realise that if I didn't say something, I could easily die where I lay, or at least be maimed for life.' He lapsed into grateful unconsciousness again but when he came round, Robbie was ready for the question.

'What aircraft were you flying?'

'Tornado.'

'It did not seem a big giveaway as we had just parked one in the sand next to their base! They clearly knew what we had been flying.'

More questions were pelted at him. Robbie's mind went back to the *Sunday Times* article that had infuriated him as he tried to relax back at his village home in Lincolnshire on the first Sunday of the New Year. It had only been a couple of weeks earlier, but now seemed like a lifetime ago. The article had detailed what the Tornados might be doing, aircraft numbers and basic capabilities. *That's what I'm going to give them.* He also recalled CNN naming airfields that missions had already been launched from. He gave them the same information. The Iraqis accepted it all. Plus a few fibs. 'I said we were flying very low at 500ft and that we tanked at 20,000ft.' None of the details were technical and he hoped he hadn't given the Iraqis anything they couldn't find elsewhere.

The questions finally came to an end. Exhausted and in great pain, Robbie was driven to a hospital. They cut off all his clothing while a softly spoken doctor asked some medical questions. 'He said I'd broken my collarbone, probably had a spinal compression injury as well as my obvious leg break. He directed the radiographer to take X-rays of my leg, shoulder and back.' While most fliers usually took off their wedding rings before a sortie, Robbie had kept his in place. 'Mine was part of me, so I had to wear it.' The hospital assistant gently wound a cord around its inside and began to ease it off. He saw Robbie looking at him. 'It's okay,' he said reassuringly. 'You'll be getting this back.'

Robbie was wheeled carefully into the operating theatre and told to breathe deeply into a mask.

'I slipped into unconsciousness for the second night.'

CHAPTER NINE

THE MISSION FROM HELL

20 JANUARY

The mental strain of flying nightly into the inferno, not knowing if you would come out the other side, was taking its toll across the Tornado force's three bases. The RAF now had around 150 aircraft – fighters, bombers, helicopters, tankers, transport and surveillance – in the Gulf, but the Tornado bombers were carrying out the most dangerous assignments under the most intense pressure.[1] Jerry Witts, in charge of the Dhahran Tornado detachment, believed it was plain common sense to share the stress as evenly as possible. 'It became blindingly obvious to me that we should have a plan to pace people. Also, to give the crews a chance to know when they'd be required to go, when they could psych themselves up and when they could relax as much as possible.'[2]

His thoughts were echoed by the Detachment Commander of the RAF Jaguar bombers operating alongside the Tornados from Muharraq, who recognised they could all be in it for the long haul. 'I couldn't ask my pilots to fly more than one sortie a day. And perhaps every fifth day, they should have a day off. The engineers also went on two equal shifts to fix the aircraft and to bomb them up.'[3] The Jaguars had largely been utilising medium-level dive-bomb attacks, avoiding the very worst of the low-level triple-A barrage, though they'd had some very close calls with the more powerful Iraqi systems capable of shelling at their operating heights of between 10,000 and 20,000 feet. And the Tornado F3 air defence crews, patrolling at around 25,000 feet, were also having to deal with Iraqi SAMs targeting them.

But for the Tornado bomber crews assembling at Dhahran, Tabuk and Muharraq for their next combat missions, there was an increasingly pervasive sense that some would not return. And that if they did survive *this* sortie, the odds were they'd catch it on the next one. Or the one after that.

Robbie Stewart's colleagues at Muharraq were certainly contemplating their immediate future. They had now lost three Tornados in as many days. Nige Risdale had kept his thoughts to himself when he overheard someone mention that Waddington and Stewart had gone down. *Oh no, there's another one! It's becoming like the Lancaster bombers in the Second World War! More aircraft, more friends lost every night.* He glanced around at the sixteen aviators clambering into their flight gear in preparation for the next dawn raid. 'I wondered who among our eight-ship would not come back from this trip.'

He knew he had to push away the dark thoughts as swiftly as possible. 'It was a momentary acknowledgement of what we were involved in, but with my single-minded psyche, it was quickly compartmentalised. My brain went back to what we were about to do.'[4] He glanced across at his friend and fellow pilot Nick Heard, who was also reflecting silently on the news of the recent loss. *Perhaps it might be* my *luck that runs out tonight?*[5]

But the attack plan for this latest raid had been well thought out; perfected by what the Tornado force had learned after three intense days of war. An hour before dawn on 20 January, the RAF would attack Al Jarrah, the Iraqi 'super-base' south-east of Baghdad, which housed three squadrons of Su-22 fighter-bombers and a squadron of air defence MiG-23 fighters. Gordon Buckley, one of the 15 Squadron Flight Commanders, knew they couldn't keep following the same attack profiles. 'I was struggling to sleep; the whole issue was playing on my mind. The preliminary attacks by the Americans, designed to *suppress* the Iraqi defences, were in reality stirring up a hornet's nest. It seemed crazy to be flying into that triple-A night after night. There had to be a better way. The risks were immense; there was so much fire and exploding lead being hurled into the air that the odds were against us continuing to get through unscathed.'

The Tornado force had to stop coming in at the tail-end of a mass attack that had already galvanised the enemy defences. Instead of being the *last* jets through, Buckley wanted them to be the *only* jets through. He believed a 'small, discrete formation package' would give them the best chance of getting in and out undetected. Discussing the problems with Paddy Teakle and Nige Risdale, they struck on the idea of sending two JP233 jets through as a surprise first attack, followed by four Tornados, each carrying eight 1,000-pounders, executing a loft attack, lobbing thirty-two bombs onto the triple-A positions and blasting open a corridor for the last two JP233 jets. The senior crews then presented the idea to the Tornado Detachment Commander, John Broadbent, who succeeded in getting headquarters approval.

In the small hours of the night, the eight-ship lined up on Muharraq's runway. Their target lay 100 miles south-east of the Iraqi capital, some considerable distance from Bahrain. They would have to fly more than an hour westwards, then cross the border and head north-east at low level for another hour before attacking the target. It was a four-hour, 1,600-mile round trip. Air-to-air refuelling along the tanker trail was going to be key.

The challenge of heading once again into the fiercest enemy fire was worsened by the probability of heavy cloud and severe turbulence along their route – and things began to go awry even before take-off. The crew of one Tornado at the rear of the formation had an engine problem and could not select reheat. There was no way they could get off the ground. The seven remaining aircraft climbed to 12,000ft for their rendezvous with the tankers. The meteorological wizards had not been wrong. They entered the heavy cloud to be tossed and bucked by powerful updraughts and downdraughts.

As he approached the Victor's right wing, Nick Heard fought to keep his lurching jet in position. He inched towards the mouth of the refuelling hose, snaking through the darkness a few feet ahead. 'I really felt under intense pressure. I was burning fuel, while also using up my allotted time to take on the fuel I needed.' Suddenly they entered clearer skies. He touched the throttle, propelling the Tornado's probe on the right-hand side of the cockpit towards the funnel. And then crunched straight through the flat metal plates that held the neck of the basket open and provided its aerodynamic stability. *Crap! This is really going to mess things up.* 'If you spoked the basket there was a real danger that some of the metal connections might break off and be ingested into your own engine, which could cause a catastrophic failure.'

These fragments being sucked through the blades could generate the destructive force of shrapnel, and cause the engine to self-destruct. In peacetime, 'spoking' would force an immediate return to base. But peacetime happened in another life. Nick carefully eased back the power, praying the whole basket wouldn't tear away and remain clamped on the end of his probe. Luckily, it emerged cleanly and the engine readings encouraged him to believe all was well. He manoeuvred through the darkness to the tanker's left wing, queuing behind Nige Risdale, who was experiencing his own dramas in the other JP233-armed jet.

He'd been three-quarters full when the Victor disappeared into a violent cumulonimbus thundercloud. 'It was like being on high-speed dodgems at the fairground, but on a corrugated surface rather than a nice smooth arena. And then being constantly battered from all sides by the other cars.' Nige dabbed on the reheat but couldn't keep the probe in the basket. 'The turbulence was throwing us around, the tanker around and the basket around. It was like trying to get cooked spaghetti up a jumping cat's arse as it runs away from you.' Another huge jolt pushed them away from the nozzle. With a soft hand on the stick, Nige nudged the power up and the probe towards the rim of the basket, then pushed it home. Once full, he made way for the next in line.

Having fouled up the right-wing hose, Nick Heard was keener than ever to get his tanks filled in a window of relative stability, and this time he engaged on the first attempt. But with the tanker now down to one conduit, it was going to be a struggle to cycle the other two aircraft of their formation through. His navigator was having similar concerns. 'I really don't think we can get this mission done without one of us going back to the tanker behind us to take on fuel.' Nick frowned. That wasn't a pleasant prospect. The rear tanker was 10 miles behind them, in total darkness and, odds on, in the same heavy cloud.

As lead crew for the seven remaining aircraft, Nige Risdale and John Broadbent were the refuelling priority. They had to top up again before heading into enemy territory.

Nick Heard was filling his tanks when Broadbent instructed him to go in search of the Victor at their rear. 'Bloody hell!' Nick muttered, disconnecting from his precious hose. 'I now had to turn out of the tanker trail and fly against the stream, making sure I was separated laterally from the oncoming aircraft, then try to reacquire another Victor in total darkness! Then I would have to join *their* formation and work my way around the rear Tornados to take on fuel. I was really thinking, *Things are not going well tonight.*' Without the aid of any night-vision equipment, it was a severe test. Even for the most experienced of crews.

The second Victor's situation was no easier, as Gordon Buckley was discovering. The wind was battering the hose so violently it was almost impossible to hook on. One of his formation did manage to connect, but radioed seconds later to report that fuel would not transfer. The fault could not be rectified, so returning to base was the only option. The eight-ship which had started the mission was now reduced to six.

After turning back, Nick Heard threaded his way past Gordon

Buckley's formation to the rear tanker's basket. With their runway denial munitions, his JP233-armed jet was a priority. He inched his Tornado forward, riding the turbulence, and pushed the probe home first time. 'Able to relax slightly for a brief moment, I was suddenly struck by the fact that it was a Saturday evening. Back at home, people were watching the football, enjoying a drink at the pub, and we were stuck on this tanker bouncing around in the darkness, the reward for which was being shot at in the very near future.'

In the meantime, three jets were still battling to refuel from one hose trailing behind the leading Victor. When time ran out for the third, John Broadbent reluctantly ordered it back to base. The eight-ship was now down to five. Nick Heard eventually eased away from the rear tanker with brimful tanks and dived into the black void to catch up with Risdale and the number three jet armed with 1,000lb bombs, already descending towards the border.

Gordon Buckley knew that refuelling was becoming increasingly dangerous. And the clock was ticking. His formation had to take enough fuel on board to reach the target at their allotted time. One crew was really struggling. 'The more times he tried unsuccessfully to connect with the tanker, the greater was the chance of him spoking and damaging his aircraft, perhaps fatally. I made the difficult decision to send them home.'

The eight-ship was now down to four.

Since Gordon had come up with the mission plan, he was determined to see it through. Summoning every last iota of skill he'd acquired from nearly 2,000 Tornado flying hours, he gently coaxed his aircraft through the tumult and into close formation with the giant Victor only a few feet away. A huge jolt threw him off the connection. Seconds after that, the same thing happened again. Time was running out. He knew if he didn't stay the distance, he'd be off the raid too. As the Tornado and the tanker bucked and swayed through the cloud banks, he managed to hook onto the hose for a third time.

But his relief was short-lived.

The skies suddenly cleared – to reveal the lead Victor dead ahead.

Gordon's tanker plunged into an emergency dive to avoid collision. His probe snapped out of the basket yet again, and the Tornado was presented with a new and drastic threat. 'The one place you must never be when tanking is above the wing line because the aerodynamic flow from the huge tanker will disrupt your own airflow. Which is precisely what happened to me – the aircraft controls went completely mushy.'

Gordon pulled back the throttles, the wing dropped and the altimeter spun like a Catherine wheel. 'I had absolutely no control of my aircraft and could only watch as it rolled left and then plunged earthwards, losing about 6,000ft.' Fighting for control, he finally managed to level it out and climbed back to rejoin the Victor. 'I gave the pilot a piece of my mind and told him to keep it steady this time! I had a final stab with the probe and basket going all over the place. I don't know how, but I finally got in; it wasn't skill, just pure luck.'

With the Tornado finally latched on, the tanker crew elected to head north. It would allow them to take on more fuel before descending to the target. But it also brought the danger zone of the Iraqi border ever closer. The plan had been to devastate Al Jarrah with a series of timed strikes by eight Tornados. Now, only three aircraft – two armed with JP233s and one with 1,000-pounders – were attacking ahead. Substantially behind them, Gordon and his navigator Paddy Teakle were left contemplating whether it made sense to make a solo dash into Iraq now they no longer had any JP233 aircraft to protect. They decided to press on. 'We had a mission and we were determined to complete it. While we would not help the attackers *that* night, if we destroyed some triple-A positions with our own 1,000-pounders, it might help others visiting the same target in the future.'

Paddy Teakle agreed. 'We decided to kill some of those gun emplacements so they wouldn't have the same intense defences next time the airfield was attacked.'[6]

As they sped over the border, an AWACS operator asked them to overfly a position where it was believed a downed American crew had ejected. They didn't hesitate. Fellow coalition fliers might be in mortal danger. Good friends had been in the same boat. Burning precious fuel they could not spare, they orbited the site, eventually turning on their aircraft lights to show their presence to any downed fliers. Seconds later their RHWR warned them that an enemy radar was on to them. It was probably coincidental, but Gordon wasn't taking any chances. With no sign of the US crew, he flicked off the lights and pushed the throttles forward, speeding up to 550mph for the dash to Al Jarrah.

The three leading Tornados had already turned sharply northeast. The target was a fraction over 200 miles ahead. Their TOT was an hour before sunrise. Nick Heard hoped the front pair would get over the airfield before the enemy gunners had a chance to open fire. This was his third operational mission and the exhilaration of combat was wearing thin. Everything was quiet as they began the final run in. *Maybe our luck is in*, Nick thought, as they sped 200ft above the desert floor. They were thirty seconds from Al Jarrah when the triple-A turned night into day. 'Bollocks,' Nick muttered. The all-too-familiar barrage of multi-coloured exploding lights blossomed around the target. 'For some reason they seemed to know where we were coming from this time. Worse, the triple-A was not only intense, it was now angled downwards instead of spraying straight up. It seemed to be aimed right at us.'

The Iraqis had changed their cannon trajectory to catch aircraft attacking at low level. Had this been triggered by information gleaned during interrogation of their captured friends? For a moment Nick was struck by how much it resembled the classic sequence in the *Dam Busters* film, when Lancaster bombers flew low over the dams into the teeth of seemingly impregnable German gunfire, before dropping their 'bouncing bombs'. He had just a little sense of the fear his forebears must have faced as streams of green and red tracer fire curved towards them through the night sky. He pushed himself against his ejection seat, gripping the controls. 'Triple-A flew past our ears as we headed in, still some distance from the target. It was awful. Really bad. I just thought, *Oh BUGGER!*'

A mile or so to Heard's left, Nige Risdale's hopes of a quiet night had also been dashed. 'The air defences at Al Jarrah were more sophisticated than the other airfields and for a third time we entered a flak firestorm on a wing and a prayer. I was convinced that the barrage was better aimed and much more threatening than anything we had experienced before.' Twenty seconds out, he deselected the autopilot and manually dipped the Tornado to head in at 180ft for the JP233 release. Gunfire rattled past the cockpit as he focused on flying diagonally across the runway ahead.

Seconds later he felt the jarring reports of the runway-cratering munitions and anti-personnel mines shooting out from the giant containers beneath their feet. 'It seemed to take a long time on this one! I could feel every single submunition come out slowly, rather than the almost machine-gun rattle I recalled from the first runs.'

Nick Heard took his Tornado through the heart of the barrage, leaving a trail of gently descending but deadly parachutes. 'We popped out the other side unscathed and couldn't quite believe our luck. We had done it again and survived! But as we completed our post-target checks, Rob, my navigator, piped up that we were now below minimum fuel to get back to the tanker with enough reserves in case the problems of the inbound flight were repeated. He jettisoned the now empty external tanks, which meant that with the weapons gone too, we were in a relatively "clean" jet apart from the Boz and Sky Shadow pods and the Sidewinder missiles.' Their aircraft was now far more aerodynamic, and would burn considerably less fuel on the egress.

Gordon Buckley and Paddy Teakle were closing in for their own, now solo, attack. Their dramatic exchanges were recorded on the cockpit cassette navigation system as they headed through the darkness towards the thundering gunfire.[7]

RRRrrrRRRrrrRRRrrr.
Their RHWR radar warner screeched a warning that a SAM system was looking at them ...

Paddy: *Turning in three minutes, avoiding the SAM 3 site.*
          Heading 350.
Gordon: *Roger.*

Paddy: *Head in for the fix.*

Teakle was now head-down in the cockpit, concentrating on the radar to update the navigation system.

AWACS: *Choctaw, picture clear.*

Using the codename of a Native American tribe, the AWACS operator told them no enemy aircraft were in the air.

Paddy: *Crossing all those roads, railroads and rivers now.*

Gordon: *There's a lot of movement down there, do we come back this way?*

Paddy: *No. We go west of here.*

Gordon: *Good. Stepping the height down and speeding up. How's the fuel?*

Paddy: *We're running on [minimum] fuel. We'll have to punch the under-wing [tanks] off in about 1,000 kilos' [of fuel] time.*

They had the bare minimum to complete the mission and get back to the tanker. They, too, would need to jettison the empty external tanks.

Gordon: *How far away is the target now?*

Paddy: *We're hitting it in eight minutes. We're about 60 miles south, at the moment.*

Gordon: *Good. I wonder what aircrew were down. Makes you wonder, doesn't it?*

Paddy: *Yep. I'm going head in for the pre-target fix. I'll use it as a confidence check [of the navigation system].*

AWACS: *Choctaw, picture clear.*

Paddy: *Fix is spot on.*

Gordon: *Roger.*

RRRrrrRRRrrrRRRrrr.

The SAM radar warning sounded again.

Paddy: *Target is at your 11 o'clock, 35 miles. The rest of the guys are approaching [the target].*

Gordon: *Setting up the escape heading of 255 degrees.*

Paddy: *Turning shortly, and pushing the speed up.*

Gordon: *When are the others on target?*

Paddy: *About thirty seconds.*

Gordon: *They're going to make the defenders really annoyed before we get there!*

Paddy: *Yep. Turning shortly. [Heading] 335. The fuel checks at 5,200 kilos.*

Gordon: *There goes the triple-A.*

Paddy: *Visual.*

'The first lot of bombs going off really did stimulate the triple-A,' Paddy recalled. 'It wasn't like the first couple of nights; it was now aimed, weaving around the heights we were flying. They were getting cleverer.'

RRRrrrRRRrrrRRRrrr.

The radar warner continued sounding its message.

Gordon   *There's the JP [JP233 weapons] going.*

Buckley could see the weapons from the Tornados ahead of them exploding.

Paddy: *Yep.*

Gordon: *There go the second lot [of JP233s]. Where are the thousand-pounders?*

Paddy: *In thirty seconds.*

AWACS: *Choctaw, picture clear.*

Gordon: *Boom, boom, boom!*

Coming in not far behind the third jet, Buckley had a good view of the first 1,000lb attack. 'The sight of the bombs exploding mid-air was shocking to the senses, but amazingly the gunfire did not diminish. I was expecting to see this "hole" in the triple-A as the guns were destroyed but there was nothing, no change at all. I now realised that *we* were going to have to attack into the same maelstrom.'

Paddy: *Okay, speeding up. Use your burners. Low loft selected. Marking the bridge.*

Teakle told Buckley to increase speed for the sharp, upward climb required before lofting the bombs. He ran through the target offsets, locating and marking them on the radar, ensuring the weapons system was as accurate as possible.

Gordon: *Switches live. Low loft light's on.*
Paddy: *Good mark on the second offset, going offset three.*
Gordon: *Speed 600 knots. Maximum dry power.*
Using the reheat well before the target, their speed was now nearing 700mph.
Gordon: *How is it on time to go?*
Paddy: *Looks good. Fifty-nine seconds to run.*
Gordon: *Looks like we're here, mate.*
Paddy: *We are not here!*

Already at the very core of the barrage of gunfire, Buckley couldn't believe the flak was so intense, so far out. 'We were at 180ft and there was triple-A coming up at us in droves, flashing lights whistling all around the canopy; it was an astonishing experience. I kept saying to Paddy, "We must be here, we need to pull up now!" He kept saying, "No, we're not there yet, keep going!" It seemed suicidal, going against everything I had trained to do in my RAF career. I was about to pull the Tornado right up into the teeth of their gunfire. At that moment I truly thought I was going to die.'

Paddy: *Forty seconds. I know the triple-A looks close.*
          You're all right. Thirty-five seconds to go.
Gordon: *Okay . . .*
Paddy: *Thirty seconds to run . . . [pause] . . . Pulling in five,*
          four, three, two, one. PULL!

The Tornado soared into the night sky. 'The barrage passed below and above us,' Teakle said. 'I could see machine-gun fire and 23mm. There was light everywhere, like we were inside a Christmas tree.' At around 1,500ft, their bombs released and began a graceful arc towards the Iraqi gun positions. The Tornado was now high and very slow. More warning sirens sounded in the cockpit. Buckley initiated the challenging loft recovery to get the aircraft back to low level.

Paddy: *Bombs all gone. It's going off all around us! There go the bombs.*

Heading away from the target, Teakle sensed the eight massive blasts over the triple-A emplacements as he monitored his instruments.

Paddy: *Height is 3,000 feet, run out heading 255. In the recovery.*

Gordon Buckley had the Tornado tipped well over on its left wing, nearly inverted, banking hard, turning and descending. Failure to recover now would lead to one thing only – the ground.

Paddy: *Jettisoning the under-wing tanks. Right, they've gone. In the descent, back down to low level, passing 1,500ft. Don't look out! Just fly the recovery.*

Pilots had to fly the recovery profile solely on their instruments, totally ignoring any potentially confusing external visual clues. Paddy was a highly experienced Qualified Weapons Instructor and had taught new pilots the drill many times. He knew how disorientating it could be. Especially at night. The manoeuvre had cost the lives of a number of Tornado aircrew. Now, in darkness and under heavy fire, Paddy felt his own aircraft plummet towards the desert floor.

Gordon: *Triple-A is still going off around us!*
Paddy: *Don't look out, mate! Just fly the plane. We're passing 700 feet, and still going down. Easy, EASY!*

Audio warnings continued to fill the cockpit.

Paddy: *Start levelling off, mate! We've 300 feet to go.*

The Tornado was still heading fast towards the ground. When Teakle had yelled, 'Don't look out!' Buckley knew it was already too late. He was totally disorientated by the gunfire which now surrounded them. 'Triple-A was flying around the cockpit. Straight green lines, red flashing dots, some going straight past, some spiralling as the operators simply waved their guns blindly in the air. I felt as though I was at the heart of a firework display. I completely lost all sense of awareness of which way the jet was pointing, or where the ground was. It was like being in a sparkling kaleidoscope at night. I had no idea if I was going up or down. Luckily Paddy had taught this loft manoeuvre to students so he could talk me out of it. If I had been with someone less experienced ... well ... it simply doesn't bear thinking about ...'

Their jet bottomed out, descending through 100ft towards the desert floor, a second or two before impact.[8] Teakle's urgent warning and cool head had saved them. On the audio recording of those moments, their rapid breathing dominates the cockpit as they climb away from the ground.

Paddy: *Wings level now, 150 feet, ease the height up,*
           Buckers. That was bloody close!
Gordon: *I don't ever want to do that again. That was awful!*
Paddy: *We were right up amongst it.*
Gordon: *We don't get paid enough for this. Well done, mate.*
           Christ, triple-A is still going.
Paddy: *Yeah, it still looks close, doesn't it?*
Gordon: *I tell you, it WAS bloody close!*
Paddy: *Five's off target. Egressing.*
Teakle told the rest of the formation they were leaving the target area.

Gordon: *I can see my cold is going to get worse soon, mate!*
Buckley joked that he might report sick for the next raid. In their elation, both men couldn't resist quoting their favourite lines from *Blackadder*.
Paddy: *Captain B, my stomach's gone all squirty!*
Gordon: *My stomach's on the floor at the moment ... Oh*
           God, I think I want to die!
Paddy: *I think we almost did ...*

It was dawn on 20 January as the four Tornados that had bombed Al Jarrah, all now with their weapons systems 'switches safe', made their way back across the border. Hooking onto the tankers in daylight was straightforward. Landing at Muharraq was not. Mist cloaked the base, bringing visibility down to less than half a mile. Nick Heard couldn't believe their luck. 'Normally in conditions like this, Air Traffic Control would talk us down using their radar, or we could use another separate, airfield-based system to guide us in. But nothing was working. Was this nightmare ever going to end? Could anything else go wrong on this trip?' One by one, each navigator used his own radar to guide his aircraft down through the thick fog. Shocked into silence, Nick Heard shut down his engine. He opened the canopy and breathed in the early-morning air, feeling the warmth of the sun that was now starting to burn off the mist. 'Normally we would jump straight out, but we both just slumped back in our seats, drained and exhausted.'

One of the ground crew plugged into his jet's intercom and asked: 'Hey, sir, where's your tanks?'

Nick was not quite ready to relive the night's events. 'It's a long story . . .'

He slowly unbuckled and climbed down the ladder. 'It was the most taxing, dangerous sortie I ever flew during my whole career in aviation. I think quite a few people were affected by that raid, and some had to take a quiet moment alone to recover.'

Walking into the Operations Room, Gordon Buckley met one of the men who had carried out the loft attack with the 1,000-pounders just ahead of them, straight after Heard and Risdale's initial JP233 drop. 'He looked utterly shattered and I asked him if he was okay.'

'I'll tell you what, Buckers, I don't have too many more of those inside me,' he replied.

'He was an experienced, senior crewman and the last person I expected to hear that from.' But Buckley also knew from his own recent brush with death that a huge amount was being asked of the men who repeatedly faced the triple-A hailstorm. Reliving the mission thirty years later with the author, Buckley's memory of the experiences was crystal clear. 'I can still see my friends' haunted expressions, and it really made me assess my own feelings. At the start, there had been a certain gung-ho excitement about what we were going to do. We were trained, we were keen, we were ready; confident in our abilities to evict the Iraqi forces from Kuwait and liberate an occupied country. We were now facing death on an almost nightly basis; the realities of war were writ large.'

John Broadbent, the 15 Squadron Boss and overall Tornado Commander at Muharraq, could see how both the losses and the continued braving of triple-A were affecting his crews. 'When I looked into the faces of my colleagues during the debrief, I could see the terrible strain etched on each one of them. And bearing in mind we had just lost our third crew, I realised that some sort of change was needed.' As the crews talked through the mission, this issue came repeatedly to the fore. Buckley thought a big question mark now hung over whether they should continue with these increasingly lethal tactics. They could endeavour to further refine their low-level tactics, of course, but did they need to? Might attacking from medium level, above the triple-A, prove more effective?

Initially, Buckley had been against any move to medium-level bombing. 'All our training, tactics, weaponry, the Tornado itself, was optimised for low level.' But he was eventually persuaded that the new tactics would be more 'palatable' if the Americans could provide the suppressive support with electronic warfare jets, anti-radiation missiles and fighter escorts to defend against Iraqi SAMs and fighters.

They reached a consensus and John Broadbent discussed the situation with the overall RAF Commander at Muharraq. 'I made the point forcefully to my own Boss, and through him to HQ: it appeared to those of us flying the mission that since the Iraqi Air Force remained grounded, had we not achieved our primary task of gaining air superiority? In that case, was it really necessary to continue to attack airfields at low level as this was costing us dear? Surely it was time to take advantage of the conditions that our efforts had created to transition to the safer environment of medium level? I still go cold thinking about that sortie thirty years on and the conclusions of my subsequent Mission Report [the official document sent to HQ immediately after every operation] told the story of what I still regard as a real horror mission:

> *The first 2 aircraft failed to achieve surprise, suggesting that the Iraqis had developed an effective early warning system. Furthermore, the resulting defensive barrage was directed at both low and medium level indicating that the Iraqis had recognised the threat posed to them by aircraft attacking from low level. It was disappointing to note that the airburst 1000lb bombs had little apparent effect on the AAA fire. Furthermore, concern was raised that the loft manoeuvre took the aircraft, not only into the heart of the AAA barrage, but as a result, tested the considerable skills of 2 of the most able and experienced pilots on the Sqn. In the light of these facts, we have conducted a review of our tactics and have decided that there is little advantage to be gained from compression through the target. If JP233 attacks remain necessary in future, they would be better conducted as pairs of aircraft sent to the target at irregular intervals. The support afforded to our missions so far has done little to suppress what has proved to be the greatest threat – that posed by AAA barrage fire. Our preferred option would be to negate the AAA by flying above it at 20,000ft plus. However, at this altitude, 2-way contact with AWACS would be essential and fighter sweep desirable. In addition, depending upon the en-route and target area SAM threat, EF1-11 or Wild Weasel [Enemy Missile Defence Suppression assets] support might also be necessary.*[9]

The casualties borne by the Tornado force in the first few days of war were not going unnoticed by Britain's American allies. When asked to comment publicly on the situation, General Norman Schwarzkopf, in overall command of the campaign, said, 'Their contribution has been absolutely superb, I am damn glad they are with us!'[10]

Lieutenant General Chuck Horner, who controlled the entire air war, was privately more frank with the overall British commander, General Sir Peter de la Billière, at the coalition headquarters in Saudi Arabia. 'Gee, Peter, I sure admire the courage of your pilots, but I'm a little concerned they ain't achieving much in relation to the risk they're taking and the effort they're putting in.' De la Billière, a former SAS commander, later recorded his reaction. 'I made some cautious reply, but from this and other comments I could tell that Chuck considered our method of operation a pretty crazy one in this environment.'[11]

The Tornado story was also gaining traction among the American press, including reporters embedded at Dhahran. Soon after Dave Waddington and Robbie Stewart had been shot down, the *Los Angeles Times* asked why the 'fabled RAF' was suffering such high losses.[12] It suggested they were the result of 'both the Royal Air Force's daring flying style and the extremely hazardous missions they have been given by allied commanders: destroying the runways that serve Iraq's air force'. This tactic, the paper continued, made the Tornados and their crews 'sitting ducks for Iraqi anti-aircraft barrages'.

What followed must have made difficult reading in certain quarters. One Tornado, it suggested, was being lost for every eighty sorties flown, whereas the Americans were flying 750 sorties per downed aircraft. But the article failed to understand – like many misinformed vocal critics at the time – that the Tornado sorties had thus far been *entirely* low level, over heavily defended airfields, and the American total included countless *relatively* safe fighter patrols plus many high- and medium-level sorties over some far more benign targets.

The piece singled out the JP233 'airfield killer' which had been used to strike Iraqi runways 'with considerable success', then made the point that Tornado aircrew knew only too well: 'The down side is that it must be delivered by pilots flying straight down the runway at extremely low altitudes – as low as 100 to 200 feet – in full range and view[13] of enemy anti-aircraft guns. Experts say the pilots cannot even take evasive action to avoid enemy fire if they want to complete their mission successfully.'

The British Air Commander tried to calm things by speaking to the press at Dhahran. 'Overall losses have been incredibly low, astonishingly low, considering the number of sorties flown and the coordination which has surrounded those sorties,' Air Vice-Marshal Bill Wratten told the media. 'I will say we have also been extremely unlucky, and bad luck does not last forever.'[14]

* * *

Back at the hotel, Nige Risdale was contemplating how any ongoing 'bad luck' might collide with his immediate future. His first mission had been a novelty, the second had seen a close call after almost colliding with another Tornado over the enemy airfield in darkness, but this latest attack was something else again. 'For me personally, that third mission was an emotional watershed. The sortie from hell, where everything that could go wrong had gone wrong.' As the Boss's pilot, Risdale felt he had to display stoicism in the face of adversity but when he got back to his room the emotions were less constrained. 'I felt totally washed out and was really worried.' He looked at the family photograph by his bed, wondering if he would get through the next mission. 'I just could not see how we would survive doing the same thing night after night. I really thought I might not see my wife and son again.'

Risdale, not known for showing much emotion even under incredible stress, felt the tears roll down his cheeks as he contemplated what lay ahead.

But he knew a phone call to Claire would straighten him out. 'She listened like the rock she has always been for me, and totally understood.' She also understood when Nige told her he couldn't call when their 2-year-old son was awake. 'I couldn't trust my emotions with him and would have broken down again. Everyone was probably suffering similar thoughts, and although most were private about their personal emotional hiccups, I don't think any of us were immune.'

Gordon Buckley was also reflecting on his own narrow escape.

'The risks were very real and people were dying. *I* had just come very close to dying. The more I relived the previous ops, the more I thought that flying through that wall of triple-A was near-suicidal.'

Their aircraft had been specifically designed for low-level bombing. It remained to be seen how much longer the Tornado force could sustain the tactic.

CHAPTER TEN

BROADCAST OR DIE

Gordon Buckley's reflections on his 'near-suicidal mission', and Nigel Risdale's of an 'emotional watershed', were being echoed by many members of the three Tornado detachments in the Gulf. But there was still a war to fight.

Seven hundred miles from Muharraq, the Tabuk detachment was planning another low-level sortie against H3, on Iraq's western border with Jordan. Just two nights earlier, the fierce wall of impenetrable flak around the airbase had forced Mal Craghill's formation to abort their attack. The prospect of returning was not a pleasant one. Dave Bellamy's formation planned to counter the groundfire threat with a variation on Buckley and Risdale's Al Jarrah tactics. Their first *four* jets were tasked with lofting – tossing – 1,000lb bombs to airburst over the triple-A emplacements, punching a hole in the defences through which the following four-ship would pepper the runways with their JP233s.

Nerves and bodies were beginning to fray. The pace of operations meant that Dave was on his third consecutive mission in three days. Then there was the gnawing uncertainty of whether his flatmate John Nichol was dead or alive. Perhaps dead was better. If he had survived, *what were the Iraqis doing to him?* 'This was the worst period of the war. News of the ongoing Tornado losses built up the stress, and we were all totally knackered. Our prospects did not look good.'[1]

Bellamy walked into the Operations Room late on the afternoon of Sunday, 20 January. The boyish grins and enthusiasm of the first day had long since evaporated. Four days into the war, every crew had experienced the terror of flying into intense gunfire. Now they had to contemplate doing it all again. And again. And again. Bellamy saw deep anxiety etched in the features of his fellow aviators. 'There were nerves and real fear in a few faces. A lot of the guys were suffering. The hardest part of those nightmare missions was that just as you were coming to grips with your own fear, you were then confronted with somebody else's right before your eyes. Some people went deathly quiet, others babbled on about something trivial. I managed to find some strength in silence and the inexplicable belief that I was not about to die.' Briefings over, the Squadron lined up on the runway.

The unease had already been registered by his Squadron Boss Mike Heath, who would be leading the mission. Heath had earlier told the press: 'I have a lot of youngsters here who are scared but know exactly what they have to do. I am immensely proud of them and my job is to make sure they carry out the mission successfully and return safely. I think we are absolutely right in what we are doing against Saddam and, while no one wants to go to war, we are prepared to fight until he gives up in Kuwait.'[2]

As countless Tornado aircrews prepared for their next missions, the merits and otherwise of low-level attack were being carefully scrutinised at increasingly senior levels. Tornado raids had thus far spread the payload of 106 JP233s[3] across a host of Iraqi airfields. Considerable damage had been inflicted by their 22,790 anti-personnel mines and 3,180 runway-cratering bombs. It appeared that the Iraqi Air Force had now lost their appetite – or were now unable – to fly. Group Captain Cliff Spink was the overall RAF Commander at Dhahran and, while his base had not suffered any losses so far, he was acutely aware of the pressure his crews were under. 'The risks the bombers were taking overflying heavily defended airfields, especially at the tail-end of missions when all the defences had woken up, were increasingly concerning me. Did we really need to continue to carry out operations that way? It seemed the Iraqi Air Force did not want to come out to play, so why continue to pursue incredibly dangerous ops which, for the moment, were apparently not needed?'[4]

It was time to consider moving the Tornados out of the devastating reach of triple-A and that difficult discussion was being fed rapidly up the chain of command.

* * *

Unaware of this heated high-level debate, the eight Tornado pilots at Tabuk brought their engines into reheat. Pushing his throttles fully forward, Pete Batson wondered what the night might bring. Their last raid on Al Asad had seen him drop a JP233 on a Mirage fighter as it came in to land. Its pilot would not have survived. He did his best to put the thought aside as he tore down the runway. At around 200mph he pulled back on the stick and felt the GR1 lift into the air. Seconds later, he raised the landing gear, ready to set a course for the tanker rendezvous.

'Come right,' said his navigator, Mike Heath.

Batson eased the column gently to starboard, to take up the new heading. It barely moved. Neither did the aircraft. He tried again. The control column would only shift one centimetre from the neutral position. The Tornado, like most military aircraft, was a truly complex jet with a multitude of interlinking systems and things could certainly go awry. Sometimes there was an easy solution, rather like turning a computer 'off and on again'; on other occasions, a crew could be in serious trouble.

'I can't come right,' he told Heath calmly. 'We can only go left.'

Batson's jet had a serious problem and he immediately radioed Dave Bellamy to hand over the lead of the sortie, then climbed to height, talking through the options with the Boss in the back seat. Heath could not quite believe his mission was about to be kiboshed by a technical fault. 'As a Squadron Commander leading a wartime sortie, I should not have been wondering what the hell had gone wrong with the plane I was flying!'[5]

The Tornado was relatively stable, and by careful use of the rudder Batson could force the aircraft to manoeuvre enough to go roughly where he wanted. But they needed a better solution. Gaining height away from the airfield, Batson started looking around the cockpit to see if there was anything obvious jamming the control column. His frantic efforts to scan the confined space while flying the heavy jet in pitch darkness met without success. The best option, Heath now considered, was to follow the straightforward and well-worn drill for dealing with any type of flying-controls restriction. 'We thought if we lightened the aircraft by jettisoning the bombs and a bit of fuel, we might be able to tip it upside down. If there was something jamming the controls, we would shake it out.'

They radioed Tabuk that they were going to dump the 1,000-pounders. Every base had its own designated jettison area, and Tabuk's was a nearby small weapons training range which Batson now discovered was permanently manned by safety staff. 'We received a message over the radio to say that the bloke who lived on the range was going to put the lights on in his shack. We were told to avoid jettisoning our bombs anywhere near him!' The lights were easy to find, and without the pressure of incoming hostile fire, they descended to jettison the ordnance and external fuel tanks safely. Batson took the aircraft back up to height and for the next half an hour they flew around, going inverted, left and right, manoeuvring and jostling the controls as best he could. Despite their efforts, the column still would not shift.

Mike Heath was unimpressed. 'We shook the plane around for half an hour but still we couldn't fix the problem.'

The options now narrowed considerably: land or eject.

Landing was going to be tricky, even for Batson, who had been flying RAF jets since 1976. 'The Tornado was still flying but it was agricultural flying, with me using a load of rudder to get it to slip sideways in a turn. The stick would move smoothly left, but I was fighting to then move it back right to a central position. My real concern now was that I might put in a left turn but not be able to get the stick back to neutral and the wings level again – we would lose control.'

Wary of the plethora of other aircraft around Tabuk, not least the fully armed American F-15 fighters lined up near the end of the runway on Quick Reaction Alert, Batson carefully prepared for his approach. The Tornado lost height as it headed towards the runway lights. Batson held the stick steady, keeping the aircraft on track for the centre line as best he could. Then the nose shifted left. He pushed the stick right but it still refused to move. A gust shifted them further left, so badly off course he had to abort the landing. Pouring on the power to climb away, Batson eased the jet around in a series of wide left turns before lining up for the strip again. The altimeter wound down through 1,000ft to 800, then 600. They were on target, ready to commit to touchdown. Batson felt the Tornado shudder slightly as he dropped the landing gear.

Five hundred feet.

Nose dead centre to the runway.

Then it shifted marginally to the left.

Batson poured on the power again. 'We tried various approaches to all the different runways for about an hour. But I just couldn't keep us in a position to make a landing while unable to make any "right turn" inputs on the control column. We were at risk of actually hitting other waiting aircraft. There was a dawning realisation that we were not going to get this jet on the ground. There was no particular fear; the outcome was rather inevitable.'

The options had narrowed further: from two to one.

Mike Heath's annoyance at missing the raid was now tempered by the knowledge that they had an even riskier undertaking ahead. 'We decided to throw the plane away.'

As Waddington, Stewart, Peters and Nichol had all shown, eject-ing could be done instantaneously with barely a thought. But Batson and Heath now had time to dwell on the prospect of being rocketed out of a fast jet into the night sky.

Mike Heath reached for their Flight Reference Cards. The stiff, white flip-book detailed every aircraft routine from engine start-up to shut-down, then all the emergency drills, clearly presented for crews under severe pressure. After the procedures to be carried out in the event of a double engine failure or undercarriage malfunc-tion, Heath found the ejection section. It contained fourteen basic commands to be undertaken '*if time and conditions permit*'. Unlike the other wartime aircrews that had recently banged out in a matter of seconds, Heath had time to study the check list.

'*Speed, 250 knots. Height, 9,000 feet*,' Heath told Batson, reading from the FRCs.[6]

'*Head towards unpopulated area.*'

They had to fly back to where they had just jettisoned their bombs and fuel tanks. Then:

Harness – tight and locked.

Oxygen mask – tight.

Visors – down.

Radio – call as required.

Throttles – idle.

Ejection position – assume.

'Roger,' Batson responded to each instruction, double-checking his visor and sitting firmly back in the seat.

They paused before completion.

Heath looked at the black and yellow handle between his legs, and briefly considered the multimillion-pound price-tag of the air-craft they were about to throw away. 'Even though it was a lot of money, that wasn't really on my mind. I just tightened my straps and prepared.' Air Traffic Control told them two rescue helicopters would be launched just before they bailed out. It was gone 11pm. After a brief discussion it was agreed that Mike would do a count-down from ten and then pull the handle. The Tornado's 'Command

Eject' system meant that both crew would leave the aircraft whoever initiated ejection.

There was just 900kg of fuel remaining when, now 9,000ft above the desert, Batson slowed the Tornado to the prescribed 250 knots (287mph) and moved the throttles to idle so it would head earthwards soon after the crew departed.[7]

Heath tightened his straps one final time. 'On a countdown of ten . . .'

Batson listened in nervous anticipation, waiting to be blasted from the calm confines of the cockpit.

'Seven . . .

'Six . . .'

Heath thought of his wife and two young children back home. 'I remember getting to five and thinking, *Oh, my God, I hope I've got the courage to do this.*'

Batson felt like the Boss was taking for ever. 'It was the longest ten seconds of my life and at one point I wondered if Mike had stopped counting!'

'Three . . .

'Two . . .

'One . . .'

Heath pulled the ejection handle. 'It was the hardest thing I'd done in my career.'

For Batson the whole sequence unfurled in slow motion. 'It seemed like a lifetime before anything happened.'

A split second of silence . . .

Then the detonation of a cartridge under the MK10A Martin Baker ejection seat as it unlocked from the aircraft and extended the telescopic tubes which guided it upwards.

An instant later, two more cartridges fired. Heath and Batson felt the straps around their thighs, legs and arms rapidly tighten, pulling their limbs taut against the seat for what came next.

Two small rockets blew off the canopy. The seat rocket motors fired, propelling them upwards. Their oxygen and G-suit cables detached and the emergency oxygen tanks kicked in. With barely half a second gone, each man felt a sledgehammer blow beneath his backside.

'There was an enormous bang and a flash,' Batson recalled. 'For an instant, I could see the canopy moving, then I was hit in the face by my aircrew torch, clipped to the canopy, which came loose and smashed into my visor. My head was forced into my lap, then, although it was pitch-black, there was this vast pool of white light from the flash of the ejection rocket's explosion.'

The seat rocket motor had kicked in, filling the cockpit with light and blasting them into the night with a thrust of around thirty times the force of gravity. They accelerated to around 200mph in the blink of an eye, tossed about like ragdolls in the jet's 300mph slipstream. As they somersaulted, over and over, another cartridge fired, releasing a drogue chute to slow the seat's descent and stop it from tumbling through the air.

One and a half seconds after Heath had pulled the handle, the leg and arm restraints were released, along with the personnel equipment connector linking them to the emergency oxygen supply. A vast orange and white canopy blossomed from its head box and guillotine clippers sliced through the straps fastening each man to his seat, allowing it to fall away into the night.

'The next thing I knew,' Batson said, 'I was dangling under my parachute and everything was silent.' The entire sequence had taken just 1.7 seconds.

Remembering his training, Batson wriggled from head to toe, reassuring himself that everything was intact and functioning, then looked up to check the canopy. All was well. During the six-minute descent he took a moment to enjoy the still of the night. 'It was a pleasant journey, really. I was able to see the circular irrigation fields and several small lights dotted around the area.' The ground soon came into view. He adopted the parachute landing position, feet and knees together, braced for the impact. Nothing happened. The seconds ticked by and still the desert swam below him. 'It was impossible to judge my height in the dark. I'd think, *There's still a long way to go*, then I thought the ground was rushing towards me and assume the landing position again but nothing would happen. I did that a few times then suddenly landed like a bag of spuds.'

During his ejection Mike Heath had managed to glance down briefly and watch the Tornado disappear on its final glide beneath him. His own descent was interrupted by the rescue helicopter appearing to fly straight at him. 'It was a moment of sheer fear. I was still looking up when I hit the desert and landed on solid rock. I catapulted forward, hit my head and knocked myself out. When I came to, the helicopter was a few miles away.'

After shaking himself out on landing, Batson ignored the dull ache in his knee. Rotor blades were drumming some distance away. Batson got out his mini-flare gun and fired two rounds into the air. Like Robbie Stewart the day before, he managed to immediately attract attention. But rather than Iraqis, an American rescue crew swooped down. A paramedic ran over and asked if he was okay.

'It's my leg that's really hurting,' Batson replied.

'Yeah, that's 'cos your foot is sticking out to one side!' he pronounced.

Batson had dislocated his knee on landing. The burly paramedic took a firm grip of his leg, twisted it, and popped the joint back into place.

Heath had also fired off his flares to attract a rescue helicopter's attention, and they were both flown to the field hospital at Tabuk. The first thing Batson did on arrival was admonish Heath on his ejection technique. 'For goodness sake, next time you count down to ten, pull the handle at eight and surprise me.' Heath managed a chuckle, but it was swiftly followed by a grimace. He had three badly bruised vertebrae which he knew would keep him out of the war for some weeks. 'In twenty-two years of flying with the RAF I have never been shot at and I have never had to eject,' he told the *Daily Telegraph* from his hospital bed. 'Now I've chalked up two firsts, both of which I could have done without.'

A subsequent investigation showed that a small electrical connector had probably become detached from its housing and jammed the control column. For Mike Heath and Pete Batson it didn't really matter. After only a couple of days, their war was already over.

* * *

Dave Waddington's war was definitely still ongoing, and he knew worse was to come. Suffering a double dislocation and concussion after his high-speed ejection twenty-four hours earlier, he had stumbled through the night behind enemy lines before being shot at and captured. He had already received some rough treatment, but at least the Iraqis had the decency to put a cast over his elbow. He had then been crammed into the rear footwell of a car and driven more than 200 miles north. Arriving in Baghdad in darkness, he was bundled into the interrogation centre. It was the building where Nichol and Peters had been mauled earlier, and it wasn't long before Dave was given the same welcome. He was blindfolded and shoved onto a metal stool. 'I could sense there were probably two or three guards behind me and a single interrogator in front. I knew what was coming and wondered how I'd deal with it.'[8]

The first thing they asked was his name, rank and service number. He answered truthfully as this was information he was required to give. But Dave knew it was just a formality for what was coming next.

'What aircraft do you fly?'

'I'm sorry, sir, I cannot answer that question.'

The truncheon cracked against his temple, his legs and his back, then again in the same three spots.

'What do you fly?'

Dave gave the same response: 'I can't answer that question.'

The truncheon came down again. 'There was a sort of acceptance on my part. It went past the stage where it hurt. It was just happening. I shouldn't have *had* to answer their questions and certainly didn't want to. So each time they didn't get the response they wanted, they would beat me, using sticks and fists.'

The deep abrasions Waddington had suffered to his face from

the blast when ejecting were still incredibly painful. During their early sessions, his interrogators decided to exploit that pain. 'They punched me incredibly hard a number of times in the face, huge hammer blows that rocked me sideways and sent stars spinning above my head. I remember the emotional shock as much as the physical pain. I realised I was totally helpless; completely in their hands. They could smash me around as much as they wanted. It was a worrying thought.'

The grilling continued throughout the night. Dave was knocked into unconsciousness on a number of occasions. 'I'd come round and they'd ask me another question then blows came again – head, back and legs. A couple of times they tried to hit my dislocated arm but it was in plaster so it didn't hurt that much. My thoughts were racing with a whole mix of emotions. Bouts of utter fear mixed with the strange sense of determination; not wanting to give in without a fight. I knew that fight would ultimately be pointless, and the end result the same whatever I did, but I wanted to resist for as long as possible for a couple of reasons. Firstly, and obviously, I didn't want to give away any information that would endanger my friends and colleagues. But perhaps just as importantly, I wanted to be able to say to myself, and others, "I held out for as long as possible; they really had to work to get me to talk." This was a huge player for me throughout the interrogation. I knew I couldn't sustain the brutality for ever, but I needed to feel as though I hadn't given up easily before accepting the inevitable. I suppose I just didn't want to appear weaker than others.'

During a welcome pause in the proceedings, Waddington was shoved into a corridor where he became aware of other allied prisoners of war around him. 'I could see under my blindfold that I was lying next to someone wearing American flying boots. There were eight or nine bodies lying around, crumpled up. I could hear American and British voices under interrogation, but I was drifting in and out of consciousness. They would finish with one guy then drag me back in.'

Each time the routine was the same. 'It was all standard stuff. It became a bit of a game with them asking me the same question,

"What aircraft do you fly?" and me just replying, "I cannot answer that question." They concentrated mostly on beating my back. I'd be knocked off my stool and thumped around until I lost consciousness. Drifting away, I remember feeling rather relieved. It meant I was getting a break from the violence. Then after I came round, they would start asking the same question again.'

'Why are you refusing to answer our questions? We don't need you to answer! We already have information from Peters and Nichol, so why don't you just tell us the same thing? We can bring them in here to talk to you if it helps?'

'I just replied again with my same stock phrase, "I cannot answer that question," but it was all starting to sound a bit daft by now.'

Like all the coalition POWs who underwent such violent questioning, Waddington felt much of it seemed unfocused. 'At one point they were beating the soles of my feet, but I still had my flying boots on. At times I wondered if they knew what they were doing – they seemed to have a simple, basic need to mete out physical violence.' Dave steeled himself for more stinging blows, but knew he was reaching his limits of endurance. 'There seemed to be no end to their violence. So what questions *will* I answer? What questions will I *not* answer? What am I prepared to *die* for?'

It was a key moment for Waddington. Alongside a determination to try to protect the Tornado crews still flying, he also dreaded betraying the identity of the female Iraqi doctor who had slipped a small strip of painkillers into his pocket while tending his arm. 'I'm not sure I could have lived with myself if I answered that question. It would have had truly terrible consequences for a person who had shown me such kindness.'

As the brutality continued sporadically through the night, his aggressors returned to the same question, the one that everyone knew signalled the end if they answered it. His resistance was slipping with the pain, the tiredness, the despondency, the captivity, the fear. 'I have no idea how long it went on, but you start to realise you can't go on avoiding the question for ever. These people are really out to hurt you.'

'What aircraft do you fly?'

'I cannot answer that question.'

The interrogator then lifted his blindfold and held up what Dave recognised as Flight Reference Cards. At the top it read: '*Flt Lt DJ Waddington*' then the title '*Tornado GR1*'.

'What aircraft do you fly?'

'Tornado.'

Dave had broken.

'Giving in to the interrogation and torture was the absolute bottom of the pit of the experience for me. I'd been shot down, didn't make it home. I was trying to resist, to retain some honour, but in that moment, I had failed.' He had tried his best to last as long as possible rather than giving in straight away to avoid the agony. 'I did what I thought was the right thing, right up to the far edge of my personal limit. It's something which goes right back in our military history, the principle, our heritage, our ethos to uphold. You don't want to be the one who falls short.'

Questions now came thick and fast, which Dave tried to resist. As his interrogators did not seem to truly understand what to ask, he tried to play the Iraqis at their own game, offering as little information as possible, giving misinformation where he could. He pretended that his youth, junior rank and inexperience meant he knew very little. His tactics came at considerable cost when the interrogator compared his answers about a basic Tornado tactic with those of the other POWs.

'Mister David! We know that you are lying to us. You will be sorry.'

'I really suffered when they caught me out lying about that. They seemed to lose all control and flew into a frenzy of violence. The worst beating of the nightmare so far.'

His name was also a problem.

'*David!* ... *Joseph!* ... Waddington, you are a Jew!'

Again and again they accused him of being an Israeli pilot, their hatred of the Jewish state fuelling their anger. 'We *know* the Israelis are flying for you!'

Dave could only tell them the truth; he knew nothing about it. But his Christian names were proving quite painful.

In Dave's mind, Robbie was still on the run, potentially on his way back home. He had no idea his friend was seriously injured and already captured. Now they wanted to know the name of his navigator. He tried his best to hold out, not wanting to hinder Robbie's escape. 'I really didn't want to give that information, but they beat it out of me too.' He waited for the moment when his courage would be tested further, when he would be forced to give away tactical intelligence that would help the Iraqis. He certainly had information on search-and-rescue procedures that could cause serious harm to others. 'Luckily, they never asked those questions, so my resolve was never tested to its limit.'

Eventually, the questions stopped and he was hopeful he had given away little of use. Battered and beaten both physically and psychologically, Dave was taken to the medical centre on the outskirts of Baghdad where, unknown to him, his navigator had just undergone a lengthy operation.

* * *

Robbie awoke in a large, comfortable hospital room with a smiling portrait of Saddam Hussein gazing benignly down on him. Judging from the bandages, the cast on his leg and minimal pain, Robbie knew that he had been well treated. He was contemplating using the pull bar above his head to move position when the door opened and a group of doctors walked in. They were led by a beaming, kindly looking man. The rest of the entourage's deference suggested that he was the senior consultant. He picked up Robbie's left hand. 'He had obviously sensed my foreboding as I'd watched my wedding ring disappear before the operation, and now, grinning with delight, he slipped it back onto my finger.'[9]

The surgeon produced Robbie's X-rays and showed him how he had fixed the bones in his leg by using two metal plates and thirteen screws. He was delighted Robbie could wiggle his toes, then explained in fluent English that he had also suffered a broken collarbone and crushed vertebrae. When they moved on, one doctor sporting the obligatory Saddam moustache stayed behind. 'You are very lucky to have been treated by this surgeon,' he said softly. 'He is the top doctor in Iraq and he was trained in a London hospital.'

Robbie had no doubt about the surgeon's concern for his well-being. The doctor left him alone with his thoughts – first and foremost, of Tange and the children. 'I imagined their dread on seeing a blue RAF uniform at the door, an image that told them without the need for any words that the worst had happened. The hot tears ran down my face again.'

He awoke from a delirious dream to find a sallow-faced medic at his bedside. The man put a thermometer in Robbie's mouth, read his blood pressure then leaned in and took his pulse. 'Me, no Iraqi, me Kurdish,' he whispered conspiratorially. Then he showed Robbie the readings as if they were top secret. 'I felt a little ray of hope that here was a man who would help me.' He drifted back to sleep, content that, in the midst of war, human kindness could still be found. When he opened his eyes, they were met with the image which would remind him that such kindness was still in short supply. 'I lay there facing this huge portrait of Saddam Hussein which hung opposite. His features had been softened by the artist to hide the fact he was a murderous tyrant who would happily kill his own people to get his own way.'

Saddam portraits and Saddam lookalikes dominated the walls and corridors of the Baghdad interrogation centre. A number of coalition prisoners were now housed there and casual brutality was the order of the day. The strike of a match and the stink of cheap tobacco in John Peters' nostrils were followed by the sharp agony of a seared wrist. Then again, on the other wrist. 'Someone was dragging on his cigarette, then carefully applying the glowing tip to my skin. He wasn't actually stubbing the cigarette out and relighting it, just touching the embers to the skin, removing it for another drag, then carefully touching it down again.'[10] Peters suddenly felt ungovernable rage. 'This was some sad, sadistic, little shit taking advantage of my complete helplessness. If I hadn't been handcuffed I would have killed that bastard.'

His navigator John Nichol was also having a tough time.

'Lieutenant Nichol, do you know that we are going to charge you with war crimes?'

The question had come with the customary kicks and slaps as Nichol lay asleep on the concrete floor of the bunker. Aching all over, stiff, bruised, flesh throbbing, he simply stared up at the Iraqi officer. 'Excuse me? I have committed no war crimes.'

'Yes, you have attacked a country you did not declare war on. You have committed war crimes. We are going to execute you.' It sounded like he meant it.

Oh well, Nichol thought.

There was a pause.

'Right,' the officer said. 'We can either execute you or put you on TV.'

Nichol contemplated his immediate future. *Broadcast or die?* The decision wasn't too difficult. 'What do you want me to say?' he eventually replied.

'I thought a TV appearance was a good deal more appealing than a death sentence, particularly since its effect would be debatable and stand a strong chance of triggering an Iraqi public relations disaster. On the other hand, I did not *want* to co-operate, or show the least willingness under any circumstances. These people were the enemy.'

'We will ask you a few questions,' the officer smiled. 'You will answer them and then you can send a message home.'

Do what you like, Nichol thought. *Shoot yourself right in the foot.*

He was taken blindfolded into a large room where a crowd swarmed around a television camera. Someone gave him a glass of water and brushed his hair. When their back was turned he ruffled it again. He wanted to look under duress. After a brief 'rehearsal' of the questions and the pre-prepared answers he was expected to give, the camera was turned on.

'How were you shot down?'

'What do you think of the war?'

Deadpan and monotone, Nichol gave the required responses. 'I was shot down by an Iraqi system. I do not know what it was. I think the war should be stopped so we can go home. I don't agree on this war with Iraq.'[11]

He hoped that by parroting the stilted English and speaking very slowly, it would be clear he was delivering words written by someone else. And by maintaining a level monotone and refusing to blink, anyone watching would know he was under duress. The Iraqis did not pick up on his charade, seemingly content to just get through the text. Then, when it was the time to give his parents a message, Nichol stared straight into the lens. 'Mum and Dad, if you're listening, everything is okay. Please pray for me. We should be home soon.'

As Nichol was led back down the corridor tears streamed down his face, soaking the crepe bandage of his blindfold. 'For me, the TV broadcasts were the lowest point; my ultimate shame. I felt as though I had let down the RAF, my Squadron and my friends. And then the thought of what my poor parents must be enduring was unbearable. I was a wreck.' In the depths of his despair, Nichol had no idea how far those TV pictures would reach, or how much they would affect his life.

* * *

Peters was also kicked awake by the guards. His blindfold was removed and an officer appeared. 'You're going on television,' he told the pilot abruptly.

'No!' Peters was not going to be used as a propaganda tool.

The slaps came in fast and hard. 'You will never see your wife and children again.' Slap.

'Is it worth it?'

Slap.

'We will kill you now.'

Slap.

One of the soldiers took his pistol out and thrust it against Peters' temple. 'You are going to die now.'

Peters was so keyed up he could almost hear the creak of the trigger mechanism. 'Okay, okay, okay,' he mumbled.

As he was dragged into the room Nichol had just vacated, Peters consoled himself that he had done his best not to co-operate. He was pushed down onto the chair and someone tried to tidy his hair. Peters knew there was little they could do with his battered face and drew comfort from the thought. 'I looked like shit and I felt shit. I was going to use that. I was going to try to refuse to say what they wanted me to say.'

As the Iraqis shouted questions and then provided the answers, Peters showed little compliance. They kept whacking him with a pistol when he refused to speak up or sit up. The pilot decided to use the injuries to his advantage. 'I wanted people to see evidence of the beatings, so turned my damaged eye towards the camera. There would be no mistaking the physical abuse.' The Iraqis cut short the questions, just demanding his name, rank and number, and confirmation that he had been shot down by missiles. Peters had done well to curtail the performance, but felt utterly humiliated. 'I hated being put on television with every fibre of every nerve. I thought I would be revealing to the world how weak I had been, how I'd given in too easily. I thought everyone would class me as a traitor. All I could think was that I was bringing disgrace to my uniform.'

As the interview drew to a close, his captors said he could send a message to his family.

'Helen, Toni and Guy, I love you . . .' A lump formed in his throat. *That's it*, Peters thought. *I've done everything they wanted. They don't need anything more out of me. I can be wasted now. I will never see my family again.* When he tried to add some words to his parents, he couldn't speak.

The interviews were broadcast on local Iraqi TV then picked up by CNN in Baghdad. Within hours, pictures of Nichol, Peters, a Kuwaiti pilot and four American POWs had been flashed around the world, prompting an unprecedented storm of global condemnation.

The harrowing images of Nichol and Peters in particular were red meat for Britain's tabloid press. The *Daily Mail* captured the public mood best. 'WHAT HAS HE DONE TO THEM?' their headline shrieked.

The Sun was less restrained: 'BASTARD OF BAGHDAD', it screamed, then demanded: 'Hang Saddam long and slow'. The faces of Nichol and Peters, its front-page opinion piece ran, 'will haunt us all for many a long day'.

Saddam could not have gifted the coalition a more perfect justification for their onslaught, especially after it was suggested that the POWs could be used as human shields at key Iraqi sites, to prevent them from being bombed. Prime Minister John Major declared the treatment of prisoners as 'inhuman, illegal and totally contrary to the third Geneva Convention'.[12] He demanded Red Cross access. 'Huge anger was aroused when captured British pilots were paraded before the camera as Iraqi propaganda,' he later recalled. 'I had met some of them in Dhahran just a few days before, and felt their plight very personally.'[13]

President George Bush echoed his words. 'If Saddam Hussein thought this brutal treatment of pilots is a way to muster world support he is dead wrong and everyone is upset about it.' Dick Cheney, the US Defense Secretary, condemned it as 'in effect a war crime'.[14]

Initially, the pictures had a positive impact on RAF morale. They now knew their comrades had not been shot out of hand by Saddam's goons. 'I am elated, now I have hope,' Dave Bellamy, Nichol's flatmate, recorded in his diary.

The news broke in Bahrain after Gordon Buckley had left the Sheraton to visit a local restaurateur he had befriended. After navigating his way through the polythene sheeting fastened across his host's front door to provide some protection from chemical attack, he was met by a beaming smile. 'They've been on the TV! They're alive and okay!'

Buckley did not have to wait long to see his fellow Muharraq fliers' beaten faces on CNN. 'It was a great relief that they were alive. Though it was obvious they were both slightly the worse for their ordeal . . .'

* * *

Helen Peters remained on tenterhooks at their home in Germany. Rolling TV coverage throughout the day had been dominated by video footage of five fliers, including John Nichol, but there was no sign of her husband. She was bathing her two young children upstairs when he finally appeared on the 5.40pm news bulletin. Fortified by a large brandy, she sat down to watch. 'It was horrible, that rush of different kinds of emotions all at once. John looked terrible. So battered; almost unrecognisable. I stood up to telephone my parents but my legs gave way.'

Although she now had confirmation that he was alive, Helen could not stop thinking that once they had forced the airmen to make the broadcast the Iraqis would have 'simply taken the boys out and shot them'.

Dave Waddington's mother Berenice was still waiting anxiously for further news of her own missing boy. She was watching TV in their neat three-bedroom, semi-detached home in Bolton when the pictures of Peters and Nichol flashed across her screen. She could not help imagining her son being similarly brutalised. 'It was horrific. They looked so terrible, so badly mistreated. Seeing them alive didn't offer us much hope.'

All that day her son John, a fireman, had used every contact he had within the RAF to try to find out more. When he finally got through to one of Dave's colleagues, his heart sank. 'An RAF officer told us that there was little chance of David or Robbie being alive because their aircraft had been seen going down in flames. No ejections had been seen. It was unlikely anyone had survived.'[15]

Berenice released a heartrending statement to the press. 'We don't know whether he is dead or has been taken prisoner. We are praying he is alive but we are prepared for the worst. All I hope is that if he has died he has done so to make a better world for our children. We believe, and he believes, that the cause he is fighting is a just one.'[16] She added that two days before hearing of his loss they had received a letter from Dave telling them not to worry. The article appeared under a banner headline: 'BLOOD AND TEARS OF COURAGE', and was accompanied by a photo of Dave and his fiancée Claire at an Officers' Mess dinner. Dave was wearing his RAF blue formal dinner jacket trimmed in silk and gold, Claire in a strapless white lace-trimmed ballgown. They looked like teenagers at a prom.

Despite the RAF officer's doleful message, Dave's sister was convinced that he must be alive. She told their mother that she would *know* if he was dead. Berenice had no idea which way to turn. 'There were so many contradictions, hope and despair. But the not knowing was the worst part; in the darkest moments it was the lack of information that was difficult to bear.'

* * *

Robbie Stewart's wife Tange was doing her best to deal with the blow of being told her own husband was missing in action. The news had reverberated around their Lincolnshire village the previous day, and the vicar had held an impromptu service. She had walked past the gravestones of All Saints into the Saxon-built tower and been startled by the packed pews within. 'There was shock and confusion on some of their faces – the whole village seemed to be moved by our situation.' They sat and listened as the vicar told the congregation of Robbie's plight. Tange held onto her son Scott and Robbie's best friend Barry as they sang 'Amazing Grace'. 'I was gripping them so tightly, coming out of the numbness of my situation and how it affected all our friends. Then I looked up into the rafters above the chancel and saw a white butterfly fluttering around freely. I wondered if it was trying to tell me something.'

Shortly after the service, RAF Marham Station Commander Jock Stirrup and his wife arrived at her house. He gave Tange a piece of advice she would not forget. 'I will only tell you information which has been *officially confirmed* by either our military, or the Red Cross.' From then on, she took everything she heard or read elsewhere as a potentially unreliable rumour. 'The thought that no one was able to confirm if they were dead kept me going. All the relatives of those missing must have held onto the same hope that their loved ones would be found alive and return to them.'

Her position was soon challenged by the flood of grainy images of Nichol and Peters. 'It was a real worry, so horrendous and so alien to everything that we had understood about life. I really hoped I wouldn't see Robbie like that.'

Then the Ministry of Defence released official pictures of Robbie and Dave which appeared alongside the other missing Tornado aircrew, Max Collier and Nigel Elsdon, in the London *Evening Standard*. The headline was sobering in the extreme: 'Be Ready for Bad News'[17] – words taken from the Prime Minister's counsel to the Commons that the nation should prepare 'to bear bad news with fortitude'.

Robbie's daughter Kirsty had gone back to board at Stamford High School. Watching the aircrew on the evening news confirmed her terrible sense of foreboding. 'It was a really horrible moment, reinforcing all the thoughts I had from the books I'd read about war, prisoners, interrogation and torture.' She could not help staring again and again at one particular image. 'John Nichol was staring at the camera and had been speaking really slowly, strangely. What was he trying to tell us? What did it mean for my dad? What would he be going through, if he was alive?'

CHAPTER ELEVEN

'STAY WITH IT!'

20 JANUARY, EVENING–24 JANUARY

Mike Toft had been on Peters and Nichol's fateful daylight raid and the outcome had continued to play on his mind. 'We were so happy to see them paraded on TV. It was clearly a terrible experience and they looked badly battered, but at least we knew they were alive. There was hope they might eventually get home. It was a real boost and it made us more determined to carry on with the job.'

Toft was now getting on with that job, in a distinctly uncomfortable and unfamiliar environment. The navigator was en route to attack an airfield 90 miles south of Baghdad. His eight-ship was about to offload 64,000lb of bombs from a height of 20,000ft. It was something he had never trained for, and it was not what the Tornado had been designed to do.[1] The mission had one unbreakable instruction from HQ: *Don't hit the mosque!* The religious site stood two and a half miles to the north of Al Najaf airbase.[2] To avoid a public relations disaster, *not even a cracked slate* would be acceptable. And an accurate strike at that height was going to be a challenge.

The Tornado weapons system was optimised for very accurate low-level attacks. Their 1,000-pounders[3] were not actually 'guided' – once they left the jet, they were on their own. But the computer aiming system had been pre-programmed to *know* precisely what the bombs' trajectory would be for the few seconds they were in the air. It also *knew* exactly where the jet was, what height it was flying at, how fast it was travelling, and what low-level winds the released bombs would be subjected to. So the computer itself would then calculate the exact moment to release the weapons.[4] The system was a huge improvement on previous versions, and on most weaponry training sorties, as long as the main computer was updated with navigational fixes, unguided bombs could be delivered to within a matter of metres of the target. And with eight of them, total destruction was almost guaranteed.

Dropping them from 20,000ft, however, posed considerable problems, not least because the aiming system was only capable of measuring wind speed and direction at the Tornado's *actual* altitude over the ground. An estimated wind speed to represent a lower altitude could be manually inputted, but the main computer still had no way of calculating how conditions would vary – and impact the flight path of the payload – during the *full* thirty or so seconds it would take to complete its journey.

Toft's formation had been told that, as their target was so vast, any dispersion due to these errors should still result in a reasonably focused spread of weapons designed to disrupt the airbase's operations. The low-level mindset had been in place since the birth of the Tornado nearly two decades before. Toft hoped he'd be able to adapt to the new environment with suitable rapidity.

Despite the lives risked and lost in pursuit of low-level excellence, old notions now had to be pushed aside. Three RAF Tornados, and one Italian version, had gone down during the execution of raids a few hundred feet above the target. But – despite misleading assertions from some sections of the media – they were not alone. The US, French, Italian and Saudi air forces had been pursuing the same low-level tactics too. Indeed, for the first few nights of the war, even the giant American B-52 strategic bombers had been flying such attacks across Iraq. One pilot remembered heading towards a chemical weapons site near Mosul, south of the Turkish border, just 50ft above the ground.[5] The B-52's wingspan was 185ft.

Now, as the losses mounted, questions were being asked across the whole coalition.

A number of American aircraft had also gone down during low-level operations, including two US Navy A-6 Intruders and two US Air Force F-15E Strike Eagles, one of the most modern combat jets in theatre. As a veteran of 500 low-level missions in Vietnam, Vice Admiral Stanley Arthur felt duty-bound to share some hard-won knowledge. From his ship in the Gulf, the Commander of the Seventh Fleet sent a carefully worded message to his senior officers. 'Gentlemen, far be it for me to dictate specific combat tactics but I must interject my early observations relative to the age-old argument of low altitude delivery versus high with a quick look at what has happened to the *multinational* [6] air forces to date. One cannot escape the fact that the current AAA environment makes low altitude delivery a non-starter.' He felt that it couldn't be successfully achieved without the benefit of surprise, and at that moment, they didn't have it. 'We learned a hard lesson in Vietnam relative to AAA,' he reminded his commanders.[7]

The French were having the same discussion. Four of their Jaguars had sustained substantial damage on an early eight-ship, low-level sortie. One pilot had a very lucky escape when a bullet from an AK-47 assault rifle passed through his helmet visor. He'd been a hair's breadth from being shot in the head, by a soldier on the ground, with a rifle.[8] Yes, it had been a lucky shot, but as the intensity of fire increased, the French decided to move their operations to 10,000ft and above. It appeared that the Iraqi Air Force may have been battered into submission during the first forty-eight hours of the air war. 'They realised fairly early on that if they were going to get airborne at all they'd be shot down,' noted an RAF planning officer in Riyadh. While the Iraqis had some truly effective jets, 'they didn't really know how to use them; their technology wasn't as good as we'd believed'.[9] In other words, perhaps the much-feared enemy fighter threat was already, largely, contained?

The growing consensus was that the risks of low-level flying now far outweighed the reward. But while all the options were still being considered, RAF Air Headquarters had ordered a mix of strategies. The Dhahran detachment would pursue a risky eight-ship night-time loft attack on Jalibah airbase, while Mike Toft and his comrades from Muharraq found themselves ordered up to more unfamiliar territory.

* * *

Instead of dropping down from the tankers, the eight Tornados felt their way gingerly up to 20,000ft. Toft contemplated their mission to Al Najaf airbase as the evening sun dipped below the horizon. It was a world away from skimming across the desert in daylight, as they had when they lost Nichol and Peters. 'The main threat to crews had been triple-A and now the aim was to fly above it. And while we knew the threat from enemy fighters had diminished, we took nothing for granted. Notwithstanding the relative safety of height, the Tornado was not designed to operate at such altitude. The primary bomb-aiming equipment was the ground-mapping radar designed for low-level operations. Now the radar was only as good as the Bomber Command radars of the Second World War.'[10]

Aircrew now had the challenge of using a radar system optimised for looking directly *at* approaching structures at low level, rather than *down* on them, and a bombing system designed to be highly accurate at 200ft, not 20,000. Mark Paisey, Toft's pilot, was also having to contend with demanding meteorological conditions. 'The weather was generally clear with little significant cloud but some ground fog was predicted to obscure features on the transit and in the target area. More importantly, there was a strong wind from the west of 70 knots at 20,000ft which would cause problems. I remember saying to Tofty that we might as well be in a Lancaster bomber because of the way we were attacking. There was very limited information for the main computer to calculate the weapons release point; especially the ever-changing winds from 20,000ft all the way down to ground level.'[11]

Leading the attack, Squadron Leader Pablo Mason was grateful for the moonless night – the shroud of darkness would provide some cover. 'We were nervous both about the sensitivity of the task and because we would be an eight-ship formation flying for the first time in a medium-level attack on the airfield. We had only ever flown out to war in the safety of low level which hid us from enemy radars.'[12] While out of range of the dreaded triple-A, they were now very much in the surface-to-air missile zone. To protect the Tornados the Americans had provided two EF-111 Raven specialist electronic jamming jets to suppress enemy radar, and two F-14 Tomcat interceptors in case any enemy fighters did manage to get off the ground.

The raid was also the first sortie for the new crew who had been sent out to replace the Two Johns. They had arrived in Bahrain direct from the UK only nineteen hours earlier. Pablo checked the time as the eight jets approached the target: 7.20pm. Ten minutes to go. 'The night was strangely quiet. My navigator gave me a final reminder that this had to be an accurate attack. If we deviated to the left by just 4km we would hit the mosque.'

A moment later their ground-mapping radar failed; they could no longer update the weapons system. Then another Tornado lost its radar too. Determined to carry on the attack, Pablo ordered an 'aerial ballet', in total darkness, and with each aircraft's external lights extinguished. He manoeuvred his own jet directly behind Toft and Paisey's. Guided only by the friendly glow of their engines just visible in the blackness, he now flew in close formation to the target. He instructed Toft to give him a precise signal when they were dropping their bombs so he could release his own manually.

The formation was now relying entirely on Mike Toft's navigation skills and the largely unpractised bomb-aiming technique. Under intense pressure to ensure the mission went smoothly, he concentrated on the green screen, trying to identify the radar offsets to feed into the main computer for an accurate drop. He became even more sceptical when the first offset – an ancient fort – had clearly disappeared 'beneath the sands of time' because nothing showed on the monitor. 'The second offset was a bend in a pylon line, an awesome aiming point from low level, but from medium level completely bloody hopeless because the pylons could not be broken out from the ground clutter.' Looking down from on high, the radar system could not differentiate between the metal structure and the ground itself. Heart racing, and only sixty seconds to target, Toft prayed that the third offset would show up. 'Without doubt, this was the most pressured I've ever been in the RAF. The first ever Tornado medium-level war mission and it all seemed to be resting solely on my shoulders.'

From the front seat, Mark Paisey could sense the tension building as his HUD counted down to weapons release. He thought a cheerful remark – 'No pressure, Tofty!' – would lighten the mood. It didn't.

The third and final offset was the nearside of a bridge over a small river. Toft peered intently at the radar screen. 'It took time to break this out from the green porridge of the display staring at me.' It finally appeared. He moved the marker over the offset and pressed the insert button, feeding the information to the main computer which registered the update. A second later the bombs fell from their aircraft.

As they made a gentle right-hand turn back towards friendly territory, Paisey counted down the seconds to impact. 'Twenty . . . ten . . . three, two, one . . .'

The pitch-black below them turned white in an instant, then a series of orange and yellow flashes marked the detonations, the shock waves expanding out, encompassing the airbase. Secondary explosions began to show. Perhaps fuel or ammunition dumps going up. Like most aircrew, Toft had only ever dropped single 1,000-pounders on practice ranges before the conflict. Now 64,000lb of high explosive were rocking the target. 'It was a terrifying sight, and a gut-wrenching moment. I thought, *What the fuck have we just done?* It was truly terrible, almost biblical destruction, and we had most likely killed many military personnel. But you had to push that reality away from your thought process. This was war.'

As the first bombs impacted, Mark Paisey watched the sky light up with the familiar red and white streaks of gunfire. 'The bombs set off heavy triple-A, both tracer and airburst reaching up to around 18,000ft. I didn't see any SAMs launch and we had no RHWR indications. Most crews were happy with their attacks and those who were uncertain ensured they bombed to the south, thus avoiding damage to the mosque.'

All eight made it safely back to base, and the subsequent Mission Report painted a rather different picture from previous raids in terms of both bombing accuracy and threat level:

> The accuracy of the attack was difficult to assess since the target was also the point of interest of B-52 aircraft shortly after our mission. This, together with the very slow delivery of damage assessment, made it impossible to draw out lessons for subsequent attacks. However, all crews agreed that the medium level option, with support, felt safer than low level overflight of defended targets.[13]

* * *

Twelve-year-old Gareth Ankerson was only just starting to realise that his father Bob's role as a Tornado navigator was part of the unfolding war on television. He'd always presumed his job was pretty much like anybody else's – a driver, say, or an engineer. As the battle in the Gulf continued, the senior boys at Brandeston Hall School had been allowed to gather in the common room to watch the evening news. Gareth saw the battered faces of Nichol and Peters in the same flying suits his father wore, but he still couldn't imagine his kindly dad being in the same situation. 'I began to make the link that my dad was doing his job, he was out in the Gulf, and these things on the news all linked together, but I don't think I had a sense of how serious it all was. Not then.'[14] Gareth had been more preoccupied with his studies after arriving back for the penultimate term at his Suffolk boarding school. The possibility of Tornado pilots and navigators becoming POWs was less pressing than the poem his English teacher had set them to learn by the end of the week.

Alone at their family home at RAF Bruggen in Germany, his mother was also grappling with the unfamiliar repercussions of the conflict. When the initial Tornado losses were reported, Chris Ankerson had admonished herself for thinking *at least it's not my husband*. 'I had naively convinced myself that everyone would come home safely. Suddenly it was all very real.'[15] She became addicted to TV news. 'I started to watch all the bulletins, although many of the wives never looked at all; they didn't want live updates about what their loved ones were doing. But I drew comfort from seeing the RAF crews I knew on TV, discussing their experiences. It allowed me to feel closer to my husband.' But the bruised images of Nichol and Peters paraded as POWs had rocked her. 'Although it was a shock, I didn't know them, I had never heard of them, so I couldn't really have any other emotion than, again, *thank God it's not my husband*. It seems wrong now, of course, but I think many of us felt that way.'

The Bruggen Station Commander made sure the wives were given regular updates from the warzone. Chris would attend the briefings and then telephone Gareth at school. It felt good sharing the latest intelligence she'd received about the Tornado force and Bob's war.

The problem was, her husband's war wasn't going terribly well. On the evening of 22 January, as the newspapers were giving full vent to their outrage at Iraqi treatment of POWs, Bob and his pilot Simon Burgess entered the briefing room at Dhahran for the final time before their first war sortie – which would take them to Shaibah airfield, south-west of Basra, at medium level. Almost a week had gone by and they were grinding their teeth. 'Lots of missions had been cancelled for various reasons and I had a sense of personal frustration about not being involved in combat ops,' said Bob. 'As a Flight Commander on a frontline squadron, I felt I really needed to be doing my share of the job.'[16] There was nothing devil-may-care about his attitude, though. 'We all knew we were flying into very high-threat environments. Anyone who was surprised by the Tornados going down must have been kidding themselves.'

As they aimed for the tanker rendezvous, their Sky Shadow electronic countermeasures pod started playing up. It was a key piece of kit, jamming Iraqi radar-guided missiles, and was more important than ever now that they were operating at 20,000ft and even more exposed to SAMs. They tried turning it off and back on again, but it was still failing after they disengaged from the Victor. Bob knew they had to return to Dhahran, but was concerned that it might look like they were 'bottling out'. He attended the debrief after the rest of the formation had safely returned, 'but I felt like an interloper'. He went to his room, deeply frustrated. 'We hadn't completed the job. There was a niggling feeling that perhaps we should have pressed on regardless. By this stage of the war, most people had completed a number of ops, but we hadn't done one. It didn't sit well.' He had also just seen the newspaper reports on Nichol and Peters. 'It put some steel into me, wanting to get the job done quicker.'

* * *

The POW images continued to unleash public indignation. 'Sir, I felt angry and sick at heart for the families of those captured airmen whose photographs dominated your front page this morning,' Mrs Geraldine Peters wrote to the editor of *The Times*. 'What can the feeling of these families be, knowing that the suffering of their loved ones is being paraded before hundreds of thousands through the media?' She then criticised the media in general for 'proliferating Saddam's hideous propaganda'.[17]

Under the headline, 'Saddam may try to break your spirit . . . he'll never break your heart,' *The Sun*'s letters page was packed with encouragement for the frontline fliers. 'I say a prayer for them every night and I also pray that the murderous bastard holding them prisoner will get his come-uppance soon,' Julie Staunton wrote from Torquay.[18]

And the gloves now came off against those opposing the

campaign. The actress Emma Thompson, photographed with a
'Stop War in the Gulf' placard at a London demonstration, was
given short shrift in the *Daily Express*. 'When men like that are
going through the living hell of war it makes me feel sick and
ashamed to hear the rantings of a silly actress about peace,' said one
of the paper's leading columnists. 'Could she look John Peters in the
eye in all his wretchedness and tell him he was wasting his time?
At times like this I wish the peace people would hop on a plane to
Baghdad and rant at Saddam instead.'[19]

The newspapers began arriving in the Gulf. While the front
pages featured the POWs, there were also reports about successful
Tornado missions keeping the Iraqi Air Force largely grounded.
After the recent losses at Muharraq, Nick Heard was buoyed by the
coverage. 'They were full of details about what *we*, the *Tornados*,
had been doing. It was gratifying to realise that people back home
understood the contribution we were making, the risks we were
taking, and were seemingly totally behind us.'[20]

The risks the crews were taking were great. Although some
Tornado raids were being carried out from medium level, low-level
sorties still continued, depending on the target and the degree of
strike accuracy required. A massive airbase could be attacked from
height, but a single structure or complex could not. On 22 January,
the Tabuk detachment were tasked to destroy an air defence control
station near the Jordanian border. Ar Rutbah was the location of
an Iraqi government facility for the manufacture of chemicals for
its gas attacks against Iran in the 1980s. Intelligence believed that it
may also have built three nerve-gas factories in the area.[21]

Squadron Leaders Garry Lennox and Kevin Weeks were spear-
heading the low-level eight-ship attack, each aircraft carrying five
1,000-pounders,[22] and planning to employ the loft profile to penetrate the target accurately. Three aircraft returned to base because
of technical faults but the other five pressed on through heavy
triple-A fire and rained twenty-five bombs down on the radar facility, breaching the bunker. Five seconds later, one of the crews saw a
fireball erupt in the distance. Closer inspection revealed a series of

fires on the nearby hillside. Garry, thirty-four, and 37-year-old Kev failed to respond to radio check-ins.[23]

News of the fourth RAF Tornado going down in combat reverberated around the RAF's Gulf bases. At Tabuk, the ground crew who had readied the jet for the mission were shattered. 'When the crew didn't return, their see-off team refused to leave the airfield,' said engineer Dean Wood. 'They just stayed there waiting for news. The Boss eventually came around and told us there was little chance they had survived. It was a terrible day and hit us ground crew hard. We kept asking for updates, clinging onto the possibility that they might appear.' Later that evening, Wood was again tasked with loading weapons and readying more Tornados for take-off. 'The crews looked ever-more nervous when they arrived. The most difficult thing was simply chatting to them. We had to appear our normal selves, trying not to make them feel any worse than they did, but what do you say to a man who has just lost two friends and is flying into something that may kill him?'[24]

Dave Bellamy knew Lennox and Weeks well. He was numbed by the loss. 'It was a very bad period of time, real stress and intense emotional pressure. You felt a sense of personal loss even though there was nothing you could have done. But my overriding thought was for their wives and kids back home. What were they going through?'

Eight months pregnant with their second child, Anne Lennox was going through hell at her parents' home in Yorkshire. When the Padre and an RAF officer rang the doorbell she knew immediately what it meant. They informed her that her husband was missing in action. There was no other news. 'My immediate reaction was anger and rage coupled with hope. He was such a strong fighter I knew that, if he could, he would come home. After that I felt numb.'[25]

* * *

The decision was finally made. The sortie against Ar Rutbah on 22 January would be the last Tornado low-level bombing mission of the war.[26] 'When we stopped flying low level and went to medium level, that wasn't because we felt we couldn't take any more losses or were hurt by public opinion,' Air Vice-Marshal Sandy Wilson, the first Commander of British Forces Middle East in the build-up to war, said. 'It was a straightforward operational decision. At that stage we didn't need to go down and drop weapons at low level.'[27] The change of strategy was endorsed at the very top of government. 'Despite the Tornado losses, it was clear by 23 January that we had achieved air superiority,' wrote Prime Minister John Major. 'To reduce the risks to our aircraft we switched to operations at medium level.'[28] General Sir Peter de la Billière, the former SAS commander who had taken over from Sandy Wilson, was more forthright. 'The reason those aircraft crashed was because they were flying low level for one reason or another,' he said in a later documentary. 'And so, one said, well is this necessary? Is this a sensible thing to do? The answer was "no", and I didn't want to go on doing it.'[29]

It was a momentous change in RAF thinking. 'Our training philosophy, our aircraft, avionics systems, weapons systems, indeed our whole procurement programme had been tailored to the pursuit of the goal of perfecting low-level tactics,' Bill Wratten, the British Air Commander, said later. 'It was our chosen style of operations and we were very good at it. It was because we were so good at it, and because low level is the most difficult operating regime of all, that our crews were able to adapt so readily to less demanding ways of waging war.'[30]

To most aircrew, the move to medium-level operations made sense. 'The absolute priority to deny runway operating surfaces to the enemy was no longer compelling,' one Tornado pilot said. 'It was clearly pointless to suffer a very high casualty rate to deny the enemy a capability which he didn't appear to want to use.'[31] Jerry Witts, the Dhahran Tornado Detachment Commander, agreed. 'At this higher altitude, things seemed much more pedestrian. Triple-A was still trying its best to reach us, but now we could look down almost contemptuously on streams of tracer as they whirled about beneath us.'

Although the bombers now transitioned to medium level, the six Tornado GR1A reconnaissance jets based at Dhahran continued their solo low-level missions gathering key intelligence on Iraqi Scud launchers.

The overriding challenge was now the difficulty in establishing the effect of the medium-level use of unguided 'dumb' bombs. A few days into the tactical shift, the Tornado's success from 20,000ft was still being questioned. The Mission Report of an eight-ship attack on an oil pumping station close to Basra on 25 January was typical of the many that were winging their way up the chain of command:

> Six aircraft delivered their weapons onto the target area. However, no damage assessment has yet been received on this target making it difficult to come to any conclusions. Given the ballistic errors inherent in the Tornado at medium level and the small size of the nominated target, it is likely that any direct hits would be by luck rather than design. We feel that the small size of the target required the attentions of PGMs [Precision-Guided Munitions] rather than dumb bombs, however accurately aimed.[32]

Although the writer of that Mission Report would not have known it, the ability for Tornados to deliver Precision-Guided Munitions was already on its way. Those involved with the RAF's oldest strike jet had been on the case for many months.

* * *

The twin-engine Buccaneer bomber had been in service since 1962, but it was equipped with the relatively modern Pave Spike laser-guided system, which could steer suitably equipped bombs onto their targets with incredible precision. Shortly after Saddam's Republican Guard had crossed into Kuwait the previous August, the Buccaneer force gently reminded RAF chiefs of its capability.[33] But they were turned down, mainly because there was simply not enough room at the region's airbases for more military jets. And more importantly, in the run-up to war, the Americans had already promised to provide any laser designation for Tornados if they moved to medium level. But the US air forces were increasingly preoccupied with hunting down Saddam's Scud missiles, which were presenting a real threat to coalition unity. They now had no jets to spare.

The ageing Buccaneer had its critics, but fliers loved it. 'There is nothing the Buccaneer cannot do,' recalled one pilot. 'I've flown well over 100 different types of aeroplane and to me the Buccaneer is the finest I've ever known.'[34] Armed with anti-ship missiles and conventional or tactical nuclear bombs, the jet was originally designed for maritime attacks. Powered by two Rolls-Royce engines, it could fly low and fast, over 670mph at 200ft and well below. In many ways it was the perfect partner for the Tornado. The previous November, despite the continuing belief that they would never be needed, the Station Commander of the Buccaneer base at RAF Lossiemouth in north-east Scotland had suggested it would perhaps be a good idea to review and refine the jet's use of Pave Spike at medium level. His Boss agreed. After a dozen training sorties deploying 1,000-pounders fitted with a laser-seeking head which used vanes to steer them onto target from 20,000ft, they had demonstrated that they were well capable of carrying out such attacks. A report went to the Ministry of Defence confirming their ability to 'spike' from both low and medium level. Again, the Buccaneer force offered its services in the Gulf.

The answer was an 'emphatic no'.[35]

'We were continually assured that the Buccaneer wouldn't be required but had done some planning just in case,' a senior engineer said. 'We were told that there was absolutely no way the Ministry of Defence would consider sending the Buccaneer to the Gulf. So we all relaxed, calmed down and all training ceased.'[36] Knowing they'd done their best to contribute to the liberation of Kuwait, Buccaneer pilots, navigators and ground crew enjoyed a peaceful Christmas. That relaxed atmosphere continued while the Tornados went to war. On 22 January, Buccaneer Squadron Commander Bill Cope, still eager to get out there, asked his Boss if it was wise to go ahead with his skiing holiday booked that week.

'Sorry, Bill, they do not want us,' was the response. 'Have a good holiday.'[37]

Only that morning, Lennox and Weeks had gone down in their pre-dawn raid.

Hours later, the Lossiemouth Station Commander was directed to the secure telephone at the War Operations Centre. His caller had one question: 'How long will it take you to deploy Buccaneers to the Gulf?'

Completely blindsided, he took a few moments to compose himself before responding. 'Three days.'

'*Cancel your holidays*,' the word went out to all required personnel. '*Return to base. Immediately.*'

The next day the Defence Secretary announced the imminent deployment of the Buccaneers. Why, Tom King was asked, was a 30-year-old aircraft being sent to war?

'Because we need to improve the standard of precision bombing,' he replied.[38]

* * *

While they waited for the ageing Buccaneers to provide some laser-guided accuracy, the Tornados continued the medium-level missions with their 'dumb' bombs.

On 24 January, Bob Ankerson was still waiting to complete a combat sortie. The day before, attending communion at a makeshift altar in the Padre's room, he'd had a strange premonition. 'I had the feeling that I wasn't going to get back from the sortie. No doubt I wasn't the only one who sometimes felt that way. There was no foundation for this feeling, it was just there at the back of my mind. But I drew comfort from my faith and beliefs; they provided me with a basis for coping with my subsequent experiences.'

Rested and with a clear conscience, he set about planning an attack on Ar Rumaylah, not far from the airfield where Nichol and Peters had been shot down a week earlier. The images of the POWs were still a talking point at Dhahran and one of Bob's close friends from Bruggen, Ivor Evans, was in no doubt about their effect. 'It was as we expected; we were up against someone who didn't take much interest in the Geneva Convention. But the pictures of the POWs just made us all even more determined.' As the leader of his own four-ship formation, the previous losses were also something to be considered, especially as Dhahran had – so far – not suffered any casualties. 'There was a feeling of relief and expectation – relief that we were avoiding the fatalities and expectation that it couldn't last.'

As Bob's formation prepared for a 3.50am take-off, their Tornados were each loaded with five 1,000-pounders, their mission to 'disrupt ops and destroy aircraft in the open'.[39] He went through the personal sanitisation process, but decided to keep his copy of a small New Testament Bible in his breast pocket.

By the time they got to the tanker, two of the four Tornados had turned back with technical issues. Bob and his pilot Simon Burgess were now leading the formation with the other Tornado piloted by Stew Gillies. Just before crossing the border, Bob's radar failed. Normally it would have meant an immediate return to base, but he was determined not to turn back yet again. 'I was completely happy with our navigation kit as I'd already managed to get a radar fix. My focus was on getting the mission done, not because it was hugely tactically important, but because I needed to complete it for myself. To *demonstrate* I could fly a combat sortie. Those previous feelings of not completing my first mission were really playing on my mind.' As they set their armament switches to live, the crew rationalised that, although they were already satisfied with their positioning, if they turned their radar off for a while, it might restart later.

As Stew Gillies and his navigator Pete Rochelle crossed the border, their RHWR showed an enemy Hawk missile installation had located them.[40] An American system, probably captured during the invasion of Kuwait, it remained at target acquisition status, so they pressed on. It did not take long for the Tornados to detect another hostile radar, this time from an SA-3 system – a highly effective anti-aircraft missile that had shot down an American F-16 fighter a few days earlier. Gillies was worried. 'This was more problematic. We had just started our attack run and knew this was probably real.' The crew immediately began chaffing, sending out thousands of metallic strands to confuse the potential missile track.

The two Tornados closed in on Ar Rumaylah as the early-morning pre-dawn glow appeared from the east. At 20,000 feet it was getting light, though still dark on the ground, with intermittent cloud obscuring their view. With nine minutes to go before they struck the airfield, a loud warble sounded on Bob and Simon's RHWR. Simon spoke rapidly. 'I've got a fighter showing on the nose. A Mirage.'[41]

'F-15s showing out to the right,' Bob responded. Their accompanying fighter escort went to investigate.

'Good lads!'

Five minutes from their objective, Bob had another go at fixing his equipment. 'I'm still trying the radar but getting sod all out of it,' he told his pilot. A few seconds later he added: 'Checking weapons package correct.'

They were closing fast on the target now, and the navigator was determined there were no excuses or hiccups that would end in another failure. 'The last thing we wanted was to get to the target and have the bombs not operate because of an incorrect switch selection. We had turned back the previous night, but we were going to do it right this time.'

'Switches live,' Simon announced calmly as they closed in, checking that all the weapons armament switches were made. 'Nothing on the CWP.'

The Central Warning Panel was clear.

'Roger,' Bob replied. 'We've got a minute to the turn.'

'Roger,' the pilot confirmed. 'Seventeen miles.'

They were now two minutes away.

'Fix/Attack is selected.'

The aircrew talked through the weapons system settings,

double-checking all was correct. They were closing fast as light seeped over the horizon.

'We've got a minute to run,' Bob said.

'Time to Go running down now.'

On their cockpit's audio recording, small hints of growing tension can be heard in the crew's voices.

'Okay,' Bob confirmed. 'Looking good.'

'Double-check. All switches live.' Simon was making absolutely certain everything was correct.

'Forty seconds to release . . .' Bob said above the low whine of the electronic equipment.

'Twenty seconds.'

A few miles from Ankerson, Stew Gillies' radar warner sounded the urgent siren of an SA-3 missile guidance, suggesting that a SAM had been fired at them. With ten seconds to go to the target, 'I had not seen a missile launch and my naive optimistic guess was that we had about twenty seconds before it hit us, so I decided to drop our bombs and evade the missile when we were lighter.'

Both jets pressed on with the attack.

'Ten seconds,' Bob called.

'Five, four, three, two, one . . .'

'Bombs gone!'

Their five 1,000-pounders fell away.

'Okay, come left.' The words had barely left Bob Ankerson's lips when an almighty explosion shook the aircraft. On the Cockpit Voice Recorder – the 'black box' – there is a loud gasp followed by the blare of the warning siren indicating serious system failures.

As Stew Gillies released his munitions, he started an aggressive manoeuvre in maximum reheat to avoid any incoming missile. 'There was a huge orange flash and an incredibly loud, angry metallic bursting sound. The aircraft rolled violently left and pitched nose down. I thought we had been hit by the SA-3.'

'Don't eject,' he told his navigator. 'I can still fly.'

'As if!' replied Rochelle from the rear cockpit. 'We are over the Republican Guard! Fly the fucking aircraft!'

Gillies was already ahead of the game.

'My plan was to limp over to the Saudi border or at least the open desert, away from the Republican Guard, and then eject.'

Sirens screaming, Bob and Simon checked their own aircraft. 'I thought we had been hit by an SA-3 from the missile site to the south of the target. There was a feeling of total disbelief.' For a brief moment the cockpit was silent. Simon had acknowledged the warnings by cancelling the cockpit attention-getters on the coaming. The lights still flashed red but at least with the alarm silenced the crew could communicate. The captions on the CWP were indicating the urgent signal of 'L FIRE'.

'Left engine fire!' Simon called, shutting it down and hitting the fire extinguisher button. 'Stay with it,' he told Bob. He didn't want his navigator to eject. The aircraft was on fire, but at least if they were flying they had a chance of scraping home.

Stew Gillies was fighting his own battle as his Tornado lurched drunkenly across the sky. Glancing out of the cockpit he spotted multiple flashes of groundfire followed by a much bigger flash from below. *Missile launch.* 'A bright orange flame appeared to be tracking us and manoeuvring. We deployed more chaff. I broke low and the missile exploded in three flashes, well away from us.'

'Stay with it,' Simon repeated to Bob. The controls appeared to still be responding to his commands, despite the spreading flames. Then, twenty-eight seconds after bomb release, something startling caught his attention. 'Check the back!' His voice crackled with tension. 'Check the back . . .!'

Bob craned his neck around. 'The left-hand side of the aircraft was now engulfed in flames. They were spreading towards the wing root near me and grew in length to around 6 feet. I realised we would not be getting home that day.' The siren activated again, indicating further major failures. 'I told Simon we were going to have to get out of the jet *very* soon.'

'Okay, stay with it,' Simon smoothly replied, trying to get every second of flight he could before ejecting. He wanted to keep going for as long as possible to get them away from the elite Republican

Guard infantry units dug in directly below them. Like Stew, he was thinking that, if they could eject in an empty stretch of desert, there was a chance of rescue.

'Two-seven-zero.' Bob steered them due west.

They jettisoned the external fuel tanks to try to stem the fire. It made no difference to the size of the blaze.

'Stay with it,' Simon urged again.

Bob understood. 'I was closer to the flames than Simon so I was more worried, but, despite the obvious risk of an explosion, we were still flying, so it was better to stay in our cocoon.'

But not for long.

'It's burning through the wing now!' Bob stared at the flames billowing from the Tornado's left wing. Sixty-four seconds had elapsed since the explosion. 'We're going to have to go!' His tone was insistent now.

'Yes, I know.' Another alarm blared out.

'I'm losing control,' Simon yelled. The jet was no longer responding to his commands. Fire was ripping through the flight control system. 'Stand by.'

'Okay, I'm ready.' Bob glanced at the altimeter: 15,000ft.

Exactly ninety seconds after they had released their bombs, the aircraft was in its death throes.

'Stand by.' Simon spoke rapidly now. 'Stand by ... eject, eject, eject!'

Both crewmen pulled their ejection handles on the third command and were rocketed upwards into the breaking dawn.

The sirens burst back into life.

Then there was silence as the empty Tornado fell to earth.

* * *

As Stew Gillies powered away from what he thought was a missile exploding below, he glanced over at the other Tornado. 'I saw the canopy, front seat and backseat ejections from the aircraft of Burgess and Ankerson. We heard nothing more from them.'

In the light of the breaking dawn he watched white vapour spill over the top of his port wing, pushing past some ragged, flapping metal. He had amber warning lights on his CWP, indicating numerous failures. The Tornado was in bad shape. 'We weren't sure where we were, being without functioning navigation kit, and we needed someone to look at us from the outside. We also needed more fuel if we were fit enough to get home.'[42]

Another Tornado pulled alongside and gave Stew the bad news. 'He could see daylight through the fin and tailplane.'

Eventually, Dhahran's runway loomed ahead and they began their final approach. At 500ft Gillies flicked the undercarriage handle to lower the landing gear. Nothing happened. He then initiated the secondary, emergency system which blasted down the undercarriage. Finally, he coaxed the stricken Tornado onto the ground. In the rear seat, Pete Rochelle remembered 'holding onto the ejection handle' throughout the whole experience until the aircraft slowed to a halt. Just in case.

Shaken, they climbed out and surveyed the damage. 'There was shrapnel under Pete's seat, holes through the cockpit, the left wing, spoiler, left engine nozzle and the fin,' Gillies said. 'And a hole the size of Desperate Dan in the tailplane.' It was nothing short of a miracle that they had been able to fly at all. And an extraordinary testament to the Tornado's resilience that it had managed to carry them the 400 miles back home. Cliff Spink, the overall RAF Commander at Dhahran, was shocked by the state of the jet. 'It looked like a total wreck and it was difficult to see how it had stayed airborne. The crew did a truly incredible job to get it back to base and on the ground. It really was an astonishing achievement.'

When they'd finished scanning the devastation, the Warrant Officer in charge of the engineering ground crew turned to Stew and Pete. 'Sirs,' he said, 'I suggest you get yourselves a strong cup of tea.'

Later, a closer inspection of the airframe and overall weapons system revealed the awful truth. Both Tornados had been blown up by their own bombs. A technical issue meant that as the second bomb had fallen from each aircraft, it had immediately detonated. Stew and Pete had been extremely lucky that their jet had managed to withstand the 1,000-pounder exploding a matter of feet beneath them.

The news of Bob Ankerson's fate came as a bitter blow to his friend Ivor Evans, also flying from Dhahran. 'No matter how much we expected that it might happen, the loss of one of our aircraft was a shock – and heightened by the fact I obviously knew Bob and his wife Chris really well. But there was little time to dwell; we were all soon back into the planning and action of the war.'

Five RAF Tornados had now gone down.

* * *

After ejecting from the stricken Tornado, Bob Ankerson had sensed a great rush of air then a tumbling sensation as he was buffeted about at 15,000ft. A few seconds later and 5,000ft lower, he was abruptly jerked upwards when the parachute automatically deployed. 'It was just getting light, and looking around I could see shadows on the ground, small arms fire and triple-A. It was flat, open desert as far as the eye could see. I just thought, *What on earth am I going to do now?*'

'Bob! Bob! Are you all right?'

He glanced around to see Simon dangling beneath his parachute. 'I'm fine,' he shouted, relieved that he could see his pilot in the gathering dawn. But as they descended into cloud, Simon disappeared. It would be some time before they saw each other again.

As the sand rushed up to meet him, Bob tried to remember his parachute drills, the lessons learned from jumping off wooden benches onto green gym mats. 'I could hear, in my head, the instructor saying, "Don't anticipate the landing. Keep your elbows tucked in, knees together and legs slightly bent. Whatever you do, don't try to fend off the approaching ground!"'

He landed without injury but became immediately aware of the deep tyre tracks around him. 'It was as if I had landed on a motor-way in the desert!'

Peering into the gloom, he noticed garage-sized shapes dotted across the landscape. 'They weren't some strange topographical feature but camouflaged tank and infantry positions. I had landed in the midst of a huge military deployment of the Republican Guard!'

Bob dropped to his knees and began bundling in his parachute, ready to bury it. Seconds later, bullets cracked above his head. He looked up to see a line of a dozen soldiers heading towards him. The shots felt unnervingly close. 'There was nothing I could do. I knelt by the parachute, put my hands in the air, and waited for them to get to me.'

* * *

Three thousand miles away, his wife tried to ignore the ringing in her ears. The doorbell sounded again and she awoke with a start. It was just before 7am. 'I knew immediately what it meant. Why else would the bell ring while it was still dark?' Chris Ankerson was on her own in their comfortable married quarters at RAF Bruggen. A myriad thoughts now rushed through her mind. She put on her dressing gown and began walking down the stairs. She stopped halfway. Where the staircase turned a corner on the land-ing there was a small window. She peered out. *A black car.* Her heart raced. Every senior officer had one. 'All aircrew wives have a deep-seated fear of a black car appearing outside their house. It meant only one thing.'

She took a deep breath and made her way slowly down the remaining five steps. Wing Commander Dusty Miller, Bob's Squadron Commander, was standing on the front doorstep. Before he could utter a word, she asked one question: 'Is he dead?'

'We don't know,' Dusty solemnly responded. He then explained that Bob hadn't returned from a mission. Chris listened in shocked silence. Someone thought they 'might' have seen ejection seats coming out of their Tornado, but there was no confirmation. An hour later, Bob's great friend Allen Snowball arrived. 'Snowy' was Gareth's godfather and Bob's 'right-hand man' in case anything happened.

Her son was at boarding school in England. Chris knew she had to get a message to him. It was dawn in Suffolk and Dusty woke up Gareth's housemaster, Richard Fuller. The headmaster was immediately informed; it fell to him to deliver any important news to his pupils. He'd previously had the unenviable task of telling children a parent had died, but never of announcing to a 12-year-old boy that his father was missing in action in a hostile land.

Gareth Ankerson was having breakfast with his friends when he was told to go to the headmaster's study on a matter of 'high importance'. He tried to gauge what it was by studying Mr Fuller's face. 'I sat for a minute thinking what had I done wrong that would be so important that I would be dragged out of breakfast by my housemaster? As I walked through the dining hall my brain was racing.' For any schoolboy, a summons to the headmaster's office could mean only one thing. 'What on earth had I done to get me into so much trouble that the head wanted to see me? It was quite a scary prospect.'

He trudged through the corridors, contemplating his fate. 'The walls looked dimmer, the wooden panels suggesting they knew what the head was going to say to me. We arrived outside the headmaster's stout wooden door – it looked so evil, sucking me in.'[43]

He was told to wait as Mr Fuller went in. Sitting outside, he could hear mumbled words and the occasional mention of his name. Then the door creaked open.

'Gareth, come in please,' the headmaster said gently.

'Yessir,' he quickly replied. 'The door was laughing at me. I could hear it whispering, *You're in trouble.*'

Gareth was directed to a large, comfortable armchair, next to Mr Fuller. The head stood behind his desk. 'Gareth . . .' He paused, his brow furrowed. 'I can't tell you this standing behind here.'

What on earth could this mean? Was this a good thing, or a bad thing?

He stepped forward and perched awkwardly on the leading edge of his desk. Gareth couldn't understand why he was being so kind. *What is happening?*

'I need to tell you something very serious . . .' The head paused, looking him straight in the eye. 'Gareth, your father hasn't come back from a mission . . .'

He hesitated.

'He's gone . . . missing . . .'

'No!' Gareth screamed. 'Not my dad. This stuff does not happen to me!'

But then reality kicked in. The television reports of war in the Gulf, the newspapers, the prisoners, the conversations back home over the summer about people dying in Tornado crashes. 'At twelve years old, a light was turned on in my head and I understood what it all meant. I broke down in tears.'

The head gave him a few minutes then continued softly. 'Gareth, we received a phone call at seven this morning. I'm afraid I don't know much detail. When your father's plane was shot down it was in flames, but the aircraft next to them did see two smaller flames shoot up out of the fire. This, I would presume, would have been your father and his pilot. At this moment we are still not sure.'

Gareth instantly latched onto the words 'two flames shot up'. He knew what ejection seats did. It was a tiny glimmer of hope that he would hold onto with all his might. But he could not prevent more tears pouring down his face.

Between sobs, Gareth managed to say that he wanted one of his close friends to be told what had happened as soon as possible. 'She knew my father well and might take it quite hard as our fathers had both served together. No one ever said this, but I somehow *knew* that the RAF itself was an extension of my own family. It was the way we lived on the base when at home, the way we mixed and spoke when back at school. So I just knew it was right for her to be told separately to the rest of the school.'

The head agreed that Gareth should get some rest in Mr Fuller's flat until he was ready to see his friends.

'Are you okay?' a bunch of waiting pupils asked. Rumours must have spread fast that something had happened to his dad.

A friend handed over his treasured Sega computer game so that Gareth would have something to occupy his mind. But he couldn't stop thinking about his father. 'Why my dad? Why not someone else? I was thinking it must all be a bad dream and I'd soon wake up. The day was going very slowly and I felt as if two years had already gone by.'

Mr Fuller reappeared, asked what he wanted for lunch and handed him a letter from his dorm mates, wishing him well and asking to see him. 'I thought it was very kind, but I was just not up to speaking to people.' The housemaster then returned with some food and his close friend who had been told the news. 'We both burst into tears then chatted for a while before she had to go back to lessons.'

Gareth was summoned to the telephone. It was his mother. Chris was still in a daze but tried to be positive. 'Dad will be fine. He's trained for this. The ejection seats are wonderful. He will be fine.'

Gareth didn't buy it. 'She tried to be happy, but when she heard my voice nothing had to be said, we just cried. I asked if I was going home. My mother shouted down the phone: "Yes! Yes! Of course! You need to be here."'

* * *

The Iraqis had taken Gareth's father to a bunker just 100 yards from where he had landed. 'I could feel my knees trembling. It was such an alien situation. It was quite a terrifying prospect that someone else was calling the shots. I had gone from being an officer flying a Tornado jet and here I was shaking like a leaf. I wondered what my captors thought of me.' He was placed on a chair outside and searched. His small Bible was taken, along with his watch, then he was blindfolded and had his hands tied. An officer arrived and asked him his name and rank. As military law required, Bob supplied the details. Other questions then followed, but Bob continued the protocol of simply replying, 'I cannot answer that question.'

'They continued asking me various questions but there was no real coercion. I wondered how long that would last.' He was then driven around a series of other buried emplacements, apparently being passed up the military command chain. 'At one stage I was asked what the "C of E" engraved on my dog tags, my identification discs, meant. I explained it was my religion, Church of England, that I was a Christian. The questioner told me not to worry, that he was also a Christian, that I'd be looked after and not harmed. I wasn't convinced.' Later, at a military checkpoint, someone reached into the car and slapped him hard across the head. 'It was probably understandable; a soldier just giving vent to his feelings but with no real purpose.' As the journey continued, so did the questions, becoming increasingly threatening at each new location. 'They told me in no uncertain terms that if I didn't answer *their* questions, they would send me to someone who would *make* me answer.'

Still blindfolded, in the last ride he was aware of someone else in the car. An Iraqi voice asked, 'What is your name?'

'Bob Ankerson.'

The question was repeated. 'Simon Burgess,' came the answer. It was the first time Bob was aware that his pilot had also been caught. They were eventually taken to what appeared to be a farm courtyard. Bob was thrown to the floor in a dimly lit room.

An interrogator arrived. 'What aircraft do you fly?' he demanded.

'I cannot answer that question.' Again, Bob gave the stock reply.

The question was repeated again and again as the Iraqi made clear he was losing patience with the airman. 'There were obviously a number of people in the room. I could hear other voices and someone else was interpreting. It was curious; while there was no immediate violence, the air of menace was all-encompassing.'

The questions, and Bob's parrying of them, went on for some time as veiled threats became increasingly unveiled.

'You *will* talk to us eventually, and you *will* tell us what we want to know. You already *know* this. It is only a matter of time.'

For a few moments there was silence before the interrogator spoke again.

'You know my nickname is The Butcher?'

It was all beginning to sound deeply unpleasant and Bob's initial thought – *'It's like being in a B-movie!'* – was soon overtaken by The Butcher's final warning.

'I am going away for five minutes. When I return, I will get the answers!'

The man returned a short while later and Bob again refused to co-operate. Then began the same procedure every other prisoner of war had endured after being shot down.

'I was on the concrete floor, blindfolded and in a foetal position with my feet bent up. They started to beat me with what felt like the edge of a wooden cricket bat. Crack! I was hit on the calves and thighs. Crack! They hit my back and across the shoulder blades.' Each strike was followed by the same question. 'What aircraft did you fly?'

Bob was determined not to give anything away and to stick to the 'rules' of name, rank and number. 'But it was bloody painful and I was in no doubt that the guy meant business.' The interrogators worked as a team. One asked simple questions in clear English, another administered the beating when answers were not forthcoming. 'You have no idea if a blow is coming – but having not answered a question, you anticipate it for a very long time . . .'

The violence continued unabated, and after one of the early sessions, the interrogator left. 'I still couldn't see, but it was obvious someone was still in the room. Suddenly, I was lifted up beneath the arms and pulled across the floor. He lifted my arm onto what felt like a concrete block. This was now really terrifying and my imagination was running rampant. What was going to happen? What was this for? I presumed they were going to break my arms on the block. But then the guard just left. Looking back, I presume he was showing some basic humanity, trying to make me more comfortable in the midst of the pain, leaning me against the block. I often thought about that man over the coming hours.'

The Butcher returned and the beatings continued. 'We had been through various training scenarios, but nothing prepares you for the reality of violent interrogation and I knew that, at some point, I would have to go down a different path.'

The questions rained down, as did the cricket bat on the fleshy parts of Bob's body. Arms, thighs, back, shoulders. 'I have no idea how long it all went on. Perhaps hours? In the end I thought, *This is bloody daft, how long can I take this?* Everyone has their own personal threshold. Was it worth being permanently injured to protect what they must know already?'

Amid the blows, the same question was repeated.

'What aircraft do you fly?'

'Tornado.'

Like every person before him, whether flier or Special Forces, Bob had broken. He gave them answers that could easily be found in newspapers or on television. He took care not to make up the information, just kept it to a minimum, developing a strategy of wandering off topic into totally irrelevant areas. 'I felt that if I was talking, I was in control of what was happening. They seemed content that their interrogation was working and I was relatively happy I wasn't being asked about vital issues.'

But it was a dangerous game, because once he had started talking, he could not say 'no' to any further questions as his captors would know they had hit on something useful. Like the other POWs, Bob struggled with the notion that he had given in and was letting his friends down. 'I promised myself I wouldn't talk about Tornado operations, especially its defensive capabilities, which could put others at risk. It was daft – back at Bruggen, when we had our regular tests about the various bits of defensive kit, I always had to work really hard to remember all the facts and figures. Now, in an Iraqi dungeon, it was like the damn things were all written on a board in front of me, clear as day. I had a real fear that I could affect the safety of my colleagues and I didn't want to find myself lacking in courage.'

* * *

Chris Ankerson had also found herself in need of courage while confronted by a dizzying multitude of tasks. Bob's parents had to be told. Arrangements needed to be made for Gareth to return. She had a house full of people. The news continued to talk of coalition losses. So many cups of tea and biscuits were consumed that someone had to get replenishments from the nearby Naafi store.[44] 'There was a lot to be done and so many people coming in and out of the quarters. Things were going on around me, Dusty making calls, friends arriving. It was all happening and I was in a daze; in fact, I was clearly in shock. I remember at one point announcing, "But it's my day to wash my hair, I need to get that done!" I realised life was going to have to go on, but at the same time, everything had changed. When Bob had graduated as an officer in 1973, I remember the reviewing officer giving the speech saying, "You will make many good acquaintances in the Royal Air Force, but only a handful of very close friends." That day, our closest friends gathered around. They were there for me and I drew such great strength and comfort from their presence.'

One of those friends was Di Evans, whose husband Ivor had been serving alongside Bob. Di had also been woken at Bruggen by a very early phone call. 'No good news comes at that hour, especially when your husband is serving in the Gulf War. I picked up the phone and the Station Commander's wife's voice immediately said, "It's not Ivor." A chill ran through my veins. *If it's not my husband, whose is it?* She then said, "It's Bob."'

As one of Chris's close friends, Di was told that the 'knock on the door' was already underway and she was to be among the next visitors to the Ankersons' home. A car would pick her up in five minutes. 'I think we were all numb and just couldn't take it all in. A huge machine of activity took over our lives as Chris's Gulf War now changed.'

And, at the back of Di's mind, an unwelcome thought was already starting to surface. 'Would that "knock on the door" be for me tomorrow?'

January 24th was the same day as the funerals of Kieran Duffy and Norman Dent, the Tornado crew killed during low-level training in Oman eleven days earlier. Bob's close friend, Snowy, was supposed to be taking a number of senior officers to the funeral in England, but a more personal mission was now ordered. He was to fly his RAF Andover transport aircraft to the UK and collect his best friend's young son from boarding school.

As he waited in his dormitory, young Gareth knew, as the man of the house now, it was his duty to get home. 'The most important thing was to be with Mum, to hug her. To look after her.'

He went to bed knowing that Snowy would pick him up the next morning. But he had a sleepless night. 'All I could see was Saddam Hussein standing at the bottom of my bed pointing a gun at my head saying: "It's your turn now. I have killed your father. You're next."'

CHAPTER TWELVE

A BOLSHIE LADY

25 JANUARY–4 FEBRUARY

In late January, General Norman Schwarzkopf updated the media on the progress of the war. Thirty-eight enemy airfields had been attacked. At least nine were rendered non-operational, and seventy hardened aircraft shelters had been destroyed out of a total of nearly 600.[1] 'By the last week in January the skies over Iraq belonged to the coalition. After two weeks of war, my instincts and experience told me that we'd bombed most of our strategic targets enough to accomplish our campaign objectives. It was now time, I thought, to shift most of our air power onto the army we were about to face in battle.'[2]

The weight of allied attacks now moved, with Tornados attacking ammunition and fuel dumps, and airfields from medium level. B-52 heavy bombers pummelled frontline positions day and night, causing huge destruction to armour, artillery and personnel. Their bombs were followed by millions of leaflets, encouraging the Iraqi military to desert their posts. 'If you come to us, we will treat you as an Arab brother,' they were told.[3]

Group Captain Cliff Spink was in command at Dhahran, which was at the heart of preparations for the expected land campaign. In the days before the war, his force had been bolstered by six recently modified Tornado GR1A state-of-the-art reconnaissance aircraft, though initially there was little concept of how they might be used. That changed as the first Iraqi Scud missiles hit home. 'There was a real fear of the indiscriminate nature of the Scuds,' he recalled.[4] 'The warheads that were hitting Israel were threatening to bring the Jewish state into the war and rip apart the carefully constructed alliance of Western and Arab nations.'

On a number of occasions, Spink found himself unnervingly close to the action. 'During one of the first Scud attacks, I was driving towards one of our Tornado sites on the airfield. I glanced over at the Patriot anti-missile battery about half a mile away. Suddenly there was the most enormous bang and flash as a missile launched. I could see the shock wave forming and spreading out, coming down the road towards me. I dived out of the car and buried myself as best I could in a dip by the road. Seconds later there was another huge explosion as an incoming Scud was hit and the remains fell onto the base about 300 yards from the Tornados. Then bits of Patriot missile debris started to clatter down around me. It was a pretty interesting experience.'

The attacks needed to be stopped and General Schwarzkopf was ordered to use every means at his disposal to counter the threat. But Saddam's troops had mounted the Scuds on tracked vehicles and used the sandy wastes to hide and fire them. Special Forces were covertly inserted into the Western Desert to seek out and destroy the launchers and their control systems, and a substantial proportion of coalition air assets were also diverted to the task. Cliff Spink's recce force now came to the fore.

With its revolutionary infra-red system, the GR1A could operate in total darkness. Fitted with VHS video recorders instead of the standard Mauser cannons, the Tornado Infra-Red Reconnaissance System (TIRRS) could also pick up information not visible to the naked eye, even in daylight. Images from the three infra-red sensors – one downward-looking and one on each side – produced a continuous horizon-to-horizon scan which was recorded onto video tapes. The Reconnaissance Intelligence Centre at base could review the tapes immediately after landing, even before engine shut-down. Imagery was also relayed to the navigator's display in real time.[5]

At ultra-low level and high speed, either crew member could hit a switch to highlight something of interest for later review.[6] Crucially, a unique capability of the GR1A allowed imagery to be replayed and manipulated mid-flight for a deeper analysis, perhaps during quieter parts of the sortie. The navigator's capacity to review the imagery while still en route and send results back to base not only enabled more responsive tasking of further intelligence gathering and battle-damage assessment, but even the potential to launch an immediate attack.

The system provided some startling capabilities. It could tell if aircraft on the ground had full or empty fuel tanks, if their engines had recently been used, and detect the heat trace of recently departed jets.[7] Commanders in Riyadh soon recognised that the Tornado's infra-red capability made it increasingly difficult for the Iraqis to hide their weapons. The tracks of recently moved tanks – and, more importantly now, missile launchers – were vulnerable to detection due to their heat signatures.

Using the in-cockpit review systems, one of the recce Tornados had reported a suspected Scud battery shortly after the first attacks. Navigator Gordon Walker and his pilot were tasked with confirming its presence. With no time to organise a tanker, the crew used four external tanks, one under each wing and two under the fuselage where bombs would normally be mounted; just enough to complete the mission.

'*Alone, unarmed and unafraid*', as their maxim had it, they took off from Dhahran at 3am and headed across the border before dropping down for a high-speed solo dash into the target area. Walker turned on the recorders and they picked up significant vehicle movement. 'We saw loads of tracks in the desert. It was like overflying Salisbury Plain [training area] seeing the army's tank tracks criss-crossing everywhere.'[8]

And sure enough, as their search continued, they located the launchers. 'We flashed over them and then headed back to friendly territory again. We thought they were firing at us, but it turned out to be the reflection of the green lights inside the cockpit on the rain outside. It was a bit spooky, though.' Travelling back to Dhahran at 670mph, Walker jettisoned all four empty tanks to lower the drag, but they still made it back with very little fuel to spare. The video tapes were rushed away for analysis. 'It appeared that we might have located as many as four Scud launchers.'

Walker was also amazed by what they could see when they played back the tape. 'It was like looking at aerial photographs of the Somme in 1915. You could see the artillery positions dug in, the zigzag of the trench patterns to the main trenches. It all looked like a classic piece of static warfare. I suppose the Iraqis fought that way because they had been fighting the Iranians for eight years and still hadn't grasped the concept of a land–air war.' The freshly analysed footage was rushed to personnel at Air HQ in Riyadh, who passed on the targeting information for immediate airstrikes.

In the first week of the war there had been thirty-five Scud attacks, then eighteen in the second. By early February they were down to one a day.[9] The recce Tornados had acquired a well-deserved reputation as 'the Scudhunters'. Despite the test of mettle, they continued their work at low level throughout the conflict, though not against heavily defended enemy airfields. In fact, an early suggestion that they should overfly airbases to assess the damage from JP233 raids was met with incredulity. *It's near-suicidal*, the planners were told. Those early low-level exploits into the heart of the triple-A fire had taken their toll on the nerves of many fliers.

One senior commander witnessed the effects for himself. 'I had gone into the crew room to grab a coffee. There were a few guys relaxing before heading off on a mission later that night. One of the aircrew was an old friend so I stopped for a chat, but his crewmate was totally unresponsive. He simply wasn't communicating, almost as though he wasn't in the room.'

The disturbed officer was clearly exhibiting '*the thousand-yard stare*', the blank, unfocused gaze of combatants who had become emotionally detached from the horrors they had witnessed. 'I was quite concerned, so asked one of my team to pop down and join me for a coffee. I didn't say why, but I asked him to look at all the crews in the room to see if he noticed anything. He immediately recognised the guy who was clearly affected by his experiences, sitting there, completely vacant. I immediately decided to take him off ops and rested him for a while.'[10]

It was not an isolated case.

* * *

John Broadbent, the Muharraq Tornado Detachment Commander, could also see the stresses building as the losses mounted. 'It was a very difficult time. Several crews were clearly feeling the strain particularly badly. This was hardly surprising – over just a few days our base had lost three crews, some presumed dead. It didn't take the brains of a rocket scientist to work out that if losses continued at that rate, you might only last a matter of weeks.'[11]

Broadbent's pilot Nige Risdale was witnessing this too. 'A few people were quietly acknowledging that they were affected by what we were doing, some more than others. On one occasion, someone asked how I could brief crews about a sortie – where we all faced the very real prospect of dying – without showing any emotion. Well, that was my job. I certainly felt those emotions, but the way I had coped was to compartmentalise them.'[12]

Not all aircrew were able to do the same.

'Frank' was a pilot who had been at the very forefront of the most dangerous low-level missions.[13] He had faced death, flying through the maelstrom to drop his JP233s over the Iraqi airfields. The triple-A had come so close that he had smelled the acrid cordite in his cockpit. He had listened to the terrified radio chatter and had to ignore the gut-wrenching effect of seeing comrades die. Frank – not his real name – had initially been able to continue on operations, somehow managing, like Risdale, to compartmentalise his experiences. Then he had come back from another intense low-level mission and seen the images of his friend John Peters repeated endlessly, relentlessly, on TV. He had *seen* the bruises on Peters' face, and *knew* they had been caused by torture rather than ejection.

A fuse blew inside his head.

A chain of images rattled through his mind. The flak bursting towards him, whipping over the cockpit; colleagues dying in a fireball. He felt the bile burn its way through the back of his throat at the POWs' plight. Then he completely lost it – screaming, crying, smashing his fists against the walls. When the medics finally got to him, he was a sobbing wreck, barely able to function. The Senior Medical Officer on the base could see he had suffered some sort of breakdown and immediately evacuated him from the region.

The next day Frank arrived at the psychiatric wing of the military hospital at RAF Wroughton in Wiltshire. He was ushered into the hands of Wing Commander Gordon Turnbull, one of the leading military psychiatrists of his generation. Three years earlier, Turnbull's team had dealt with the fallout from the Lockerbie bombing. Pan Am 103 had been blown up by Libyan terrorists at 30,000ft over the Scottish town, killing 270 people. RAF Mountain Rescue teams had spent weeks combing the hillside for survivors, and then body parts. Many had paid the price with post-traumatic stress disorder.

PTSD – the direct consequence of a range of severe traumatic episodes – manifested itself most commonly in disassociation, flashbacks and nightmares. Gordon Turnbull had recently visited America to study their treatment of Vietnam veterans, which further fuelled his determination to assemble a team capable of treating the inevitable psychological casualties of the Gulf conflict. His pioneering success with Lockerbie gave him the credibility to persuade senior commanders to allow him to lead the treatment. At first, there was considerable resistance to this initiative from some senior officers, who, as Turnbull put it, 'still believed that trauma reactions were evidence of psychological frailty'. He fought hard to enlighten them, and did not have to wait long to put his experience to good use.

Frank's official service flying record was immaculate; he was regarded as one of his cohort's best pilots. Twenty-four hours earlier he had been flying frontline operations, into the teeth of enemy fire. Now he found himself being driven in pouring rain through the front gates of a military psychiatric hospital. The car stopped and Frank stepped hesitantly onto the forecourt, looking around at the rolling hills. Supported by a nurse, he shuffled through the doors.

Waiting to greet him, Gordon Turnbull was enraged by what he saw. Someone in the Gulf medical facility had scribbled: 'Acute Melancholia with Hysterical Features' on a scrap of card and hung it around his neck on string. It bounced against Frank's olive-green RAF flying suit as he entered the hospital. 'I felt my blood boil,' Turnbull said. 'As if this poor fellow hadn't been through enough, he had flown all the way back to the UK with a diagnosis of his condition, a wrong one I was fairly sure, scrawled on a piece of cardboard for all to see. It might just as well have said "*unclean*". Forget the First and Second World Wars, I felt as if we had regressed to the Dark Ages.'[14]

The pilot barely acknowledged his new surroundings.

'I had rarely seen such a broken figure. He was hunched over and could barely walk. He looked at me, I imagine, much as he might have looked at an Iraqi interrogator. The whites of his eyes were visible above and below his irises, a sign he was producing too much adrenaline.' Turnbull well knew that 'steely-eyed pilots' could absorb a lot of stress, but, like every other human being, they had their tipping point. 'I had long suspected there was a dangerous rigidity to the highly developed defence mechanisms within pilots, one that would take a great deal to break, but when they did go, the collapse would be the equivalent of a dam bursting.'

Convinced that Frank represented the 'bow wave' of hundreds of cases from the Kuwaiti offensive, Turnbull and his psychiatrist colleague later got to work. 'Let me start, Frank, by telling you that you are perfectly safe here,' he told the pilot. 'Nothing is going to happen to you.'

Frank's eyes briefly met his. 'I'll never fly again, will I?' He started weeping. 'My career's over, isn't it?'

'We're not going to make any assumptions about what brought you here, nor do we make any assumptions about your future, Frank,' the psychiatrist said. 'We know that something traumatic happened to you. I'd like to try to understand what it was.'

'It scared the shit out of me.' The pilot faltered, wiping tears from his eyes, speaking barely above a whisper.

'What you say stays with us. I'm not taking notes.'

Sobbing and barely glancing at them, Frank said, 'Flying is everything to me. My mates are everything to me. I've never experienced anything like this. I'm not a coward. I just want to be with my mates.'

'And we want you to be back with them,' Turnbull told him. 'But the more you can tell us about it, the better.'

Frank looked at the doctor, held his gaze, then slumped back in his chair and exhaled. 'When I saw them on TV, I just snapped. John Peters and I know each other pretty well. It was the bruises around his eyes. Those weren't from any ejection. I just felt this incredible anger. And then the world started to close in on me. Thoughts, images, everything . . . it just seemed to explode inside my head. I couldn't take it any more. That's when I just . . . lost it.'

'It was a panic attack,' Turnbull said gently. 'It's a perfectly normal reaction, Frank, considering everything that happened.' At the word 'normal' the psychiatrist could see relief flood across Frank's face. 'Your experience was a stress reaction. Not only is it normal but it's as old as the hills. You are safe here, Frank. Nothing bad is going to happen to you.'

* * *

While Frank started his psychiatric treatment in England, the families of the prisoners of war were undergoing their own mental and emotional challenges. Chris Ankerson had no idea if Bob was alive or dead. 'How long was our ordeal going to last? Weeks, months, a year? We simply had to try our best to cope with each stage of the awful journey.'[15] Gareth Ankerson's earlier nightmare about his father's death still haunted him. 'Mum and I had to consider the worst. How would our lives change if my dad had been killed? Our only hope was that the two flames that had shot out of the fire of their jet were my father and his pilot. But how long would we have to wait to find out?'[16]

Three days after Bob was reported missing in action, his Boss, Dusty Miller, rang the doorbell again at their married quarters in RAF Bruggen. 'Chris, I need to speak to you.'

Oh no, is this it? Chris could see the grave look on Dusty's face. It was bad news, but not of the kind she expected. 'Sorry, Chris, you're not going to believe this, but Robert's flying pay is being withdrawn.'

At first Chris had breathed deeply, thankful it wasn't the worst news, then digested the meaning of Dusty's words. The Ankersons were victims of a regulation which decreed that if an airman was missing in action, and ergo unable to do the job they were paid for, their specialist flying pay, perhaps a third of their salary, would be stopped. Chris was devastated. 'We had Gareth's boarding-school fees, bills, shopping. And a mortgage! It was simply shocking. Truly astonishing.'

But that was not the worst of it.

'Dusty then told me that Robert's salary would also cease to be paid into our joint bank account. It would now be sent directly into the RAF Bruggen administrator's care and I would be issued "an allowance" – if and when I needed cash. I was now required to present myself to a junior clerk to beg for access to our own money! I was absolutely livid. It was an archaic Second World War regulation which some faceless bureaucrat had initiated. It appeared "ladies" didn't have the financial acumen to deal with their missing husband's salary.'

Chris and Dusty spread the family financial documents across her living-room floor. 'I was furious but I needed to deal with it. After several calculations I thought, *Yes, we should be able to manage, as long as I am careful.* But I was so angry. I didn't know if my husband was alive or dead, yet they were now stopping his pay. How dare they?!'

Chris called their UK bank to explain what had happened and the manager quickly came to the phone. He was one of many who had watched the war unfold on the news. 'Mrs Ankerson, we all know what has happened to your husband,' he said. 'We are so sorry to hear about your situation. But please don't worry about anything. Be assured that I will personally ensure everything will be fine with your finances.'

It seemed that a civilian bank manager was more sympathetic to the plight of those missing in action than the military establishment that had sent them to war.

Tange Stewart faced a similar nightmare after her husband Robbie had gone missing in action on 19 January. Like Chris Ankerson, she had no idea how long her situation would last. 'I would wake up every morning and, just for a second, forget what we were going through. Then, quick as a flash, I'd be brought crashing back to reality.'

Tange had not received Robbie's payslip at the end of January, so picked up the phone. 'My bank manager said Robbie's pay had initially come through, but it had then been recalled, so he presumed I'd be receiving Robbie's pay by some other means. I was speechless; really annoyed and worried. How was I meant to cope without any money? More calls were made, voices were raised. Messages were sent flying up the military chain of command and, eventually, I received Robbie's pay.'

It seemed the issue had been resolved until she received a letter from Archie Hamilton – the Armed Forces Minister who had announced in a radio interview that Nichol and Peters were probably dead. It stated that she would only be paid Robbie's salary for thirteen weeks, after which she would get a certificate to claim a pension and life insurance. 'I said no one would be giving me any such *certificate* until they could prove my husband was dead!'

The bureaucratic short-sightedness forced Tange to confront

the possibility of Robbie never returning. 'It was really difficult to cope. As the days dragged by, I began to think years into the future. How to get the children through their education, then perhaps I could travel out to Iraq to find out what had happened to Robbie, if he was still alive? I just didn't know how to think or react.'[17]

Chris Ankerson went one step further. She had been told that the head of the RAF, Air Chief Marshal Sir Peter Harding, would visit RAF Bruggen. 'I'd had enough and requested a personal meeting with him. I had decided not to take any more of this nonsense. I was going to become "*the bolshie lady*".'

The Chief of the Air Staff was not having a good day. He arrived late for their meeting in the Officers' Mess after the ground crews' wives had given him a piece of their mind over the Gulf airmen's working conditions and financial allowances. Chris was not in the mood to take any prisoners. 'I poked him in the chest and said: "How dare you take my husband's money from me!" This wasn't something you normally did to the RAF's most senior officer, but I was so angry with "the system". I had always toed the party line, been meek and mild, but I just flipped and told him exactly what I thought.'

Harding exploded. 'What do you mean? Who told you this?' He already knew about the archaic rules and had specifically told his staff that they should be ignored.

'Hearing me tell him that, despite his orders, they had been implemented was clearly a shock. A ripple seemed to go through his waiting Staff Officers. Sir Peter turned to them and said, rather forcefully, "Sort this all out. Now!" There was quite a bit of scurrying around and the matter was quickly resolved.' But not entirely. Bob's full salary would still have to be paid into the care of the RAF Bruggen administration team and *then* issued to Chris on request. It appeared that wives of those missing in action still could not be *completely* trusted to manage their own affairs.

* * *

As Harding tried to keep up morale on the home front, the spirits of the Tornado force were lifted by the move to higher altitudes, albeit with questionable effectiveness. On 26 January an eight-ship attacked an ammunition dump 170 miles south of Baghdad. While the munitions had rained down on the general target area it had not been a great success. Yet again, the Mission Report told a familiar story:

> A majority of bombs had impacted between the sheds. Indeed, only one of the [190] storage sheds was clearly seen to have been destroyed. It was disappointing to see such an apparently small amount of damage for the effort involved.[18]

That disappointment, it was hoped, would soon be reversed. On the same day as the ammunition dump attack, the first two Buccaneers carrying Pave Spike laser targeting pods set off to join the Tornados in the Gulf, fulfilling the Defence Minister's promise to 'improve the standard of precision bombing'. With the desert camouflage paint still drying on their airframes, they left RAF Lossiemouth in Scotland for the nine-hour, non-stop journey – honouring their Station Commander's commitment to be ready to go to war within three days.

The force's 140 personnel had been inoculated, equipped with chemical warfare suits, issued personal weapons and asked to make wills. Bill Cope, the Squadron Boss, departed with his most experienced crew at 4 a.m. arriving at Muharraq later that day. Their arrival was somewhat underwhelming. 'If we had expected a welcome for bringing a much-needed additional capability to the RAF element in-theatre we were to be disappointed,' Cope later said.[19] That night he went for a drink with the Jaguar Detachment Commander in the top-floor bar of the Sheraton Hotel, where they were quartered. What was the drill for a Scud attack? Cope asked. Do we go down to the basement?

'Not really,' his friend replied. 'If a Scud hits the hotel it will be coming vertically downwards at about Mach 5 and will probably pass through all floors before ending up in the basement. So most people rush up here for a beer while watching the Patriot missiles launching from Dhahran across the causeway.'

Cope considered the advice carefully while sipping his beer.

With the Buccaneers in place, the Tornados from Pablo Mason's formation at Muharraq were pulled off war sorties for a rapid training programme. The navigator who had released the bombs on the Tornado's first ever medium-level mission now formed part of the team for the first precision strike. Mike Toft had mixed feelings. 'I was a bit miffed that we were not continuing to "do our bit" as the war went on around us. But on the other hand, I was slightly relieved that we wouldn't be putting our pink bodies in harm's way for a few days.'[20]

As the end of January approached, the ageing Buccaneers and the Tornados flew a number of practice missions, establishing the best way to operate in concert. Using its Pave Spike targeting pod, the Buccaneer navigator identified the target on a small cockpit TV screen and the system then focused a laser beam on the target. The Tornados carried standard 1,000lb bombs fitted with a special nose attachment consisting of a 'seeker head' linked to guidance vanes, or 'wings'. The head could 'see' the Buccaneer's laser spot on the target and when the bombs were released, their seekers could track the laser and send signals to the small canard 'wings' which moved, allowing the bomb to 'fly' precisely towards the laser spot placed on the target.[21]

By early February, the Tornados had a precision targeting capability.

* * *

While Tornado pilot Frank's comrades were flying to war, Wing Commander Gordon Turnbull was attempting to reconnect him to the world he had known before his collapse. He used the same formal psychological debriefing he had utilised after the Lockerbie disaster, ensuring the pilot talked in detail about his experiences.

Frank was told that all his conversations with the psychiatric team were in total confidence. He had the freedom to say exactly what he was feeling because nothing was on the record. He had been allowed to call his wife at his home base and to let her know that he was safe and would be coming to see her and their child very soon.

The key for the psychiatrists was to understand exactly what had happened to Frank in the lead-up to his breakdown. The pilot had to recall and recognise the specific events in what they called the 'cognitive domain phase'. 'To give us all the information we needed to help him, Frank had to respond to our simple *"who, what, why, where, when questions"* in order to establish a timeline.'

Frank talked about the night-time raids and the unbelievable stress that aircrew faced flying into the triple-A. Turnbull was shocked and began to realise that the JP233 sorties were nothing like the sanitised attacks he had seen on TV. Frank went on to tell them about the high attrition rate in the Tornado force and how it had affected some of the aircrew. He talked about the fears and feelings he experienced during the combat missions. He had been able to handle the stress of war until the 'trigger moment' occurred – his utter distress and revulsion at the television pictures of the brutalised POWs, which also made him terrified of what would happen to his wife and child if he was shot down. 'Frank had been constantly reliving the missions, seeing the flak, seeing the explosions, replaying the movie again and again in his head. We were into classic flashback territory.'[22]

'We told him that the flashbacks were "unprocessed memories" with his mind presenting them again and again as a way of trying to find an explanation for events that defied reason.' Turnbull also explained his 'Pint Pot' theory where levels of stress grew inside until it 'overflowed with a physical force of enough power to knock somebody off their feet'. Frank's particular 'Pint Pot', they explained, had already been filled to the brim by his previous experiences. 'To anyone else, the sight of Peters and Nichol on TV, although distressing, would not have had the same impact. That it had done so with Frank was down to the fact that he knew them so well.'

The key for the pilot was to understand what had happened to him, to 'demystify the event' and hasten his recovery. Turnbull was amazed at how quickly he got it. 'As soon as he started to understand that it was his personal emotional connection to Peters and Nichol that had caused the fuse to blow, Frank made a remarkably swift recovery.' The flashbacks and nightmares formed the cornerstones of his PTSD; without either of these symptoms the condition began to diminish.

Within days his state had improved considerably. Turnbull now had an even greater ambition: to help fulfil Frank's earlier wish to get back to his Squadron. 'This had been his number one priority. To the best of my knowledge there had never before been a case of an RAF pilot returning to flying duties in the wake of a breakdown during combat operations.'

Turnbull now needed to convince his own Boss that Frank was ready to return to duty. After examining the pilot, the senior medic concluded, 'Well, this is remarkable. He appears to be fixed.'

Frank was sent back to his home base for re-evaluation flying the Tornado, before a return to normal duties. Perhaps even in the warzone.

* * *

With her husband missing in action and her only son back at boarding school, Chris Ankerson allowed herself to be absorbed by the news; reading the papers, watching television or listening to the radio. The daylight hours were usually fine, as friends visited regularly. But darkness brought the most troubling thoughts, and, one night, the pent-up emotions eventually spilled over. 'I lost all control. It wasn't one particular incident, just everything tumbling down on top of me.'

It was 3am, and there was only one thing for it. She phoned her friend Di Evans.

Di's husband, Ivor, was also serving in the Gulf, and she had stayed with Chris for the first few days of her ordeal. 'This huge machine of activity took over our lives and the news played constantly on TV. Chris had slept like a baby every night and I kept going into her room to see if she was okay. I was wide awake and unable to even have a nap. I eventually went home to sleep in my own bed. A few days later, the phone rang again in the middle of the night. I obviously thought it was now my turn for the "knock on the door". But Chris's teary voice just said, "What am I, Di – am I a widow or a wife? What am I?" I told her to come around immediately.'[23]

As Chris walked over, she bumped into two armed RAF policemen.

'Morning, Mrs Ankerson,' they said. 'Is everything okay?'

Everyone on base was very aware of her circumstances.

'I'm fine, I'm fine, thank you,' Chris said between sobs. 'I'm just going to Mrs Evans' house.'

'Do you need us to escort you there?'

'No, I'll be fine. Thank you.' She continued on her way. 'It was those tiny human touches which made such a difference.'

Di knew that Chris had arrived. 'I didn't need to worry where she was; I could hear the terrible crying as it got nearer to my front door.'

They chatted through the early hours until they both remembered that Princess Diana was visiting Bruggen that afternoon on a morale-boosting trip and they were both scheduled to meet her. They snatched some sleep then dressed for the visit. 'Princess Diana was so delightful,' Chris said. 'So kind and understanding. It was important to us that people outside our military bubble understood what was happening. It wasn't just our husbands at war. We were part of it all, too.'

Fluctuating emotions were also assailing Tange Stewart. With no reports of an ejection from Robbie's aircraft, in her darkest moments she feared he had perished along with Dave Waddington. Then the *Daily Express* splashed a story saying two Iraqi 'peasants' had overpowered the navigator and 'sold' him to the authorities for £15,000; the bounty that Saddam had put on captured airmen.[24]

The piece also quoted an 'RAF source' speculating that Robbie might have been injured and unable to defend himself. Although the story appeared to be based on conjecture, it contained some curiously accurate details, though Tange could never have known that at the time.

The next day the press pack appeared in her small village, eager for more information. Tange refused to give any interviews. Fortunately, her teenage children Kirsty and Scott were at home when the story broke. 'The phone went crazy and all the press kept knocking at the front door,' Kirsty said.[25] 'There were TV cameras, with lights shining on our house. The press intrusion was really difficult. We were a very private family and the notion of us being on the front pages was really difficult.'

Kirsty's young mind was turning once more to darker thoughts. 'I was thinking of all those spy novels again. I eventually told Mum that I didn't want Dad to be alive and suffering. I would rather he was dead and at peace and I was now more scared than ever. If he was alive, he could be being terribly tortured and I couldn't bear that thought.'

With no idea how close to the truth she had been, Kirsty returned to boarding school wearing her father's old jumper as a reminder of his touch, 'and I clumped around in a pair of his flying boots trying to feel closer to him'.

School was a helpful diversion, although she struggled in some lessons. 'My mind drifted but the teachers were so understanding. In one English class, we were meant to be writing an essay about *Macbeth* but I just stared out of the window. The teacher saw me and quietly suggested I write about how I was feeling instead. I wrote a poem about missing Dad. Which really helped.'

Amid the emotional and financial turmoil, the Queen stepped forward and requested a meeting with some of the families of the missing aircrew. Berenice Waddington was still struggling with the uncertainty of whether her son David was alive or dead. 'I spent most of my time simply hoping and praying, and little else. Then our liaison officer rang to say the Queen would like to meet us. At first,

I said, 'No, I'm not really up to it. But they eventually persuaded me, promising to make all the arrangements.'[26]

Uniformed drivers collected the families from across the UK and drove them to RAF Marham in Norfolk. Berenice and her husband Jack were spirited down from Bolton, while another RAF car wound its way through the icy Lincolnshire lanes with the Stewarts. The day before, Kirsty had been taken to buy new clothes; a maroon skirt, cream tights and red velvet shoes. She was now finding the journey a great challenge. The Officers' Mess had informed them they would provide a packed lunch. They wanted to make the occasion as special as possible. 'As a 13-year-old, I thought a packed lunch meant a sandwich, a KitKat and a can of Coke. But the Mess, trying to be really kind to us, had provided an expansive finger buffet on huge platters covered by silver cloches! We were eating in the back of the car while trying to avoid the gourmet smoked salmon, asparagus spears and prawns spilling onto our posh new clothes.'

Tange picked at the food while eyeing the frost-covered hedgerows and ploughed fields. 'Everywhere was white and icy, and as the scenery flashed by I thought, *That view is exactly how I feel inside.*'

Jock Stirrup, RAF Marham's Station Commander, escorted the families around the base. To help them understand what the airmen had been doing, they were shown the planning areas and the aircrews' flying kit in the locker rooms. Berenice Waddington had a difficult moment. 'We saw David's peg where his flying suit would hang. It was empty. There was just his name pinned to the wood. That really hit us both hard. It spoke volumes about our situation.'

Aside from the Waddingtons and the Stewarts, the base also hosted the families of the first Tornado crew to go down – Nigel Elsdon's parents and Max Collier's wife Molly with their three sons. With no official confirmation that any downed aircrew were dead or alive, all the airmen were currently listed as MIA. Berenice found it strange. 'We met a lot of the other families, which was very moving, but it was an unusual gathering of people. None of us knew if our loved ones were alive or dead.'

It would be many weeks until they each found out the truth, but the awkwardness of not knowing was forgotten when the Queen entered the Officers' Mess bar, where the families had assembled.

Primed with the knowledge that Her Majesty always made the running in any small talk, Scott Stewart had decided to help her and prepared his own discussion beforehand. Drawing confidence from being dressed in his missing father's new, light-grey pinstripe suit, the 16-year-old schoolboy bowed then launched into a ten-minute speech about the support they had received from the people of Coleby and how they were coping. Her Majesty listened intently. Tange thought she looked pleased having someone actually talk to her. 'I was very proud of Scott. The whole day was a huge boost to our morale. Taking us out of ourselves; a real relief from our ongoing worries. The Queen was simply wonderful, so friendly and approachable.'

Kirsty found it a strange experience going from their 'Stewart bubble' into a group suffering the same emotions. 'I realised that many other people were affected by the Gulf War and my child's world was a lot larger than I knew.' Dressed in her smart new outfit, Kirsty curtsied gracefully as the Queen approached. 'She was really lovely and we chatted about my netball at school and how she cheered Prince Charles on when he had played sport. It was all very surreal.'

* * *

While it was cold and frosty in Lincolnshire, the clear weather in the Gulf had been assisting the planning for the first laser-guided bomb (LGB) attack. The Pave Spike system could only be used in daylight and clear skies. Night-time bombing was out as the target could not be identified, and any changing cloud cover could mean that the laser beam would not reach the target nor perhaps be spotted by the seeker head. On 2 February, it was time to see if the

Tornado could become the first RAF jet to drop a Precision-Guided Munition in war. The target was a bridge that spanned the River Euphrates halfway between Baghdad and Basra, just north of the town of Samawah.

Four Tornados, each equipped with three 1,000lb LGBs, were given the task of destroying the bridge. A pair of jets would fly with a Buccaneer that would laser-designate for both. After the short break in combat operations, Mike Toft readied himself for the sortie. 'It was time to go sausage side again. The bridge was on Highway 8; one of the key supply routes. In preparation for the ground war, we needed to take out the bridges to hamper the Iraqi capability to get reinforcements down to their front lines. It was my third mission and yet again there was a huge change in tactics. We were now going to war at medium level, *and* in broad daylight. It was not a comfortable feeling.'[27]

With clear weather now forecast over Samawah, they were given the final go-ahead after breakfast. Faced with their first operational sortie, nerves were evident among the Buccaneer force. 'It was a tense moment for all of us because the crews that came out [to theatre] were very scared,' said the Buccaneers' senior engineering officer. 'No one had been in combat before or knew what to expect. Some had false bonhomie and others snapped at the ground crew. The ground crew understood the tension the aircrew felt and handled them like eggs. We all knew that success or failure of the Buccaneer would depend on how well the aircrew did.'[28]

There was a great deal at stake. Thanks to the Pave Spike's recording system, there was no hiding place. 'These videos would be used to demonstrate to the world that this was indeed pinpoint bombing designed to minimise loss of life,' said one officer. 'Accuracy was a political necessity.'[29]

Nearly every member of the Buccaneer detachment headed out to see off the first raid. 'It was quite emotional,' one airman remembered. 'You get very attached to the aircrew because you work with them day in and day out. You get to know their little habits and what they like and don't like. They picked up their helmets and walked out to the aircraft. We were so nervous we just sat there and didn't know whether to speak to them. Always in the back of your head was, *please let them come back*.'[30]

It had been a tumultuous week for Bill Cope. Only a few days before he had been packing his salopettes to go skiing with his wife; now he was holstering a loaded pistol ready to lead his Buccaneers on their first raid. 'I believe most Squadron Commanders have a mental image of how they think they will go into battle for the first time. Typically, it will be to lead the crews we have trained with for months or even years. On my first mission the reality was rather different. As we transited over Iraq, heading for the bridge, I wasn't leading at all, the Tornados were. We were at high level not low level and over land, not over sea.'[31]

Like the Tornado crews, the Buccaneer airmen now found themselves in uncharted territory. Some way from their target they met dense cloud. With their antiquated navigation equipment, it was vital that they stayed with each other. If they got lost, the mission would fail. 'Visitors always assume that the Middle East is in burning sunshine,' said Cope. 'Not so. I was in cloud staring at a Tornado's wingtip. I listened to lots of Soviet radar systems just as I had in the simulator at home, but these were real signals coming back from real enemy radars. The thought running through my mind was, *It's not supposed to be like this*.'

With 50 miles to go, the cloud suddenly gave way to open skies and the jets, in arrow formation, found themselves in broad daylight, directly over enemy territory, a brown landscape under flat grey light. With a minute to go, the flak opened up below them, but there was no time for fear; the Buccaneer crews needed to positively identify the target. Amid the incredible concentration of fire, the navigators picked up the bridge over the Euphrates and set their individual target designators on either end. Heavy traffic continued across, unaware of what was about to happen. Satisfied with the target acquisition, they signalled to Pablo and his number two. Six 1,000-pounders sailed towards the target, the canard wings on the munitions guiding them towards the laser spot.

After a nerve-racking wait, a huge blast billowed from one end of the bridge, completely enveloping an Iraqi lorry. Another detonation then hit the opposite end. Pablo was delighted. 'The Buccaneers had done the fine-tuning and our bombs did the work. It was pure weapons aiming to perfection. We blasted our target.'

Within hours, the results of the sortie were being signalled up the chain of command. Group Captain Cliff Spink was at a meeting at Air Headquarters in Riyadh. 'I was in Air Vice-Marshal Wratten's office when one of his team burst into the room. The Boss looked up to see what was so important. His Staff Officer produced a communication detailing the immediate results of the first LGB attack – the bridge had been dropped exactly as planned. The Buccaneers' Pave Spike system operating alongside the Tornados had worked perfectly. There was utter delight in the room. And a real sense of relief. We had demonstrated that this new bombing technique, something the Tornados had never really trained for, was a great success on its very first outing.'

The film of the strike was also shown to the personnel back at Muharraq. 'They were amazed at the video and the results, but the biggest reaction of all was when we showed it to the Tornado guys at the debrief,' recalled the lead Buccaneer navigator. 'They had no idea until then what they had done, how effective it had been. It was fantastic to actually see the results. It was a big lift for them.'[32]

The ground crew were also amazed. 'That really brought it home. Good Lord, we were actually killing people, and a lot of guys grew up,' said one.[33] 'Seeing it on the television screen made me painfully aware that people were going to die because of what we were doing. As engineers we were responsible to the aircrew who pushed the buttons. I found that difficult, but eventually accepted that the bridges were crucial. And we saw the effect that knocking those bridges down was having on Iraqi soldiers in Kuwait. Supplies weren't reaching them.'

The next morning the *Daily Telegraph* ran the headline: 'Buccaneers Claim Laser Bomb Success'. 'The other good news, at least in our minds,' Mike Toft thought after reading the piece, 'was that we had not lost a Tornado for the last ten days.'

The mission was the advent of precision weaponeering for the Tornado. This was not good news for the Iraqi leader, who, according to the *Daily Express*, was taking tranquillisers to get over the headaches from the relentless aerial bombardment. 'Sinking Saddam Is Under Sedation,' the front page read on 4 February.[34]

But there was also an unforeseen psychological impact on the Tornado crews who now began dropping bombs with clinical accuracy. During an attack on another bridge across the Euphrates, Gordon Buckley rolled the jet to look for his bombs' strike. 'A lorry drove onto the bridge and I actually felt a bit sick. In an aircraft, you feel isolated from the mayhem you cause. I thought, *God, I've just killed him*. The bomb exploded right on target and seconds later the truck drove out of the smoke and debris. I was pleased he had survived – that was one lucky Iraqi.'[35]

Buckley's concerns about killing others were brought back to the fore after bombing an airbase. 'You need to see this film, it's amazing,' the Intelligence Officer had said on his return. The black and white footage showed the laser marker hovering over the roof of the base's Pilot Briefing Facility – the reinforced concrete bunker where aircrew could plan operations in what was previously believed to have been relative safety. 'There was a flash of light outside the PBF; I was told this was someone opening then closing a car door,' recalled Buckley. 'Although you couldn't see a person, you could then see a door opening and closing at the side of the PBF as they walked in. I was watching someone like me – probably aircrew – walk into their PBF as I had done many thousands of times back home. Then all four walls simply exploded outwards as our bombs hit home. Whatever, whoever, was in that PBF was instantly obliterated. That really affected me. There was a war to be fought and the targets were legitimate, but it really brought home the reality of what we were doing.'

* * *

Still facing his own very personal consequences of war, Robbie Stewart was recuperating in an Iraqi military hospital. A fortnight into his stay, he told one of the doctors treating his shattered leg that he was feeling much better. It was a huge mistake. He was bundled into a truck along with his crutches and thrown into the grim Mukhabarat prison complex, where, unbeknown to him, all the other POWs were now being held by the much-feared Iraqi Intelligence Service, the 'secret police'.

His welcome here was rather different to that of the smiling London-trained surgeon he had woken up to after his surgery. A guard threw him over his shoulder, carried him to a cold dank cell, flung two blankets on the floor, and dropped Robbie to the ground. He then grabbed him by the neck and pulled his face close. 'My child,' he hissed, drawing his index finger across his throat and pointing at Robbie. 'You!'

The metal door clanged shut, echoing down the corridor. A bar was pulled across, then chains, and finally a key turned in the lock. 'The closed door had shut out all the light. I thought of Tange and how she would have hated to be enclosed like this. The floor was cold and hard and I could not get warm with the two blankets they had given me. I pulled them up to my nose and dropped into a very unsettled sleep, dreaming that I was back at home with my family.'[36]

Robbie steeled himself for the coming days.

CHAPTER THIRTEEN

'MISSILE LAUNCH!'

4–24 FEBRUARY

By early February, 22-year-old Mal Craghill, the Tornado force's youngest navigator, was a veteran of the conflict. He had flown a number of raids, witnessed the mental distress of some of his companions, and lost friends in battle. Now, Mal and the Tabuk aircrew were waiting for the next major development in their Tornado's warfighting capability: the Thermal Imaging Airborne Laser Designator.

The TIALD pods were the up-to-the-minute version of the ageing Buccaneer's Pave Spike. In late 1990, it had still been in the research-and-development stage. Only two prototype pods existed. But with the imminent onset of war in the Gulf, the RAF had ordered Ferranti to speed up production in case precision targeting became necessary. It had done.

In the third week of January, four Tornado crews had arrived to undertake trials at the Aeroplane and Armament Experimental Establishment at RAF Boscombe Down in Wiltshire. On 2 February they made the inaugural drop of a laser-guided bomb targeted by

a British-built laser pod.[1] Four days later, the two prototype pods
were flown out to Tabuk. With its infra-red capability, unlike Pave
Spike, it enabled laser targeting at night. Tornado crews would soon
deploy laser-guided bombs under cover of darkness.

In the meantime, those without Buccaneer Pave Spike support
continued with the Tornado's bombing system, optimised for
low-level operations, for the ongoing medium-level attacks. On
6 February, Craghill and his pilot Mike Warren prepared to hit an
airfield south of Baghdad. Its proximity to the capital meant they
would be entering what was solemnly referred to as the 'Super
MEZ' – the Missile Engagement Zone. Saddam had sited a host of
SAM batteries around the capital, including the battle-proven SA-3
and the giant SA-2 which had knocked Gary Powers' U2 reconnaissance jet out of the sky at 70,000ft over the Soviet Union in 1960.
It may have been ancient, but it was still effective. To help smooth
the way, Craghill's formation was accompanied by two Tornados
equipped with ALARM anti-radar missiles and American EF-111
aircraft armed with powerful radar jammers.

The night was still and clear as their eight-ship refuelled at the
border then pushed on towards Baghdad. Craghill's pre-war training had focused on the visual characteristics of the Iraqi SAMs
as well as their technical capabilities. 'Knowing the colour of the
missile's rocket flame, and the typical salvos fired, meant we might
be able to identify what was being launched. Two missiles in quick
succession with a short-burning blueish flame would probably be
an SA-8, two missiles a few seconds apart with a longer-burning
yellow flame were likely SA-6.'[2] To control the missile, a radar
ground station locked on or 'illuminated' the aircraft, working out
its precise position, and updated the missile while in flight, guiding
it close enough to the target for the proximity fuse to detonate the
warhead with its lethal shards of shrapnel.

Approaching the Super MEZ, Craghill now watched in amaze-
ment as salvos of SA-8, SA-3 and SA-6 missiles were fired off
without any guidance. 'The Iraqis wanted to be seen to be doing
something, but didn't want to attract the attention of the anti-radar

missiles and get themselves killed in the process.' Some of the SAM operators would not be so timid. Seconds later, his RHWR showed 'SA-2 TA' – Target Acquisition.[3]

'This was not necessarily a big deal. "Target Acquisition" had become relatively common and I continued to prosecute the attack while monitoring the RHWR screen.'

Then an audio alarm sounded and the display switched to 'SA-2 TT' – Target Tracking. This was a major escalation. The Iraqi operator was clearly unaffected, or unconcerned, by the presence of jammers and anti-radar missiles. He was using his own radar to track their aircraft, updating his target information in preparation for a launch. The bearing indication flashed on Mal's display, showing the direction of the threat. Craghill dispensed chaff and confirmed to Mike that the jamming pod was responding correctly. 'We both assumed that was as far as it would go. We now had only a few miles to run to weapons release; less than ten seconds. Then, the unthinkable happened.'

The alarm switched abruptly to a ferocious warble. Craghill saw 'SA-2 MG' – Missile Guidance – on his RHWR. The Iraqi operator had locked his system onto their aircraft and was about to launch. 'I looked out of the cockpit in the direction the RHWR showed the threat was coming from. A fraction of a second later I saw an almighty flash as a massive missile came off its launcher. It was a gloriously clear night and I could now see that an SA-2 was on its way up to us.'

The deadly 35ft-long SA-2 Guideline missile was accelerating to its maximum speed of Mach 3.5 (2,685mph). Craghill made a snap decision to complete the bombing run then defend against it without the extra weight of their weapons.

'Press on with the attack,' he said quickly. 'The pod is jamming.'

He felt Mike weigh up the advice – albeit for a microsecond.

'Roger.'

'With just a couple of seconds until bomb release, everything now happened very rapidly. Our actions were completed on instinct, with no time to register any emotion.' Craghill made a rapid radio call to say they were defending against an SA-2, broadcasting their location to cue their radar jamming support. 'Although there was nothing they could do to protect us from *this* missile, they could begin jamming the appropriate radar frequencies so that if we defeated the SA-2, it was less likely that we would be engaged in a follow-up attack.' They monitored the burning rocket plume throughout its flight. 'It was a curious feeling watching this huge missile track towards us. I wasn't particularly scared over those three or four seconds; I just knew we had to defeat it. The consequences of not doing so were unthinkable.'

Two seconds later, their five 1,000lb bombs released and Mike pulled the jet into a violent right-hand turn. Blind to the other seven aircraft in their formation, and relying again on the 'big sky' theory, they plunged down through the darkness towards the missile. 'When the shit hits the fan, your response has been hardwired after years of training. We did the drills instinctively, without thinking. Mike manoeuvred as hard as possible to make it harder for the missile to follow our flight path, while I called out the heights, checked our Sky Shadow pod was jamming, and kept dispensing chaff, hoping to break the missile's lock.'

There was a bright flash as the SA-2's 195kg fragmentation warhead detonated behind them and its shrapnel blossomed. Craghill felt the shock wave rock their Tornado. Although seemingly unscathed, they were still in real danger. 'The manoeuvre had taken us from 20,000ft down to 13,000ft. This close to Baghdad, it put us within reach of an awful lot of triple-A systems. Mike put the jet into a climb on full afterburner, uncomfortably highlighting our position in the darkness, but essential to regain height and momentum in case of another attack.'

Later, safely back on the ground, they discussed whether prosecuting the attack had been the right thing to do. 'We decided it was. What saved us was our training and that we trusted each other to do what was required. That, and probably a huge dose of luck. But it had been a close call and we had come pretty close to being shot down. Or worse. There was little time to dwell on it; there was a war to be fought and we were back on a mission the following day.'

* * *

Just a few miles from where Mal Craghill and Mike Warren had almost been shot down, the coalition prisoners of war had been gathered in one of the most feared locations in Iraq. The Mukhabarat prison in Baghdad, run by Saddam's secret police, was relentlessly cold, dark and depressing. From floor to ceiling, the cell's ice-cold chocolate-brown tiles numbed the brain and turned the stomach. In some crude designer joke, the tiles matched the only thing that broke up the prison's rectangular boxes – the 'toilet'. Embedded within its dark, noxious hole was a mass of ancient darkish-brown excrement. There was no furniture in the cells, not even a piece of foam to lie on, just two thin blankets which provided little respite from the chill.

Robbie Stewart had been transported to the prison from his hospital bed. 'The floor was freezing and rock hard. I thought the draught on my face was from an open window, but soon realised that the breeze was actually cold air falling from the freezing tiles on the walls.' His cell boasted two plastic bowls, one for water and one for food. Very little of either was forthcoming. The only light came from a narrow window covered by an iron grille high above him which cast criss-cross shadows over the floor and walls. Robbie was clearly just the latest in a long line of tortured souls who had inhabited this space. A series of strokes had been scratched onto the brown tiles, batches of six struck through with a single diagonal line – the classic record of time endured there by its previous inhabitants. Robbie was in no doubt that for the many thousands of Iraqis incarcerated here over the years, there would have been no happy ending.

The passing hours turned into passing days. Robbie's stomach would rumble as he waited for any sign of human contact. As the shadows blurred, the hatch in the heavy steel door would be drawn back and flatbread and something masquerading as soup thrust through. 'We got a single miserly meal per day. The liquid was very hot but extremely thin, with streaks of fat; it was reasonably

A Victor tanker trails its hoses ready for a Tornado armed with laser-guided bombs and its accompanying Buccaneer 'Pave Spike' targeting aircraft to refuel before crossing the border into Iraq.

At the end of the war, Steve Hicks' friends carry his coffin to an awaiting aircraft for his final journey home. From left, Pablo Mason, John Broadbent (OC 15 Squadron) Nige Risdale, Steve Barnes, Dave Cockerill.

Former prisoners John Nichol and Rupert Clark face the media after being reunited with their families at RAF Laarbruch.

Dave Waddington and Robbie Stewart are finally reunited with their families at RAF Marham after seven weeks of captivity. From right: Kirsty, Robbie, Tange and Scott Stewart; Dave Waddington and his fiancée Claire.

John Peters and John Nichol take a Tornado airborne again for a first flight together after their release from captivity.

Jerry Witts enjoys his first beer in the 31 Squadron crewroom on landing back at RAF Bruggen after flying some of the Tornados home from Dhahran.

Robbie Stewart, left, and Dave Waddington plan their first Tornado sortie together after returning from captivity.

John Broadbent at Kuwait international airport after the ceasefire with some of the captured Iraqi weapons.

General Sir Peter de la Billière (right), the UK forces' commander, alongside General Norman Schwarzkopf, the overall coalition commander, arriving at Heathrow Airport in 1991 following the end of the war.

Three Tornados from the Muharraq detachment in late 1990 armed with JP233 runway denial weapons. Very few Tornado aircrew had actually flown the jet loaded with this weapon prior to the build-up to the conflict.

Simon Burgess, left, and Bob Ankerson prepare for a training sortie together after the war. Sadly, Simon would be killed in a flying accident a few years later.

John Nichol presents former Prime Minister Sir John Major with a signed Tornado print as thanks for being the Guest Of Honour at the 25th anniversary reunion of the Gulf War POWs in 2016.

Philippa and Jeremy Green, whose father Bill was killed in a Tornado accident before the war started, with the trophy the family presented to 27 Squadron in his, and his navigator Neil Anderson's memory.

Kirsty Stewart about to go flying with her father Robbie during a Tornado training sortie.

A 'Diamond Nine' formation of Tornados pictured during the final days of the Tornado's RAF service in February 2019.

The RAF POWs during their annual reunion and celebration in 2019; most are looking older, greyer, balder, rounder and wiser. From left: Dave Waddington, Rupert Clark, Robbie Stewart, John Peters, John Nichol, Bob Ankerson.

A post-war formation of the RAF's major combat aircraft involved in Operation Desert Storm. From top, Tornado F3, Buccaneer, Tornado GR1, Jaguar.

Two Tornados taxi out ready for an early evening take-off from RAF Marham in 2018.

salty and edible. I sipped it slowly, letting it warm me as the heat reached my stomach.'4 Time passed more quickly if you savoured every scrap.

There was little to hear, bar the occasional sound of footsteps in the corridor and the rattle of a key in a lock. He found a piece of old soap in a corner and used it to write Tange's name on the wall. 'I had no picture, but these few letters projected her image whenever I looked at them.' He would fall asleep beneath the thin blanket, dreaming of his wife. 'Tange was making tea. I was dressed in my yellow prison suit. We would be chatting then I'd turn to leave. "Where are you going?" she'd ask. "I have to be back in Baghdad," I'd reply, then I'd wake up and, depressingly, I was back in my cell.'

The same surreal dream, of being back among loved ones while still dressed in yellow prison garb, was shared by almost all of the POWs during their ordeal.

Robbie was unaware of it at the time, but his friend and pilot was only a few metres away, separated by thick prison walls and solid steel doors. Their captors, perhaps still convinced that David Joseph Waddington had to be an Israeli pilot, had thrown him into what appeared to be a 'punishment cell'. 'There was a metal grille at the end of the cell on the outside wall, but it was covered over so no light could enter. When they first threw me in, I looked at the single electric light and thought, *If they turn that off, I'll be in real trouble*. After a couple of hours, I was plunged into darkness as the light went out. It rarely came on again over the next three weeks.'

Dave nonetheless managed to measure his area of confinement – around 5ft wide and 12ft long. On the couple of occasions when the dim light flickered on, it revealed a dank chamber with a foetid hole in one corner that passed for a lavatory. As the weeks ground by, Waddington began to struggle with the darkness. 'It was horrendous. The intense boredom was made infinitely worse by the fact that I couldn't see a thing. I became very concerned for my state of mind. How long could I survive like this?'

As well as the coalition prisoners, the Iraqis also kept some of their own in the cells. 'One of the worst aspects was the terrible noises people made,' John Nichol said. 'You could hear the pitiful screams of other prisoners enduring God knew what torment. One night I woke up to hear an Arab man being dragged past my cell. He was screaming for mercy as they beat him over and over again. It sounded like the Iraqis wanted to punch and kick him to death. In between the prisoner's pleas, I could hear the guards' threats and curses. His pitiful mewling was fuelled with the anguish of total mental breakdown.'

During one particularly suffocating stretch, Dave Waddington found himself drawn away from his internal battles by those yells and screams outside his steel door. He was momentarily sustained by the reminder that he wasn't the only one struggling. But it did not take long for him to descend once again into the echoing void. 'It was miserable, worse than the broken arms, worse than the torture. All that pain was fleeting but the darkness was interminable.'⁵

The guards took great pleasure in making Waddington's life as miserable as possible. After being treated for his injuries at the previous hospital, he had arrived at the prison in bare feet, wearing only a surgical gown and his underwear. After asking for another blanket two guards opened his door, letting in some precious light. They dropped a blanket to the floor then both urinated on it before kicking it inside his cell. 'I tried to air it as best I could and it eventually dried out a bit. I managed to get a screw off the grille and used it as a basic needle to help fashion a pair of rather fetching moccasins for my freezing feet.'

Bob Ankerson had decided that the best way to get through his POW ordeal was to become the 'grey man', anonymous and undemanding. 'I avoided aggravating the guards and tended to be ignored in terms of some of the bad treatment others were clearly enduring.'

As days turned to weeks, the night-time tedium was broken by the endless coalition bombing raids on the capital. Through the tiny gaps in the metal grilles, most of the POWs could see the green and red flashes of triple-A fire soaring into the sky, alongside the blazing orange of exploding ordnance. Bob was constantly uplifted by the allied offensive. 'To my ever-present question of how or when victory might happen, there was no answer. So part of my defence mechanism to cope with this extreme, unknown and potentially violent situation was to deal with it moment by moment. My immediate future was measured in minutes and hours. Not days. In fact, I didn't know what the future held. Or, if I had any future at all.'

Bob, too, had no contact with other prisoners, and little idea of what was happening outside his cell. For the most part, the doors rarely opened, and the prisoners languished in their own squalor and their solitary journey to starvation. But he wasn't so desperate for company that he wished the footsteps coming down the corridor would stop outside his door. The sound of the key being turned in his lock was the last thing he wanted to hear. 'Were you going to be taken away to be interrogated or beaten? You'd hear another cell door being opened then sounds of people crying out in pain. Then you thought, *Is it my turn next?* It was a terrible existence.'

The Iraqis appeared obsessed with their belief that Israeli pilots were bombing them from American and British jets. As Dave Waddington knew all too well, any hint of Jewish blood was ruthlessly challenged. The Mukhabarat seemed increasingly intent on following the unappealing example of the German Gestapo, starting with a demeaning physical examination. One by one the POWs were dragged out of their cells. Bob was taken to a brightly lit room and ordered to drop his trousers. 'It was a really disturbing experience; your mind races as you have no idea what is about to happen. But it became clear that they just wanted to check for circumcision; looking to see if any of us were Jewish.'[6]

Blindfolded and still wearing his hospital pyjamas, Robbie Stewart was subjected to an even more intimidating experience. Two burly guards lifted him out of his cell and dragged him along the corridor to the basement. 'Suddenly I felt my pyjamas pulled down together with my underpants. What were they going to do? I was truly petrified.'

He could feel people staring at his exposed genitals for several minutes before his clothes were replaced and he was frogmarched back the way he'd come. 'I was actually pleased to be back in my cell. It sounds really strange to say now, but I felt more secure locked away from the guards.' But they could still strike fear into their charges. One who had taken a particular dislike to Robbie would stand outside his door shrieking. He would order Robbie to get to his feet, then lie back down again, knowing the airman had a shattered leg. And yet he was also capable of moments of haunting lyricism. 'He had a wonderful, melodic voice, singing mournful and haunting Arabic songs long into the night. In the morning, he would revert to his spiteful self.'

After his own circumcision check, Dave Waddington was catapulted back into his ongoing nightmare. 'At one stage, I don't think I saw any light for a couple of weeks. I began developing a "strobing" behind my eyes, whether they were open or closed. It would drive me crazy. Sometimes I'd hammer on the door just so the guards would open the hatch to see what was wrong, even though I knew they'd go mad and punch me in the face. It was worth it just to see something other than blackness.' Like most of the POWs, regardless of their prior beliefs, Dave found himself turning to God for comfort. 'I'm not a particularly religious person, but I prayed an awful lot. I even returned to my Catholic upbringing, making rosary beads out of wool torn from my blanket. When I was really down, when I couldn't stand it any more, something would happen to boost my spirits, like the light coming on for a minute or a guard coming round with an extra piece of bread.'

There was always hope.

A few days into his incarceration, Robbie was taken to another part of the prison to have his broken leg re-plastered. The doctor was accompanied by a guard in a smart green suit. Robbie held the man's gaze for a moment. 'That was a mistake; his eyes narrowed and the muscles around his jaw went taut.' Robbie recognised him as the jailer who went out of his way to make his life a misery. It did not bode well.

The doctor removed some thick bandages from a brown case. His sidekick leered and drew a long-bladed knife from his jacket pocket. Robbie felt the touch of cold steel against his cheek, then the blade slide down towards his neck. Desperate not to catch the guard's eye again, Robbie focused on the doctor plastering his leg. The blade disappeared back into the suit. Only to be replaced by a pistol, which he held inches away from Robbie's face, and loaded with a theatrical flourish. Robbie felt the cold, hard muzzle against his forehead then the unmistakable sound of the weapon being cocked. 'The doctor seemed oblivious to the nutter with the gun. For all he was concerned, this man could have been a nurse wiping my brow.'

'I am going to shoot you,' the Iraqi rasped.

Robbie stared down at his fresh cast, refusing to believe that they would go to the trouble of fitting it if he was about to be executed. He closed his eyes and waited. The muzzle was removed, then the butt crashed into the side of his head. He looked up in time to register the guard pulling back his arm, preparing to deliver another punishing blow. 'The scene became somewhat surreal as the guard continued to pistol-whip me, while the doctor continued to plaster my leg.'

Eventually the guard grew bored and the doctor completed his task. Robbie was thrown back into his cell, with a throbbing skull and the smell of drying gypsum. 'Later, I slipped into my dreams, escaping to the hills of Scotland where Tange and I had enjoyed so many walking holidays.'

* * *

While the POWs battled with cold, hunger and despondency, their colleagues at Muharraq spent their time between missions in the comfort of the Sheraton Hotel. It was a bizarre existence. 'The contrasts of living in a five-star hotel and flying war missions really were stark,' Gordon Buckley recalled. 'One moment, we were flying ops over enemy territory, dropping sophisticated weapons, destroying infrastructure, killing people, then a few hours later we would be by the pool ordering a club sandwich and a beer. It was difficult to reconcile at times. Especially when the worst happened. You never knew when reality would hit.'

The crews were also living cheek by jowl with the press. Most of the aircrew were relatively happy with the set-up. Nick Heard enjoyed the company of people who offered a very different perspective from military life. 'The media guys became friends and generally played a fair game, respecting when to talk to us, when to give us space, especially if we had lost a jet. Our socialising meant things were said over a beer we would never want to appear in print, but they rarely crossed that line, and on the odd occasion one of them did, it was the rest of the media guys who brought them up sharp.'

After one incident where an off-the-cuff remark appeared in a newspaper, the Detachment Commander warned the press pool in no uncertain terms that if boundaries were not respected, they would be evicted from the base and have no access to any crews. Mike Toft remembers a slightly different version of events. 'One of the newspaper reporters overstepped the mark and he found himself thrown, fully clothed, into the hotel swimming pool by some very angry aircrew. He deserved it, and the matter was resolved.'[7]

By mid-February, with no aircraft from Muharraq lost in more than three weeks, things had settled into a routine, underpinned by the Pave Spike-enabled precision bombing. 'We gained confidence in what we were doing,' Heard said. 'Working from the Sheraton was surreal at times, but I enjoyed the contrast between ops and then having the ability to unwind with a beer or do some exercise.'

One of the TV reporters, Tony Birtley, enjoyed both the exercise and the drinks with the RAF fliers. Tornado pilot Rupert Clark, now a veteran of fourteen missions,[8] was renowned for his mathematical skills and his prowess on the squash court. Birtley challenged him to endless games, and emerged from most encounters with only a sweat-drenched shirt and drooping shoulders to show for it. John Broadbent, the Tornado Detachment Commander, was also on Clark's hit list. 'Rupert was a lot better player than me,' he said. 'But he was generous enough of spirit not to destroy my morale too comprehensively. Our matches became an important way for me to relax.'[9]

Clark's sporting expertise and brainpower were coupled with tremendous talent as a marksman. The Cambridge University graduate, fondly referred to as 'Posh Git' by his Squadron mates, had represented Great Britain Under-18s in the international rifle championships.[10] Neither that nor his successes with a squash racquet ever went to his head. The press corps found him down-to-earth, and he would often share a beer in the small hours with Birtley and his fellow reporters.[11]

Clark was in a good place. He had married before deploying on operations and his wife was expecting their first child. He shared a hotel room and a Tornado with his affable navigator Steve Hicks, who, with two young children of his own, had a few tips about fatherhood ready to pass on.

Hicks, twenty-nine, was a popular member of the Squadron and a good friend of navigator Mike Toft. They lived within spitting distance of each other in the RAF Laarbruch married quarters. Deployed for three months in the Gulf, they had shared long chats and many cigarettes outside the Squadron's buildings as they contemplated how the war was progressing. Steve had previously served as an Air Electronics Operator on Nimrod maritime patrol aircraft and was affectionately known as 'Diddley-dit' because of his Morse Code skills.

* * *

Operations continued apace and, on 10 February, a Dhahran crew dropped the base's 1,000th 1,000lb bomb. The final unguided weapons were dropped two days later.[12] While laser-guided bombing greatly improved targeting results, the system was certainly not infallible. Weapons could veer off course if there was a technical fault, perhaps with the seeker system, or if sudden cloud cover obscured the target, and hence the laser beam. And because some attacks were now on bridges near population centres, occasional tragedies did occur. During one early LGB attack on the Euphrates river crossing in Falluja west of Baghdad, a 1,000lb bomb failed to guide and hit the crowded marketplace causing terrible devastation, and as many as 130 deaths.[13]

It later transpired that perhaps three bombs had failed to guide. Pre-attack planning had taken that possibility into consideration so the approach track was along the river in the hope that any errant munitions falling short would land in the water.[14] Two had, but the third veered into the built-up area where the cost borne by civilians, as is so often the case, was horrendous.

Hamid Mehsan, a Falluja merchant, lost his son, brother and nephew in the incident. He later described what he saw to a British journalist: 'A bomb hit just over there and as soon as it exploded, the old buildings fell down. The people were buried, and I saw the men digging with their shovels to bring out the dead. I saw people without their throats. Some they did not find: my son Omar was never found, we found only his head.'[15]

Although it would be of no comfort to those whose lives had already been shattered, precision bombing now allowed the allied air forces to prepare the battlespace for the approaching invasion. The Tornados were ordered to focus on taking out the enemy airfields, and especially their hardened aircraft shelters as intelligence had suggested that when the ground war began, the Iraqis might launch kamikaze-style attacks using aircraft loaded with Saddam's chemical weapons.[16] The bombers were tasked with ensuring the remnants of the Iraqi Air Force remained firmly grounded.

While the RAF continued its attacks on airfields, other allied forces were targeting Iraqi military 'command and control' facilities, but horrific tragedies involving civilians still occurred. At 0430 on 13 February, two American F-117 Stealth bombers each dropped a huge 2,000lb laser-guided bomb on what was believed to be an Iraqi military command bunker in the Amiriyah district of Baghdad. It was actually sheltering hundreds of civilians. The bombs cut through 10 feet of reinforced concrete before detonating. The destruction was catastrophic. Reports vary, but it is estimated that around 400 people – mostly women and children – were killed. It was a stark reminder of the brutality of war, and how it was the innocent who often suffered most.

As preparations for the ground war continued, the scale of RAF attacks rose from six to twelve aircraft: eight Tornados, each armed with two 1,000lb LGBs, supported by four Buccaneers. Shortly before dawn on 14 February, the jets took off for Al Taqaddum airbase, 40 miles west of Baghdad. As they would be entering the area of the Baghdad 'Super MEZ', they had USAF Wild Weasel and EF-111 aircraft on hand, specifically designed to deal with the threat posed by enemy radar systems.[17] American F-15 fighters also patrolled the area.

There had been much discussion about tactics, so the lead navigator who planned it had sought John Broadbent's advice. With the enemy fighter threat eliminated, support from accompanying US anti-missile aircraft, and their own jamming pods, the Squadron Boss was content the SAM threat could be dealt with. 'Attack directions sometimes had to be compromised by the overriding requirement to ensure accurate identification of weapons release points. Al Taqaddum offered featureless approaches from all but one direction. By this stage of the war, we had been delivering LGBs from medium level for almost two weeks in a relatively benign environment, so when the navigator came to me to discuss his choice of attack direction, his reasoning was perfectly sound.'[18]

Two hours and twenty minutes into the mission, the airfield's two parallel 12,000ft runways came into view. Pablo Mason was first over the objective, scoring a direct hit on the selected HAS. With their RHWRs untroubled by missile threats, the rest of his formation followed, sending their laser-guided bombs down onto the aircraft shelters. A few minutes later, the next four bombers and two laser-designator Buccaneers began their final run in.

Nigel Risdale was leading, with John Broadbent in the navigator's seat. They were halfway down the delivery run when their accompanying Buccaneer crew reported that cloud cover made it impossible to identify the target. Risdale pulled out of the stream.

Nick Heard was next, coming in from the west with the early-morning sun on his face. 'We were wary as we knew the target would be hot territory inside the Super MEZ. As we approached at height, the airfield disappeared under our nose so you lost sight of the target. It didn't matter as the Buccaneer's laser pod would be guiding our bombs. There was a *bump, bump* as the bombs came off and descended into the HAS.'

Heard pulled away to the north and the rest of the attack followed in.[19]

Rupert Clark and Steve Hicks were experienced operators. The morning sun was glinting off the ribbon of the Euphrates far below as the pair prepared to release their munitions. The clock had just passed 8.42am when the Al Taqaddum runways appeared. Their target was a HAS on the south-east corner of the airfield. Five seconds before dropping, Rupert noticed a brief burst of signals from an enemy radar on his RHWR.[20] He glanced quickly outside then back at the screen. There was no visible sign of any missile launch or further indication of radar activity. They pressed on.

Just after weapons release,[21] an urgent shout rang out over the radio. 'Missile launch! Missile launch!'[22]

Their attention was immediately diverted from the attack.

'Two missiles airborne. Heading for the formation.' The frantic warning came from one of the accompanying Buccaneer crews who had seen the initial blasts from the ground as the missiles left their rails.[23]

Clark and Hicks instantly scanned the ground, looking for the rocket flame and smoke trail of an attacking SAM. Nick Heard dipped his wings in turn. 'I was looking down, searching to see if I could see anything coming our way. We had no idea who was being targeted.'

All eyes were on stalks. 'The words "missile launch" really got our attention,' said John Broadbent, now some distance from the target. 'Everyone was heads up, looking out of the cockpit, searching for the incoming missiles.'

'SAM! SAM! SAM!' A split second later a sharp-eyed American

fighter spotted what everyone was looking for: two plumes gunning skywards.

Pablo Mason saw them streaking up towards a Tornado. 'I saw two puffs of black smoke just off my port wing as I was running south, and the last of our team was running onto the target.'

Rupert Clark hadn't initially seen the missiles heading towards his aircraft. But suddenly his RHWR screamed a warning: 'Missile Guidance'! His heartbeat quickened. Powered by solid-fuel rocket motors, the pair of SA-3 missiles had already reached their maximum speed of 2,300mph.

'Break left!' Hicks shouted while releasing chaff. Clark was already ramming the throttles into full power, lowering the Tornado's manoeuvring flaps and throwing them into a tight turn. But the missile was too fast. 'We were going through north, when there was this huge explosion and I felt the blast wave hit the aircraft.'[24]

The first missile exploded a few feet off the port side of the Tornado and fragmentation from the 60kg warhead peppered the fuselage.

'You okay?' Clark shouted back to Hicks. He didn't have time to register the lack of response. 'I saw the second missile coming up at us vertically, waggling as it guided onto me. I pulled on the stick as hard as I could. There was nothing else I could do. The missile disappeared from view, going behind and to the right of the aircraft. Then there was another explosion.'[25]

A smudge of smoke appeared as the second SA-3 detonated, sending more shards of shrapnel into the jet. 'When the second missile hit, the whole cockpit was shattered. The instruments were gone, as were both engines.'[26]

Pablo Mason had a clear view of what had happened. 'I saw the SA-3 missile explode on the other side of their jet. I could see the aircraft was still intact as it came out of the second blast, and was still flying.' The jet dived northwards looking 'strangely graceful' as it faded further into enemy territory. Descending, now with no power, Clark attempted to glide as far as he could, away from the danger area. He again called Hicks. There was still no reply.

Nick Heard searched the sky for further SAMs. 'I could see the trails of where the two missiles had come up from the ground intersecting with the trail of smoke from a jet heading gently down. We didn't know who it was. I just kept manoeuvring my jet to check if anything else was heading towards us, but also so I could keep an eye on the descending aircraft to see if anyone ejected.'

Clark's secure HaveQuick radios were down so he could not communicate with Heard or anyone else in the formation. He watched the altimeter unwind as the Tornado descended through 15,000ft. He knew ejection was inevitable but delayed as long as possible, increasing the distance from the launch site.[27] The aircraft became less and less responsive to his inputs until eventually there was nothing more he could do.

'Steve, are you okay?'

There was still no reply from his navigator.

Clark pulled the handle, ejecting them both. 'I got a massive kick up the backside as my seat fired. I was fully conscious and remember thinking, *When are all these explosions going to stop?* Suddenly there was dead silence, no noise at all, and I was hanging from my parachute in clear blue skies. The trouble was, it's Iraq below you.'[28]

When Pablo Mason called the entire formation to check in, it was clear to navigator Mike Toft who was missing. '*Fuck!* All I knew was that Rupert and Steve were in serious trouble. I was immediately thinking, *Are they alive? What's happened?* This latest loss really hit us hard, especially as we had been incident-free for so long.'

The downed aircraft's approximate position was relayed to the AWACS as the surviving crews reluctantly turned south for home. Nick Heard could still see the consequences of the missile attack. 'We just watched the smoke trail of the descending Tornado, still desperately hoping to see some ejections. There was nothing.' It was another ominously quiet transit back to Muharraq. 'I had joined the RAF with Rupert and we'd gone through officer training together. Hicksy lived a few doors away from me on the married patch. I was friends with them both. I now presumed I'd just seen both killed.'

Nige Risdale and the Boss also shared a silent flight home. 'The only thing we could hope for was that they had managed to eject. It may sound cold now, but there was nothing else to do, apart from hope.' John Broadbent was also numb. 'The journey back to base seemed interminable. It was our first loss since 20 January, and all the more shocking for that.'

When the formation arrived at Muharraq, Heard and a close friend of Hicks were sent to the Sheraton to pack up the aircrew's personal belongings. 'It was a sad task,' Heard said. 'Sorting through all their kit – shirts, family pictures, books, socks – to be sent home to their loved ones. I was reminded of how many times it must have happened during the Second World War to the men in Bomber Command.'

The military personnel were not alone in being devastated by the loss. The journalistic contingent shared their distress. Some had become trusted listeners to the men going into battle. Among them was Ian Henry of the *Sunday Express*, who had spent long hours chatting and drinking with Clark. 'Rupert was a man of obvious dedication to his chosen career,' Henry wrote three days after the incident. 'He was anxious not to give away any details which might help the enemy, but also anxious to help readers understand the risks he and his colleagues undertook. Their faces will be two more that will be sorely missed. It leaves a real gap in the banter around the poolside bar.' He then added: 'As professional fliers the brave crews of the RAF may be steeled to the acceptance of losses, even the loss of close friends. I knew Flight Lieutenant Clark only fleetingly, but I find it hard to bear that his smiling face is absent.'[29]

Clark's regular squash partner Tony Birtley was distraught. With tears in his eyes, he sought out one of 15 Squadron's Flight Commanders, Gordon Buckley. It was Buckley's day off, so he was enjoying his regular club sandwich and a beer by the pool. 'Rupert and Steve have been shot down,' Birtley sobbed. 'The rest of the formation saw their aircraft get hit by a SAM and they didn't eject.'[30]

Buckley was shattered. 'It hit us all really hard. We had thought we were over the worst of the air threat, but now it appeared that two more mates had been killed. The morale took a real downturn and it was a harsh wake-up call. The risks were still very real every time we crossed that border.' Before the war had started, Buckley had snapped a picture of Steve Hicks sitting at the hotel bar. 'It was a great photo. Hicksy was grinning the way I always remember him; he had a really infectious smile . . . That image remains emblazoned on my memory thirty years on.'

* * *

The next day, 15 February, at 2.30pm, Baghdad Radio announced that Iraq would leave Kuwait. The capital's streets filled with crowds celebrating the end of the war. 'Air-raid sirens wailed, and Baghdadis fired rifles into the air,' the *Los Angeles Times* reported. 'People gathered in excited groups to discuss the news.'[31]

Saddam said he would abide by the UN resolution for unconditional withdrawal of his troops. But then came his conditions: all allied forces would withdraw from the region, war reparations would be made to Iraq, and the Kuwaiti royal family would be replaced by a new government. In addition, Israel would pull out of the occupied Arab territories. It was, said President George Bush, a 'cruel hoax'. The American leader went on to say: 'Until a massive withdrawal begins, with those troops visibly leaving Kuwait, there will be no let-up in the offensive.'[32]

The streets of Baghdad fell silent again as the next raids came in.

Indeed, the bombings grew in intensity. It was becoming clear that the ground assault was near. A flurry of further diplomatic activity began with Tariq Aziz, the Iraqi Foreign Minister, flying to Moscow for peace talks on 21 February. Saddam also considered it an appropriate moment to make a bellicose speech. 'The mother of battles will be our battle of victory and martyrdom,' he said over the airwaves. 'They want us to surrender, but of course they will be disappointed.'[33]

On this occasion, President Bush did not feel obliged to respond in person. Instead, the White House issued a statement: 'Our forces remain on a steadfast course. The liberation of Kuwait continues.'[34]

Ground attacks against Iraqi tank, artillery and infantry positions intensified. In response, Saddam ordered his troops to set fire to more than 300 Kuwait oil wells. A dark, noxious cloud hovered over the looming battlefield.[35]

* * *

For the prisoners in Baghdad, the days of confinement rolled on. The marks etched on their walls showed they were now deep into February. They had learned to live with the stench of their own sweat and excrement, the dirt under their nails, matted hair, body lice and the interminable cold. And the chocolate-brown tiles. The monotony was broken only by the nightly bombing of Baghdad. 'Lying on my favourite spot on the cell floor, I could see up through the window bars and into the night sky,' John Nichol recalled. 'It never really occurred to me that this might prove any danger to us. I could see the tracer arcing into the sky and the detonations of the coalition bombs. I came to rely on the bombing as a sign that I was not alone. It was comforting, the way a train passing in the night was comforting when I was a young boy, tucked up safely in bed. I was starving and must have lost a couple of stone, I lived in fear of the footsteps stopping outside my steel door, and I was terrified by the screams of pain and suffering of those around me. But I wasn't alone. My friends were in the skies above us, continuing the fight.'

Dave Waddington's weight had also plummeted; he was always last in line for his measly helping of food. Nearly three weeks into his nocturnal existence, the guards dished out boiled rice instead of the usual slimy soup. It was the prisoners' first solid food since arriving at the Mukhabarat jail. Dave waited anxiously as he heard the helpings gratefully received in the other cells. 'By the time they got to me they'd run out. All I got was a tiny piece of pitta bread. I was devastated and almost burst into tears. I was trying to work out how long it would be before I starved to death.'

Dave's mind slipped into oblivion during the long hours of gloom.

'I remember praying, "Wouldn't it be good if this building was hit by the coalition bombing so the Iraqis had to move us?"'

He was about to be granted his wish.

As he lay on his blankets in the pitch darkness, Robbie Stewart also prayed for the war to finish. It was 23 February and the night was unusually quiet.

'Suddenly, there was a low moaning rush followed by an unbelievable roar like some demented banshee screaming with toothache,' he recalled. 'I could hear the crackling of sound waves and then an enormous explosion. The walls shook, the ceiling fell in and the flap on the steel door was blasted open. I could see flames through the small window as I cleared my ears from the impact pressure.'

Terrified of instant obliteration, Robbie put his plastic water bowl on his head and shouted, 'Incoming!' 'There was a short period just before each explosion when I wondered if my name was on that particular bomb.'

As each one fell, the air parted. It sounded like a high-speed train thundering through a station. The explosions reverberated through the building, undermining the walls and shaking free the brown tiles. In the middle of the attack, Dave Waddington realised with some irony that his prayers had been answered. 'I was absolutely scared stiff. It was much worse than being shot down; you could hear each bomb a fraction of a second before it hit. I didn't know whether I was going to be alive or dead in the next few seconds. I just lay there thinking, hoping, *Please let me survive*. There was absolutely nothing I could do; it was truly terrifying.' Another explosion bowed his steel prison door inwards. Like his navigator, Dave sat in the corner with his plastic water bowl over his head.

As he listened to the screaming detonations and felt the shock waves resonate through the building, John Nichol also grabbed his plastic bowl. He had used it to save some water for his first wash in four weeks, and readied it now in case a fire broke out. With around half a pint of water, it was unlikely to provide much protection, so he quickly tore a square out of his tattered blanket, padded the inside of his larger food bowl and placed it on his head. Given his paltry resources, it was the best protection available; he was grateful for anything in the maelstrom. 'The whole building was shaking. I could hear rubble falling and I thought the floor was going to collapse. Everybody was yelling at the tops of their voices to be let out. I was petrified, waiting for the fourth bomb to hit the bullseye. I resigned myself to the notion I was about to die.'[36]

Bob Ankerson was also cowering in his cell. 'We were the "target for tonight" and it was a curious experience. I actually felt quite tranquil. I put my trust in the hands of God, simply thinking, *Thy will be done*. My faith had provided me with comfort through the ordeal so far; I could only wait to see what transpired next. But as I curled up in a ball on the floor, I had the biggest knot in my stomach.'

The last of the four bombs exploded almost on top of the POW block, blowing in walls, ceilings and doors, freeing some of the prisoners from their weeks of isolation. Rapid, disjointed and manic chatter broke out through the shattered prison, between comrades rendered incommunicado for the previous weeks.

Nichol recognised Rupert Clark's distinctive public-school accent, amazed to hear someone from his own Squadron. Clark had been captured a few minutes after ejecting and sent to the Mukhabarat jail after some truly horrific beatings, during which his leg had been broken.[37] It had taken four American 2,000-pounders to discover he was with his RAF comrades.

'Rupert! Good to hear you, mate!' Nichol shouted.

'John Nichol,' he replied. 'How are you? We thought you were dead!'

'How's Steve Hicks?' Nichol asked.

After an emotionally charged silence, Rupert replied: 'Steve's dead.'

Clark described how they had been shot down nine days earlier, and that Hicks had been killed in the initial blast. Nichol listened with a heavy heart. He and Steve Hicks had both served in the ranks before being commissioned as officers. They shared an unspoken bond.

Nichol then remembered he had seen his old friend Simon

Burgess, Bob Ankerson's pilot, in one of the courtyards of a previous prison. 'Budgie Burgess,' he called. 'Are you in here?'

'John Nichol,' Burgess shouted back. 'How are you, mate? I haven't seen you since you were pissed at that airshow last August, running around with a tea towel on your head. I bet you regret that now!'

Laughter echoed among the dust and debris.

Bob Ankerson heard his pilot's voice for the first time since the day they ejected. 'Are you all right, Simon?'

'Yes, I'm okay.'

Bob was delighted. 'We were both still alive and in it together.'

Robbie Stewart listened to everyone 'talking excitedly as if they were in their back gardens leaning over the fence'. Then, through the chatter, he heard a voice that brought tears to his eyes. 'Has anybody seen Robbie Stewart?'

'Hi Dave, I'm here!' Robbie replied, overjoyed. 'The thin Bolton accent floated up through the chaos. Dave Waddington was just down the corridor. It felt fantastic knowing that he was alive.'

Dave experienced conflicting emotions. 'Joy that Robbie was alive, happiness that we were still together, but sadness that he hadn't got away.'

The Iraqi guards had now recovered from the shock of the bombing and used crowbars to open some of the cell doors. Prisoners were dragged downstairs and out of the ruined building. Eventually one of them unlocked Bob Ankerson's door and he was led over the piles of rubble and pools of water veined with leaking kerosene. He was pushed onto a bus crammed with other evacuated prisoners in their drab yellow suits with 'POW' emblazoned on the front. All the seats had been removed but it was still crowded. Bob spotted a tiny gap. 'As I flopped down, my hands went to the floor and touched the hands of the POW next to me. For just a few seconds we gripped hands and both had a moment of human comfort. It was an immense morale boost. He was a complete stranger but we were both in it together. I was back among friends. No longer isolated.'

Being less mobile than most, Robbie was delighted to get out of his cell. A diminutive Iraqi guard entered, pulled the navigator's arms over his head and carried him out in a fireman's lift, over chunks of masonry and down stairwells dripping from the ruptured water pipes. Robbie was thrust at two brawny guards who grabbed an arm each and started running him across a stretch of concrete covered in rubble. With his broken leg still held together by plates inserted five weeks earlier, Robbie gritted his teeth through the excruciating agony. 'Just when I thought I would collapse from pain and lack of breath, they stopped and pointed to the incredible destruction.'

'This is what your American friends have done,' one guard hissed, pushing Robbie up against a wall. The guards moved back, then unslung their AK-47 rifles. 'I had the terrible feeling that this was how it was all going to end,' Robbie said. 'They raised their rifles. I was suddenly very calm and unafraid. I had talked to Tange about the prospect of me not returning, about the kids' education and their lives after my death. I was a Christian and now facing two AK-47s. I looked to God for extra strength and found it as I stood waiting for the bullets.'

Robbie stared at the gun barrels aimed at his chest, bracing himself. The seconds ticked by. The guards lowered their rifles and hustled him towards the bus. A few yards from the open door, they let go of him and stood back. Without his crutches, Robbie tottered towards the open door. The bus moved forward a few yards, just beyond his reach. Robbie swivelled right and hobbled after it. Just as he was about to get on, the driver put the vehicle in reverse. The guards laughed uproariously at the infantile game. Finally, Robbie lunged for the doorway and was pulled inside. 'Collapsing on the floor, I felt the hands of the person next to me. He touched my fingers then squeezed them, giving me a wonderful feeling of companionship in this dreadful predicament. I returned the squeeze.'

There was a clatter at his feet. His crutches. Followed by the unmistakable sound of a body being thrown down next to him. A Kuwaiti pilot who had been shot down in the early stages of the war. The Iraqis hated him intensely, blaming him for Iraq's predicament.

Robbie listened as they proceeded to beat him ferociously. 'It was an awful sound, a deep groan spilled out as they kicked and punched him. Then I made out the noise of my crutch hitting his body as he screamed in pain. We sat there, unable to move, as they pounded him until I heard a crack as my crutch snapped in two. The beating stopped and the guards muttered contentedly and left.'

The bus doors finally closed and it headed away, taking the prisoners to another unknown destination, and an uncertain future.

* * *

The menacing cloud from the oil-well fires over Kuwait spread like a gathering storm across the horizon. From the shoreline of the Gulf, all the way along the border to the Western Desert, great holes were blasted through the Iraqis' defensive sand berms to create gaps for the armoured assault force. At 4am on 24 February, in driving rain, the first US Marines crossed the border into Kuwait under the covering fire of 155mm howitzers. Their progress was fast and the resistance minimal.[38]

Not far from the Marines, the Challenger tanks of the British 1st Armoured Division also advanced into battle. Three hundred miles to their west, a French light division and the US 101st Airborne pushed through the open desert as part of the surprise 'left hook', to come in behind the heavy Iraqi troop concentrations. Across Saudi Arabia 150,000 troops and 1,500 tanks began their advance, heralding the start of the ground war to retake Kuwait.

At 10pm local time in Washington, 6am in Iraq, President Bush appeared on television. 'The liberation of Kuwait has now entered the final phase. I have total confidence in the ability of the coalition forces, swiftly and decisively, to accomplish their mission.'[39]

CHAPTER FOURTEEN

TERMINATE THE WOLFPACK

24 FEBRUARY–5 MARCH

As lives were lost on the battlefield, life outside the region continued as normal.

Sue Toft was heavily pregnant with their second child when her navigator husband Mike had been summoned to war. They both knew he would not be there for the birth. 'I could never have left the theatre of ops,' he said. 'I had a duty to my friends, my pilot, Mark, my Squadron; we had a mission to complete. It might sound cold, but I was more use with them than back in Germany with Sue. More importantly, there was absolutely no suggestion from Sue that I should return.'

As February dragged on, Sue was moved to the military hospital in Germany in preparation for the birth. Returning safely from each raid, Toft would call the ward for an update. Then, just before the ground war started, 'We were in a Japanese restaurant by the hotel. A few hours earlier, we had been on combat ops. I was now enjoying a beer and a fantastic meal. It was surreal. In another few hours I would head back out on ops and perhaps put my life on the line. I was living in truly strange times.'

Leaving his noodles and beer, Mike headed once more for the telephone, armed with a fistful of coins. 'After the previous false starts, my tired wife was brought to the phone with our new daughter in her arms.' A sharp gurgle and an indignant squeal suddenly echoed down the line. 'The midwife had pinched the baby's toe to make her cry so I could hear! It was a wonderful moment and quite a contrast to the reality of war.'[1]

Toft went to bed a happy man. The next morning, he was assigned a mission near the Super MEZ in Baghdad. The Muharraq Detachment Commander was waiting in the Operations Room to congratulate him on his new arrival. With a broad grin, Toft handed the DetCo an official 'Leave Pass' requesting six days' compassionate absence, starting immediately. 'When we returned from our mission, the Leave Pass was in my locker annotated with the single word "Refused".'

But there was also a handwritten note taped to a chilled bottle of Moët & Chandon champagne:

Sorry about the leave, Tofty. Perhaps the attached will help wet your new daughter's head. Many congratulations and best wishes. Dave Henderson. Muharraq DetCo.

There was also a promise that, once the war was over, Toft would be one of the first to return home. After debriefing, his formation retired to the bar to raise a toast. As they clinked beers, his pilot Mark Paisey looked him in the eye. 'Tofty, we now have all the more reason to get back safely!'

It was a sentiment echoed across the region as the conflict entered its final, decisive phase. There was still a deep-seated fear that Iraq would use chemical weapons against allied ground troops. Satellite imagery had shown Su-25 Frogfoot ground-attack aircraft at Shaibah airbase, only a few miles north of the Kuwaiti border. The Frogfoot was more than capable of delivering chemical munitions. Precision bombing was required to destroy its runway, and the Tornados were once again called into action.

The two prototype Thermal Imaging Airborne Laser Designator (TIALD) pods had been rushed into service and were now based with the Tabuk detachment. Their superior night-time targeting capability had quickly been battle-proven. Ten Tabuk crews were rapidly trained on the new equipment and round-the-clock operations were now available to mission planners.[2]

Dave Bellamy led his TIALD-equipped formation towards Shaibah airfield 700 miles east of Tabuk. He was initially puzzled by an unexpectedly early sunrise. 'As we got closer, the glow became a red pinprick of fire. That single fire became two or three, then ten or twenty. It was countless oil-well fires, and it looked like hell on earth.'

Bellamy then noticed streaks of light rising from the desert out to his right – the launch of hundreds of rockets targeting Iraqi troop positions. The rockets arced out in front of them before descending away to his left where the desert sparkled as the munitions exploded. The ground attacks were clearly intensifying. Five minutes out, Bellamy heard a Texan drawl issuing orders over the radio as further targets were identified. 'Then the ground bubbled up in red flame, like jam bubbling in a pan. It was giant B-52 bombers, unseen in the darkness, each dropping eighty-odd 1,000lb bombs.'[3]

Minutes later, the Tornados sent their TIALD-guided bombs into Shaibah, blasting huge craters at each intersection of the runway and taxiways. The Frogfoots would no longer be able to take off, and the threat of imminent chemical attack was diminished.

Bellamy's formation's egress took them north along the border. 'On one side we saw street lights and neon strips at petrol stations in Iran, while on the other, the landscape burned with bomb blasts and fires around Basra. It was an apocalyptic vision, like watching a movie with no soundtrack. An astonishing, silent image of war.'

After landing, Bellamy recorded his memories in his diary: 'It was a rare trip and those images of the battlefield are fixed in my mind for ever.'

And, as the war neared its denouement, more personnel were entering the fray.

* * *

It was with a sense of foreboding that Wing Commander Gordon Turnbull had dropped off his young sons. 'I watched all three walk into school with a lump in my throat, then headed to RAF Brize Norton for my flight to the Gulf.'[4]

He only had himself to blame. A few days earlier, his Boss had called about the Tornado pilot Gordon had treated after his breakdown in the early days of the war. 'Frank has just successfully carried out his first operational mission back in the Gulf.'

Before the psychiatrist could express his delight, his Boss went on, 'Of course, Turnbull, you realise what this means, don't you?'

'I told him I reckoned I did. I was to visit the main bases with an eye firmly looking out for signs of underlying combat-stress reactions.' At the RAF's main transport base in Oxfordshire, Turnbull boarded a huge Tristar capable of carrying over 300 passengers. 'There were only fifteen of us. The jet was loaded from floor to ceiling with ordnance. Shells wrapped in plastic like flat-packs of giant soup cans. Their pointed noses stretched from the cockpit to the tail.' He squeezed between the shells and into a seat, wondering what the future might hold.

His first port of call was Frank's Tornado base. He was anxious to see how he'd readapted to combat operations. Turnbull was met by the Squadron's Commanding Officer, who told him that the Tornados were about to go 'downtown'. They walked between the austere bunkers to the operation's briefing. 'I was keen to see how the crews dealt with the pressure of imminent combat. But having a shrink sit in on a pre-mission brief was huge. I tried to imagine how my presence would have gone down at a pre-mission briefing of a Bomber Command squadron during the Second World War.'

'How's Frank getting on?' he asked the CO.

'You can see for yourself.' They stepped into the concrete interior of the air-conditioned facility. 'We're here.'

The pair stood at the back as Turnbull learned that the formation was to strike a command and control bunker close to Baghdad.

He noticed considerable tension in the room, few questions asked and 'brief flashes of humour'. He also spotted Frank at the front, scribbling notes.

Turnbull counted the jets taking off, then, ninety minutes later, counted them all back without loss. He uttered a quiet prayer of thanks. Afterwards, 'the atmosphere had changed completely. The debriefing was characterised by noise and full, highly detailed descriptions of the mission. This was not just a technical download but a psychological one too, in which the Tornado crews were ventilating emotions. They were processing the information of the shared experience they had just been through. This was all good, healthy stuff.' He stepped outside the bunker with the CO, who lit a cigarette.

'Did you find what you expected?'

'I don't really know what I expected,' Turnbull replied. 'But I'm amazed.'

'In what way?'

'At their ability to switch emotions on and off,' he said. 'It's like a cloak they slip on and off. Remarkable.'

Turnbull heard the heavy bunker door clank open behind him.

'Good to see you looking so well,' Turnbull said as he and Frank shook hands.

'I am well,' Frank replied, smiling at his therapist. 'I just wanted to thank you for everything you did.'

'I didn't do anything,' Turnbull said. 'It was really all down to you.'

There was nothing else to say. With a hesitant smile, Frank thanked him again and left, a very different person to the broken man who had come through Turnbull's door three weeks earlier.

He knew that senior RAF officers still remained deeply sceptical about allowing psychiatrists onto bases. 'I concluded my visit would be a one-off, but it had been invaluable nonetheless. Far from being ostracised by the crews, I felt in a quiet kind of way that I'd been made welcome. With the ground offensive underway, we could all now hope for a swift conclusion to the conflict. With any luck there would be no need to deploy large numbers of psychiatrists to the front line.'

Turnbull now concentrated on his next mission. The missing RAF prisoners of war. Although it was still not known who was alive or dead, Turnbull had been adamant that any captured aircrew would need thorough psychological debriefing when freed. 'Going home immediately, I warned, would almost certainly prove disastrous. These people needed to decompress.'

The RAF eventually agreed, and as the prisoners' ordeal continued, Gordon prepared for any repatriations.

* * *

When the ground war began, the POWs had been evacuated from the shattered Mukhabarat prison and driven through the devastated streets of Baghdad. Their new destination was the notorious Abu Ghraib prison, run by the Ba'ath Party and home to countless thousands of political prisoners and criminals. Spread over a vast site, it had a well-deserved reputation for torture and extrajudicial killings.

The POWs were led in silence through its long, cold corridors, carpeted with bird droppings, and past hundreds of barred cells. Hobbling now on his one remaining crutch, Robbie Stewart was hustled into a freezing cell measuring 10 feet by 6. Piling in behind him came Dave Waddington, Bob Ankerson, John Nichol, Rupert Clark, an Italian Tornado pilot and the Kuwaiti pilot battered with Robbie's other crutch. After weeks of solitary existence, and despite the threat of what future Abu Ghraib might hold, the prisoners were overjoyed to be in each other's company. 'It was bliss,' said John Nichol. 'This was the first time I had really been with any friends since being shot down. It was like being at a very small, very crowded party.'[5]

Nichol helped Robbie to the floor then sat down himself, placing Robbie's broken legs over his own to provide some relief from the cold. Robbie immediately felt the body warmth and shared spirit.

'It was so uplifting all being together, it soon deteriorated into schoolboy gabble. We were excited, cracking jokes and forgetting our dire predicament.'[6]

The stories poured out, from being shot down to torture. It was a healing moment. The aircrew were bursting to share their bottled emotions – the humiliation, fear and pain of interrogation. 'Sitting in solitary confinement, everyone had reached the same conclusion,' said Nichol. 'That they had given in too readily.' But it soon became clear that every one of them had broken at pretty much the same time. The cold cell walls and floor became momentarily forgotten as the men chatted in hushed voices through the dark hours of the night.

Bob Ankerson was among those who felt the burden of self-reproach and guilt begin to lift. 'It was an amazing night. The joy and relief of being together, able to talk, just to be alongside a friendly face was incredible.'[7]

Nichol too was delighted. 'We were in prison, beaten to shit, we still didn't know if we were going to survive, but we were on a fantastic high.'

They had barely snatched twenty minutes' sleep before Abu Ghraib came to life. The chatter of its many thousands of prisoners, punctuated by the angry bark of guards, warming up for the day ahead. For weeks the POWs had grown used to meagre helpings of cold, slimy food, but when their door now clattered open, a guard appeared with a steaming washing-up bowl filled with leek soup, another with dark, sweet tea, and some flatbread. 'We had the most extraordinary scene of seven starving men standing in a circle passing the bowl around, each offering it to his neighbour, very politely saying "after you",' said Robbie. 'Small sips were taken, though each of us actually wanted to guzzle the lot. The bowl was then passed on, with another "after you".'

Later that morning, all the POWs were moved into the central courtyard to sit in the blazing sun, cross-legged and heads down. To help pass the time, the guards wandered around casually punching or whipping a POW across the head or back with their regulation lengths of hard-rubber hose. Throughout the day, each prisoner was taken for further interrogation.

With the invasion underway, their captors' questions had become increasingly focused. 'What can you tell us about the ground offensive? Where will the main allied thrust come? Will there be a seaborne invasion or a frontal assault on Kuwait City? Where would paratroopers be used?'

The airmen were clearly ill-equipped to answer, but the Iraqis were undeterred.

'I am giving you one chance to save your life,' Nichol was told as he sat once again in front of an interrogator. 'Tell me something about the ground offensive so I can save your life.'

'I was really trying very hard to come up with *anything* I could tell him since he seemed perfectly calm and serious. But I had nothing to give. My ignorance must have been obvious as he eventually let me go.'

At the end of an eventful day, the POWs were marched to yet another section of the prison and locked in solitary confinement once more.

* * *

There was one man who knew precisely how the ground war was progressing, and what was planned for the coming hours. From the basement of his command bunker in Riyadh, General Norman Schwarzkopf listened to a flurry of incoming reports. Major assaults had been preceded by thirty-minute artillery barrages which saw 10,000 shells and half a million bomblets rain down on the enemy front line. M1A1 Abrams main battle tanks equipped with mine ploughs smashed through their defensive positions, sometimes burying Iraqi soldiers alive in their own trenches. Following units streamed north towards Kuwait City. American armour also pushed into the desert from the west in surprise attacks on the Iraqi flank. One of Schwarzkopf's key objectives, aside from retaking Kuwait, was now to inflict such damage on the Republican Guard that they would never again pose a threat to their Arab neighbours.

He was woken later to be told that radio intercepts suggested that Iraqi troops were being ordered to abandon Kuwait City. The US Marines were attacking Kuwait International Airport and were within 10 miles of the capital. Fearful that the Republican Guard might slip through his grasp, Schwarzkopf urged his commanders to push forward hard, especially the heavy divisions coming in from the west in the 'left hook' through the desert. By nightfall, a massive armoured force was arrayed against the largely unsuspecting Republican Guard, who, seven months earlier, had been at the spearhead of the Kuwait invasion force. Schwarzkopf was content with their progress.[8]

Saddam Hussein realised his options were now severely limited. The only effective offensive weapon left in his arsenal were Scuds. One was fired on the morning of 25 February at Dhahran, where a substantial part of the Tornado force was based alongside thousands of allied forces. It was intercepted by a Patriot missile. That evening, another Scud was picked up heading towards the base, but its trajectory suggested it would land just beyond the Patriots' protective umbrella. It hit the periphery; coming down on a US accommodation block, killing twenty-eight and injuring eighty-nine. It was the worst single coalition loss of life during the entire war.[9]

* * *

Life inside Abu Ghraib was as grim as any of the other Iraqi jails the POWs had experienced. Dave Waddington had lost his homemade blanket moccasins in the violent evacuation from the Mukhabarat prison. Luckily, he had found some plastic bags in his cell to wrap around his feet. They served a dual purpose. 'On the few occasions we were allowed out of the cell to use the "toilet", they protected my feet from the overflowing pits of urine and faeces. And when they wouldn't let us out, I could pee in one of the bags, tip it out of the window, then turn it inside out and pop it back on my foot.'

Isolated in their cells, the prisoners could hear the misery. One evening, the guards targeted an Iraqi civilian and did not relent for eight hours. 'His screams echoed and rolled around the prison,' Nichol said. 'The cries were unearthly – lingering, agonised, banshee wails interspersed with sharp yelps of pain. Because the noise was rasping, playing continually on the edge of our nerves, it was impossible to sleep.'

The next morning, Robbie Stewart saw the prisoner tied to a post in the courtyard below their cells, as the guards set about him again with their rubber hoses. He watched as the man's skin became streaked with livid red welts. 'His cries grew weaker and I wondered how much longer he could last. I was also wondering how long the war would last and if we would ever be released.'

The POWs were eventually paired up in cells and Nichol was partnered with Larry Slade, a US Navy F-14 Tomcat backseater. Their cell also overlooked the courtyard where many of the beatings took place. Three Arab inmates waved up at them from their window opposite. Nichol and Slade waved back. A surreal hand-signal conversation took place: the inmates mimed dropping bombs from an aircraft and gave the two airmen a thumbs-up. There were suddenly angry shouts from below and guards pointing furiously at the POWs' windows.

'Shit,' said Slade. 'They're coming to get us.'

A minute later, in a nearby cell, Robbie heard aggressive voices and boots pounding up the stairs. His cell door burst open, framing two huge Iraqi guards who demanded to know if they had been communicating with the Arab prisoners. 'We shook our heads and backed slowly to the wall. They slammed the door and went to the next cell.'

Bursting in on Nichol and Slade next, the guard screamed, 'Were you looking out the window?'

'No, no. Not us,' the pair replied in unison.

The guards thundered on.

A few minutes later they were back. With menace. They started on Slade first, punching him to the ground as Nichol looked on. 'It was as bad, if not worse, than anything in the interrogation. They were kicking the shit out of him. I was watching from the corner, frozen with horror. It was a concerted, merciless avalanche of furious blows and thudding kicks. There was no escape.'

Nichol knew with some dread that he would be next. The assault on Slade went on and on until the screams died out and he lay motionless. The Iraqis gave him a couple more kicks, then advanced towards Nichol. 'They punched and kicked me until I fell, then started kicking me in the face. I could feel the blood streaming down my cheeks and mouth in a hot torrent. I remember lying there, watching the bright red drops spattering down onto the dull grey concrete.'

Barely conscious, Nichol was pulled upright. As the blows continued, he raised his arms to protect his head.

'Keep your hands down!' a guard screamed. 'I'm going to break your face.' The Iraqi laid in with another frenzied attack.

'What were you signalling?' he demanded.

'We were just waving,' Slade mumbled through his broken lips.

'Right,' the guard said. 'You're dead.' He took out a pistol and pulled back the slide to load a round.

'You two, stand together.'

Nichol was shoved up next to the American.

'You are now going to die,' he said.

Both airmen looked down the barrel of the loaded weapon. 'For a number of seconds, the Iraqi stood quivering with rage, knuckles white, the slack taken up on the trigger. We were a heartbeat away from death. He pulled the trigger. *Click*.'

There were no rounds in the pistol. The guard had removed the magazine. He sneered at the POWs' petrified faces, then walked away.

The Iraqis returned later that evening with their rubber hoses, smacking them against the wall, demanding to know which cell the POWs had communicated with. The two airmen caved in. 'We felt terrible. With a burning sense of shame we told them.'

Ten minutes later, screams echoed from the opposite side of the courtyard.

'That was a very low time for us, Larry and me. We were responsible for those screams. But we had had enough for one day.'

* * *

Unknown to the POWs, Norman Schwarzkopf's ground troops were giving the Iraqi army an even more vigorous pummelling. Feeling the weight of the allied force arrayed against him and the inevitability of defeat, Saddam played his last card. On 26 February he publicly stated that Kuwait was no longer the 19th Governate of Iraq, and that his forces were going to leave the Emirate 'by the end of the day', thus fulfilling the UN diktat.

But the Americans paid little heed.

Schwarzkopf knew that the hour of reckoning was upon the Republican Guard and urged his troops forward. 'The Iraqi retreat was disintegrating into chaos. Large units were all trying to make it to Basra but were finding the Euphrates bridges down, and, as we'd anticipated, convoys were bunching up in the extreme south-east corner of Iraq.'[10] As the general had envisaged, the enemy was being driven into a small pocket where they could be decimated. 'Until we destroyed the Republican Guard, our job was only half done.'

By 27 February the retreating enemy columns tearing north up the eight-lane highway out of Kuwait were being hit non-stop, both by the tanks coming in from the west and the US Marines from the south. Once the airborne assets joined the fray, the road was quickly dubbed the 'Highway of Death' as the shattered vehicles and bodies piled up. 'The road out of Kuwait to Basra was an awful sight,' recalled a Tornado F3 navigator patrolling overhead. 'There was no way they could get off it to do anything, they were just slaughtered. It was better they died on that road than our boys, we were all acutely aware of that. But it didn't reduce the horror of what we saw.'[11]

The Americans set about the task of inflicting such pain on Iraq's armed forces that they would be permanently crippled. The coalition stacked up its air power, rotating eight fresh aircraft to attack every fifteen minutes, relentless in their destruction of as many Iraqi Republican Guard units as they could place in their gunsights.[12]

In between these attacks, Black Hawk helicopters equipped with loudspeakers flew over the battlefield, telling the Iraqis: 'Get out of your vehicles. Leave them behind and you will not die. We will let you go home.' A great many Iraqis had already abandoned their positions and thousands of POWs were being taken. After just four days of fighting, 3,000 of Iraq's 4,300 tanks had been destroyed, as well as 2,140 of its 3,100 artillery pieces.[13] The press was quickly onto the scent of victory. 'Saddam's outgunned elite smashed in armoured duel',[14] the *Daily Express*'s headline ran.

Like the Iraqis on the road to Basra, the POWs in Abu Ghraib felt the war had reached an apocalyptic moment on the night of 27 February. The sonic boom of jets was a constant overhead as the final air attacks went in. Nichol hunkered down in his cell, huddled up with Larry Slade, still dazed and covered in dried blood from their beatings. 'Explosion after explosion thundered incessantly nearby, until the air itself felt exhausted. It was terrifying. The bomb blasts seemed to be getting closer and closer. There was no way this prison would withstand a direct hit, or even a near miss.'

The pandemonium went on throughout the night, with little sound of opposition from the Iraqi triple-A. The enemy, it seemed, had lost the will to fight.

* * *

That same night, the Tornado TIALD force was again ordered up to hit Iraqi airbases. Now well versed in laser bombing, Mal Craghill and his pilot Mike Warren were told to strike the Al Habbaniyah helicopter hangars, west of Baghdad. They flew 500 miles northeast, destroyed the target and returned to Tabuk, two hours and fifteen minutes after taking off. After so many weeks at war, it had been a largely unremarkable mission.

'We had just got back to our accommodation after the debrief and put the BBC World Service on the radio,' Craghill recalled.

'Suddenly the newsreader announced that it was all over, a ceasefire had been agreed. I was bloody delighted; it appeared that Kuwait had been liberated and we had survived! Mike and I had dropped the last RAF bombs of the war.'

The ceasefire codeword was broadcast across all coalition aircraft radios:

'*Terminate Wolfpack. Terminate Wolfpack.*'[15]

It was approaching 5am in Iraq when President George Bush made his announcement from the White House. 'Exactly 100 hours since ground operations commenced, and six weeks since the start of Operation Desert Storm, all United States and coalition forces will suspend offensive combat operations. Iraq's army is defeated. Our military objectives are met. Kuwait is once more in the hands of Kuwaitis.'[16]

Jerry Witts, the Tornado Boss at Dhahran, woke up to find that one of his rival Squadron Commanders had pinned a note to his door: '*Bush declares cessation of offensive action. Last one back to Bruggen is a cissy!*'[17] Like the many servicemen in Saudi Arabia, Witts immediately headed off in search of illicit alcohol to celebrate the victory.

Over in more liberal Bahrain, the morning briefing at Muharraq airbase was laced with booze. A Buccaneer pilot was having breakfast when he spotted his navigator. 'He had the glazed look in his eyes he has when he's pissed; it was a look I knew very well. "It's all over," he said. It was Guinness and Macallan whisky at nine o'clock in the morning. By eleven I was out of my tree.'[18]

Mike Toft was delighted with the news, especially as he had been promised a spot on one of the first flights home once the war ended. 'There was a real sense of relief. It was a strange sensation as we had been living on the edge for six weeks. But ultimately it was simply a case of, *Thank God it's all over.*' Toft went in search of the clerk to book himself on the next transport aircraft out. He had an appointment to meet his new daughter.

At Tabuk, Dave Bellamy and his pilot Trevor Roche were woken at 5.20am as the Tannoy blared, 'Ceasefire declared. All missions now on a two-hour standby.' Minutes later a friend entered their room with a bottle of Johnnie Walker Red Label whisky. Soon the whole detachment had wind of the ceasefire and the pre-dawn merriment began.

Bawdy singing and boozy cheers greeted Bellamy at the Lightning Club. 'It was hearty handshakes, smile after smile, and a time to see everyone happy again. It was good to see the guys throw off the shackles of fear and uncertainty.' At some point the celebratory photographs took on a wintry aura when a foam fire extinguisher was discharged into the throng. The sun was beating down as Bellamy led a gaggle of merry airmen across the tarmac to breakfast. They no longer had to force down food, worrying about what might lie ahead over enemy skies. On the way they passed one of the base's most senior officers, 'pissed as a fart, in flying suit and moccasins, trying to pour out a glass of home-brew while balancing the plastic container on his head'.

There were more photos, a bonfire, drinking. 'A barbecue went ahead in scorching sun. Lots of people wanted pictures of the aircrew. I was unsure if we deserved it and felt like a prize poodle on show.' Eventually Bellamy slipped back to his quarters. 'I didn't feel like celebrating with full vigour while my flatmate John Nichol was still captive. I was sunburned, exhausted and emotional. I lay down with tears rolling down my cheeks and slept the sleep of paupers, content to be alone.'

When he awoke a few hours before midnight on 28 February, the base had fallen silent, no jets taking to the air, just the muffled sound of contented men snoring behind closed doors. Bellamy called his girlfriend. 'My conversation was stilted and tired. It had been so long since we had last spoken that I had forgotten how to communicate. We didn't really know what to talk about, we had been living such different lives for six weeks.' He finished the call then went to find the Intelligence Officer.

'Have they released the POWs yet?' Bellamy asked.

'Hopefully over the next forty-eight hours,' he was told.

'I truly hope he is safe,' Bellamy wrote in his diary. 'The war won't truly be over until I know what has happened to John.'

In the meantime, the British newspapers trumpeted the news of the victory. 'Surrender!' or 'Victory!' ran the headlines in almost every edition.

'It has been a very remarkable military campaign,' Prime Minister John Major told a press conference. 'I doubt there have ever been any campaigns better organised by the military than this one; it has been a supreme success for them.'[19] He too, had not forgotten about the British prisoners of war. 'We want them back immediately,' he said. 'There is no question of any delay.'

February 28th was a terrifying day for the families of all the missing airmen. Only now would they discover whether their loved ones had survived. Chris Ankerson had become used to 'living in the limbo' of not knowing whether Bob had ejected or gone down in his Tornado. 'The end of the war meant I'd soon receive the news. Good or bad. It was a terrible prospect.'[20]

The feeling of dread gripped Tange Stewart. Ever since the RAF liaison officer had appeared at her friends' dinner party, she had clung to the fact that Robbie had not been *confirmed* dead. It had been reported that the Iraqis would hand over prisoners or the remains of the deceased once ceasefire negotiations had concluded. 'They were the most truly horrendous days of the whole experience.'[21]

Berenice Waddington felt the same. 'The wait was so tense. Was David alive and a POW, or had he died in the Tornado crash?'[22]

For 12-year-old Gareth Ankerson, the weeks at boarding school without any new information had led him to a very dark place, and as February came to an end he was struggling. 'My confidence in my father being alive had been totally destroyed. I lost faith that I would ever see him again. I kept thinking how I said goodbye with just a hug, telling myself, *That's no way to say goodbye to someone who is going to die.*'[23]

* * *

The night of heavy bombing over Abu Ghraib had merged seamlessly into a cacophony of small arms fire and explosions on the morning of 28 February. Hunkered in their cell, John Nichol turned to Larry Slade and asked: 'What the hell's going on?'

'One of three things,' Slade replied. 'One of our guys has been shot down close by, they've got hold of him and they're celebrating. Or, there's a battle going on outside and some of our Special Forces are coming to get us. Or ... the war is over ...'

Moments later the prisoners were bundled out of Abu Ghraib and onto a bus. An air of menace accompanied the diminutive guard with his Saddam moustache who patrolled the aisle. Robbie Stewart again made the mistake of catching a guard's eye. The man knelt beside his seat, stroked the back of his neck, then grabbed a clump of hair and ripped it out. Fighting back the pain, Robbie kept his head bowed. 'He strutted off, then returned to stroke my hair once more, then karate-chopped me across the back of my neck.'

The man strolled around the bus looking for more victims. 'On his next return, I glanced at Bob Ankerson across the aisle, who was bent over with a lovely tuft of hair ripe for pulling. I thought to myself that the guard should go for Bob this time and give me a break.' He pulled out yet more of Robbie's hair. 'My hair was long but this was not the way to cut it. I whimpered in pain then suddenly realised what he was after. I shouted out louder and moaned, holding my head. This seemed enough to satisfy the sadist who wandered away.'

The bus eventually moved off. 'If you had been standing a little distance from that bus,' John Nichol said, 'you would have seen the prayers coming out of it, wraithlike, rising up to the heavens.'

A few hours later the POWs arrived at yet another prison on the outskirts of Baghdad. After being forced to run yet another gauntlet of yelling, punching, kicking soldiers, they were shoved back into solitary confinement in tiny, dank cells. Nichol counted 750 ticks on the wall marking the days endured by a previous occupant. His spirits drooped again.

However, despite the occasional screams that echoed around the stone corridors, the POWs soon began to detect a calmer atmosphere. Robbie Stewart dared to hope that the war might be over.

'There was no bombing and I knew something had changed. The guards talked with excitement in their voices.' Later in the day a bowl brimming with food was pushed onto the floor and the delicious aroma of lamb filled his cell. 'Something had definitely changed. I could make out rice, vegetables, slivers of meat and a bone. With great deliberation and utter pleasure, I slowly scoffed the lot. Using my tongue I delved into the core of the bone and retrieved the delicious marrow. I certainly slept well that night.'

As Robbie listened to allied jets coming in over Baghdad, like the rest of the POWs he still had no idea that a ceasefire had been ordered. 'The bangs I heard were not from bombs but supersonic booms. Was this a new tactic? Or were some of the lads having a bit of fun. Whatever the reason, I was desperate not to let my hopes rise.'

A few days later, on Sunday, 3 March, there was a tangible change in the guards' demeanour. For the first time in six weeks, the airmen were allowed to wash, albeit using the same barrel filled with warm water and the accumulation of the previous users' dirt. 'The scum didn't matter,' said John Peters. 'It was a marvellous feeling after weeks of grime just to feel the warm water coursing down my body.'[24] Robbie took the opportunity to wash his underpants, 'which had been worn back to front, inside out and upside down'. He was given a new yellow suit with 'PW' stitched on the front and doused with a can of perfume. 'Hope was in the air and it was a tremendous lift to think about home, the notion that the ordeal might soon be over.'

On 4 March, John Peters was given laces for his plimsolls which he hoped could only mean one thing: he was going to be released. He heard a group of Iraqi officers touring the building.

One entered Peters' cell and simply said, 'The war is over, you are going home in ten minutes.' Peters could not quite believe what he was hearing. He had been convinced that he would never see his wife and two young children again. 'It was the first confirmation I'd had of the secretly hoped-for fact. They had said it, it was undeniable. And it was tremendous. A rush of emotion and relief ran through me. I had no thoughts of whether we had won or lost, only the thought of going home.' He was taken outside and joined a group of nine Americans to eat some pitta bread, cheese and tomatoes. But there was no sign of his navigator John Nichol or any other RAF POWs.

The ten men were handed over to the International Red Cross and spirited out of Baghdad to the Jordanian border, then passed to British and American embassy officials under the glare of television camera lights and a barrage of media questions. Their ordeal was over. More importantly, Peters could now pass on the names of all the POWs he had seen or heard in the various prisons. Sadly, he could also confirm those who were not being held. Although details could still not be officially confirmed, the list was quickly flashed back to the UK and German Tornado bases. Family liaison officers were dispatched to pass on what little news was available, good and bad.

* * *

Mike Toft was also on his way home. His Detachment Commander had fulfilled the promise he made after the birth of Mike's daughter and the navigator was offered a seat on one of the first VC10 passenger jets flying out of the region after the ceasefire. He boarded with the bottle of Moët & Chandon safely stashed in his kit. As they flew over Greece, Toft was asked if he would like to go to the cockpit, where he was handed the radio headphones. The VC10 captain had been told the reason for his early return and arranged a telephone-patch over the RAF's high-frequency radio monitoring system, straight to Mike's married quarters. It was a very expensive method of communication and the captain had used his own credit card to book the call.

Mike's eyes welled up and his words caught in his throat. Finally, he managed a simple, 'Hi, babe, I'm in the air, on my way home, see you when I land.' He went back to his seat a contented man. A few hours later, he was on the ground. 'It was an incredible experience to land on home soil, back from war. Sue had driven down to meet me. It was simply fabulous, quite indescribable. As I stepped down onto the airfield, there were my girls.' Reliving the events thirty years later with the author, Tofty's voice again cracks at the memories. 'I had survived. I was home to my family. I had all three of them in my arms. The war was over.'

* * *

Like John Peters, Bob Ankerson had been given plimsolls with shoelaces and 'for the first time in the whole ordeal, I allowed myself to believe it might be nearing the end'. But Ankerson and the remaining POWs had to wait one more night before they too were taken out to a waiting bus.

Robbie limped towards it using his single crutch and was finally reunited with his pilot, Dave Waddington. The elation of release was still tempered by worry. Waddington was not yet ready to believe it was all over. 'I hoped that the guards were telling the truth, but we simply did not know for sure. This was Iraq and the brutal regime of Saddam and his sons. Another ending was possible. We could just as easily be lined up in Baghdad's main square and be shot to show that Saddam was still in charge. One thing was certain, this was going to be the end, one way or another.' Robbie gripped his friend's hand, trying to convince him that in fact they were being freed.

After what they had all suffered, Dave remained unconvinced. 'I thought Robbie was actually trying to tell me, *If I don't see you again, if this is it mate, good luck* . . . I was still very nervous.'

Directly in front of them sat John Nichol, whose face was still badly bruised from the beating in Abu Ghraib. As they passed through the bombed streets, Robbie watched the navigator stare out of the window like a child in a sweet shop. 'Nichol could not contain himself any longer and blurted out, "Cor, look at all that damage!" as we passed the clinical destruction of buildings across Baghdad.' The guards started to give him a few hostile stares so Robbie told him to pipe down. 'We then drove in silence through the streets, marvelling at the accuracy of the missiles until we stopped at our destination.' They had arrived at the Baghdad Novotel and the care of the International Red Cross.

The POWs had been freed so quickly because of Norman Schwarzkopf's ceasefire demands. 'Number one was the immediate release of all prisoners of war as well as a complete exchange of information on troops listed as missing in action and the return of any remains. It was essential that I account for everyone. There was no way I wanted a repetition of the POW and MIA agony of the Vietnam War.'[25]

In the days following the ceasefire, Tange had devoured the newspapers and watched television in the hope of discovering something about Robbie. Newspaper reports suggested that some POWs were dead. The *Evening Chronicle*, Nichol's local paper in the North East where his parents lived, splashed, 'Have They Murdered John?' Then added: 'Reports Claim British Aircrew Tortured and Killed'.[26] The line was followed up the next day in a *News of the World* piece headlined: 'Stormin' [Norman] Battles to Get Pilots Back'. The report contained the paragraph: *'Military intelligence sources have been told two airmen, probably British, have been tortured to death by Saddam's brutal interrogators. Their identities are not known.'*[27]

The words began to gnaw at Tange Stewart. 'We simply didn't know what to believe. It was a very bad time for everyone. A lot of POW names had already been released. And the worry of not knowing was simply impossible to bear.'

John Peters' list of the airmen he had heard in the prisons had been examined and some details were being passed on. Of course, Peters had only seen a few prisoners, so without definitive confirmation – which meant the release of bodies – it was impossible to be sure who had survived. It was a dire situation for all concerned. In desperation, Tange called the RAF Marham Station Commander, Jock Stirrup. He was in a meeting but his assistant took him the phone. 'Are you leaving us until last to tell because Robbie and Dave are dead?' Tange demanded. Stirrup told her there was still no further news. 'I feel so bad about that now,' Tange said, remembering the events thirty years on. 'The poor man had so much on his plate and he would obviously have already told us what he knew. But I was simply beside myself with worry.'

It was now 5 March, and later that day she saw their RAF liaison officer walk past her kitchen window. He was in full uniform and carrying a briefcase. 'I immediately realised that Robbie must be dead and he was bringing official paperwork that I needed to sign.' Tange ushered him in and waited. He opened the briefcase and pulled out a bottle of champagne. 'He's alive!'

'It was an utterly wonderful, wonderful feeling. Tears flowed. It was such an incredible release from the ordeal.'

Waiting at school, Kirsty Stewart had slumped into a bean bag watching the news in her common room when the house matron appeared. 'Kirsty, come with me please, I have someone to see you.'

Kirsty felt her chest tighten as she entered the room and saw Lesley Norris, a trusted family friend. 'She was the person I had chosen to give me any news, good or bad. Now she was standing there, looking at me. I just stopped in my tracks. I presumed she was going to tell me my dad was dead. She took hold of me and gave me a huge hug. But it felt like the "wrong type" of hug for bad news.'

'Is Dad dead?' the schoolgirl asked.

'No! He's alive,' Mrs Norris said. 'I've come to tell you your dad's alive.'

Kirsty broke down in tears.

Within an hour she was back in Coleby, reunited with her mother and brother. Villagers armed with champagne arrived and a huge celebration began. Once again, the community assembled in the All Saints Church, beneath the ringing bells.

In Bolton, Dave Waddington's mother had not strayed far from home since the ceasefire had been called. The phone rang.

'I grabbed it and our liaison officer said, "Are you sitting down?"'

'Oh my gosh. We all looked at each other. Which way was the news going to go?

'He said, "Your son is alive!"'

'Well! We just screamed our heads off. We were overjoyed, and overcome with relief. At last we knew. We were dancing around, shouting, hugging each other.

'I then heard the liaison officer say, "I tell you this, Mrs Waddington, there are grown men in the room with me crying their eyes out."

'So we all cried together. It was simply marvellous – David was alive. It was the best moment of our lives. Nothing will ever surpass that.'

At around the same time, Chris Ankerson heard the doorbell ring at their home in Germany. '*Oh, oh,* I thought, heading downstairs, just as I'd done six weeks before. The Station Commander's wife stood outside. She had a huge grin on her face and just shouted, "Bob's alive!" I was overjoyed. But I knew that, at the same time, other families across the Tornado force were receiving the worst news possible.'

* * *

Very few of the POWs in the second batch got much sleep during their first night of freedom at the Novotel. After a breakfast of hot croissants, coffee, honey, jam and boiled eggs, the POWs were hustled through the scrum of waiting press and onto a bus. They arrived at Baghdad's Saddam Hussein International Airport to find the gates bolted. There was an interminable wait before they opened and hundreds of former Iraqi POWs poured out. Only then were the airmen allowed to board a Swiss Air passenger aircraft chartered by the Red Cross.

Nichol looked out of the window and realised that leaving was not going to be straightforward. 'As we began taxiing out, the Iraqi soldiers who had been loitering around ran towards their gun emplacements and trained the barrels of their weapons directly at our civilian airliner. It may have been no more than an empty gesture of defiance but a graveyard hush settled over the interior of the aircraft. We were very, very vulnerable.'

'No, they wouldn't dare . . .' one of the POWs muttered.

'They can't be . . .' another said.

'But what have they got to lose?'

As the jet rolled down the runway, the long gun barrels tracked it until the wheels left the tarmac. Finally, a tremendous cheer went up.

The jet was still in Iraqi airspace when two American F-15 fighters approached, pulling victory rolls before coming in close, firing off brilliant infra-red flares in celebration. One of the pilots lowered his mask, punching the air in celebration. Moments later two Tornado F3s joined the passenger jet on the other wing. Nichol grinned as this time, in more restrained fashion, the RAF fliers gave a gentle wave to their comrades. 'Somehow the sight of those friendly aircraft, shepherding us home, brought our freedom into sharp focus. The four fighters escorted us into Saudi airspace and as we crossed the border another huge cheer went up. We were finally liberated.'

Looking out of the windows as they taxied in at Riyadh's enormous military airbase, the POWs could see a huge reception lined up on the tarmac. There were thousands of American troops waving, clapping and cheering at the return of their jailed comrades. Several of the British airmen had tears in their eyes when they saw their fellow RAF personnel formed up in uniform, standing rigidly to attention in the 30°C heat. 'That brought a lump to my throat all right,' recalled Nichol. 'But it was important not to let rip the waterworks just yet; there was too large an audience.'

Standing at the top of the steps Robbie Stewart gratefully stepped through the cabin door into brilliant sunshine. Below him stood General Schwarzkopf, at the head of a long line of VIPs including the British Ambassador, the RAF's most senior officer Air Vice-Marshal Bill Wratten, and the Prince Regent of Saudi Arabia. 'It was a truly amazing spectacle,' Robbie said. 'Certainly not what I had expected.'

As the former POWs reached the bottom of the steps, General Schwarzkopf gave each a crunching handshake. 'Welcome home, you guys,' he said. 'You've done a great job.'[28]

CHAPTER FIFTEEN

GOING HOME

MARCH–APRIL 1991

After shaking hands with General Schwarzkopf, the returning POWs were quickly ushered onto a waiting RAF Hercules and whisked away to a nearby military airfield where a group of RAF 'minders' had assembled to look after survivors.

Despite the fact that it was now known that a number of the missing aircrew were *definitely* alive, there was still no formal confirmation of those who were dead. Every eventuality had to be catered for. John Nichol's Flight Commander Gordon Buckley was among those standing in the mid-afternoon heat. 'We thought that each POW would need a "minder", a friend, who could identify with him, help him through the early stages of getting back to freedom and readjusting to normal life. I was there for John, but, sadly, we still didn't have full details of who was coming out of the prisons. So all those still listed as MIA had someone on the tarmac. It was just a matter of us all waiting.'[1]

Nick Heard stood alongside his fellow Tornado aircrew, wondering if *his* charge would arrive. He had last seen his friend Rupert Clark and his navigator Steve Hicks moments before their Tornado was shot down on 14 February. 'The Iraqis had never released any comprehensive information about prisoners, so I was asked to be Rupert's prospective minder – even though I truly believed I'd seen him die. And no one had told us who was on the Hercules, so we just waited to see who would walk off the back. We presumed that not all of the missing crews we were sent to meet would be coming home.'

As the British POWs settled into the Hercules' uncomfortable mesh seats for the ten-minute flight, a crew member handed John Nichol a British newspaper. 'You probably need to see this,' he said. A few days old, one story reported his parents being battened down at their home in the North East. A second suggested he had been tortured to death alongside John Peters. For Nichol, totally unaware of the worldwide coverage *their* war had garnered, the news was shattering. 'It was appalling. I pictured my parents sitting in a darkened house, shuttered up like a bunker, while the press prowled about outside. It was more than I could take. I found it hard to control myself.' He threw the paper aside as the noise of the Hercules' engines dropped in pitch and it lurched into its descent.

Heard and Buckley watched the wide-bellied aircraft bounce onto the runway and taxi in. The minders smoothed their green flying suits as the rear hydraulic ramp descended. All eyes were fixed on their colleagues stepping down onto the shimmering tarmac.

Buckley spotted John Nichol and ran over. 'It was a truly warming sight to see our friends, still in their yellow prison overalls, walk out to freedom.' He gave Nichol a big hug then stepped back. 'You stink! And you need to get rid of that prison garb too.' Despite the ribbing, Nichol was delighted. 'It was incredible to see so many of my friends standing there. And, in Buckers, I could not have wished for a better escort home.'

Heart racing, Nick Heard peered into the group. Another familiar figure limped towards him with a huge smile lighting up his distinctive, angular face. 'When Rupert walked out of that aircraft in Saudi, with John Nichol and the others, I was simply gobsmacked. I had been convinced he'd not survived that missile strike. I rushed over, grabbed hold of him and simply hugged him. Bloody hell, it was amazing!'

Dave Waddington, Robbie Stewart, Bob Ankerson and his pilot Simon Burgess were also collected by their waiting friends. As the survivors filed out, five other RAF officers remained stationary, looking on. Steve Hicks, Garry Lennox, Kevin Weeks, Nigel Elsdon and Max Collier were not coming home. Their bodies would be repatriated on a later Red Cross flight. 'It was at that moment we finally discovered who had not made it,' Buckley said. 'So, sadly, their five minders, now unneeded, departed back to their bases.'

The survivors boarded the VC10 for the three-hour flight from Riyadh to the British military base on Cyprus. As Buckley chatted to Nichol, he realised that the navigator 'had absolutely no idea how the war had been fought, the cost, the results, or how his Squadron at Muharraq had fared'. In the meantime, he and his fellow minders had more pressing questions. 'As military aircrew, we wanted to know what they had endured in captivity. What the Iraqis had done to them.'

Nichol suddenly had other matters of importance to focus on – his favourite dish, chicken tikka masala, and a lot of chocolate, all washed down with gin and tonic. 'The transition from the hideous nightmare of imprisonment to the absolute normality of crew-room banter with my mates had happened in a handful of hours. Even then, I did not completely relax until we touched down at RAF Akrotiri.'[2]

They were driven the three miles to the five-storey, 200-bed military hospital on the southern Cyprus peninsula. Robbie Stewart and the others were light-headed with their newfound freedom. 'We felt like schoolboys set free for the first time, giggling on the bus, making jokes about anything that entered our heads.'[3]

Ushered into a reception room, they were greeted by Gordon Turnbull, who had rapidly set up a facility for psychiatric treatment and medical checks. Turnbull had staked his career on the issue when he made the case with his superior just after the ceasefire. 'I told him we needed to debrief the POWs. That whatever happened, our unit needed to get to the POWs first. If we could take care of them immediately, there was a good chance we could help them come to terms with their experiences early enough to prevent the imprint from causing long-term problems.'

'How do you know it will work?' his Boss asked.

'I don't know,' Turnbull replied. 'But you saw what we achieved with one Tornado pilot. With the right support we can help others too.' He then handed over his proposal for treating the airmen. 'The bottom line is, if they go back to the UK, if we succumb to the public relations imperative to reunite them with their families, then we've lost them.' His Boss had agreed, and Turnbull got to work.

'What do you guys want?' Turnbull asked as he greeted the men. Nichol had an immediate request. 'The thought that my parents might still be wondering if I was truly alive, and were worrying themselves sick, was consuming me.' He was taken to a phone and, after a few failed attempts, got through. 'The first sound of my dear mother's voice pushed my long-suppressed emotions over the edge. It was the sound of freedom at last. I simply broke down. Tears streaked down my face.'

Robbie Stewart was also ushered to a phone and dialled his home in Lincolnshire. After a couple of rings, a familiar voice answered. 'Hello . . .?'

Robbie could hardly get his words out before he too broke down in tears. 'Just to hear Tange was all I needed. It was out of this world. I could hardly believe that I had got through it all, I was alive, albeit injured, but at last I was now free.'

For the first time in six weeks, Tange no longer had to worry. 'Hearing his voice was just so overwhelming. We were all sobbing. The reality of what we had been through hit hard; it was such a wonderful sensation. I no longer had to live each day wondering if my husband was alive or dead.' Amid the tears, she told Robbie how supportive the villagers of Coleby had been, and about the family's meeting with the Queen. 'He simply couldn't understand why we'd seen her and was just flabbergasted to hear he had been national news.'

The shock of realising that their POW story had received global coverage was something they would all have to come to terms with. 'Incarcerated in a cell, alone, isolated,' Robbie remembered, 'I simply had no idea of the coverage, the publicity, and the horror that our captivity had aroused.'[4]

The early March weather in Cyprus brought warm sunshine and blossoming flowers. Robbie was just surfacing from a blissful night's sleep between crisp, clean sheets, when a smiling nurse dressed in an immaculate military uniform brought him breakfast. 'It was quite a contrast to the previous six weeks. I realised I had quite a bit of adjusting to do.' He strolled onto the balcony, luxuriating in the glorious weather. Breathing in the rich Mediterranean air, relishing its distinct saltiness, his thoughts turned to the family he longed to see. But he knew there was work to be done first.

Gordon Turnbull led the former prisoners through the process he had designed to help them deal with their experiences. 'Their brains had done whatever was needed to survive their interrogation and captivity. Now that those survival skills were no longer needed, I explained that they had to de-orbit.'

The POWs were going to have to relive their experiences, and be open about how they were affected. Not everyone was happy at the prospect, nor about being detained for five days by a 'shrink', John Nichol foremost among them. 'The only reason I'm going along with this,' he said, his face barely an inch from Turnbull's, 'is because you're a senior officer and we've been ordered to. I want you to know that my colleagues and I think this scheme of yours is a shite idea and it won't work. I just want to get home, to be with my family. We all do. Sir!'[5]

Nichol's words were a challenge to Turnbull. He'd had success with Tornado pilot Frank, managing to get him back on combat operations, but what if that was a one-off fluke? *Do I have the wherewithal to re-equip them for normal life?* The last thing he wanted was a confrontation, so he spoke to the navigator in a soft voice. 'Please, John, just watch this space.'

Nichol stormed off.

Turnbull had got the message. The task of rehabilitating the POWs was not going to be an easy one.

* * *

While the ex-POWs were coming to terms with life away from captivity, those still on duty in the Gulf remained deeply suspicious of Saddam Hussein's intentions. Combat air patrols continued to be flown, ever vigilant for a resurgence of aggression. And respirators were still carried in case the dictator was foolish enough to deploy any of the chemical weapons he retained. 'For those who were flying, it was a case of everybody being on their best behaviour,' said a Tornado F3 pilot. 'We had to be very careful because people were fatigued and the last thing we wanted at that stage was to lose an aircraft through aircrew error.'[6]

John Broadbent, the Muharraq Tornado Detachment Commander, certainly noticed the change in attitude. 'We took a break from flying for a few days, but it soon became obvious that we should get back into the air, if for no other reason than to keep ourselves current. I found it quite remarkable how reluctant some crews were to undertake anything particularly demanding, especially if it involved low flying. Having survived combat operations, they didn't want to risk themselves unduly in peacetime.' It was a sentiment that most aircrew could identify with.

After the ceasefire, teams of army engineers began clearing the battlefield and inspecting the damage. Nigel Risdale and John Broadbent were offered the chance to join them in an RAF Chinook helicopter. 'We flew up the coastal strip of Saudi and into Kuwait,' said Risdale. 'The oilfields were still burning furiously and the rolling black smoke created a massive, ugly blanket over a huge area, creating a truly horrific picture. Putting aside the obvious environmental damage, it seemed to underline the spiteful nature of the regime.'

'We headed a short way up the "Highway of Death" at low level,' Broadbent recalled. 'It was a very sobering experience. I'd seen some images on TV but wasn't fully prepared for the reality. Mile after mile of destroyed vehicles stretched to the horizon, some still smouldering, plenty of civilian cars and trucks in the mix, presumably looted by the fleeing Iraqi ground forces. If I'd had any doubts about the effectiveness of air power and conversely the vulnerability of ground forces in a permissive environment before that short flight, I certainly didn't afterwards.'

The journey became an education for the Tornado fliers, who would never normally see the results of their 'handiwork'. Inspecting the hardened aircraft shelters they had bombed, almost identical to the ones housing his own squadron of Tornados back at RAF Laarbruch, was a revelation to Broadbent. 'The damage was nothing short of devastating. We had fitted our LGBs with post-impact delay fuses so that they would penetrate the roof of the HAS before exploding inside. The blast of a 1,000lb bomb in a confined space was enough to utterly destroy the contents of the HAS and often blow off the giant steel – supposedly blast-proof – doors. It must have been absolutely terrifying to be on the receiving end of our bombs.'

They also had the chance to inspect some of the damage the initial JP233 raids had caused. The results they saw at one area of an airbase were inconclusive; there was minimal evidence of the mass destruction to the runways and taxiways they could get to. It appeared some of the cratering munitions may have punched straight through the surfaces, the subsequent explosions absorbed by the sand rather than causing the huge 'upheave' expected on the European soil and clay substructure they were designed to be used against. Of course, it was not known what repairs had been carried out, or how the anti-personnel mines had disrupted those operations. All that was known for sure was that the Iraqi Air Force had effectively been grounded in the first few days of the war.

'We also managed to crawl over a multitude of Soviet-era military hardware,' said Broadbent. 'Not surprisingly, I was particularly interested in the triple-A pieces and SAMs that had engaged us during our missions. I couldn't help wondering what the operators had thought as we thundered overhead in our Tornados, whether they'd been as scared of us as we were of them.'

The level of deliberate devastation caused by the Iraqis was shocking at every level. A female RAF officer on another battle-zone flight over the suburbs of Kuwait City stared in disbelief. 'Imagine seeing a house that's been burned out, with a car turned over in the drive and a swimming pool that's black and has pieces of furniture floating in it. Then try to imagine a whole city like that.'[7] Worse, the occupation had seen numerous acts of rape and torture, and the killing of more than 1,000 Kuwaitis.[8] Saddam's secret police, the Mukhabarat, who had taken such pleasure in their work on the POWs, had been deployed to Kuwait with brutal intent. An American woman married to a Kuwaiti described random acts of violence that included shooting people just to steal their car. 'Rape became commonplace, with soldiers breaking into houses to violate women. Suspected resistance fighters endured inconceivable barbarity at the hands of skilled Iraqi interrogators who used electric drills, acid and knives to obtain confessions. Often, innocent people, having survived such depravity, would be taken home and shot in front of their families as a warning to others.'[9]

* * *

Tucked away from the destruction in the eastern corner of Saudi Arabia, a calmer existence had returned to Tabuk. Mal Craghill had completed 22 operational missions, dropped 89 bombs, including 17 laser-guided, and two JP233s. 'In just a few short months the Tornado force had undergone a massive transformation, from a Cold War, low-level, primarily nuclear strike force, to a highly accurate, medium-level laser-guided bomber and one of the most experienced combat forces in the world.'[10]

Craghill and his pilot Mike Warren had been part of an astonishing air armada deployed to the Gulf. At the start of the conflict, 2,430 allied aircraft had been based in the region, or close enough to project air power into it. The RAF initially contributed 135 aircraft: 18 Tornado F3 fighters, 46 Tornado GR1/1A attack and recce aircraft, 12 Jaguars, 17 tankers, three Nimrods, 31 Chinook and Puma helicopters, seven Hercules and one HS125 transport aircraft. Countless other transport and supply aircraft flew missions in and out of the region. By the start of the land war, a further twelve Buccaneers and more Tornado GR1s had flown into theatre to support the precision-guided bombing attacks. Around 3,000 RAF personnel were deployed across the Gulf.[11] When the cease-fire came into effect, the allied forces had flown 110,000 sorties, of which the RAF flew over 6,100 – the largest number of any nation except the US.[12]

After sixty hours of operational flying, Craghill and Warren decided they had earned some post-war relaxation. 'The time was spent panic tanning,' said Warren. 'Everybody was concerned that they should be as bronzed as possible when they returned home. Others were very busy packing up equipment. People said they were bored and couldn't wait to get home, but I think it was a good idea that we had that period at the end of the war. It gave you a chance to settle yourself, wind down, relax a bit and get a few of the war stories out of your system.'[13]

A week after the war ended, Craghill and Warren said goodbye to the aircraft that had served them so well. 'For me, the Tornado had performed wonderfully. It never let me and Mike down when we needed it most. The losses, although all traumatic, were lower than we probably expected considering the dangerous nature of the missions we undertook. I had always felt "solid" in the Tornado. If one can ever feel so; it was a reasonable environment to go to war in.'

Mal's Squadron boarded a transport aircraft for the journey back to RAF Laarbruch. 'There was an enormous cheer as we got airborne. It was a six-hour flight and the big surprise was that the RAF presented everybody with a small bottle of red wine to drink with the meal. I thought I was dreaming . . .'

* * *

The returning troops' flight path took them over the RAF hospital in Cyprus where Gordon Turnbull was still searching for a breakthrough moment with his reluctant patients. He brought all seven POWs together for a group debrief. Since the standard military mindset was to bottle up emotions, it was always going to be a gamble.

He removed his Wing Commander rank tabs and placed them on the floor. There were a couple of approving nods from the men sitting on hard plastic chairs arranged in a semi-circle in the airy hospital room overlooking the sea. Turnbull gave a brief history of post-traumatic stress disorder, arriving at his experiences with the RAF Search and Rescue teams following the Pan Am 103 bombing over Lockerbie which had killed 270 people a few years earlier, scattering bodies across the countryside. 'I was able to describe how men I knew, men renowned for *not* cracking under pressure, had cracked in a number of cases. Given that the Mountain Rescue teams were known to be uniformly tough, this seemed to impress the aircrew.' Then Turnbull told them that PTSD was categorically not about flaws in the character of men who went into battle. He also described how their Tornado colleague Frank had gone 'back into the fight' after his rehabilitation programme.

The sound of lapping waves filled the silence; Frank's story was shocking news to the POWs. They had no idea that some of their fellow fliers, some of their close friends, had suffered such debilitating mental assaults. There was a murmur of approval as they began to comprehend the complexity of their situation.

At their next session, Turnbull noticed that one of the POWs was silent and withdrawn as the others discussed what had happened to them in the interrogation centre. A tear trickled down his cheek. One of the group put a hand on his shoulder. 'What's wrong, mate?'

At first the airman refused to say, but then admitted, 'I feel guilty.'

'Guilty about what?' the man next to him asked.

'Guilty about giving in to the interrogation. I told them more than my name, rank and service number. I told them a lot. Nothing that would have compromised operational security ... I don't think ...' he said, weeping openly now. 'But I just feel so bloody guilty.'

Recognising a breakthrough, Turnbull remained silent, allowing their stories to unfold. 'What happened next was amazing. One by one, all the others confessed to feeling exactly the same way. I was totally spellbound. What, I wondered, would have happened if this hadn't come out? This man, all of them, would have been living a lie, and it would have eaten away at them.'

The psychiatrist listened as the men began discussing the reality of their interrogation and beatings – that they all knew they would break at some point. How they had all felt a 'need' to suffer before the inevitable happened. Militarily, it was a mostly pointless gesture. But from the perspective of personal honour and integrity, it had been crucial to them all that they had endured as much violence as individually bearable before giving in.

As he watched the excited and impassioned discussion, Turnbull also noticed something wonderful begin to happen. 'A voice I'd not heard since we'd started the debriefings was now animatedly engaged. A voice with a strong Geordie accent. I looked up and caught John Nichol's eye, and this time he gave me an almost imperceptible nod. I realised that if I could win over sceptics like John Nichol, the guys on the front line who really mattered, then there was every chance the therapy could work on anyone.'

Despite his complaints, Nichol had listened carefully to the psychiatrist's words, that there was 'nothing unmanly' about PTSD. 'He told us the most important thing was to talk about our experience and not to bottle it up or ignore the feelings. Being military aircrew, we were sceptical about baring our souls, but, in retrospect, everyone agreed that the whole process was necessary.'

Robbie Stewart found the group debriefings tremendously helpful, especially listening to others' experiences. 'I had no real problems mentally; although I was beaten, I wasn't really tortured. But unknown to us, Gordon Turnbull led the POWs back into the world we had left the previous August. His gentle probing and sympathetic manner opened the closed doors in my mind and released pent-up feelings. All this was done without me realising at the time.

Only years later could I look back and see the help which prevented me from suffering from any PTSD.'

The POWs had been well cared for; emotionally, psychologically and medically. The same could not be said for every soldier, sailor and airman who fought in the Gulf. It was a time before 'mental health' was openly discussed in the military, and the vast majority of the forces would return to their homes and loved ones with no decompression or debriefing at all.

After a few days in hospital and the mentally draining psychological debrief, everyone was suffering from cabin fever. Nichol and Rupert Clark decided to organise an 'Escape Committee' in order to have a proper drink. They persuaded a medic to covertly transport them the 3 miles to the Officers' Mess on the other side of Akrotiri airbase, 'only for one quiet beer', they promised. The pilots, navigators and minders walked into the long bar, which was overflowing with fellow fliers – crews of RAF passenger jets, tankers and transport aircraft using Cyprus as a hub to supply the Gulf. Given the former POWs' international press coverage, they were instantly recognised. A huge cheer went up, followed by clapping and back-slapping as they waded into the gathering.[14] 'I shall never forget the moment we walked into that bar,' said Buckley. 'The sea of green flying suits was overwhelming and the camaraderie was intoxicating. As were the pints of Cypriot beer.' Those drinks flowed even more freely when the President of the Mess invited the new arrivals to drink at the Mess's expense. They needed no second bidding, and 'one quiet beer' was rapidly followed by a dozen considerably louder ones.

In the increasingly convivial atmosphere, Nick Heard felt the constant pressure of operations ebb. 'It was simply awesome to be part of that gathering with so many crews in the bar from other aircraft. The party just got bigger and bigger. We could not wait to get home, but before then, many brandy sours needed to be sunk. It was an incredible night.'

The Tornado crews met friends they had trained with. The reunions required further drink to be taken. 'What could be better therapy, we asked ourselves, than to be back in an RAF bar with your mates, a few beers and a fair sprinkling of attractive women,' Nichol said. Unfortunately, the POWs' 'Escape Committee' had not fully comprehended their sensitive status on base amid the ongoing terrorist threat. During a shift change at the hospital, their absence was discovered, triggering a huge security alert. Searches were launched, but no one thought that the first place to look should be the Officers' Mess bar. 'We returned to the hospital rather the worse for wear,' Nichol admitted. 'And a bit ashamed at having caused the people who were looking after us so much trouble. It was a good night, though.' As one of those responsible for the POWs, Nick Heard was given a dressing-down by a senior officer. 'She was decidedly peeved that most of her POWs were missing and told the minders we were going to be in a lot of trouble for being part of it. We decided that we could easily accept any bollocking, bearing in mind the risks we'd all been taking in the skies of Iraq over the previous six weeks at war.'

The former POWs completed five days of therapy before flights home were arranged. Some were allocated RAF HS125 VIP jets. Looking down on the snow-capped Alps, Robbie Stewart knew he was in the lucky group. 'There was something surreal about sitting comfortably in a business jet, sipping a drink, cruising past Italy and then over France when only a week earlier we had been prisoners in Baghdad, fearing for our lives.'

On a damp, misty Norfolk afternoon, Tange, Kirsty and Scott Stewart were driven to the 27 Squadron HQ and ushered quietly into the Wing Commander's office. Kirsty stared out as the HS125 came in to land. 'It taxied towards the Squadron site and finally the door opened and the steps came down.'

Waiting to step down onto home soil, Robbie was bemused by the reception. 'Most of our ground crew were lined up waving, and I could see our Station Commander, Jock Stirrup, and other senior officers waiting to greet us.'

He hauled himself out of his seat and made his way awkwardly towards the open door.

Remembering the moment thirty years on, Tange Stewart begins to weep. 'I watched my darling husband hobble down those steps and I was utterly shocked. When he left us he had been fit and tanned. Now here he was, his hand resting on his minder's shoulder for balance, looking pale, drawn and weak.'[15]

The image is also fixed in Kirsty's mind, who was also in tears reliving the events. 'It was agonising to watch my dad limp out of the aircraft. He was really thin, almost wizened, struggling to walk. I was horrified. For much of the experience I felt I had been living in a surreal nightmare. Now it was all shockingly real.'[16]

Robbie limped slowly down the path to the HQ building, still holding onto his friend for support. When he reached the entrance, he was pointed towards the office where his family were waiting.

'The door opened and Dad hobbled in,' said Kirsty. 'He took one step forward then tried to "run" – unsuccessfully – towards us. We all fell into each other's arms and hugged. It was the most amazing, wonderful moment of my life. At last I knew he was alive.'

Recalling the reunion, Robbie – and the author – also descend into floods of tears. 'This was the moment I had been dreaming about and will treasure always. To see their faces, so relieved to see me but still unsure of my wellbeing. Few words were spoken, we just cried and hugged. Just being able to touch each other was all we wanted. The kids hung on so tightly, as if determined never to lose me again. Tange looked beautiful but had a weariness in her eyes. She had coped with so much trauma alone.'

Tange gripped her family tightly. 'We were all in tears, but back together again. It was all over.' A few miles away in their Coleby village, the bells of All Saints Church rang out once more. This time in celebration.

* * *

As operations in the Gulf wound down, the battle-scarred Tornados arrived back at their bases in dribs and drabs. Their once pristine, sand-coloured livery was now stained with the heat and smoke of intense, wartime flying. A small patch could be seen on a few, covering the hole of a triple-A strike. Four Tornados had been lost in training before the war, another with a technical malfunction at Tabuk, and six went down over enemy territory.

There had clearly been some issues with equipment failures. Like all military aircraft, the Tornado was a complex mix of electronics, computerised systems, hydraulics, flying controls and all manner of military hardware crammed into a small airframe which could fly, under fire, at over 700mph in rain, sleet, snow or desert conditions. Some missions had certainly been lost to technical problems, but the incredible teams of dedicated engineers had fought tirelessly to keep the aircraft ready for battle and, despite some challenges, the force had carried out more than 1,800 war sorties delivering over 100 JP233s, 123 ALARM missiles, along with 4,200 'dumb', and nearly 1,000 laser-guided, bombs.[17] It had been an incredible achievement by all involved, on the ground and in the air.

Seven Tornado aircrew had died during training for the conflict, and five in battle. A total of forty-seven British servicemen lost their lives during the war to liberate Kuwait. John Broadbent had presided over some of their final journeys home.

'The war had been over a few weeks and most of the British forces had returned to their peacetime locations, leaving my detachment one of the last in theatre. As one of the few senior officers in the region, it fell to me to oversee the remaining coffins onto their RAF transport aircraft for repatriation to the UK. One of the dead from my own Squadron, Steve Hicks, was among them. I'll never forget waiting with our small bearer party that was to carry Steve onto the RAF Hercules. We stood there staring at the coffins all neatly lined up and covered in Union Jacks. I have never felt so humbled. Or so sad.'

* * *

As the cost was still being counted, things moved on apace for the survivors. Whether arriving home via RAF transport, or in a Tornado, each returning squadron was welcomed back to its base by joyous crowds, VIPs and emotional families.

On arrival at RAF Laarbruch, Mal Craghill was presented with a drink, and a challenge. 'Before I reached the bottom of the steps, I had a bottle of champagne in one hand and a bottle of beer in the other. I was then faced with the conundrum of how to shake hands with the Chief of the Air Staff!'[18]

Jerry Witts, who had commanded the Tornados in Dhahran, was also confused by all the attention. 'It was a beautiful day flying across the snow-covered Alps, then the green fields; all the lovely things you don't see in the desert. We'd had a tip-off there would be a reception, but I didn't expect the RAF Germany Band and half the station personnel waving flags. It was all a bit over the top, really. I remember standing up in the Tornado and saying to Adie, my navigator, "God I'm embarrassed. What do I do now?" He told me I should just try getting out.'[19]

John Peters arrived back at RAF Laarbruch in style on another RAF business jet. He had already spoken to his wife Helen at length by phone, and been through Gordon Turnbull's full psychological debrief. *I'll be fine*, he told himself.

Walking towards the HQ building, he saw Helen holding their daughter Toni in her arms. 'The ground began to quiver and dissolve. Guy came toddling out from behind her, down the stairs towards me, his thick mop of hair shining. "Daddy!" he shouted. I gathered him into my arms, hugged him in a long, long hug. I had worried so much in prison that he might have forgotten me, it was fantastic that he still recognised me. I was overwhelmed. Then Helen was in my arms and we held one another long and close. It felt like for ever since we had parted. Toni had only been two months old when I left, a little baby. Now she looked completely different; a diminutive grown-up, her character emerging. Completely adorable and pretty. My happiness at being with them again was almost unbearable.'[20]

Most of the reunions were continued with vigour in the various bars which dotted each RAF station. After an emotional reunion with his wife, Nick Heard headed to the Officers' Mess. 'It was a wonderful, memorable time, but at the back of my mind the occasion was marred by the thought that we had lost a number of friends and there would be no homecoming celebrations for their families. So there was a striking contrast to the happiness in the bar that day. There was joy, laughter and celebration for some of us, while not far away in the married quarters, there was incredible grief and sadness. That was the reality of our war. I was one of the lucky ones; I was back home with my wife. Not everyone who had flown the Tornado to war was that lucky.'

* * *

While the survivors enjoyed reunions with loved ones, and the bereaved began to make arrangements for funerals. In the UK and across the Atlantic, questions began to be asked as to why the coalition's victorious army had not continued along the road to Baghdad and knocked out Saddam Hussein while the allies had him on the ropes. The clamour from armchair-generals and analysts calling for the dictator's destruction grew.

James Baker, the Secretary of State, later explained precisely why he thought it was a terrible idea. 'Removing him from power might well have plunged Iraq into civil war, sucking US forces in to preserve order,' he told the *Los Angeles Times*. 'Had we elected to march on Baghdad, our forces might still be there.' He also cautioned that an American occupation would lead to Iraq fracturing along ethnic and religious lines, with the majority Shia taking over from Saddam's Sunni-led regime and the Kurds in the north seeking autonomy. More importantly, it would play directly into the hands of the fundamentalist Shia-dominated Iranian theocracy. 'The mullahs could export their brand of Islamic fundamentalism with the help of Iraq's Shiites and quickly transform themselves into the dominant regional power.'[21]

General Norman Schwarzkopf also dealt fulsomely with the concept of 'regime change' after the war to liberate Kuwait which had worldwide support, and nine UN resolutions authorising the coalition's actions. 'The resolutions that provided the legal basis for our military operations in the Gulf were clear in their intent: kick the Iraqi force out of Kuwait. We had authority to take whatever actions were necessary to accomplish that mission, including attacks into Iraq. We had no authority to invade Iraq for the purpose of capturing the entire country or its capital.'[22] Like Baker, he knew that the costs of governing and security would be prohibitive. With some prescience, Schwarzkopf then said: 'I am certain that had we taken all of Iraq we would have been like the dinosaur in the tar pit, we would still be there. We, not the United Nations, would be bearing the costs of our occupation. This is a burden I am sure the beleaguered American taxpayer would not have been happy to take on.'

Although no one knew it then, Baker and Schwarzkopf were offering a remarkably accurate vision of the future – when the idea of regime change was revisited in 2003.

The British Prime Minister also had to fend off criticism that Saddam was still in situ, arguing that the war had severely weakened the dictator. 'It put the world on notice of his potential to do harm,' John Major said. 'It set a pattern for peacekeeping and allowed the United Nations to begin a weapons inspection programme which did much to limit Iraq's chemical and nuclear weapons capability. And above all, although it may be unfashionable to think in such terms, it was morally the right thing to do. It gave a signal that the world expected certain standards in international behaviour and would act to enforce them.'[23]

Within days of the war ending, the lights had returned to Baghdad for the first time in two months. Iraqi television came back on air, schools opened and the water supply was restored. But with no sightings of Saddam since the ceasefire, rumours abounded of his death or that he had fled to Algeria seeking asylum. Then, on the evening of Sunday, 3 March, a familiar face appeared on Iraqi television: 'a 45-second videotape of smiling Hussein meeting his aides', the LA Times reported. 'The message was clear. Someone is running Iraq and that someone is Saddam Hussein.'[24]

Despite the firepower arrayed against him, Saddam had survived. As he would for more than a decade longer.

* * *

Saddam Hussein's immediate future was of no interest to the Tornado crews who had hastened his forces' eviction from Kuwait. It was back to business as usual. At least that was the plan. But it was difficult for those who had been at the heart of the action. And, for those who had not.

'The bonding had been so strong, it took me three or four weeks to get over not being with my people,' one of the medics from Muharraq remembered. 'It was difficult readjusting. You found that people who were out there talked together in huddles. It was a shared experience. There's a divide between us and people who were not out there.'[25]

Tornado engineer Dean Wood had spent the war at Tabuk. He too hankered after the action. 'It was so wonderful to be home safely with my wife and young children. To put it all behind me,' he said. 'But I quickly realised I was really missing all those fellas I'd been with. We had lived and worked side by side amid a war; every hour of every day together. We'd had colleagues killed. Lots of things remained unsaid between us, but we all felt the same emotions. And we instinctively knew how the others felt. I missed the bond we had shared, the camaraderie of war. We missed it so much that just a couple of days after we returned, we all arranged to go out together for a bit of a drinking session. Our wives were not too happy about that! But it was difficult for those who had not been there to understand what we had gone through.'[26]

What Dean Wood and those Gulf War veterans could never have imagined as they enjoyed their drinks, and the initial days of peace in March 1991, was that they, and their Tornados, would return to combat operations in the Gulf region on countless further occasions over the following decades.

'The dust created by the turmoil of the Gulf War soon settled as everyone returned from their post-war holiday and the Squadron tried to return to some sense of normality,' Gordon Buckley said. 'In hindsight that was never going to happen. Too much had gone on in people's personal lives and wartime experiences. I often thought about the bombs we dropped; I can still see that Pilot Briefing Facility exploding, annihilating everyone inside. You don't want to kill anyone but that's what happens when you go to war. It's what needs to be done. Part of being a Tornado crew is destruction and killing.'

That destruction and killing would eventually continue through the whole operational life of the Tornado.

Nigel Risdale shared Buckley's perspective. 'When I was training in 1982 and had first seen those shiny new Tornados in a hangar, ready for the possibility of a nuclear war, I could never have conceived we would fight a regional, limited conflict in the desert. Yet in truly trying circumstances the Tornado force had done an incredible job of adapting to constantly changing requirements, carrying out missions the vast majority of people had never trained for, or perhaps even heard of before. But we adapted quickly to the new tactics and weapons. That's what the RAF had always been about and it was truly gratifying to be part of it. And the Tornado itself performed magnificently too. To have a machine that was so flexible, adaptable, becoming more capable with each new development, was just astonishing. It was a great aircraft and proved itself in an environment it was never designed for.'

Risdale had been among the many aircrew who had flown straight home to an emotional reunion with his family. 'I was really proud to have been part of those early Tornado war operations but, now, life had to go on.'

A few weeks after returning, he was back in the UK visiting friends and family. 'I was walking through a bright, modern shopping centre in Northampton with my wife and young son. We were just passing the time, browsing the shop windows, when the most bizarre and curious feeling washed over me. I looked around at all these people rushing about, living their "normal" lives; shopping, eating, going to and from work. It dawned on me that my own life had changed irrevocably. These people had no idea what I – and more importantly my family – had gone through just a few weeks before.

'When you have been through an experience like war, life-threatening and life-defining, it concentrates the mind and you realise what is important. And what is not. I had faced death and survived, some of my friends had not. At that moment, looking at the crowds rushing by, I suddenly realised what was important in my own life – holding hands with my wife and son. Nothing else mattered.'[27]

* * *

Not every child was able to hold a much-loved father's hand. On 27 March 1991, an RAF VC10 flew the officers and airmen from Steve Hicks' Squadron to Cornwall for his funeral. All wore full dress uniform and black armbands. Steve had left final instructions that if anything were to happen to him, he was to be buried in the area he considered home after his time based there on Nimrod maritime patrol aircraft. He had also requested he be laid to rest in sight of the sea.

Steve's Squadron Commander, John Broadbent, was among those waiting at the Norman church of St Eval near Padstow. With its strong connections to the RAF in the region going back to the Second World War, and only a mile from the coast, it would be the perfect resting place.[28]

Thirty years after leading his Squadron to war, the experience still plays on Broadbent's mind. 'Not many days go by that I don't think about that time. Steve's death in particular still haunts me. He and Rupert Clark were number four in my own four-ship formation, so I saw it as very much part of *my* job to do the best I could to keep *them* safe. In that, I failed. I still wonder: if only ... if only ...? As his Boss, what could I have done differently? What *should* I have done differently?

'I asked his Flight Commander, Gordon Buckley, if he'd give the eulogy. It should really have been me, but I was afraid that my emotions would get the better of me and I'd break down. I felt Steve deserved more dignity than that. I was very relieved and grateful when Buckers agreed to take on that heavy responsibility.'

The mist was hanging on the wooded landscape and a stillness had settled in the air as the hearse, carrying the casket draped in a Union flag, passed through the discreet security cordon and stopped outside the church. The uniformed pallbearers, all RAF friends of Steve, moved forward to lift the coffin onto their shoulders, then slow-marched down the aisle past the countless memorials to the many others who had already given their lives in the service of their country. Coming to a smart halt, they lowered the coffin, stationing their comrade's body in front of the altar.

Gordon Buckley had arrived early, to sit at the front. He kept his eyes straight ahead as the others filed in. When the time came, he walked to the lectern and turned to face the congregation. 'I couldn't believe it – the church was packed to overflowing. People crammed, standing and sitting, in every space. It was very hard; I thought, *How the hell am I going to do this?* Then I looked down and into Steve's widow's eyes. I knew I had to do it for her, and his two young sons. At that moment, I realised the true enormity of what we had all been through. There were now wives without husbands, children without fathers.'

Tears and moments of laughter filled the deep-vaulted ceiling as Buckley spoke warmly about the man who had gone from being a sergeant and Air Electronics Operator on Nimrod maritime sur- veillance aircraft, to an officer and fast-jet navigator. They heard about his humour, his caring nature and his devotion to his family.

A later obituary expanded on his contribution to the RAF:

Steve was a worker, a man who could be relied upon to com- plete any task well. He was not slow in voicing his opinions or prodding someone's shoulder in defence of others. He was a successful ingredient in the formula that is XV Squadron. In the Gulf, his contribution was exemplary. He was generous to a fault and a loyal person, devoted to the Squadron; a man of principles, of truth. We pray that he may rest in peace, and we extend our love and friendship to his wife and two children.[29]

The last hymn was sung, then Steve's friends gently lifted him back onto their shoulders for his final journey. He was buried in the churchyard, overlooking the sea, as an RAF bugler sounded the 'Last Post'.

At 3.25pm a Nimrod aircraft roared overhead, then the howl of Rolls-Royce RB199 engines was heard as four Tornados approached through the thinning mist. Directly over the cemetery the lead aircraft pulled up vertically in full reheat, soaring away from the remaining three jets, signifying a missing man; a departed comrade. It climbed upwards, the orange flames of its afterburners lighting up the grey sky.

A hush fell over the mourners as the thunder of engines slowly ebbed into the distance. The long moment of silence passed, then John Broadbent marched up to the grave, saluted, paused, about-turned and walked away. Each officer followed in turn, saluting their fallen comrade. After bidding a final farewell, they left Steve in sight of the crashing ocean. Just as he had wanted.

EPILOGUE

'OUR STORY HAD COME FULL CIRCLE'

1991–2020

The Tornado had proved itself in war, and those who had flown it in combat now presumed they would enjoy the peace. The following decades would show their presumptions were sorely misplaced, and many would deploy on countless more military operations.

'I think that because the Gulf War, and the use of air power, had been so successful, there was a sense that this was the new world order. Perhaps this was our role from now on?' said Gordon Buckley. 'Politicians must have looked at the incredible military power they controlled, thinking that we could be deployed around the globe to police trouble spots and ensure a more stable world. Of course, it didn't work out like that . . .'[1]

For nearly thirty years, the Tornado would be an integral part of Britain's military operations, from Iraq, to Kosovo, Afghanistan, Libya, Syria and back to Iraq again. Wherever there was a need for combat air support, a Tornado would normally be found nearby.

Sadly, not all those who had been bloodied in the jet's first battles in 1991 would survive to see the aircraft eventually retire in 2019.

* * *

The Tornado force had initially returned to the routine training designed to counter the Cold War threat. But that threat no longer existed. The continuing demise of the Soviet Union had brought with it the demolition of the massive standing armies of the Communist era. The British government, in turn, embarked on a grand cost-cutting defence review as part of the so-called 'peace dividend'. Personnel would be reduced by around 18 per cent across the Armed Forces. The RAF was about to lose around 20,000 people; the nine squadrons of the Tornado force would be reduced to six, and its bases in Germany from four to two.

It would be the end of an era.

Only months after returning from captivity, John Peters and John Nichol made their final flight together as three of RAF Laarbruch's four Tornado squadrons were disbanded. 'In the whole of our professional lifetime, a squadron had never been decommissioned, yet now, in the space of a few days, three of them disappeared,' said Nichol. 'It was an emotional time, as though most of your family was emigrating to Australia.'

The family might have been splitting up, but not before a drink-fuelled final dinner.

Nichol had been tasked with ensuring the evening went with a bang. He took his duty seriously. 'I'd ordered thousands of pounds' worth of fireworks. Rockets the size of champagne bottles took off like surface-to-air missiles. The sky lit up like those Iraqi airfields on the first night of the war. Our Squadron's war trophy had been set up outside the Officers' Mess for the grand finale. We loaded the four-barrelled Iraqi triple-A gun with some serious pyrotechnics. It brought back quite a few memories to those watching when they blasted off.'

The Two Johns then set off for a ski trip in Garmisch, the delightful German town in the foothills of the Zugspitze where Robbie Stewart's family had learned of Iraq's invasion of Kuwait. The pair spent a week enjoying the slopes, raising the odd glass to absent friends, and reminiscing before heading off to their new bases, Nichol's in England and Peters to RAF Bruggen in Germany.

Snow flurries rode along the bus's headlight beams as it pulled to a halt outside Peters' new station. Nichol helped his pilot unload his kit. 'That's it then, that's the end of us,' he said as Peters scooped the skis onto his shoulder. They shook hands, slightly awkwardly, then hugged. 'As the bus pulled away I looked back and could see JP standing in a pool of light, with the snow falling around him. We would never share a cockpit again.'[2]

Jenny Green had said her goodbyes to the RAF before the Gulf War started. Her husband Bill had been killed flying a Tornado training mission a fortnight after Iraq's invasion of Kuwait in 1990 and his body was never recovered from the North Sea. The following January, from her new civilian home, she had watched the first mission take off from Muharraq, the same airbase from which Bill should have led his Squadron to war. When the first losses were reported, Jenny knew exactly what their loved ones would be facing. 'It was a very poignant time, seeing all the Tornados, wondering what might have been. The worst had already happened to me, but I knew other people were now going through what I had. Everything changes. In the words of many widows, you feel excommunicated; a bad omen. My security pass was taken away and I was required to move out of our married quarters. I don't think they wanted to be cruel, but the RAF needed to move on quickly. Other people were waiting to take over our house.'

For Jenny and Bill's 17-year-old son, Jeremy, it was a time of intense change. 'After Dad died, and as a teenager heading into adulthood, you have to grow up,' he said. 'You have been exposed to the harsh realities of life. It was a very difficult time for us all and you lose a little bit of your youth but, in reality, we had to carry on, get back to a new "normality" and focus on what really mattered. We had lost a father and husband so, in a way, you feel the need to become "the man of the house". But at the same time you are still a kid who has lost his dad and you feel guilty about moving on. And I could see that Mum really suffered with a lot of the archaic rules in the aftermath of Dad's death. She had to deal with all the financial aspects, the funeral, the social aspects. She had been a military wife all her married life. Now, she was out of that community.'[3]

'There was a sense that we were no longer wanted,' said Jenny. 'No one *set out* to be hurtful, it was just the way it was. After twenty-three years as an RAF wife, I was simply no longer part of that structure.' Within two months, the family was out of their military home, forced to start anew when they hadn't really had a moment to mourn. 'It is a time when you hardly feel able to put one foot in front of the other, yet you have to uproot your children and move.'[4]

As the war went on, Jenny was struck by the lack of central co-ordination to help and support those at their lowest ebb. Shortly after the ceasefire, she wrote to every RAF widow she knew asking if they wanted to get together to discuss a plan to help the next generation. 'Thank goodness someone is finally doing something about this,' was the universal response.

At the first meeting, a year after the war ended, twenty-six of them gathered, passionately determined to help formulate a new policy. 'There were huge gaps in the way the RAF dealt with widows at that time, in terms of housing, information, pensions and the immediate aftermath of bereavement. The military just didn't realise how let down we widows felt. No one had ever told them. I think the RAF really wanted to get this right, but did not know *how* to truly help.' Jenny set up the RAF Widows' Association and the group began designing training sessions for the officers nominated to liaise with any next of kin, and bereavement packages for widows explaining their rights. 'We provided comfort, friendship and someone to talk to who knew what the new widow was going through. Sadly, we had a unique understanding.'

Anne Lennox's husband Garry had been killed alongside his navigator Kevin Weeks when their Tornado had crashed during the last low-level attack of the war. She was heavily pregnant with their second child when she was eventually given the news that Garry had not survived. 'I'd hoped beyond hope that he would come home. I knew that if he possibly could, he would get through it. And it all seemed to no avail. Then I just began to feel a bit numb.' Surrounded by pictures of her family and late husband, Anne talked about how the imminent birth of her son, and protecting her young daughter, took over her life. 'I had to be strong for the children. Someone once said to me, they didn't know how I survived, given that I'd had a bereavement, I had to move home, and have a baby. But I managed it.'[5]

Although it was too late for Anne Lennox, the RAF Widows' Association began to address a number of lingering issues. 'One of the first problems we dealt with,' said Jenny Green, 'was that rather than having to leave your home within a few weeks or months of your husband's death, widows can now stay in their married quarters for two years if needed.'

* * *

Not long after the first three squadrons disbanded, the Tornado was back on operations over Iraq. Given Saddam Hussein's previous history, it should not have come as a surprise.

Shortly after the 1991 conflict ended, the Kurds in northern Iraq and the Shias in the south, encouraged by American promises, had rebelled against the dictator, seeking secession. They were brutally suppressed. Although the West once again drew back from direct involvement, 'safe havens' were created, enforced by British and American aircraft policing 'no-fly zones'. They provided little security. Under the ceasefire agreement, Saddam was not allowed to use fixed-wing aircraft above the 36th parallel in the north or below the 32nd parallel in the south. But he was still free to use his helicopters and troops. Yet again, he attacked his own people with breathtaking savagery. Many thousands were killed, tens of thousands displaced.

In August 1992, two years since the first F3s had arrived to deter Saddam from invading Saudi Arabia, a detachment of six Tornado

GR1s returned to Dhahran, tasked with overseeing the no-fly zones. 'We had all assumed that Iraq was consigned to the *"been there, done that"* pile,' Mal Craghill said as his Squadron deployed. 'But the reality was that less than two years later I was back, conducting Operation Southern Watch sorties, trying to prevent Saddam Hussein from persecuting his own people. In reality, little was being achieved. We saw troop movements, fires burning and reported them back. But nothing was really done. Basically, the Iraqi army was burning the Marsh Arabs out of their homes so they could massacre them. We certainly felt helpless at first.'[6]

Monitoring operations soon turned into direct action, and in early 1993 100 coalition aircraft attacked Iraq's rebuilt air defence systems which had been targeting them in the skies of southern Iraq. Mal Craghill found himself over enemy airspace once again, dropping bombs on the same facilities he had pulverised two years earlier.

He would go on to serve another seven tours in the region over the following years.

While Craghill had returned to the fight, others were training the next generation of fliers. Among them was Simon Burgess who, alongside Bob Ankerson, had fought in vain to keep his Tornado airborne after a bomb had detonated prematurely. After ejecting, both men had spent the rest of the war as prisoners. Five years on, Simon was still flying fast jets, but now using his experience to teach trainee pilots at RAF Valley in Wales.

On 13 February 1996 he was programmed to fly a routine sortie to assess local weather conditions.[7] He powered down the runway and the Hawk jet lifted off, then, due to an engineering fault, almost immediately became uncontrollable, rolling towards the ground. Simon ejected but sadly it was outside the ejection seat parameters and he was killed. He was twenty-eight.

Simon was buried with full military honours in Humberston, Lincolnshire. Many Gulf veterans were among the 200 who filled the church. The service was relayed to as many again who were standing outside.[8] Shots from the firing party rang out as his coffin was lowered into the ground, and as the 'Last Post' faded a flypast of two Tornados followed by four Hawks roared overhead. In time-honoured tradition, one of the Hawks pulled vertically out of the formation in the 'missing man' salute.

A number of the mourners were former Second World War RAF prisoners of war. 'We old veterans have a great respect and regard for our new Gulf War friends,' one said. 'We share their sense of loss at the death of this young pilot. It was very obvious that the wider family of the Royal Air Force were also mourning the loss of a highly respected and popular officer.'[9]

The sound of the jet engines soon faded, but the words etched on Simon Burgess's headstone speak of what he left behind:

> BELOVED HUSBAND, SON & BROTHER
> LOVED & REMEMBERED ALWAYS
> FLY HIGH AND FLY FREE

While some from the 1991 Gulf War Tornado community decided to stay on and make a career out of the service, others decided to try something new. When navigator David Bellamy's Squadron was disbanded as part of the defence cuts, he decided to resurrect his idea of pursuing a career as a civilian Electronic Warfare Instructor for a major defence contractor. 'I resumed my studies with a summer school in 1991 at Norwich University. We had a guest presenter for one section – a British-Iraqi lecturer. He proceeded to give a speech about the war, accusing the coalition pilots of revelling in the bombing, wearing mirrored sunglasses, and cheering as they killed people. He could not have been more wrong.

'The war to liberate Kuwait was a just war and I was proud to have flown the Tornado as part of it. It was a cornerstone of my life. It took me a few years to "come down" from the war-fighter I had become in 1991. In fact, I don't think I really calmed down until the birth of my daughter three years later.'

Shortly after the war Bellamy had married, and asked his wartime pilot Trevor Roche to be in the guard of honour and to give a reading. His friend happily obliged.

While Dave had been working in 'civvy street', Roche had furthered his credentials as one of the RAF's outstanding pilots when he took on several flying jobs that culminated in serving as a test pilot for the newest generation of combat aircraft which would eventually replace the Tornado. Trevor left the RAF in 1998, joining British Airways and eventually captaining one of the huge Airbus A320 passenger jets. But he also continued piloting vintage aircraft for a civilian display company. He would go on to fly thirty-seven different types, from a 1909 Blériot monoplane, the oldest airworthy flying machine in Britain, to Spitfires and Hurricanes.[10] Roche loved the sound of engines and the freedom of flight.

* * *

During school holidays in the 1980s, Robbie Stewart's young daughter Kirsty had frequently accompanied her father into the planning room at RAF Marham, poring over maps and listening to the Tornado aircrew discuss tactics. 'Dad really enjoyed planning his sorties and some of that certainly rubbed off on me. I loved the notion of aviation; the sights and the smells. And I loved spending time with Dad and his friends on the Squadron.'[11]

It was perhaps unsurprising that only a few years after Robbie's return from captivity, she announced that she wanted to join the RAF. Furthermore, she wanted to become a fast-jet pilot. They took her seriously. In the years before what is now known as the 'First Gulf War', the RAF had egregiously banned women from becoming pilots or navigators. But attitudes had rightly changed, and in 1994, after qualifying on Tornados, Jo Salter had become the first RAF female fast-jet pilot. Kirsty followed in her footsteps four years later. She was coming towards the end of her training when Al Qaeda terrorists flew hijacked passenger jets into the Twin Towers of the World Trade Center and the Pentagon during the 9/11 attacks in 2001. She had no doubt that the Tornado would spearhead the conflict which would surely follow this devastating strike at the heart of America.

Gordon Buckley's navigator Paddy Teakle had also remained on the front line, and in 2003 was commanding a Tornado squadron in Kuwait, still monitoring the no-fly zones. By then, his Tornado GR1 had been transformed into the superior GR4 with advanced night-vision and navigation capabilities. The conversion was the beginning of a series of significant enhancements that would give the aircraft the ability to fire Brimstone anti-armour precision missiles and drop advanced precision-guided bombs, as well as incredible reconnaissance and targeting capabilities with the new RAPTOR and Litening pods.[12]

It was quite a change from hurtling towards enemy fire at ultra-low level in the pitch darkness, which came as a relief to Teakle and the crews now facing another war. 'The Tornado had truly become the multi-role combat aircraft it had originally been conceived to be.'[13]

Teakle was crewed with a young pilot who had been in his teens when Paddy was dropping JP233s on Iraqi airbases from 200ft. As they crossed the border into Iraq on a 'familiarisation' mission early in January 2003, twelve years after Teakle had first entered the country, an order came to attack an air defence facility near Tallil airbase in response to an infringement of the no-fly zone. 'So within minutes of the very first operational sortie of his life, my young pilot found himself dropping two laser-guided bombs onto an Iraqi bunker, and I found myself attacking facilities at an airfield back where it had all begun for me in 1991.'

President George W. Bush, the son of George H. W. Bush, was intent on achieving what his father had chosen not to do after Kuwait had been liberated during the First Gulf War. There was unfinished business to be dealt with. Teakle began to witness another massive build-up of forces in the Gulf, and was given command of the Tornado Combat Air Wing in the coming conflict.

There were many who had warned of the dangers of 'regime change' in Iraq in the wake of the first conflict. But others still lamented the lack of ambition in 1991. Among them was Margaret Thatcher, the Prime Minister who had been dramatically ousted from power two months before the conflict.

In the following years, she showed no reluctance in expressing her ongoing disapproval of the way the First Gulf War had ended, telling one documentary maker, 'When you are dealing with a dictator, he has got not only to be well and truly defeated, but has got to be seen to be defeated *by his own people*.'[14] She went further during a later victory celebration in Kuwait, openly lamenting the failure of Britain and America to wipe out Saddam Hussein. 'I only wish that I had stayed on to finish the job properly. Perhaps then we wouldn't be where we are today, with this cruel and terrible man securely in power.'[15]

The scene was set for the Second Gulf War.

Paddy Teakle and the Tornados went to war in Iraq again on 20 March 2003. 'The fear of the unknown for me was entirely missing: this was now familiar ground. Among the team, however, things were different, as for many this was their first taste of combat. I could feel their excitement and trepidation.'

The first three days of the war went well; the combat novices quickly showed their mettle. But on 23 March tragedy struck. An American Patriot missile battery mistook a Tornado returning to Kuwait as an enemy aircraft. Flight Lieutenants Kev Main and Dave Williams were killed instantly when the 90kg warhead detonated, bringing down their aircraft. As the Tornado Detachment Commander, Teakle had to lead from the front. 'I visited aircrew and ground crew in their workplaces and encountered a wide raft of emotions: shock, disbelief, anger even, but what shone through above everything was resilience, stoicism and resolve. The team had taken a heavy hit but it had come out fighting and more united and determined than ever before.'

Main and Williams would be the last Tornado combat deaths, but not the last deaths in the conflict. Norman Schwarzkopf and James Baker's previous words of warning soon proved prophetic. An invasion, they had said, would end in America occupying a disunited country with unresolved enmities, and, in the ensuing chaos, there would be civil war at great human and economic cost. They were right.

Kirsty Stewart was among those in the Tornado force who had heard the news about the tragic 'blue-on-blue' with dismay during her training. In 2006, she joined her first squadron, walking into the very same office at RAF Marham where fifteen years earlier the family had waited for Robbie's return to freedom. 'It felt as though things were coming full circle. When I'd been on the site in the late 1980s, helping Dad on the Squadron, the trees surrounding the hardened aircraft shelters were just saplings, now they were enormous firs, dominating the landscape. The image really struck home. Time had marched on.'

The 2003 invasion and 'regime change' had indeed heralded long-term occupation. The capture and execution of Saddam Hussein only seemed to spur on the insurgency. And Tornados were once more at the heart of the action when Kirsty Stewart deployed on operations in 2006.

Supporting coalition troops from medium level, she knew her operational tour would be very different to her father's war of ultra-low flying into a storm of triple-A and SAMs. But the first time she entered hostile territory, she experienced a strong connection with the past. 'Not long after crossing the border, I glanced down at my moving map display and saw the word "*Tallil*". I suddenly realised the significance of where I was. It was a surreal moment. It was a clear day and I could see the whole airfield. I realised that below, still buried in the sand, was my dad's mangled Tornado GR1. Somewhere down there he had regained consciousness after his traumatic ejection at 600mph. He had been lying on the sand weeping, looking up to where I was now flying, worrying about me as a young girl and his family back home. On that patch of earth he had realised that his injuries were so bad, that his only option was to attract the enemy's attention and deal with the terrible consequences. That part of our family's personal story had come full circle and I felt really close to Dad in that moment. But it was astonishing to think that I was still fighting an ongoing conflict; a conflict he had nearly died in *sixteen* years earlier. It was all rather sad.'

Around the same time, Pete Batson was also finding his wartime experiences coming into sharper focus. The former Tornado pilot was now teaching new aircrew at RAF Cranwell in Lincolnshire.

A few years after Saddam Hussein had been eventually defeated in the second Gulf conflict, and as part of the peace dividend, young Iraqi military pilots began to arrive in Britain for training. It was a curious turn of events. 'When I was an instructor in the 1980s, we had taught Iraqi student pilots when their country had been our friend in the region,' Batson recalled. 'They would sometimes come to my house for dinner or a drink and I never gave it a second thought. But I then went on to fight against them in 1991.'

Now, Iraq was once again an ally and the next generation of Iraqis were already back in the British training system.

A framed map of Batson and Mike Heath's raid on Al Asad airbase – when Batson had instinctively bombed an Iraqi Mirage as it came in to land – hung in the student headquarters. Examining the target map of their homeland, the new intake asked Batson about his memories of the 1991 war. 'The young Iraqis were all very pro-British, which was strange given that I and some of their other instructors had been attacking their country. Some of their relatives had been pilots, one had actually been the senior officer in charge of the air defence system around Al Asad, so he would certainly have been trying to kill me. This gave me pause for thought about what war actually meant. The deaths and suffering. My mind turned to the Iraqi Mirage I'd dropped the JP233 on. It was entirely possible that I might have killed one of my students' relatives. It had been war, it was what was required, but it certainly felt surreal talking to them about it all. It was curious how it all turned out, and I wondered what the future might bring for this latest batch of Iraqi aircrew, and their country.'

Pete Batson was soon to be reminded of the slender thread by which life hung. His own Gulf War had come to a frustrating end when a technical fault meant he'd had to eject from his Tornado with his Squadron Boss, Mike Heath. While Mike managed to return to Tabuk to shepherd his men through their last few war sorties, Batson's injuries meant he did not recover in time to fly into battle again. Heath's leadership qualities saw him pass up the ranks, rising to Air Vice-Marshal. But his military service had been interrupted by a number of skirmishes with cancer. He had fought it off successfully on each occasion, until it returned with a vengeance when he was working at the United States Central Command in Florida.[16] He decided to return to the UK and retire, but on 17 November 2007, while preparing to leave, he was struck by a massive heart attack and died. He was fifty-seven.[17]

'He was very highly regarded,' a post on a military website read. 'One of the most friendly and approachable senior officers I have ever been privileged to meet. Always keen to chat in the bar – and liberal with the use of his bar book!'[18]

Mike Warren was another Tornado pilot who utilised his hard-won spurs to teach the next generation of aircrew. He and his navigator Mal Craghill had dropped the last RAF bombs of the war in 1991. After returning, their Squadron was disbanded and Mike eventually moved on to instructing duties.[19] He finally left the RAF and became an airline pilot, building a new life at the family home in Ormskirk, Lancashire, with his wife, 7-year-old daughter and 4-year-old son.

On 24 February 2008, a cold front had come in from the Atlantic, bringing rain to Manchester, no doubt making the 156 passengers who boarded Mike's Airbus A320 shortly after lunch even more delighted with the promise of warmer temperatures in Cyprus. As co-pilot, Warren offered the holidaymakers comforting words of welcome as they departed. For two hours they cruised over Europe in skies he was all too familiar with after his Tornado days. They had crossed the Alps and were heading down to southern Europe when Mike suffered a heart attack. The Purser rushed to the cockpit to administer first aid, frantically trying to keep him alive while the Captain diverted to Istanbul airport. They made an emergency landing just after 8pm and waiting paramedics immediately came on board. There was nothing they could do to save the 43-year-old former RAF aviator. He was already dead, just days before his little boy's fifth birthday.[20]

Thirty years after they flew into battle together, Mal Craghill still has the fondest memories of him. 'I feel genuinely privileged to have been crewed with Mike. Not only was he a very good pilot and a great friend, he was one of life's truly lovely people. I never met anyone with a bad word to say about him. We certainly had our share of "*holy shit!*" moments during the war, but I never worried that we wouldn't come out the other side because I trusted him completely. His cheeky grin is sadly missed at our annual Tornado reunions.'[21]

* * *

The Tornado that Mike and Mal had flown continued to perform peerlessly in its GR4 upgrade, demonstrating its adaptability as one of the most capable ground-attack aircraft and flying combat operations in a number of different theatres of war.

In Iraq, the invasion and occupation had come at a tremendous cost. From 2003 to 2011, 4,431 US personnel were killed,[22] thirty times more than the 1991 war. By the time the Tornado and British ground forces withdrew from Iraq operations in 2009, 179 UK service personnel had lost their lives.[23] The plight of the Iraqi people was harder to quantify; estimates of civilian deaths range from around 100,000 to nearly half a million.[24]

And after the post-9/11 war to expel Al Qaeda and the Taliban from Afghanistan, the Tornado had entered the fray in 2009 in support of the 10,000 British troops deployed to contain the resulting insurgency in Helmand Province. Then, in 2011, it also deployed over Libya in the battle to oust Muammar Gaddafi. The 3,000-mile return trips from RAF Marham to the southern Mediterranean were the first attack missions flown from UK soil since the Second World War.

But the new breed of Tornado did not just excel on the battlefield. In 2014, its reconnaissance capabilities were employed to provide imagery for those tasked with countering the floods which had devastated areas of the UK. Then in August that year, three GR4s were deployed to Chad to help track down the 276 schoolgirls kidnapped by the Islamic terror group Boko Haram in northern Nigeria.

It was all very different from 1991, hurtling along, only feet above the desert floor. The aircraft designed amid the threat of Cold War nuclear Armageddon now wore a coat of many colours.

* * *

Dave Bellamy had flown his last Tornado sortie with Trevor Roche in August 1991, just days before he left the RAF. 'I asked the Boss if I could swap pilots so that I could fly one final time with Trev,' he said. 'The Boss replied, "There's no keeping you two apart!"

'Trev did a high-speed fly-by over the Squadron HQ, then the champagne was broken out after we landed. There were smiles and laughter, but also a sinking feeling of knowing that something important was over.' Trevor had also eventually left the RAF to be an airline and civilian display pilot. Dave's subsequent work as an Electronic Warfare Instructor took him the length and breadth of the Middle East.

On 1 July 2012, he was instructing clients in Abu Dhabi in the complexities of radar jamming. Returning to his hotel suite, he made a drink and tuned in to BBC Radio 2 via the internet. At the turn of the hour the news came on. Only half listening, he heard the news-reader announce that a Gulf War veteran had been killed flying a vintage aircraft. 'Immediately the hairs went up on the back of my neck. There were only a few people that this could be. The more they said, the closer it got. And then they said his name.'

Trevor Roche had been one of the star attractions at a summer aircraft display in Bedfordshire, piloting a 1923 de Havilland DH53 Humming Bird monoplane. After taking off in blustery condi-tions, he was making a level turn close to a copse of fir trees when the classic machine plummeted to the ground. Trevor was killed instantly. The subsequent Air Accident Investigations Branch report concluded, 'It seems likely that the loss of control was the result of a combination of the challenging operating and handling charac-teristics of the DH53, the turbulent effect of the trees and the gusty wind conditions.'[25]

As the news sank in, Bellamy paced his room. 'I was furious and ended up smashing up a dining chair in my hotel suite. After everything we had done together, I could not accept his death with-out anger. Foolishly, you think if you had been there, things would be different. Losing Trevor was monumental, it really knocked me sideways for some time. After all that truly life-threatening danger in the war, he died in a peacetime accident, flying a vintage aircraft. That is when I cracked and my world collapsed around me. I finally understood what many others had been through losing a loved one.'[26]

Trevor's wife Katie had made Bellamy promise to keep her husband safe during the war and now asked him to deliver his friend's eulogy. Dave readily accepted. 'Trevor was my "other brother", my brother in arms. I was devastated. But he died doing the thing he loved: flying. That's all I can hold onto.'

The first line of his obituary in the *Telegraph* said it all:

Squadron Leader Trevor Roche, who has died aged 52, was a former RAF fighter pilot and flew so many types of aircraft, from pre-First World War monoplanes to Airbus airliners, that his career aloft encompassed almost the entire history of aviation.[27]

With the RAF's last Tornado training fatality occurring in 2012, forty-five aircrew had been lost – seven on wartime operations and thirty-eight in training.[28] By the early 1990s, the RAF had been losing around ten aircrew a year in accidents away from the battlefield.[29]

Inevitably, it meant that the RAF Widows' Association's numbers increased. And so did Jenny Green's awareness of the archaic injustices of the military system, particularly the rules governing military pensions for the surviving spouse, which legislated against any remarriage or committed relationship. 'It all seemed terribly unfair,' Jenny said. 'If you found love again, and remarried or cohabited, then you lost your late husband's Armed Forces Pension, and, if you had one, your own War Widows Pension. But having a different lover each week was deemed to be okay! It was totally ridiculous; old-fashioned and insulting.'

Furthermore, the rules changed depending on when and how your husband had actually died. Baffled by the discrimination, Jenny, by then also the chairwoman of the War Widows' Association, and her colleagues threw all their energy into upending the legislation. 'Our groups had significant support for the campaigns because we occupied the moral high ground. I confess I loved the political challenge and the fight to rectify a wrong. Together, we continued chipping away at the many anomalies in the rules and gradually managed to get a lot changed.'

Enlisting the support of the national press, the various groups mounted an energetic campaign to heap pressure on the then Prime Minister David Cameron to revise the system. In 2014, as Tornado crews risked their lives against ISIS in Syria and Iraq, Jenny and the War Widows' Association succeeded in overturning the injustice. Just before Remembrance Sunday, *The Times* reported that all widows in receipt of their military pension would be allowed to keep it, whatever their personal circumstances: 'The landmark move, which will affect up to 300,000 current and future widows over the next four decades, followed almost ten years of lobbying and campaigning by the War Widows' Association.'[30]

Sadly, the new legislation did not apply to all, and the association is still campaigning on behalf of the 300 or so who had remarried *before* the change came into force. Having already chosen to surrender their pensions to pursue love, they have not had them reinstated and are still left out in the cold.

Another battle won, Jenny could give more attention to her own family. 'At the time of a loved one's death, you can't believe you can rebuild your life. But you have no choice other than "to cope", to move on. I have been lucky enough to rebuild a good and useful life. I am also enormously proud of my children; they coped with everything so well and were very helpful to other children who tragically found themselves in the similar situation of losing a father.'

Her grandson William Green, named after his Tornado pilot grandfather, has inherited his love of aviation. 'He looks so much like Bill; it is so very special to spend time with him. I took him to see the Harrier jets at RAF Wittering carrying out training flights. He was really taken by the sights and the sounds, asking if he could learn to fly too. I said he probably needed to ask his mum and dad . . .'

* * *

Like Bill Green, Jerry Witts was a truly inspirational leader. As the Tornado Detachment Commander, his empathy and charisma helped carry the Tornado force in Dhahran through difficult times. He later reflected on all that had passed in the 'blur' of the six-week war:

'Twenty-one Scud attacks and as many false alarms. The losses, the POWs. The hits and, not too often, the misses. The fatigue, frustration and fear. The exhilaration and excitement. Mission by mission, target by target, we were part of an unstoppable force. Old myths were dispelled and new tactics evolved. Through it all, the ups and the downs – and there were plenty of both – there was a constant feeling of massive support from home. It was very gratifying, not to say humbling, to know that people cared for us all. My own [memories] will always include the simple bravery and fortitude of our families back at home. The sheer guts of the [engineers] loading bombs as bits of Scud rained down. Watching young, inexperienced aircrew grow so quickly into seasoned campaigners. Most of all, the feeling of immense personal privilege to have shared such company and commanded such people.'[31]

The pictures of Witts at the annual Gulf War reunions show a smiling, contented man surrounded by his friends and fellow aircrew. Those at the British Embassy in Washington also welcomed his affability during his later posting as Air Attaché in the United States. During a ceremony on the White House lawn, he gave a sideways nod to his humble Wiltshire roots when he was heard to murmur, 'Not bad for a ploughman's grandson!'[32]

Then, aged sixty-one, Jerry was diagnosed with corticobasal degeneration. In his habitually indomitable style, he helped raise funds for much-needed research into the brain disease, even as his own health deteriorated. In later years he became totally immobile, and his only movement was the blink of an eye.

In 2020, as the world became gripped by the coronavirus pandemic, his wife contracted Covid-19 and Jerry had to be taken into a nursing home. On 3 June, aged sixty-nine, the Squadron Commander who had done so much to care for his men died of pneumonia. Isolated because of the Covid restrictions, he was far from the bosom of his friends and family.

After his death, one of his officers from the Dhahran days told *The Times* obituarist: 'Throughout all the troubles, Jerry stood tall, taking a pragmatic view at all times. His leadership was outstanding and I do not know any one of the 400 of us out there who would not follow him anywhere.'

In normal circumstances, many hundreds of his military friends would have flocked to pay their respects at his funeral. Because of the ongoing constraints, only one was able to do so.

Alongside just a handful of his immediate family, his Gulf War navigator, AJ Smith, read Second World War fighter pilot John Gillespie Magee's poem, 'High Flight'. All those who had flown the Tornado to war with Witts could fully relate to the words:

Oh! I have slipped the surly bonds of Earth
And danced the skies on laughter-silvered wings;
Sunward I've climbed, and joined the tumbling mirth
of sun-split clouds, and done a hundred things
You have not dreamed of .[33]

Most American forces had left Iraq in 2011, but when Islamic State took over huge swathes of the country three years later, they were forced to return. RAF Tornados joined them, back in the skies where it had all begun twenty-three years earlier.

Flying out of Cyprus from 2014, the jets were striking ISIS units that at one point had threatened Baghdad itself. Their bombs and missiles now targeted lone gunmen, terrorists planting roadside IEDs, bomb factories and even small barges transporting weapons and personnel across rivers. Over the following five years ISIS was gradually pushed back to a final redoubt in north-east Syria.

But the Tornado's legendary status as a battle-proven machine eventually proved no match for ongoing defence cuts. It was time to finally stand down. It was announced that the remaining squadrons were to be disbanded, the jets broken up, sold for scrap and spare parts.

On 26 January 2019, two Tornados flying from Cyprus carried out the aircraft's final strike missions. Armed with Brimstone missiles and

500lb Paveway II bombs, the pair hit Islamic State positions in Syria.[34] In the previous five years, the Tornado had been responsible for a third of the 4,315 casualties inflicted on the ISIS extremists by the RAF.[35]

Among those carrying out the final operations was 27-year-old Nathan Shawyer. Nathan had not been born during the first Tornado attacks in Iraq in 1991. He flew home from Cyprus with the retiring aircraft in February 2019. 'I'm the last ever Tornado pilot to be trained by the RAF. After everything that's come before, it's quite a thrill, quite an honour,' he said. 'It was an absolutely awesome machine to fly. The Tornado has given us [countless] years of fantastic service, been all over the world and done a lot of things for the United Kingdom.'[36]

James Heeps was one of the Squadron Commanders of the final detachment to take to the skies over Iraq. He had been a young boy glued to the television news reports of those first strikes in 1991. 'I never dreamed that nearly thirty years later I'd be one of the last Squadron Commanders taking the Tornado out of service on operations,' he said on his return to RAF Marham. 'For over a third of the Royal Air Force's existence, this aircraft has been the backbone of its ground-attack fleet. We've grown up seeing it, now we've served on it, and taken it to war; there's an emotional connection. As I shut the engines down today there was a little bit of sadness as well.'[37]

The jet was not going to pass into history without an appropriate farewell, and on 14 March 2019 many hundreds of personnel associated with the Tornado, ranging in age from eighteen to over eighty, descended on RAF Marham to send it off in style.

The day began with a formal parade in front of Sir Stephen Hillier, the Chief of the Air Staff. A Tornado pilot himself, Hillier had been rushed out to Dhahran in late January 1991 as a 'battle casualty replacement' after Bob Ankerson and Simon Burgess had been brought down by their own bombs and captured by the Iraqis. He went on to fly fifteen combat sorties during the First Gulf War, then deployed on countless other operations across the region over the following years, eventually rising to the highest position in the RAF.

After the parade, a lone Tornado took off to perform one final display. Breaking a few minor aviation rules, the crew made a number of low-level passes over the cheering crowd, culminating in a screaming flypast at around 100ft and some 600mph – exactly as it would have done during the first missions of the Gulf War in 1991. Despite many of the crowd ducking, and the constant shriek of car alarms prompted by the blast of high-speed turbulence, no one complained.

'If my eyes are just a little bit glassy, it's not just down to the wind that's blowing today here at Marham ...' Air Chief Marshal Hillier told a television news crew.[38]

Later that evening, in one of the RAF's newest hangars built to house its very latest acquisition, the F35 Lightning, hundreds of Tornado men and women gathered for dinner. At one end stood a brightly lit Tornado GR4, repainted in the grey and green 1980s Cold War camouflage, and surrounded by many of the weapons it had carried over the course of its incredible lifetime. The volume of chatter among those who had served on the jet grew in direct proportion to the amount of alcohol consumed as they relived their tales of war and peace.

As the formalities drew to a close, Sir Stephen rose to his feet. He recounted his own final flight a few days earlier, when he had flown a series of flypasts over iconic Tornado sites. As he led the last formation over Tain Air Weapons Range in Scotland, the Range Safety Officer's voice could be heard on the radio.

'Tornado flight, are you ready for a message?'

'Go ahead,' Hillier replied.

'Tornado, as you depart Tain Range for the last time, can I just say what an honour and privilege it has been to serve the Tornado force over the past decades.'

The Range Officer then continued with his regulation weapons safety check.

'So Tornado – for the *final* time – I ask you to confirm you are all now *switches safe*.'

There may have been a slight crack in the Chief of the Air Staff's voice as he told the story.

'In that time-honoured way which we all know so well, the radio calls rippled up through the formation.'

'Three, switches safe.'

'Two, switches safe.'

'One, switches safe. Thank you, Tain. Tornado is en route.'

Everyone in the audience, many with tears in their eyes, knew this was the last goodbye for the faithful aircraft that had flown an astonishing 186,000 hours on combat operations.

'So tonight, at this splendid dinner,' Hillier continued, 'and in front of the Tornado force present and past, I conclude simply by echoing those words from that final flight.

'For the very last time, and for the whole Tornado force, I say, *Tornado, we are switches safe, and we are going en route.*'

Hundreds of chairs scraped back as the audience rose as one to give a lengthy standing ovation to 'The Boss', and to the aircraft they loved.

* * *

For those who have experienced the dangers, excitement, fear and loss of combat, there is a shared, inner understanding. A sense of comradeship and conviction.

This book began with an account of the twenty-fifth annual reunion of the Gulf War POWs, their colleagues, and some of the loved ones of those who had not returned. After being contacted by the author, President George H. W. Bush, the man who had set the liberation of Kuwait in motion in 1991, sent the group a personal letter:

It is with humility and pride that I send warmest greetings to all those gathered. I wish I could be with you to convey my personal respects and my gratitude; I hope you know I have never forgotten the important role you played in this multinational effort.

Too often it is said we have no heroes. Not so! We do have heroes and each one of you – aviators and soldiers of clear purpose who put service ahead of self – is a hero in the truest sense of the word. Your service and gallantry will long be remembered, and all freedom-loving peoples owe you a lasting debt of gratitude.

This United States Navy man and former Commander-in-Chief salutes you and sends you best wishes for a memorable gathering to celebrate duty, honor, and liberty.[39]

A Second World War pilot who had seen action himself, President Bush's words were warmly received. 'I would never take anything away from those who went after me,' Nick Heard said. 'But I doubt there is much to compare to that first week of the war in 1991. Night low-level operations, into the heart of incredibly heavily defended airfields. Those intense images of the domes of the triple-A we had to fly into are still imprinted on my brain.'

Coming home relatively unscathed, Mal Craghill admitted to 'enjoying' the war. 'That's not to say I don't recognise the suffering, and the loss of some close friends, but we were doing the job we were trained to do, the job we wanted to do. We were given the chance to put our hard-earned skills to the test. We did *exactly* what was asked of us – Kuwait had been liberated from enemy occupation. That was the task; that's what was done.'

Images of the war frequently appear in Gordon Buckley's mind. 'I lost some great friends and the memories are still very fresh. The guys waving us off on the first night, a Tornado on the runway in front of me going into full reheat. The incredible triple-A. Some images bring a smile to my face too, as I remember the camaraderie and excitement. Others bring sadness as the sense of loss takes over. I find that Steve Hicks' smiling face flashes up ever more regularly.'

Thirty years after the war ended, navigator Mike Toft has his own reflections on the conflict. 'What makes military people serve, fight, risk their lives? It's certainly not the money or the glory. It's not really Queen or country. In the end it's your mates, standing – flying – on your left and right. They rely on you, and you on them. We fight together, we celebrate together, and sometimes some of us die together. Being part of a unit with a combined purpose was incredible. I was part of a great force, with some exceptional friends and colleagues; a solid team flying a solid aircraft. I was very, very proud to have served alongside everyone on the Tornado.'

* * *

The legendary Tornado developed exponentially from its original design during the Cold War as a conventional and nuclear bomber to be deployed in extremis against Soviet targets. Its inventors built a machine that may not have been blessed with the beauty of the Spitfire or the rugged, imposing presence of the Lancaster, but it did have something else: stoicism, endurance and the ability to adapt to the challenges of the times, whether against a heavily defended enemy airbase filled with fighter jets, or a lone suicide bomber hiding in a mudbrick compound.

Yet the men and women who built and serviced the jet, and those who took it into the skies in peace and war, outshone its myriad technological advancements. While always part of a vast team, each was an individual – a father, son, mother or daughter prepared to give their lives for each other, and in the service of their country.

When Bill Green was killed in a Tornado accident in the build-up to the Gulf War in the summer of 1990, his son Jeremy was just a teenager. Voice cracking at times, Jeremy relived his experiences when talking with the author. 'Thirty years on, the memories of my dad are still strong. In the years after he died, I would think of him every single day. Then, late one night, I suddenly realised he hadn't come into my mind. And, as time went on, I began to realise, *I haven't thought about Dad for a couple of days now.* It was a painful, perhaps guilty, realisation that I was moving on.[40]

'For years afterwards, my sister Philippa and I would see friends enjoying time with their fathers. Perhaps learning to drive, moving home, helping with DIY. We didn't have any of that. We missed out on an important part of life's experience. On one tragic day in August 1990, everything had changed. But wherever we are in the world, the family always makes contact on the anniversary of his death to remember him, to raise a glass in celebration of a good life.

'I knew a girl at university whose father had also been killed in an RAF flying accident when she was only two years old. We had a ridiculous argument about the worst time to lose a parent. She thought *my* situation was worse as I had grown up with my dad; he was an integral part of my life when he was killed. But I thought *she* had had it far worse than me, as she had never really known her own father. She'd never experienced the love I had. I had been lucky to spend time with this amazing person; a wonderful, kind, family man. And even though our time together was cut short, I cherish every moment.

'Growing up on a Tornado base, the RAF becomes part of your life, part of your family. I knew all the jet's capabilities and its role; it was a truly amazing aircraft and I was fascinated by it as a machine. But for me, the son of a Tornado pilot and Squadron Boss, I was staggered by what the crews themselves did; their manifest love of flying, their incredible skill and expertise. Their unique bravery flying the Tornado in war – and while training during peace – was truly astonishing.

'A year after my father died, his Squadron arranged for me to have a flight in a Tornado. I think they wanted me to have a sense of what Dad's job had been; to feel a part of his life. A memory of him to hold onto. It was a truly wonderful experience and it gave me a connection to Dad; a very real sense of the excitement and exhilaration of fast-jet flying.

'In those brief moments aloft, flashing over the countryside at high speed and low level, I began to understand why my father had loved such a dangerous job, why he loved being part of a team. Why he truly loved flying the Tornado.'

Bill Green's body was never recovered after the accident, but the much-admired Squadron Commander's legacy lives on in the hearts of all who served with him. However, as Jeremy quietly made clear, the full consequences of military service affect no one more than the beloved of the fallen. 'My son William knows what his grandfather did, that he flew Tornados; that he died in a flying accident. We didn't really talk about the circumstances that much, but he obviously picked up on some of the family conversations. A few years ago, when he was around six or seven, someone asked him what he wanted for Christmas. William said he wanted a submarine, so he could go to the bottom of the North Sea to find his missing grandad.'

IN MEMORIAM 1979–2019

Pilot: Flight Lieutenant (Retd)
Russ Pengelly (BAe)
Navigator: Squadron Leader John Gray
12 June 1979 – Irish Sea
XX950 – Panavia MRCA

Pilot: Squadron Leader
Michael Stephens
27 September 1983 – Norfolk, UK
ZA586 – Tornado GR1

Pilot: Flight Lieutenant Ian Dixon
28 October 1983 – Norfolk, UK
ZA558 – Tornado GR1

Pilot: Flight Lieutenant Michael Barnard
Navigator: Flight Lieutenant John Sheen
12 December 1985 – North Sea
ZA610 – Tornado GR1

Pilot: Flight Lieutenant Steven Wright
Navigator: Flight Lieutenant John O'Shea
10 May 1988 – Berge, Germany
ZD808 – Tornado GR1

Pilot: Flight Lieutenant Colin Oliver
Navigator: Flight Lieutenant
Anthony Cook
9 August 1988 – Cumbria, UK
ZA593 – Tornado GR1

Pilot: Flight Lieutenant John Watts
Navigator: Lieutenant Ulrich Sayer GAF
9 August 1988 – Cumbria, UK
ZA329 – Tornado GR1

Pilot: Flight Lieutenant Mike Smith
Navigator: Flight Lieutenant
Alan Grieve
13 January 1989 – Wiesmoor, Germany
ZD891 – Tornado GR1

Pilot: Flight Lieutenant Stephen
'Alfie' Moir
21 July 1989 – North Sea
ZE833 – Tornado F3

Pilot: Major Dennis Wise USAF
Navigator: Flight Lieutenant
John 'Stan' Bowles
14 August 1990 – North Sea
ZA545 – Tornado GR1

Navigator: Squadron Leader
Gordon Graham
14 August 1990 – North Sea
ZA464 – Tornado GR1

Pilot: Group Captain William Green
Navigator: Squadron Leader
Neil Anderson
16 August 1990 – North Sea
ZA561 – Tornado GR1

Pilot: Flight Lieutenant Kieran Duffy
Navigator: Flight Lieutenant
Norman Dent
13 January 1991 – Masirah, Oman
ZD718 – Tornado GR1

Pilot: Wing Commander Nigel Elsdon
Navigator: Flight Lieutenant
Max Collier
17 January 1991 – Talil AFB, Iraq
ZA392 – Tornado GR1

Pilot: Squadron Leader Gary Lennox
Navigator: Squadron Leader
Adrian 'Kev' Weeks
22 January 1991 – Ar Rutbah, Iraq
ZA467 – Tornado GR1

Navigator: Flight Lieutenant
Stephen Hicks
14 February 1991 – Al Taqaddum AFB,
Iraq
ZD717 – Tornado GR1

Pilot: Flight Lieutenant Stuart Walker
Navigator: Flight Lieutenant
Nigel 'Norm' Orme
8 July 1994 – Akrotiri, Cyprus
ZH558 – Tornado F3

Pilot: Flight Lieutenant Peter Mosley
Navigator: Flight Lieutenant
Patrick Harrison
1 September 1994 – Perthshire, UK
ZG708 – Tornado GR1A

Navigator: Flight Lieutenant
Martin 'Jesse' Owens
10 March 1995 – North Sea
ZE789 – Tornado F3

Pilot: Squadron Leader
William Vivian
Navigator: Flight Lieutenant
Derek Lacey
15 June 1998 – North Sea
ZE732 – Tornado F3

Instructor Pilot: Flight Lieutenant
Greg Hurst
Student Pilot: 2 Lieutenant
Matteo Di Carlo ITAF
21 January 1999 – Nottinghamshire, UK
ZA330 – Tornado GR1

Pilot: Flight Lieutenant
Richard 'Dicky' Wright
Navigator: Flight Lieutenant
Sean Casabayo
14 October 1999 – Northumberland, UK
ZD809 – Tornado GR1

Pilot: Flight Lieutenant Kevin Main
Navigator: Flight Lieutenant
David Williams
23 March 2003 – Ali Al Salem AFB, Kuwait
ZA710 – Tornado GR4A

Navigator: Flight Lieutenant (Retd)
Mike 'Wolfie' Harland (BAe)
14 November 2007 – Norfolk, UK
ZA554 – Tornado GR4

Pilot: Flight Lieutenant
Kenneth Thompson
Navigator: Flight Lieutenant
Nigel Morton
2 July 2009 – Argyll and Bute, UK
ZE982 – Tornado F3

Pilot: Flight Lieutenant Hywel Poole
3 July 2012 – Moray Firth
ZD812 – Tornado GR4

Pilot: Flight Lieutenant Adam Sanders
Navigator: Squadron Leader
Samuel Bailey
3 July 2012 – Moray Firth
ZD743 – Tornado GR4

ENDNOTES

Major Characters

1 Data provided by Les Hendry, 31 Sqn Senior Engineering Officer.
2 Many squadrons are actually designated by Roman numerals. They are presented throughout the book in this way for ease of understanding.

Foreword

1 There had obviously been many other conflicts in the region, perhaps most notable between Iraq and Iran. But this phraseology is regularly used in the media.
2 The extracts have been edited and abridged from Sir John Major's full speech delivered that night.
3 'Defence Estimates' 1989; some of the total number included new aircraft replacing those being phased out so the actual figure of aircraft at the time was around 2,000.
4 Operation Desert Storm was the international codename for the mission. The British codename was 'Operation Granby'.
5 The date of the start of the conflict is variously described as both 16 and 17 January. When the first attacks commenced in the early hours of what was 17 January in the region, it was still 16 January in America. Hence the disparity.
6 There were two female American POWs but they were not at the reunion.
7 The extracts have been edited and abridged from Michael Fallon's full speech at the dinner.
8 At the time, the RAF had no female aircrew on combat operations.

Prologue: Seven Seconds

1 Robbie Stewart, private diary and John Nichol interview.
2 Pablo Mason, *Pablo's War* (Bloomsbury, 1992).
3 Dave Waddington, John Nichol interview.
4 National Defense University Washington DC Research

Directorate; Daniel K. Malone, 'Roland: A Case For or Against NATO Standardization?' (May 1980).

5 John Peters and John Nichol, *Team Tornado* (Michael Joseph, 1994).

6 Memories about the exact value and number of the sovereigns vary.

7 John Peters and John Nichol, *Team Tornado* (Michael Joseph, 1994).

8 Charles Allen, *Thunder and Lightning* (HMSO, 1991).

9 The figure for the wartime maximum-all-up weight of the aircraft varies between publications and individual memories.

10 John Peters and John Nichol, *Tornado Down* (Michael Joseph, 1992).

11 Michael Napier, *Tornado Over the Tigris* (Pen and Sword, 2015).

12 Ibid.

13 Michael Napier, *Tornado GR1: An Operational History* (Pen and Sword, 2017).

14 Peters and Nichol, *Team Tornado*, op. cit.

15 Ibid.

16 Aeronautica Difesa (Iraq 1990).

17 Napier, *Tornado Over the Tigris*, op. cit.

18 *Air Power Review: First Gulf War 25th Anniversary* (RAF, 2016).

19 Although 'parallel track' formations were meant to be standard across the Tornado force, differing separations were used depending on the mission or individual squadron tactics. These distances and timings are approximate.

20 Tange Stewart's letter is edited for brevity and clarity.

21 Events reconstructed from Stewart/ Waddington personal accounts and the Tornado Cockpit Voice Recorder recovered from their crash site.

Chapter One: The Birth of 'The Fin'

1 Robbie Stewart, private diary and John Nichol interview.

2 *Department of Defense Dictionary of Military and Associated Terms* (2001).

3 Ian Black, *RAF Tornado: Owners' Workshop Manual* (Haynes, 2014).

4 Ibid.

5 Napier, *Tornado GR1*, op. cit.

6 Black, *Owners' Workshop Manual*, op. cit.

7 Ibid.

8 Ian Hall, *Tornado Boys* (Grub Street, 2016).

9 Black, *Owners' Workshop Manual*, op. cit.

10 Ibid.

11 BAE Systems Tornado First Flight 1974: https://www.youtube.com/ watch?v=yIFul_xyP38

12 Jeffrey Quill, *Spitfire: A Test Pilot's Story* (Crecy Classic, 1983).

13 Hall, *Tornado Boys*, op. cit.

14 United Press International report, October 1984.

15 Dave Waddington, John Nichol interview.

16 *Superjet: Secrets of the Tornado*, Forces TV, 2019.

17 Black, *Owners' Workshop Manual*, op. cit.

18 Ibid.

19 Napier, *Tornado GR1*, op. cit.

20 Peters and Nichol, *Team Tornado*, op. cit.

21 Ibid.

22 Ibid.

23 Napier, *Tornado Over the Tigris*, op. cit.

24 Ibid.

25 Peters and Nichol, *Team Tornado*, op. cit.

26 Napier, *Tornado GR1*, op. cit.

27 Black, *Owners' Workshop Manual*, op. cit.

28 *Hansard*, House of Commons, 25 July 1990.

Chapter Two: The Gathering Storm

1 Alastair Finlan, *The Gulf War 1991* (Osprey Publishing, 2003).
2 Ibid.
3 Margaret Thatcher Foundation: https://www.margaretthatcher.org/
4 Ibid.
5 Norman Schwarzkopf, *It Doesn't Take a Hero* (Bantam, 1992).
6 Robbie Stewart, private diary and John Nichol interview.
7 Tange Stewart, John Nichol interview.
8 Kirsty Murphy (née Stewart), John Nichol interview.
9 Stan Morse, *Gulf Air War Debrief* (Aerospace Publishing, 1991).
10 Allen, *Thunder and Lightning*, op. cit.
11 Ibid.
12 Ibid.
13 Ibid.
14 Ibid.
15 Dave Waddington, John Nichol interview.
16 Bob Ankerson, personal account and John Nichol interview.
17 Chris Ankerson, John Nichol interview.
18 Gordon Buckley, personal account and John Nichol interview.
19 Mike Toft, personal account and John Nichol interview.
20 Pete Batson, John Nichol interview.
21 https://assets.publishing. service.gov.uk/government/ uploads/system/uploads/ attachment_data/file/530766/ Army_FOI_2016_77154___ Number_of_Iraqi_cadets_ trained_in_Britain_from_1992_ to_1988_plus_5_Iraqi_officers_ staff_training_1970_and_1980.pdf
22 Peters and Nichol, *Tornado Down*, op. cit.
23 Military Aircraft Accident Summary, 1990: http://www. ukserials.com/pdflosses/ maas_19900814_za464_za545.pdf
24 David Bellamy, private diary and John Nichol interview.
25 RAF Laarbruch Station Magazine, September 1990. Edited for clarity.
26 Jenny Green, John Nichol interview.
27 Jeremy Green, John Nichol interview.
28 Military Aircraft Accident Report: http://www.tornado-data.com/ Production/MAAS%20Reports/ ZA561.pdf
29 Ibid.
30 Bob Ankerson, personal account and John Nichol interview.
31 Black, *Owners' Workshop Manual*, op. cit.
32 Finlan, *The Gulf War 1991*, op. cit.

Chapter Three: 'Everything's Changed'

1 Precise numbers varied across the squadrons.
2 Mike Toft, personal account and John Nichol interview.
3 Nigel Risdale, personal account and John Nichol interview.
4 Peters and Nichol, *Tornado Down*, op. cit.
5 Ibid.
6 Allen, *Thunder and Lightning*, op. cit.
7 Ibid.
8 Gordon Buckley, personal account and John Nichol interview.
9 *Royal Air Force Historical Society Journal* 32 (MOD, 2004).
10 *Air Power Review*, op. cit.
11 Some very basic handheld GPS systems were available but they were not integrated into the Tornado navigation system.
12 Some NVGs (night-vision goggles) were in theatre by this time. But no crews were properly trained on

them and, in general, they were not compatible with the cockpit lighting, or with the ejection seat system and low-level combat operations. Some pilots did have a set but they were not in operational use.

13 Paddy Teakle, correspondence with John Nichol and his personal account, edited for clarity.

14 Nigel Risdale, personal diary and John Nichol interview.

15 Information supplied by Rob McCarthy, who took part in the flight.

16 Schwarzkopf, *It Doesn't Take a Hero*, op. cit.

17 Ibid.

18 John Major, *The Autobiography* (HarperCollins, 1999).

19 Ed Herlik, *Separated by War: An Oral History by Desert Storm Fliers and Their Families* (Tab Aero, 1994).

20 Peters and Nichol, *Tornado Down*, op. cit.

21 Kirsty Murphy (née Stewart), John Nichol interview.

22 Tange Stewart, John Nichol interview.

23 Napier, *Tornado GR1*, op. cit.

24 Finlan, *The Gulf War 1991*, op. cit.

25 Schwarzkopf, *It Doesn't Take a Hero*, op. cit.

26 Major, *The Autobiography*, op. cit.

27 Mike Toft, John Nichol interview.

28 Mark Paisey, personal diary and John Nichol interview.

29 Chris Ankerson, John Nichol interview.

30 Allen, *Thunder and Lightning*, op. cit.

31 Finlan, *The Gulf War 1991*, op. cit.

32 John Broadbent, personal account and correspondence with John Nichol.

33 Major, *The Autobiography*, op. cit.

34 Allen, *Thunder and Lightning*, op. cit.

35 Finlan, *The Gulf War 1991*, op. cit.

36 Major, *The Autobiography*, op. cit.

37 Opening Statement, James A. Baker, Senate Foreign Relations Committee, 19 May 2010.

38 Napier, *Tornado GR1*, op. cit.

39 Michael Napier, *Blue Diamonds* (Pen and Sword, 2015).

40 Allen, *Thunder and Lightning*, op. cit.

41 Napier, *Blue Diamonds*, op. cit.

42 Allen, *Thunder and Lightning*, op. cit.

43 John Nichol interview.

44 Letter from Mark Paisey to his mother dated 13 January. Edited for brevity and clarity.

45 Morse, *Gulf Air War Debrief*, op. cit.

Chapter Four: The Wolfpack

1 David Bellamy, personal diary and John Nichol interview.

2 These official figures vary according to sources.

3 Gordon Buckley, personal account and John Nichol interview.

4 Not all these missiles 'locked' – this term is used for ease of reading.

5 Morse, *Gulf Air War Debrief*, op. cit.

6 Mal Craghill, personal account and John Nichol interview.

7 Gordon Buckley, personal account and John Nichol interview.

8 Ibid.

9 This is an edited and condensed version of the actual signal (supplied by 9 Sqn Historian, Sqn Ldr Dicky James) to ensure it is more easily understood.

10 Peters and Nichol, *Tornado Down*, op. cit.

11 Jerry Witts' account is constructed and edited from: *Thunder and Lightning* (Allen), the *RAF Yearbook Special: Air War in the*

Gulf (IAT Publishing, 1991) and *Tornado GR1* (Napier). There are some discrepancies in the various accounts; resolved here as far as possible.

12 Allen, *Thunder and Lightning*, edited for brevity.

13 Schwarzkopf, *It Doesn't Take a Hero*, op. cit.

14 The Operations Room: Desert Storm – The Air War Day One (2020): https://www.youtube.com/watch?v=zxRgfBXn6Mg&feature=youtu.be

15 Nick Heard, personal account and John Nichol interview.

16 *Air Power Review*, op. cit.

17 Allen, *Thunder and Lightning*, op. cit.

18 Ibid.

19 Jerry Witts.

20 Major, *The Autobiography*, op. cit.

21 Morse, *Gulf Air War Debrief*, op. cit.

22 The Operations Room: Desert Storm – The Air War Day One, op. cit.

23 This is a slightly different time to the 'H-Hour' which is when the mass attacks occurred, and is cited by Norman Schwarzkopf as the opening shots of the war.

24 The Operations Room: Desert Storm – The Air War Day One, op. cit.

25 Morse, *Gulf Air War Debrief*, op. cit.

26 The Operations Room: Desert Storm – The Air War Day One, op. cit.

27 Nigel Risdale, personal account and John Nichol interview.

28 Mission Report, supplied by John Broadbent.

29 Paddy Teakle, John Nichol interview.

30 Napier, *Tornado Over the Tigris*, op. cit.

31 There were also a couple of reports by crews who attacked in TFR mode that, when the canisters jettisoned, they experienced a TFR pull-up over the target.

32 Allen, *Thunder and Lightning*, op. cit.

33 The Operations Room: Desert Storm – The Air War Day One, op. cit.

34 Jerry Witts.

35 Mike Warren, quoted in Allen, *Thunder and Lightning*, op cit.

36 Paddy Teakle's account is collated from *Separated by War* (Herlik), correspondence with John Nichol, and Forces TV documentary *Air War in the Gulf*.

37 Peters and Nichol, *Tornado Down*, op. cit.

Chapter Five: Gin-clear Skies

1 Herlik, *Separated by War*, op. cit.

2 Dave Waddington, John Nichol interview.

3 Robbie Stewart, private diary and John Nichol interview.

4 The full text of the letter has been edited and abbreviated for clarity.

5 Nick Heard, personal account and John Nichol interview.

6 Gordon Buckley, John Nichol interview.

7 Mike Toft, personal account and John Nichol interview.

8 Mark Paisey, personal diary and John Nichol interview.

9 *Air Power Review*, op. cit.

10 Peters and Nichol, *Tornado Down*, op. cit. Some detail has been edited for clarity and continuity. Some further reflections have been added by John Nichol.

11 Mason, *Pablo's War*, op. cit. Some detail edited and abridged for clarity.

12 Morse, *Gulf Air War Debrief*, op. cit.

13 Mason, *Pablo's War*, op. cit.

14 Peters and Nichol, *Tornado Down*, op. cit.

15 Individual recollections of the final moments of attack differ slightly. Resolved as far as possible here.

16 Peters and Nichol, *Tornado Down*, op. cit.

17 Mason, *Pablo's War*, op. cit.

18 Peters and Nichol, *Tornado Down*, op. cit.

19 Mason, *Pablo's War*, op. cit.

20 *Hansard*, House of Commons, 1991.

21 Tange Stewart, John Nichol interview.

22 Kirsty Murphy (née Stewart), John Nichol interview and personal notes.

23 Herlik, *Separated by War*, op. cit.

24 Peters and Nichol, *Tornado Down*, op. cit.

Chapter Six: 'My God, We've Lost Another One'

1 Peters and Nichol, *Tornado Down*, op. cit.

2 The DetCo had actually used Nichol's correct name 'Adrian' but, for ease of explanation, 'John' is used in the text.

3 David Bellamy, private diary and John Nichol interview.

4 Pete Batson, personal account and John Nichol interview.

5 Morse, *Gulf Air War Debrief*, op. cit.

6 Robbie Stewart, private diary and John Nichol interview.

7 Dave Waddington, John Nichol interview.

8 Peters and Nichol, *Tornado Down*, op. cit.

9 Allen, *Thunder and Lightning*, op. cit.

10 Ibid.

11 Morse, *Gulf Air War Debrief*, op. cit.

12 Allen, *Thunder and Lightning*, op. cit.

13 It was not clear what this missile was – but every possibility had to be countered.

14 Batson was given information later that it was a Mirage F1EQ multi-role jet, optimised for both ground-attack and air defence operations.

15 Allen, *Thunder and Lightning*, op. cit.

16 This is an edited and abbreviated version of the full letter.

17 Berenice Waddington, John Nichol interview.

18 Peters and Nichol, *Tornado Down*, op. cit.

Chapter Seven: 'The Bad Stuff'

1 Peters and Nichol, *Tornado Down*, op. cit. Some quotes edited for brevity and this is a condensed account of their interrogation.

2 Morse, *Gulf Air War Debrief*, op. cit.

3 Peters and Nichol, *Tornado Down*, op. cit.

4 Schwarzkopf, *It Doesn't Take a Hero*, op. cit.

5 Allen, *Thunder and Lightning*, op. cit. Some quotes edited for brevity.

6 Morse, *Gulf Air War Debrief*, op. cit.

7 'Halabja: Survivors talk about horror of attack, continuing ordeal', *Ekurd Daily*, 2008 – edited for brevity.

8 Allen, *Thunder and Lightning*, op. cit.

9 Ibid.

10 Schwarzkopf, *It Doesn't Take a Hero*, op. cit.

11 Ibid.

12 Jim Corrigan, *Desert Storm Air War: The Aerial Campaign Against Saddam's Iraq in the 1991 Gulf War* (Rowman & Littlefield, 2017).

13 Mal Craghill, personal account and John Nichol interview.

14 It later transpired that the airman had suffered from a tonic-clonic seizure – a form of epileptic fit.

15 Dean Wood, private diary and John Nichol interview.

16 There are differing accounts of the exact words. This is Craghill's version.

17 Allen, *Thunder and Lightning*, op. cit.

Chapter Eight: 'Please Let Him Be Dead'

1 Letter abbreviated and edited for clarity.

2 Robbie Stewart, personal account and John Nichol interview.

3 Dave Waddington, John Nichol interview.

4 Kirsty Murphy (née Stewart), John Nichol interview.

5 Tange Stewart, John Nichol interview.

6 Berenice Waddington, John Nichol interview.

7 Reported in the *Evening Chronicle*, 19 January 1991.

8 Ibid.

9 TV News Pool report from 19 January.

10 *We Were There – Tornado Force*, Forces TV, 2015.

Chapter Nine: The Mission from Hell

1 *Royal Air Force Historical Society Journal* 32, op. cit.

2 Allen, *Thunder and Lightning*, op. cit. Some quotes edited for clarity.

3 Ibid.

4 Nigel Risdale, personal account and John Nichol interview.

5 Nick Heard, personal account and John Nichol interview.

6 Herlik, *Separated by War*, op. cit.

7 Transcript of Teakle's tape reproduced in Herlik, *Separated by War*. Dialogue edited here for clarity.

8 The cockpit recording of the attack showed that the radalt had 'unlocked' which happens at 100ft – it is unclear what height the crew actually bottomed out at.

9 'Attack on Ubaydah Bin Al Jarrah Airfield – 20 Jan 91', Mission Report, supplied by John Broadbent.

10 *RAF Yearbook Special: Air War in the Gulf*, op. cit.

11 General Sir Peter de la Billière, *Storm Command: A Personal Account of the Gulf War* (Harper Collins, 1992).

12 'British Fliers Suffering Higher Rate of Losses', Kim Murphy and Douglas Frantz, *Los Angeles Times*, 1991.

13 Clearly, in darkness, the Iraqi gunners could not actually 'see' the Tornados.

14 *Los Angeles Times*, op. cit.

Chapter Ten: Broadcast or Die

1 David Bellamy, private diary and John Nichol interview.

2 Con Coughlin, *Daily Telegraph*, January 1991.

3 *Royal Air Force Historical Society Journal* 32, op. cit.

4 Cliff Spink, John Nichol interview.

5 Mike Heath's account was retrieved from: http://www.ejectorseats.co.uk/tornado_down.html in June 2019. The website is no longer active.

6   Tornado FRC Ejection card – edited for brevity and clarity.

7   Report on the Engineering Investigation into the Accident of Tornado GR1 ZD893, Ministry of Defence, 1991. Supplied by Pete Batson.

8   Dave Waddington, John Nichol interview.

9   Robbie Stewart, private diary and John Nichol interview.

10 Peters and Nichol, *Tornado Down*, op. cit. Edited for brevity.

11 Interview is an edited account of the full version.

12 *Financial Times*, January 1991.

13 Major, *The Autobiography*, op. cit.

14 *Financial Times*, January 1991

15 Berenice Waddington, John Nichol interview.

16 *Daily Record*, January 1991.

17 *Evening Standard*, January 1991.

Chapter Eleven: 'Stay With It!'

1   Some personnel had practised 'level' bombing techniques from medium altitude, but they were few and far between. The Tornado could actually perform 'dive bombing' from that height which could be remarkably accurate and a few missions were conducted. But a heavily laden jet, rapidly descending into heavy triple-A, was not something many wanted to try.

2   The name of this target appears differently in some documents.

3   The Tornado had a couple of other weapons at its disposal, but none were suitable for this environment. There was a proposal to use cluster bombs against some targets but plans did not evolve.

4   This is a very basic explanation of the Tornado weapons system.

5   Herlik, *Separated by War*, op. cit.

6   Author's italics.

7   Corrigan, *Desert Storm Air War*, op. cit.

8   http://aviateurs.e-monsite.com/pages/1946-et-annees-suivantes/premiere-mission-jaguar-sur-le-koweit.html

9   Allen, *Thunder and Lightning*, op. cit.

10 Mike Toft, personal account and John Nichol interview.

11 Mark Paisey, personal account.

12 Mason, *Pablo's War*, op. cit. Some quotes edited for brevity.

13 Mission Report, supplied by John Broadbent.

14 Gareth Ankerson, personal account and John Nichol interview.

15 Chris Ankerson, John Nichol interview.

16 Bob Ankerson, personal account and John Nichol interview.

17 *The Times*, January 1991.

18 *The Sun*, January 1991.

19 *Daily Express*, January 1991.

20 Nick Heard, personal account and John Nichol interview.

21 Anthony Cordesman, *Iraq and the War of Sanctions: Conventional Threats and Weapons of Mass Destruction* (Praeger, 1999).

22 Napier, *Tornado GR1*, op. cit.

23 'Statement on the Loss of RAF Tornado Aircraft in Combat during the Conduct of Air Operations against Iraq'. This was the official brief given by the RAF in 1991.

24 Dean Wood, private diary and John Nichol interview.

25 John Nichol interview, *BBC Breakfast*, 2001.

26 The 20 Squadron official Gulf War history: https://sites.google.com/site/raflaarbruch/home/laarbruch-squadrons/no-20-squadron/20-sqn-history-whilst-at-laarbruch

27 Allen, *Thunder and Lightning*, op. cit.

28 Major, *The Autobiography*, op. cit.

29 *The Gulf War*, BBC, 1996.

30 *Royal Air Force Historical Society Journal 32*, op. cit.

31 Al Byford, personal account.

32 Mission Report, supplied by John Broadbent.

33 Graham Pitchfork, *The Buccaneer Boys* (Grub Street, 2013).

34 Allen, *Thunder and Lightning*, op. cit.

35 Pitchfork, *The Buccaneer Boys*, op. cit.

36 Allen, *Thunder and Lightning*, op. cit.

37 Pitchfork, *The Buccaneer Boys*, op. cit.

38 Ibid.

39 The account of this mission is constructed from: Bob Ankerson's private account and John Nichol interview; RAFC Cranwell 20th Anniversary of Operation Granby commemorative brochure; Ankerson/Burgess Cockpit Voice Recorder tape; Gordon Thorburn, *A Century of Air Warfare with Nine (IX) Squadron, RAF* (Pen and Sword, 2014).

40 Ibid.

41 Dialogue constructed from the recovered 'black box' Cockpit Voice Recorder from their aircraft and from Ankerson's personal testimony.

42 Thorburn, *A Century of Air Warfare*, op. cit.

43 Gareth's account is constructed from a school essay he later wrote about his experiences, and his interview with John Nichol.

44 The on-base 'supermarket', the Navy Army and Air Force Institution.

Chapter Twelve: A Bolshie Lady

1 Morse, *Gulf Air War Debrief*, op. cit.

2 Schwarzkopf, *It Doesn't Take a Hero*, op. cit.

3 *Los Angeles Times*, January 1991.

4 Cliff Spink, John Nichol interview.

5 This is a very basic explanation of a very complex and technologically advanced process.

6 The actual phrase used was 'event'.

7 Black, *Owners' Workshop Manual*, op. cit.

8 John Godden, *Shield and Storm* (Brassey's, 1994). Some quotes edited for clarity.

9 Schwarzkopf, *It Doesn't Take a Hero*, op. cit.

10 The senior commander asked not to be named, or the base identified, in order to protect the person involved.

11 John Broadbent, correspondence and interviews with John Nichol.

12 Nigel Risdale, personal account and John Nichol interview.

13 Professor Gordon Turnbull, *Trauma* (Corgi, 2011). Frank's account is constructed from Turnbull's writings on the case. Some details have been edited and disguised.

14 Ibid. Some quotes edited for clarity.

15 Chris Ankerson, John Nichol interview.

16 Gareth Ankerson, personal account and John Nichol interview.

17 Tange Stewart, personal account and John Nichol interview.

18 *Air Power Review*, op. cit.

19 Pitchfork, *The Buccaneer Boys*, op. cit. Some quotes edited for clarity.

20 Mike Toft, John Nichol interview.

21 This is a very simplified explanation of laser-guided bombing – the actual practice was far more complex and required close co-ordination.

22 Turnbull, *Trauma*, op. cit. Quotes edited for clarity and brevity.

23 Di Evans, correspondence with

John Nichol – quotes edited for clarity.

24 *Daily Express*, January 1991.
25 Kirsty Murphy (née Stewart), John Nichol interview.
26 Berenice Waddington, John Nichol interview.
27 Mike Toft, personal account and John Nichol interview.
28 Allen, *Thunder and Lightning*, op. cit. Some quotes edited for clarity.
29 Ibid.
30 Ibid.
31 Pitchfork, *The Buccaneer Boys*, op. cit.
32 Allen, *Thunder and Lightning*, op. cit.
33 Ibid.
34 *Daily Express*, February 1991.
35 Gordon Buckley, personal account and John Nichol interview.
36 Robbie Stewart, private diary and John Nichol interview.

Chapter Thirteen: 'Missile Launch!'

1 Napier, *Tornado GR1*, op. cit.
2 Mal Craghill, personal account and John Nichol interview.
3 This is just a précis of the various indications on the RHWR.
4 Robbie Stewart, private diary and John Nichol interview.
5 Dave Waddington, John Nichol interview.
6 Bob Ankerson, personal account and John Nichol interview.
7 Mike Toft, personal account and interview with John Nichol.
8 Allen, *Thunder and Lightning*, op. cit.
9 John Broadbent, correspondence and interview with John Nichol.
10 Tony Gallagher, *Daily Mail*, February 1991.
11 Ian Henry, *Sunday Express*, and Allen, *Thunder and Lightning*, op. cit.

12 Napier, *Tornado GR1*, op. cit.
13 It was never completely established which Tornado formation, if any, might have been involved; indeed, there had been suggestions that some incidents like this might have been caused by failed Iraqi ground-to-air missile systems, though this seems unlikely. Information on this incident gathered from various crews in the region and from: https://www.hrw.org/reports/1991/gulfwar/CHAP3.htm#P141_23985. There are conflicting reports about the exact date and the number of casualties. There is no doubt an incident occurred.
14 Again, there are conflicting accounts and memories. There is little doubt that at least one bomb could have hit the marketplace.
15 Ed Vulliamy, 'Limbs and lives blasted away by allied bombs,' *The Guardian*, 3 May 1991.
16 Morse, *Gulf Air War Debrief*, op. cit.
17 Mason, *Pablo's War*, op. cit.
18 John Broadbent, John Nichol interview.
19 Nick Heard, personal account and John Nichol interview.
20 Martin Bowman, *Jet Wars in the Nuclear Age: 1972 to the Present Day* (Pen and Sword Aviation, 2016). Some quotes edited for clarity. This account is constructed from various sources.
21 One 1,000lb LGB had actually remained stuck on the rail.
22 Nick Heard, personal account and John Nichol interview.
23 Mason, *Pablo's War*, op. cit.
24 Bowman, *Jet Wars in the Nuclear Age*, op. cit.
25 Ibid.
26 'Pilot tells of escape from Tornado blaze', *Daily Telegraph*, 11 March 1991.
27 Ibid.

28 Ibid, and Bowman, *Jet Wars in the Nuclear Age*, op. cit.

29 Ian Henry, *Sunday Express*, 17 February 1991 – edited for brevity.

30 Gordon Buckley, personal account and John Nichol interview.

31 *Los Angeles Times*, February 1991.

32 Ibid.

33 Ibid.

34 Ibid.

35 Morse, *Gulf Air War Debrief*, op. cit.

36 Peters and Nichol, *Tornado Down*, op. cit.

37 *Sunday Express*, 5 January 1992

38 Schwarzkopf, *It Doesn't Take a Hero*, op. cit.

39 United Press International, February 1991.

Chapter Fourteen: Terminate the Wolfpack

1 Mike Toft, personal account and John Nichol interview.

2 Napier, *Tornado GR1*, op. cit.

3 David Bellamy, private diary and John Nichol interview.

4 Turnbull, *Trauma*, op. cit. Some passages edited for brevity.

5 Peters and Nichol, *Tornado Down*, op. cit.

6 Robbie Stewart, private diary and John Nichol interview.

7 Bob Ankerson, RAF Police interview 1993, and John Nichol interview.

8 Schwarzkopf, *It Doesn't Take a Hero*, op. cit.

9 Morse, *Gulf Air War Debrief*, op. cit.

10 Schwarzkopf, *It Doesn't Take a Hero*, op. cit.

11 Allen, *Thunder and Lightning*, op. cit.

12 Morse, *Gulf Air War Debrief*, op. cit.

13 Ibid.

14 *Daily Express*, February 1991.

15 20 Squadron official Gulf War history, op. cit.

16 *New York Times*, March 1991.

17 *RAF Yearbook Special: Air War in the Gulf*, op. cit.

18 Allen, *Thunder and Lightning*, op. cit. – edited for clarity.

19 John Major Archives: www.johnmajorarchive.org.uk

20 Chris Ankerson, John Nichol interview.

21 Tange Stewart, John Nichol interview.

22 Berenice Waddington, John Nichol interview.

23 Gareth Ankerson, personal account and John Nichol interview.

24 Peters and Nichol, *Tornado Down*, op. cit.

25 Schwarzkopf, *It Doesn't Take a Hero*, op. cit.

26 *Evening Chronicle*, March 1991. The newspaper actually used Nichol's Christian name 'Adrian'.

27 *News of the World*, March 1991.

28 Peters and Nichol, *Tornado Down*, op. cit.

Chapter Fifteen: Going Home

1 Gordon Buckley, personal account and John Nichol interview.

2 Peters and Nichol, *Team Tornado*, op. cit.

3 Robbie Stewart, private diary and John Nichol interview.

4 Ibid.

5 Turnbull, *Trauma*, op. cit.

6 Allen, *Thunder and Lightning*, op. cit.

7 Ibid.

8 Eric V. Larson, *Misfortunes of War: Press and Public Reactions to Civilian Deaths in Wartime* (Rand Corporation, 2007).

9 Finlan, *The Gulf War 1991*, op. cit.

Edited quotes. Using her American passport, Dina actually managed to escape Kuwait before the war started.

10 Mal Craghill, personal account and John Nichol interview.

11 Around 7,000 in total served in the region during the crisis.

12 *RAF Yearbook Special: Air War in the Gulf*, op. cit. Slightly different figures appear in other publications.

13 Allen, *Thunder and Lightning*, op. cit. Edited quote.

14 Peters and Nichol, *Tornado Down*, op. cit.

15 Tange Stewart, John Nichol interview.

16 Kirsty Murphy (née Stewart), John Nichol interview.

17 Figures vary depending on the publication consulted. These are amalgamated from the *RAF Yearbook Special* (1991) and *Gulf Air War Debrief* (Morse).

18 Allen, *Thunder and Lightning*, op. cit.

19 Ibid. Edited quote.

20 Peters and Nichol, *Tornado Down*, op. cit.

21 James Baker III, *Los Angeles Times*, 1996.

22 Schwarzkopf, *It Doesn't Take a Hero*, op. cit.

23 Major, *The Autobiography*, op. cit.

24 *Los Angeles Times*, 4 March 1991.

25 Allen, *Thunder and Lightning*, op. cit. Edited for clarity.

26 Dean Wood, private diary and John Nichol interview.

27 Nigel Risdale, personal account and John Nichol interview.

28 http://www.lannpydar.org.uk/steval/raf%20links.html

29 *Laarbruch Listener* Magazine, May 1991 – edited for brevity and clarity.

Epilogue: 'Our Story Had Come Full Circle'

1 Gordon Buckley, personal account and John Nichol interview.

2 Peters and Nichol, *Team Tornado*, op. cit.

3 Jeremy Green, John Nichol interview.

4 Jenny Green, private diary and John Nichol interview.

5 Anne Lennox, John Nichol interview, 'Gulf War, Changed Lives', *BBC Breakfast*, 2000. Edited quotes.

6 Mal Craghill, personal account and John Nichol interview.

7 Military Air Accident Summary, 14 May 1998.

8 RAF Ex-POW Association Newsletter No. 60, 1996.

9 Ibid. Edited quote.

10 *Daily Telegraph* obituary, 24 July 2012.

11 Kirsty Murphy (née Stewart), John Nichol interview.

12 Black, *Owners' Workshop Manual*, op. cit.

13 Paddy Teakle, 'No Ordinary Job: A Personal Perspective', published in *Air Power Review* (RAF, 2018). Edited quotes.

14 *The Gulf War*, BBC, 1996 (author's italics).

15 *The Guardian*, 6 March 2001.

16 https://www.justgiving.com/fundraising/heathy

17 https://www.pprune.org/military-aviation/366836-5-marathons-5-days-memory-late-avm-mike-heath.html

18 Ibid.

19 https://www.pprune.org/military-aviation/315261-co-pilot-michael-warren-dies-during-plane-flight.html

20 *Daily Mail*, 25 February 2008.

21 Mal Craghill, correspondence with John Nichol.

22 US Department of Defense: www.
    defense.gov/casualty.pdf
23 Ministry of Defence: www.gov.uk/
    government/fields-of-operation/iraq
24 https://www.bbc.co.uk/news/
    world-middle-east-11107739
25 BBC News, March 2013.
26 Dave Bellamy, personal account and
    John Nichol interview.
27 *Daily Telegraph* obituary, 24 July
    2012.
28 'Tornado: In Memoriam 1979–
    2019', document produced by Wing
    Commander Gary Coleman.
29 John Nichol – Flying Authorisers
    Course, 1994.
30 Deborah Haynes and Sam Coates,
    The Times, November 1991.
31 *RAF Yearbook Special*, op. cit.
    Edited quotes.
32 This section constructed from the
    Telegraph and *Times* obituaries,
    July 2020.
33 John Gillespie Magee Jr (1922–
    1941), August 1941.
34 *Daily Telegraph*, 5 February 2019.
35 Craig Hoyle, FlightGlobal,
    November 2014, and: https://

www.edrmagazine.eu/
the-end-of-tornado-gr-4-role-in-
op-shader-tornado-gr-4-retirement-
its-effect-on-the-air-war-on-terror.
There are some conflictions
regarding the precise numbers of
casualties and dates of final strikes.
RAF Typhoons and Reaper UAVs
were responsible for the other
deaths.
36 BBC News, January 2019.
37 Forces TV, Ministry of Defence,
    2019.
38 Sir Stephen Hillier, correspondence
    with John Nichol.
39 Letter to John Nichol from
    President George H. W. Bush.
    Edited contents.
40 Jeremy Green, John Nichol
    interview.

In Memoriam

1 Information taken from 'Tornado:
   In Memoriam 1979–2019',
   document produced by Wing
   Commander Gary Coleman.

BIBLIOGRAPHY

BOOKS

Allen, Charles, *Thunder and Lightning* (HMSO, 1991)

Black, Ian, *RAF Tornado: Owners' Workshop Manual* (Haynes, 2014)

Bowman, Martin, *Jet Wars in the Nuclear Age: 1972 to the Present Day* (Pen and Sword Aviation, 2016)

Cordesman, Anthony, *Iraq and the War of Sanctions: Conventional Threats and Weapons of Mass Destruction* (Praeger, 1999)

Corrigan, Jim, *Desert Storm Air War: The Aerial Campaign Against Saddam's Iraq in the 1991 Gulf War* (Rowman & Littlefield, 2017)

Crawford, Neta, *Costs of War* (Brown University's Watson Institute for International and Public Affairs, 2001)

de la Billière, General Sir Peter, *Storm Command: A Personal Account of the Gulf War* (HarperCollins, 1992)

Finlan, Alastair, *The Gulf War 1991* (Osprey Publishing, 2003)

GEC Ferranti, *TIALD – The Gulf War* (GEC Ferranti Defence Systems Ltd, 1991)

Godden, John, *Shield and Storm* (Brassey's, 1994)

Hall, Ian, *Tornado Boys* (Grub Street, 2016)

Herlik, Edward C., *Separated by War: An Oral History by Desert Storm Fliers and Their Families* (Tab Aero, 1994)

Herriot, David, *The Tornado Years* (Pen and Sword, 2019)

Larson, Eric V., *Misfortunes of War: Press and Public Reactions to Civilian Deaths in Wartime* (Rand Corporation, 2007)

Major, John, *The Autobiography* (HarperCollins, 1999)

Mason, Pablo, *Pablo's War* (Bloomsbury, 1992)

Morse, Stan, *Gulf Air War Debrief* (Aerospace Publishing, 1991)

Napier, Michael, *Blue Diamonds* (Pen and Sword, 2015)

Napier, Michael, *Tornado Over the Tigris* (Pen and Sword, 2015)

Napier, Michael, *Tornado GR1: An Operational History* (Pen and Sword, 2017)

Peters, John and Nichol, John, *Tornado Down* (Michael Joseph, 1992)

Peters, John and Nichol, John, *Team Tornado* (Michael Joseph, 1994)

Pitchfork, Graham, *Buccaneer Boys* (Grub Street, 2013)

Quill, Jeffrey, *Spitfire: A Test Pilot's Story* (Crecy Classic, 1983)

Schwarzkopf, Norman, *It Doesn't Take a Hero* (Bantam, 1992)

Thorburn, Gordon, *A Century of Air Warfare with Nine (IX) Squadron RAF* (Pen and Sword, 2014)

Turnbull, Professor Gordon, *Trauma* (Corgi, 2011)

MAGAZINES

Air Power Review: First Gulf War 25th Anniversary (RAF, 2016)

RAF Yearbook Special: Air War in the Gulf (IAT Publishing, 1991)

Tornado GR 1974–2019 (Air Media Centre, HQ Air Command, 2019)

PICTURE CREDITS

Integrated

pp. x–xi map © Liane Payne

p. xv Tornado GR1 © Berry Vissers / Squadron Prints Ltd

pp. 425–6 Tornado GR1 and Tornado F3 © Berry Vissers / Squadron Prints Ltd

RAF squadron crests reproduced with permission of the MOD

Plate sections

1. Tornado test flight: Rob McCarthy; Tornado cockpit © Simon Whittaker
2. Ankersons: Bob Ankerson; Toft and Paisey: Mike Toft; Tornado © Ian Black
3. Bellamy and Roche: Dave Bellamy; John Major: David Ailano; Waddington and Stewart: Robbie Stewart
4. Murharraq formation: John Broadbent; RAF Laarbruch: John Nichol
5. Refuelling: Wilbur Wilson via Les Hendry Dhahran archive; engineers: Andy White
6. Bill and Jenny Green: Jenny Green; Teakle and Buckley: Gordon Buckley
7. Rear cockpit: Tommy Tank
8. Front cockpit © Ian Black

9. Tornado formation: Mike Toft
10. Groundcrew in NBC © Ian Black
11. Weeks and Lennox: Tabuk photo archive via Matty Mathieson; Craghill and Warren: Mal Craghill
12. Anti-Aircraft fire © Patrick de Noirment / REUTERS; Heath: Tabuk photo archive via Matty Mathieson; Batson: Pete Batson
13. Hicks: Rupert Clark; Stewarts and HM Queen Elizabeth II: Robbie Stewart
14. Chris Ankerson and Princess Diana: Bob Ankerson; crash site: Robbie Stewart
15. Nichol in former cell © Mike Moore / *Daily Mirror*
16. Nichol and Clark on aircraft: John Nichol; low-level flying: Dave Bellamy
17. Hicks' coffin: John Broadbent
18. Nichol and Clark and the media: John Nichol; Waddington and Stewart reunion: Robbie Stewart
19. Peters and Nichol: John Nichol; Witts in crewroom: Jerry Witts via Les Hendry Dhahran archive; Stewart and Waddington: Robbie Stewart
20. Broadbent: Nige Risdale; De la Billière and Schwarzkopf © Dennis Stone / Shutterstock
21. Three Tornados © Mike Lumb; Burgess and Ankerson: Bob Ankerson
22. Major and Nichol: John Nichol; Robbie and Kirsty Stewart: Robbie Stewart; Philippa and Jeremy Green: Jenny Green
23. Diamond Nine formation © Stuart Norris; POW reunion: John Nichol
24. Post-war formation © Ian Black; Tornados at sunset © Mark Ranger

INDEX

Read on for an extract from
John Nichol's previous book

LANCASTER

LANCASTER –
The Forging of a Very
British Legend

Chapter 1: *'I've got a strange feeling about this bloody Munich job'*

Late afternoon, Sunday 7 January 1945. The leaden skies spread from horizon to horizon. Ground crews had been working the snow ploughs all day to keep the runways clear.

Now, at last, the snow had abated and the job was on.

Dusk was falling fast as the drab green Fordson crew-bus took the seven men out to their giant Lancaster bomber: one of sixteen from their base scheduled to be part of this operation, scattered at their dispersal points around RAF Metheringham, 12 miles south-east of Lincoln.

Metheringham was a new, purpose-built affair, which had risen from the flat, windswept Lincolnshire farmlands and become operational a year earlier. It was a nondescript place, playing host to bleak Nissen huts and a concrete block of a control tower – one of hundreds of such bases dotted across eastern and southern England. Lincolnshire – 'bomber county' – had the lion's share, being the best-placed platform for taking the war to the enemy.

The Fordson's engine stuttered in the cold as it reached its destination. Jettisoning their last cigarettes, nerves taut, the aircrew disembarked, the oldest of them twenty-six, the two youngest still only nineteen. Breath pluming in the frigid air, they stamped their feet and rubbed their hands, glancing at one another, waiting for nerves to settle, focusing on the task ahead. They did their best to echo their driver's cheery smile as she waved goodbye and walked the short distance to the looming beast that lay in wait for them.

In service since 1942, before many of the crew had joined the Royal Air Force, their four-engined Lancaster bomber was just one of 7,377 built to serve in Bomber Command. What the crew could never have known was that over half – an astonishing 3,736 – would be lost during the course of the war. Towering on its undercarriage over 20ft above them, the Lancaster was the spearhead of the British assault into the heart of Nazi Germany; its upper surfaces were coated with camouflage greens and browns, and matt black on its lower flanks, belly and the undersides of its wings. The ghostly attire of the night bomber.

They each climbed the short ladder through the square door on the starboard side of the Lancaster, just aft of the wing: Jim Scott, twenty-three, the pilot and captain; Bob Dunlop, also twenty-three, the bomb-aimer who doubled as front gunner; Ken Darke, twenty-one, the navigator; Harry Stunell, the wireless operator, also twenty-one; Les Knapman, the flight engineer and 'old man' of the crew at twenty-six, whose responsibility was to ensure the smooth running of the aircraft, as well as covering for the pilot.

The mid-upper gunner, Jack Elson, was one of the 19-year-olds. The other gunner, and the 'baby' of the crew, was Ron Needle. He held the loneliest position of all, far from the rest of his friends in the rear gun turret at the back end of the aircraft, hence his nickname of 'Tail-End Charlie' or, more colourfully, 'Tail-Arse Charlie'.

They boarded in silence and without ceremony. Many crews had long-established rituals from which they dared not deviate – relieving themselves on the rear wheel of the aircraft, perhaps. Their ground crews complained that this rotted the rubber, but toilet facilities were minimal once airborne. Others would give voice to a particular song before embarking. The Andrews Sisters' 'Shrine of St Cecilia' was particularly popular; its lyrics spoke to the souls of all bomber crews.

> *I kneel in my solitude, and silently pray*
> *That heaven will protect you, dear, and there'll come a day*
> *The storm will be over and we'll all meet again*
> *At the Shrine of St Cecilia.*

On a night such as this, their voices – some quivering, some firm – could ring out with the resonance of a choral mass.

Many carried mascots or talismans, some personal, some for the entire aircraft, and woe betide them if by chance they left their lucky charm behind.

But that wasn't the way things worked on this Lancaster.

Ron Needle, in particular, had no time for superstitions. 'I've always accepted life as it is. What will be will be.' It was a good philosophy for a young man who had to face death on a near-nightly basis. In the job they'd volunteered for, boys had to grow up fast.

The down-to-earth Brummie had volunteered for the RAF eighteen months earlier, as soon as he'd reached the age of eighteen.

I saw my first enemy aircraft one Wednesday afternoon whilst in the back garden at home. The Luftwaffe bombed the Royal Orthopaedic Hospital in Northfield on 23 November, 1940. I was around 100 yards away as it unfolded. That was the point I decided to join the RAF and fight back against the Germans. Boy, I was angry! I really wanted to take the war back to Germany.

Ron was going to get his wish. He exchanged a quick, tight grin with his friend, wireless operator Harry Stunell, whom he'd got to know well over the months they'd been together, dubbing him 'a gentleman with a great sense of humour'. Humour was a great weapon against fear, as long as you always treated fear with respect.

It was a short climb into the Lancaster, a brisk prelude to a long and dangerous journey, in which evasion in a crisis was far from straightforward. For Ron, the Lanc would always remain an 'elegant and very beautiful aircraft'. For some of his older colleagues, the fact that it wasn't easy to get out of the Lanc in an emergency counterbalanced its other undoubted virtues. Apart from the main door, the only exit (other than a sea-ditching hatch roughly midships on the top of the fuselage, not designed for a parachute escape) was the tiny forward hatch, just 22 inches by 26, tucked under the padding where the bomb-aimer lay in the nose of the aircraft when dispatching his deadly payload.

At least Ron, as rear-gunner, had the possibility of rotating his turret to one side in an emergency and bailing out backwards from his Perspex bubble. *If* all went well. *If* he had time to firstly open the doors behind him and reach into the aircraft for his parachute (it was too bulky to wear in the turret), stowed on the bulkhead. *If* he could then connect it to his harness, in the midst of the chaos and confusion. There were a lot of *if*s for the men flying Lancasters in Bomber Command.

This was his crew's eleventh sortie. They'd scraped through their tenth only forty-eight hours earlier. On a night run against a pocket of enemy troops near Bordeaux, all hell had broken loose. They'd been caught in anti-aircraft fire. Their first bombing run had been aborted, so they'd had to go again, their Lancaster shuddering as the flak hammered and burst around it, far too close for comfort, buffeting the men so violently that Ron Needle's only thought had been, *Let's get the hell out of here.*

At last, the payload had gone, and, relieved of its weight, the Lanc had leapt skywards, leaving the airmen's stomachs hollow. The thought of being shot at while carrying fourteen 1,000lb high-explosive bombs – a typical load for such a target – wasn't a comfortable one for any of them. However often you flew, you knew that every time could be the last. Each sortie was like 'going over the top' for the troops in the trenches in the First World War. You could never leave anything to chance – but, at the same time, you knew that so much was entirely out of your hands.

They'd got home safely – no injuries, no damage to the aircraft – but very shaken. They all knew that, in their line of business, survival was never something to be taken for granted. Never far from their minds was the thought that, whenever they lifted off from the runway, death was 'the eighth passenger' in their Lancaster.

* * *

The briefing room that afternoon had been blue with cigarette smoke. Everyone had groaned when the briefing officer drew back the security curtain that covered the map, and revealed the red cotton line marking their route.

Munich.

A long run; four hours or so there, another four back.

Though they didn't know it yet, this was to be the last major aerial assault of the war on the heart of a city already pulverised by over seventy raids during the previous five years. The Western Allies, having achieved near-total dominance in the air by this stage in the conflict, were pushing their point home, softening up the Germans to facilitate the Russians' westward advance.

Ken Darke, along with the other navigators, made notes on routing and heights; pilots paid close attention to the route and other elements of the attacking formation. They were all familiar with the routine. 'It was a totally normal day,' Ron recalled. 'We'd had breakfast. We had such good food as aircrew; bacon, real eggs, not the powdered variety! Tea, toast and jam. We really were well looked after. Then we would just wait to see what the day would hold. It was just another day in Bomber Command.'

The briefing over, the time had hung heavily. There were checks to be run, the ground crews busy about their cherished aircraft, night-flying tests to be completed. However often you did it, your nerves tingled and you longed for the moment of takeoff. After checking the guns and ammunition, rear-gunner Ron could only wait. 'We would just hang around and chat. But you never really talked about what we were going to do, what we might face. I suppose no one wanted to really acknowledge what we might be feeling. Even if you felt it, you could never admit to being afraid.'

Once aboard their Lancaster, Ron turned left – all the others turned right – and clambered aft through the narrowing fuselage, past the Elsan, a bucket-like toilet, slotted into its place midships and fitted with a lid that, in theory at least, stayed clamped down on its contents when not in use. For the duration of the flight, Ron was separated from the rest of the crew, firstly by a set of double swing doors on the fuselage, and then by the sliding doors of his capsule. All communication would be by intercom. Squeezing himself into the turret protruding from the tail, his back was now to the rest of the aircraft and he would face outwards, without the advantage of knowing what he was flying into, until the crew – hopefully – landed back at base, over eight hours later. It was the loneliest spot on earth. And one of the most cramped.

With its 102ft wingspan and four mighty Merlin engines, each as big as a car, the Lancaster's 69ft-long fuselage was essentially built around its giant 33ft-long bomb bay. The interior of the aircraft, barely 6ft across, and 6ft high at best, was traversed near the centre by the twin steel spars, to which the wings were attached. These spars narrowed the gap between floor and ceiling to just a couple of feet, creating a letterbox-like space the crew had to clamber through when moving forward or aft. To compound their difficulties, they had to squeeze in between the equipment racks and crew stations, which narrowed the interior further, taking care that their heads and bodies didn't connect with jutting metalwork.

You might be secure enough in your confined crew position, but moving around was hard enough in normal circumstances. Moving around in flight, in darkness – and the Lancaster was a night worker first and foremost – and wearing a bulky flying suit, was much tougher, even when you were accustomed to it, as these young men were. Moving around while under attack or on fire – well, that was something else again.

Ron's role was one of the most vital to the safety of the Lancaster. Sitting on a leather padded seat, knees bunched up, in an area about the size of an oil-drum, exposed to the night sky on all sides through his flimsy Perspex turret, his job was to scan it ceaselessly for danger. His gloved fingers were never far from the triggers of his four 0.303-inch Browning machine guns. The Lancaster wasn't built for comfort, but Ron's electrically heated flying suit kept the worst of the chill at bay – if it worked. Sometimes one side was burning hot, the other bone cold. But that was the kind of thing you got used to. Cold was always a problem in a Lancaster.

Ron waited for his pilot to go through the cockpit checks. Everything had to be in perfect order before takeoff. The pilot was the boss, the 'skipper', even if other crewmen outranked him. On Ron's Lancaster, his pilot Jim Scott was a flying officer, while the navigator Ken Darke was a more senior flight lieutenant. None of that mattered now. Ken would take orders from Jim for the duration of the flight. Everyone would watch everyone else's backs. That was the way to survive, unless survival was taken out of your hands by German anti-aircraft guns or by the deadly fire of Messerschmitt or Junkers fighters.

Once all the checks were completed to the skipper and flight engineer's satisfaction, Ron heard the low growl of the four Merlin engines as they each burst into life, finally giving vent to a deep-throated roar as the huge aircraft lumbered towards the runway. Through his turret, he could see about twenty well-wishers who'd gathered to wave them off.

The squadron commander was there, the ground crew who looked after the aircraft on the base and all but mothered it, and a group of WAAFs [members of the Women's Auxiliary Air Force] who worked round the base, as radio operators, parachute packers, drivers and debriefing officers.

I always drew comfort from seeing them – there was a sense of us all being in it together. They knew what we were facing; they'd seen so many eager young crews set out on an op and fail to return home. As we sped down the runway, all I could see was the blackness of the concrete, a slight glow from the snow, and all those people waving, disappearing from view.

Ron hadn't felt any sense of foreboding before taking off that day, beyond the usual nerves and adrenaline rush that came no matter how often you flew. That apprehension almost always disappeared, if you were lucky, the minute you set your mind to the task in hand. But his mate, the wireless operator, 21-year-old Harry Stunell, couldn't suppress an obscure sense of foreboding. Each Lancaster crew was a tight-knit bunch, seldom fraternising seriously with other crews. The ever-present threat of death made men chary of close friendships. But Harry did have a friend in a fellow wireless operator, and, in the crew room before the flight that afternoon, as they stood by the kit lockers, he confided, 'Bill, I've got a strange feeling about this bloody Munich job.'

Bill Winter had already noticed that his buddy, normally so cheerful, had been a bit long in the face that day, and now did his best to reassure him. It was Harry's father's birthday, wasn't it? Maybe Harry was just desperate to be celebrating with his dad in a pub at home in Brighton. Bill, the calm, good-natured son of a policeman, patted his friend on the back. 'We all get these feelings sometimes. You'll be okay.'

'Tonight feels different. I don't feel happy at all,' Harry replied.

But he had to keep his feelings to himself. The unspoken golden rule was that you never let on misgivings to your crewmates. And the rest of them, like Ron, seemed to feel this was just another operation: dangerous, of course – they all were – but routine. They'd spent the time before boarding chatting idly about what they'd do when it was over, whether to go to the pub for a few pints of weak wartime beer, or have a drink in the mess, or, if there was time, visit friends or family away from the base. There was still a life to be lived, away from the war in the skies over Germany.

Harry quietly took his place a short way aft of the navigator's station, exchanging a grin with Ken Darke, who'd already squeezed his 6ft 2 frame into position.

Ken was twenty-two years old and a London bank clerk in civvy street. Fair-haired and handsome, but also bookish and reserved, he was the brainbox of his family, and dearly loved by them. He had settled down in the RAF, found his niche, and made friends quickly with fellow airmen and WAAFs. As the war progressed, the backgrounds of air crews had broadened: initially, the RAF had looked to the middle classes and the public schools for its ideal recruits. Now, everyone mixed in, more or less happily. Harry had been an upholsterer before joining up; Ron, a butcher from Birmingham. Nobody cared about backgrounds or schooling. Least of all the senior echelons of Bomber Command, for, as casualties mounted to unprecedented levels, they could no longer pick and choose who would fly their aircraft to war.

Ken drew the curtains round his cubby-hole to shut in the light from his desk-lamp and spread out his charts. At 6ft 2, he was lucky to have the luxury of the navigator's space. There were rear-gunners even taller than he was, but their knees must have been jammed under their chin.

Jim powered up the engines, waiting for the takeoff signal as their roar reached a crescendo. Then the green light flashed and he released the brakes. Ron's chest pushed against the controls of his Browning machine guns as the craft thundered down the runway. He felt the tail-wheel lift beneath him first, which always gave him a curious sense of elation, then the main wheels left the ground, as the Lanc lifted into the night sky, soaring with a lightness that belied its size.

RAF Metheringham grew tiny beneath them as they set course to join the rest of the 50-mile-long bomber stream, bound for the Bavarian capital.

It grew colder as they climbed, dropping around 2 degrees for every 1,000ft. As they crossed the French coast at about 7.45 p.m., the temperature at 19,000ft was bitter. The men in front could benefit from the Lancaster's heating system, which was at its most efficient there, but Ron Needle, exposed to the freezing outside air in his Perspex turret, was grateful for his heated flying suit and thick gloves.

Time passed both too slowly and too fast; suddenly, it was only forty-five minutes to target. As they drew closer, Jim urged them all to keep a look out for enemy fighters. Ron kept his eyes even more strictly peeled for enemy aircraft – Messerschmitt 110s and Junkers 88s, whose cannon were more powerful and had a longer range than his machine guns. To his relief, none came. If they had, the Lancaster's wonderful manoeuvrability might just have kept them out of trouble, but he was glad they didn't need to put that to the test right now. Their experience two days previously, when attacked by a German fighter, had been bad enough. Hopefully, tonight would be different.

Light sparkled off the sheen of the upper surface of the wings and their aircraft jolted and shook in the turbulence of the bomber stream. The full attacking formation they were part of that night comprised nine Mosquitos and 645 Lancaster bombers. The black skies around them were crowded and dangerous. Stunell recalled that 'tension was at concert pitch, reaction speeds intensified. Young lads who had not long ago feared our strict headmasters, were now flying into the Third Reich, which was presided over by one of the biggest bullies of all time'.[8]

Ron could hear the voice of the bomb-aimer over the intercom: 'Route markers ahead, Skipper.' Though he was aware of the glow in the sky, he couldn't see what Bob Dunlop could: the brightly coloured red, green and yellow indicator flares dropped by the Pathfinder Force that had preceded them to mark the route and the target itself. He didn't look directly at the glowing sky. Gunners never did. 'Bright lights affect night vision. It takes about ten minutes for eyes to adjust to the dark.'

The skies above Munich began to glow as the fiery rain of bombs from the aircraft at the head of attack force began to fall. Harry Stunell pushed any forebodings to one side, moving up to look out from the cockpit onto what he remembered as a huge boiling sea of flame, an Impressionist landscape daubed with lurid orange and red brushstrokes. Beneath him, Pathfinder aircraft were swooping down to replenish burnt-out target flares, in order to ensure subsequent bombs were concentrated on the heart of the city. Munich was ablaze.

Near him, the pilot kept a watchful eye out for other Lancasters in the stream, jostling for position to commence their attack runs. Collisions happened at moments like this, or, worse, you could be on the receiving end of bombs falling from a Lanc above you. Some would drop their payload out of sequence, some too early. The darkness was bursting into a maelstrom of noise and flame, and, coupled with the roar of the engines and the stabbing brightness of the searchlights, you could never be sure of anything. Stunell decided he didn't want to see the horrors unfolding below and returned to his station.

Their Lancaster was approaching the target. Bob's voice, striving to be calm, talking to Jim, crackled in Ron's intercom, too: 'Steady ... steady ... right a bit ... steady ... correct left a tad ... steady ...'

Ron prayed it wouldn't be a dummy run again.

'Keep her there. Right!'

A moment's silence, then: 'Bombs gone!'

The Lancaster's load, a massive 4,000lb 'Blockbuster' bomb, escorted by 954 4lb incendiaries, hurtled towards the stricken city. The Blockbuster, as the name suggested, was designed to blast structures apart, leaving them exposed to the incendiaries that would ignite the exposed and shattered interiors. War from the air was a brutal business.

Released of its burden, the pilot had to control the aircraft as it leapt upwards – another instance of potential risk if someone was flying above you.

Then came the moment they all loathed.

'Hold her for the photo.'

It meant keeping straight and steady for a few seconds while the camera behind the bomb-aimer took automatic flash shots of their run through its own small porthole on the floor. How the crewmen hated those few seconds, vulnerable to attack and unable to manoeuvre. The pictures were vital, mandatory. Analysed back home, they served a dual purpose: proof that the Lancaster had done its job; and material to assess the success of the raid. But those brief moments seemed like the longest of the entire flight.

It was then that disaster struck.

A bomber stream should fly to its target on one course, and return home by another. No marker lights showed on any aircraft, and, apart from the blazing target and the pale glow of the moon, it was dark – too dark to see fast-moving allies close by.

Ron had heard the 'bombs gone' announcement, and was thinking, *Good, now we can go home*. Jim Scott, holding the Lancaster steady for the photo-run, had suddenly caught sight of something out of the corner of his eye. A giant, dark shape, heading straight for them. He grappled with the controls to avoid the collision, but it was too late. With a roar, their aircraft was flipped out of control and, engines screaming in protest, started to plummet earthwards, towards the burning city they had just bombed.

Harry Stunell's foreboding hadn't been misplaced.

Ron's only thought was: *What the hell is going on?*

Endnotes

1 See *In the Middle of Nowhere* by Richard Bailey.
2 Bombers were scattered at individual 'dispersal points' around the main runway – this made it impossible for an enemy fighter or bomber to destroy several aircrafts at once.
3 The Andrews Sisters were a hugely popular close-harmony girl band of the war years. 'The Shrine of St Cecilia' dates from 1942, and its lyrics, dealing with a town ravaged by an undefined storm 'from up above', which has miraculously spared the Shrine of St Cecilia, would have had direct appeal to bomber crews. St Cecilia is the patron saint of music.
4 Ron Needle, *Saved by the Bell*, and John Nichol interview.
5 Miles Tripp, *The Eighth Passenger*; and see John Nichol and Tony Rennell, *Tail-End Charlies*.
6 Mel Rolfe, *To Hell and Back*.
7 Information from Lincolnshire Aviation Heritage Centre, East Kirkby.
8 Quoted in Rolfe, op. cit.